MARKETING

Nigel Hill B.Sc (Econ), M.Phil, PGCE, Dip.M., MCIM

BUSINESS EDUCATION PUBLISHERS LIMITED

1989

© Nigel Hill 1989

ISBN 0-907679-24-2

First published in 1989
Reprinted 1990
Reprinted 1991

Design by Flora Pearson of Computer Design, Durham

Published in Great Britain by Business Education Publishers Limited,
Leighton House, 10 Grange Crescent, Stockton Road, Sunderland,
Tyne and Wear, SR2 7BN

Tel. 091 567 4963

Printed in Great Britain by Athenaeum Press Limited, Unit 3, Mill Lane Industrial Estate, Newcastle upon Tyne.

Tel. 091 273 7737

This book is dedicated to
Janet, Christopher and Nicholas

The Author

Nigel Hill B.Sc (Econ), M.Phil., PGCE, Dip.M., MCIM.

Nigel Hill is Marketing Director of JPD Associates Ltd., a company with interests in managemment consultancy, training and manufacturing. He has had experience of sales and marketing in consumer and industrial markets, and in manufacturing and service industries. He currently acts as a consultant to a number of companies as well as presenting management development seminars on marketing. Nigel has taught students on BTEC, degree and post experience courses. He has written a number of articles and two books on marketing.

Acknowledgements

I would like to express my gratitude to colleagues and friends who have provided help, constructive comments, polite corrections or brutal criticism as required. I would like to thank Paul Callaghan for his encouragement, help and feedback, and, above all, for running a publishing company which is not submerged in bureaucracy and red tape. To Jane Russell, Tom Harrison, Moira Page, Kathryn Martin and Caroline White who edited and punctuated my anarchic prose, to Flora Pearson who provided the illustrations and who designed the cover, I am greatly indebted. I would also like to thank the companies whose good marketing practices have given us so many examples to highlight, especially Volkswagen (UK) for their generous provision of information. Last, but not least, I would like to thank my long suffering wife and family for their support and understanding.

All errors and omissions remain the responsibility of the author.

N.H.

Huddersfield, June 1989

Preface

This book has been written to provide a comprehensive coverage of Marketing at an introductory level. It assumes no previous marketing knowledge on the part of the reader. The text has been structured to take the student in a logical manner through the marketing tasks which face typical organisations operating in today's business environments. Following an explanation of the marketing concept, the book takes the student through the three key steps of the marketing process. Firstly, the organisation must understand its potential customers, their needs and their priorities. Secondly, it must develop a product or service which meets those customers needs more effectively than do any offerings from competitors. Thirdly, it must inform potential customers that the product or service exists and demonstrates how it does meet their needs better than competing products or services. Finally, the book examines some special aspects of marketing such as the application of the marketing concept to non-profit making organisations.

The inclusion of a range of practical, problem based assignments provides an opportunity for students to engage in active learning tasks. The assignments also provide the basis of an in-course assessment programme.

This text is particularly appropriate for students studying marketing at BTEC National Level and for the marketing element of A Level Business Studies. It should also prove of value for students undertaking introductory marketing courses at BTEC Higher Level and those pursuing professional qualifications such as the Certificate of Chartered Institute of Marketing and the CAM Certificate.

Table of Contents

PART ONE: ANALYSIS

This book is divided into three parts. The first part of the book is the logical starting point not only for a marketing book but also for the work of a marketing manager or marketing consultant. Good marketing is almost always based on a thorough and accurate analysis of the situation faced by the company.

Margaret Crimp describes the purpose of marketing very clearly:

'The object of the marketing process, taken in its entirety, is to locate a target group of consumers or users who have an unsatisfied need which could be met by a branded product.'

(Margaret Crimp: The Marketing Research Process).

To find a group of consumers with an unsatisfied need requires the ability to explore, identify and interpret customers' behaviour, attitudes and preferences. It relies on a deep understanding of those customers and the society in which they live. The first part of this book will describe and explain how marketing managers carry out these analysing tasks. As Crimp says, a good analysis will *'define a target group in the market and specify the characteristics of a product to suit this group'.*

This part further examines how markets and consumers are analysed. We look at how customers are divided into groups and at the kind of research techniques that marketers use to carry out this exploration of their markets. Part Two of the book considers the marketing mix and Part Three special aspects of marketing strategy.

Chapter 1
What is marketing?

Introduction

I wonder what you would say if you were asked to define marketing using only one word? It is not easy. The task is made more difficult by the fact that most people already think they have a pretty good idea of what marketing is. After all, we are constantly coming up against examples of marketing.

A mail shot may have come through the letter box this morning, we see advertisements on the television and in newspapers and magazines. New products are being introduced all the time. Most of us have been asked at some time to participate in a market research survey and a sales person may recently have tried very hard to sell us something. Have you also noticed that more and more companies are making an effort to tell customers how hard they are trying to give a good service? At one time the Marks and Spencer 'no questions asked' guarantee was unmatched by other stores. It is now becoming the norm on the high street. Companies everywhere are trying to give customers what they want and are paying more attention to the little details that lead to customer satisfaction. Most hairdressers, for example, will offer their customers a cup of coffee while they are having their hair done.

In this first chapter we will define marketing, we will consider the beliefs which underpin the marketing concept and we will examine the planning process which results in marketing activities coming to fruition. The chapter will be sprinkled with examples of companies which are successfully implementing the marketing concept.

1.1 A definition of marketing

So what about that one word definition of marketing? Many people reply with the word 'advertising'. This is an understandable response since we see so much of it. Marketing, however is not advertising. Nor is it promotion, nor is it selling. Some people say research (that is market research), but that still does not cover it. Others say service, which is getting much warmer but still is not quite right. We will return later to our one word definition.

1.1.1 Meeting the needs of customers

Marketing is about organising the company to meet the needs of customers, not just today and tomorrow but also in five or even ten years time. It is about supplying customers with well designed, good quality, reliable products, at a price which they consider to be fair. It is about providing the level of service before, during and after the placing of an order that customers have a right to expect. Marketing therefore is all about making the company outward looking or customer oriented. To do this you have to be able to put yourselves in the customers' shoes, (or, even better, inside their minds) in order to really understand what they want and what they feel about things. Only in this way can the firm organise itself successfully to meet the needs of customers.

1.1.2 Marketing is a philosophy

Marketing should be seen as a philosophy. It is a way of thinking, from the customers' perspective, about how the firm can meet the needs of customers.

So what about that one word definition?

If marketing is a philosophy, the problem with the words given at the start of section 1.1.1 should be clear. They are all functions or activities. They are things that marketing people do. They design and place advertising, they sell products, they carry out market research and they provide good customer service. They are all part of the marketer's job, but they do not describe the outward looking philosophy which enables those activities to happen effectively.

My one word definition is 'serving'. That little word sums up the customer oriented philosophy which must go right through the whole organisation if it is to be successful in the long run in meeting the needs of customers. Although the marketing department is responsible for planning marketing strategies and activities, everybody in the organisation has some role in helping to implement them. Staff of all levels have some impact on the organisation's ability to keep its customers satisfied. It is a key responsibility of marketers to ensure that this marketing philosophy, about serving customers, is the spirit which motivates the behaviour of everyone in the organisation however little contact they have with customers.

This is perfectly illustrated by an extract from 'Iacocca', the autobiography of Lee Iacocca who ran the Ford Motor Company in the 1970's and rescued the Chrysler Motor Company in the 1980's, very much as a result of implementing marketing principles. In his book, he illustrates his understanding of the marketing philosophy by relating a little incident which occurred in a restaurant when he was young. The food was good, the surroundings were clean and comfortable but the family's meal had been somewhat spoilt by the surly, offhand attitude of the waitress. At the end of the meal when it came to bill settling and tipping time, Iacocca's father called the waitress over and said:

'Now I'm going to give you a REAL tip. Why are you so unhappy in this job? Is anyone forcing you to be a waitress? We're out for a nice time and you're wrecking it. If you want to be a waitress you should work on being the best damn waitress in the world. Otherwise, find yourself another line of work.'

A little harsh maybe, but if organisations are going to be successful in the long run everyone in the organisation must strive to be the best damn waitress, fitter, cleaner, receptionist, designer (or any other position), since the most successful organisations will usually be those whose staff take the most trouble to serve their customers. These ideas concerning the role of all staff in delivering good customer service will be developed more fully in Chapters 9 and 14.

1.1.3 Inward looking or outward looking?

Many businesses are not at all outward looking. They are inward looking or 'product oriented'. They think not in terms of customers' needs and preferences but in terms of their own products, their own activities and their own priorities. They think that the key to success in business lies inside their organisation. Some believe that the key is to be an efficient producer, enabling the company to cut its costs and therefore sell at a lower price. A well known exponent of this 'production concept' was Henry Ford, who pioneered mass production, in itself a very good thing, but then became carried away with more and more economies of scale. Everything in the company was built around the need for production efficiency. Ford was famous in the 1920's for its slogan, 'you can have any colour as long as it's black'. It was more efficient to produce only black cars and as a result Ford did sell the cheapest car on the market. However, General Motors wondered if customers would prefer more choice. They offered red cars and blue ones, and several other colours and many additional, unnecessary luxury items inside the car. All this added to the cost, and General Motors could not compete on price with Ford, but their sales kept on growing. By the 1930's they had overtaken Ford and they have never lost their position as the world's leading manufacturer of cars, a position that was based quite simply on giving customers what they wanted.

Some companies see the ability to sell hard as being the key to success in business. Whether in manufacturing or retailing the company must sell its products. It must keep the stock moving. This view could be seen in the 'pile 'em high and sell 'em cheap' philosophy of Jack Cohen in the early years of Tesco. It is not however, the company's philosophy today. Following the trend in food retailing set by companies like Sainsbury's and Marks and Spencer, Tesco now places much more emphasis on high quality merchandise and an appealing shopping environment, even though this must add to the company's costs and therefore its prices. The leading supermarkets know that consumers today demand quality and are prepared to pay a little more to obtain it.

According to the product concept of Henry Ford, a business is a goods producing process. According to the selling concept of Jack Cohen it is a sales operation. According to the marketing concept it is neither. The marketing concept sees the business as a customer satisfying process.

We can contrast the inward looking product and sales oriented approach with the outward looking marketing oriented approach in the following way. Imagine that someone is starting a new business. The thought processes of the inward looking entrepreneur might go something like this:

This new electric hammer would be a good idea

Let's make some

Let's make 1000

Let's charge £ 1 each

Now let's try and sell them.

The outward looking entrepreneur would tackle the exercise in a very different way. His thoughts would develop thus:

Let's find out what people want,

Let's find out how many they want,

Let's find out how much they will pay,

Let's decide if it's profitable,

Now let's make them.

Management writer Peter Drucker has said that

' the aim of marketing is to make selling superfluous'

Put simply, marketing is about ensuring that the organisation provides products that people want to buy. Selling is concerned with persuading people to buy the products that the organisation offers.

1.1.4 Defining marketing

We have now established that the core of the marketing philosophy is about keeping customers satisfied. We have suggested that the best way to do this is to look forward to find out what customers want so that the organisation can organise itself to provide the products that customers want to buy.

In effect, marketing is a kind of matching process. It seeks to learn what people want and then tries to match the resources of the company to supplying those wants. Of course, this does not mean that companies can supply whatever people want. A private school cannot suddenly turn itself into a private hospital if there is more demand for medical care than for education. Organisations have to be realistic about their abilities. They have to concentrate in areas where their strengths lie, a principle we will develop in section 1.4.

There are two more factors which should be accommodated in any definition of marketing. Firstly, marketing is a creative process. It is about getting noticed in the market place by doing something different or novel. In the nineteenth century, Ralph Waldo Emerson coined a very famous phrase:

'If a man build a better mousetrap, then even though he live in a wood, the world will beat a path to his door.'

In the nineteenth century, with demand for most products outstripping supply, Emerson's remark may have had some validity. However, in today's highly competitive markets Emerson's beliefs are most certainly outdated. However good a firm's product, and however closely it meets the needs of customers, it will not be a success if it does not get noticed. In the real, competitive business world, though marketing will make selling much easier, it rarely makes it superfluous. As we will see in Chapter 4 on marketing research, Chapter 7 which looks at new product development and Chapters 10 to 13 which examine marketing communications, creativity can be a very important factor in marketing success.

The second factor is the importance of profitability. Companies are not in business primarily to make products, to sell products, to be market leader or to win awards for export achievement, design or quality. They are in business to make money. Marketing has a vital role to play in generating profits. In the long run it steers the company towards potentially profitable market opportunities. In the shorter term, as we will see in Chapters 5, 6 and 8, it is concerned with adding value to the company's product or service so that it sells at a good, profitable price.

We can therefore define marketing as a creative process which seeks to identify and satisfy customer needs profitably by matching company strengths to market opportunities.

1.2 The marketing process

1.2.1 A short story

In the early years of this century a man made an appointment with the chief of a well known New York advertising agency. He walked in and asked quite simply if the agency was capable of making for him the world's best ever advertisement for shampoo. Not inclined to modesty, the advertising man replied that of course his agency could do that - it was the world's best advertising agency. 'Good', said the client, getting up to leave, 'get on with it and let me know when you've finished.'

'Hold on a minute' said the agent. 'Where's the product? What's it like? What does it do? What colour is it ? What's the packaging like?'

'We'll have to wait and see said the client. I'll know the answers when you've come up with the advert'. And he took his leave.

The agent was flummoxed. This was not at all the normal way of going about things. Where should he start? Not knowing anything about shampoo he decided that the first job was to educate himself. He found out all about it. His staff went and asked people which shampoo was best, how they used it, what problems they had with it, what kind of packaging they found most convenient and attractive. They used the answers to design an advertisement for a fictional product - the ideal shampoo.

They contacted the client who came back in and was delighted with what he saw. He went away and had the shampoo made and packaged according to the ideal formula. The agency then promoted it. The client's name was Alberto Culver and his company has been extremely successful in the American shampoo market ever since. That story has almost passed into marketing folklore. Alberto Culver followed to the letter the marketing process outlined in section 1.1.3, starting with 'Let's find out what people want'. He was outward looking, concerned only with 'doing the right things.'

1.2.2 Doing the right things

Inward looking, product oriented companies tend to be obsessed with efficiency. Peter Drucker defines efficiency as 'doing things right', and maintains that managers in most companies are motivated, assessed and rewarded on the basis of 'doing things right'. Of course, companies do not want to be inefficient, but Drucker insists that there is another, more important criterion upon which performance should be judged. This is effectiveness, which he defines as 'doing the right things'. There are two aspects of effectiveness, the long term and the short term. An effective organisation (or an effective manager within an organisation) will be concerned over the long term with providing products that customers want to buy. This ability to spot the most potentially profitable marketing opportunities has never been more important than in today's highly competitive and rapidly changing markets. It is this process of analysing market opportunities and identifying the most suitable ones which forms the subject of Part One of this book. In the short term 'doing the right things' means organising the company to deliver satisfaction in all its dealings with those customers. These tactical, 'marketing mix' matters are covered in Part Two of this book. According to Drucker it is being effective that enables a company to prosper in the long run.

As shown in Figure 1.1, companies which are both ineffective and inefficient will not last very long at all. However, even the most efficient of companies cannot prosper in the long run if they are not also effective. A company operating in a declining market for example can expect to do no better than decline less slowly than its competitors as the market slowly disappears. As it is explained in more detail in Chapter 7, if it is to grow rather than die slowly it must do other things, the right things. It must identify newer products and enter markets which are growing rather than declining.

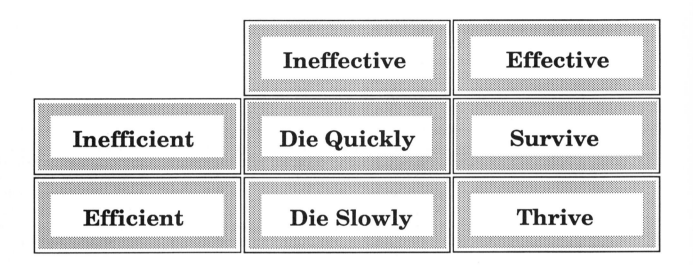

Figure 1.1 The efficiency - effectiveness matrix.

In contrast, companies which are 'doing the right things' often do not need to be particularly efficient to do quite nicely. In a growth market it is relatively easy for a company to grow. If the market is getting bigger a company which is a relatively poor performer can still increase its sales, even though it may be losing market share. Moreover, sales are likely to be profitable because in growth markets demand often outstrips supply, with the result that buyers are often happy to pay premium prices simply in order to receive supplies. In a declining market, where supply is greater than demand, suppliers will be fighting fiercely to retain their market share, often price cutting, at the expense of profits, in an attempt to win business from the competition.

Of course the ideal position is to be both effective and efficient. The most alert organisations will always be alive to changes in their marketplace and if necessary they will enter new markets in order to remain effective, as demonstrated by the following two examples.

1.2.3 Doing the right things out of town

In the early 1970's the British milk and dairy products market was not as buoyant as it had been. There were a number of reasons, including competition from the EEC milk lake, cuts in free school milk and growing health fears regarding cholesterol. Dairies therefore faced two choices. They could look inwards, tighten their belts and become more efficient in the hope of weathering the storm. Many chose this alternative. Many dairies' profits did decline over the ensuing years and many dairies disappeared altogether.

A second, more risky option was to look for newer, growing areas of need into which the profits from the dairy market could be invested while the going was still good. One company which chose this option was a medium sized regional dairy based in Yorkshire called Associated Dairies Ltd. They pioneered the hypermarket concept in the U.K. Being the first to move food shopping out of the town centre was a very bold move, but it paid off. Asda is now the third largest food retailer in the country and others have followed them into superstores based out of town.

A more recent arrival to British out of town shopping is IKEA, a Swedish furniture retailer with almost a hundred stores in twenty countries. IKEA opened its first British store in October 1987 in Warrington and its second in Neasden, west London in September 1988.

IKEA was founded in 1943 by Ingvar Kamprad as a small mail order furniture operation and opened its first out of town furniture store in 1953. It was soon spreading overseas, firstly to Switzerland and then across western Europe, with West Germany now its biggest single market. It now has stores in such far-flung places as Iceland, Kuwait, Saudi Arabia, Hong Kong and Australia.

The success of IKEA is based firmly on doing the right things. Like Asda it has been prepared to take the risk of breaking new ground with its huge out of town furniture superstores. IKEA's smallest stores cover 160,000 square feet, three times the size of the biggest stores operated by its two main British rivals, MFI and Harris Queensway. More importantly the company is effective in terms of exploiting market opportunities at the right time. According to Birger Lund, the managing director of IKEA (UK), as well as identifying the growing preference of the British shopper to visit out of town superstores the company has also spotted a gap in the British furniture market. According to Lund, the best, high quality furniture is extremely expensive in Britain, but the low cost alternative is very poor quality. IKEA aims to fill that gap in the middle with good quality reasonably priced furniture.

As well as getting its planning right, IKEA does the right things from day to day to keep its customers satisfied. Correctly identifying the trend towards shopping (especially for clothing, durables and luxuries) being viewed by the public as a leisure activity rather than a chore, IKEA ensures that a visit to one of its stores will be as pleasant and interesting an experience as possible. The stores have a restaurant, selling both English and Swedish food (including reindeer steaks), a video room, a supervised children's playroom and huge car parks (large enough for 11,000 cars at the Neasden store). In view of the fact that only seven months after the opening of the Warrington store its millionth customer walked through the door, IKEA must be doing something right.

1.3 Marketing planning

If the company is going to do the right things and become genuinely customer oriented, it will need to adopt a very thorough planning and control system for its marketing activities. In this section we will look briefly at the function of such a system.

1.3.1 Situation overview

Nobody can plan effectively unless they know exactly where they are starting from. The most common way of analysing the current situation of a business is to perform a SWOT analysis (see Figure 1.2) which examines its internal strengths and weaknesses and the external opportunities and threats which it faces in the immediate and more distant future. It is here that market analysis and market research techniques, discussed in Chapters 2 and 4 are most useful in helping companies to spot the best potential opportunities. The purpose of the external analysis is to alert the company to possible threats as well as to opportunities. The directors of the company must steer it towards opportunities and away from threats.

However, as suggested earlier in this chapter, marketing is not about simply identifying the most lucrative market opportunities and automatically pursuing them. To succeed in any market, organisations must exploit their strengths to the full. To stand a chance of beating the competition they must do things they are good at. Therefore the situation analysis forms the basis of the whole marketing planning process whose purpose is to match the internal strengths of the company with external market opportunities. As Crimp says, the company must locate a group of customers with an unsatisfied need which could be met by that company. It is the accuracy with which a company can match its internal strengths with external opportunities which will be primarily responsible for its success in the marketplace. As an example, it was not difficult in the 1970's to identify the fact that North Atlantic scheduled flights represented an enormous opportunity but it was not one which was most appropriate to the relative strengths and weaknesses of Laker Airways which, as a small company, was always going to be vulnerable in any price war with the established transatlantic airlines which were much larger.

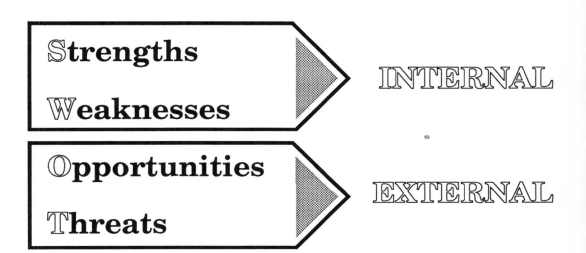

Figure 1.2 SWOT analysis.

1.3.2 Setting objectives

The matching process should lead logically to a statement of company objectives, which should be stated as precisely and in as much detail as possible, otherwise it can be impossible to monitor a company's progress towards achieving them. For example, a publisher of diaries might decide to enter the growing personal organiser market. The objective could be to secure a firm footing in the market, but stated in this way it would be impossible to know when it had been achieved. A much better objective would be to gain a 20% share of the personal organiser market within two years. This could be quantified in monetary or volume terms and interim targets could be set, against which progress could be monitored, and, if necessary, remedial action taken. The larger the company the more important it is to have detailed and unambiguous targets so that all company personnel can strive effectively for that common goal.

1.3.3 Formulating a strategy

Having decided where it wants to go, and defined it accurately the company has to decide how it is going to get there. A strategy is required, just like the man driving his car from London to Leeds has to have a good idea of the route he must take.

Of course, a marketing strategy has to be realistic and consistent with the strengths and weaknesses of the company. As shown in Figure 1.3, it will cover the medium to long term. It will concentrate on salient developments such as the planned dates for the introduction of new products or the opening of new outlets, major changes to existing production capabilities such as the planned raising of quality levels through the implementation of a new quality assurance system, important changes in the organisation of the sales force or perhaps a new distribution initiative.

1. STRATEGIC ASPECTS

.....up to 10 Years

- **Broad Objectives**

- **New Products**

- **New Markets**

- **New Initiatives**

2. TACTICAL ASPECTS

........less than 1 Year

- **Short Term Activities**

- **Doing it better than the Competition**

- **Adding Value**

- **Effective Promotion**

Figure 1.3 Marketing strategy and tactics.

1.3.4 Annual operating plans

The most detailed work in the marketing planning process comes at the stage of developing the annual operating, or tactical plan. It will include short term sales and promotional targets and detailed budgets. Operating plans are usually concerned with the marketing mix, or the 'Four P's' of product, price, place (in other words, distribution) and promotion. They will be examined at length in Part Two of this book. Some people suggest that there should be a fifth 'P' standing for people because, as suggested at the beginning of this chapter all the employees of a company can have a significant effect on its ability to deliver satisfaction to customers. Chapters 9 and 14 will examine the role of people in more detail.

As suggested in the diagram, tactical plans are all about competing in the marketplace, or 'doing it better than the competition'. They often revolve around the concept of adding value in the eyes of customers and will also devote a great deal of attention to working out ways of effectively promoting the company's products in the marketplace.

1.3.5 Controlling the marketing plan

As the plan is implemented it must be continuously monitored to ensure that the organisation remains on course. This is often done by setting targets on a monthly or quarterly basis for product lines, departments or key individuals such as sales people. If the organisation is not on course the cause of the poor performance must be identified. It may be concluded that the company, or parts of it, should have done much better, in which case corrective action should be taken as soon as possible. In some cases it could be the plan which is inappropriate and needs amending. This would usually be due to a major environmental, economic, political, technological or competitive development which was not foreseen and has occurred since the writing of the plan.

1.4 Marketing - a trivial or a vital pursuit?

1.4.1 What makes companies successful?

In the past few years much research has been done and many books have been written on the subject of what makes companies successful. The first of these books was In Search of Excellence by Peters and Waterman, which has now sold over a million copies worldwide. They spent a considerable amount of time getting to know around fifty of America's top performing companies before committing pen to paper on the subject of why they were so successful. Of course, many factors in addition to marketing were seen to be vital in company performance. Corporate culture (i.e. teamwork, enthusiasm, dedication of the staff) was very important as was the role of the chief executive in setting the standards. Innovation had played a crucial role in the success of many companies, as did tight financial controls. However, Peters and Waterman, and other more recent authors of similar studies, have all agreed that good marketing is a vital factor in business success. Moreover, by good marketing they do not mean creative advertising, aggressive selling, clever market research or quality products though each of those may be useful. By good marketing, Peters and Waterman mean that companies follow the outward looking marketing philosophy outlined at the start of this chapter. Peters and Waterman define this as 'being close to the customer'.

This is a very interesting way of looking at it. Some companies, such as service companies are by necessity close to their customers because the nature of their work involves a considerable amount of customer contact (see Chapter 6). The larger the company and the longer the chain of distribution between producer and consumer, the less customer contact there will be. Therefore a large manufacturer of consumer goods who sells through retailers may have virtually no direct contact with users of its products. It will have to find other ways such as market research, exhibitions or demonstrations to get to know its customers.

It is logical that being close to customers will help any company to give customers what they want. Companies which are naturally very close to their customers are frequently very good at marketing without having a marketing department. As Charles Ames says, it is the substance rather than the trappings of marketing which matters. The case study which follows illustrates how a company which did not have the trappings of marketing but was certainly close to its customers became extremely successful.

1.4.2 Pure genus

Just before Christmas 1979 two very poor, rather bored 30 year old Canadians, Chris Haney and Scott Abbott were sitting round the kitchen table. They invented a board game. It took them forty-five minutes, and several bottles of beer. They liked board games and they liked quizzes, and they needed some money so they decided to market their new game, forming a company, Horn Abbot Ltd. in January 1980 to do so.

Not having bothered much with the trappings of marketing they had already made a number of mistakes. They were unaware of the fact that sales of traditional board games were lower than they had been for many years as computer games became more popular in North America. 1982 was the year of Pac-man. Retail sales of video games and software reached $2.1 billion in the USA. The leading board game companies were in trouble.

Secondly, they had come up with an idea that was going to be incredibly expensive to produce. The board and the counters were OK but the 1,000 questions in six categories? How long would they take to develop? The answer to that question turned out to be over a year, until spring 1981 to be precise. It was also very expensive to manufacture with one thousand cards to be printed and collated for each game. It was November 1981 before the first trial batch of 1,100 games was ready to be launched.

Trivial Pursuit also broke several other rules in the games market. Firstly it was very expensive, retailing at $29.95, seen as an exorbitant price for a board game. Even that price wasn't high enough since it had to wholesale at $16 which was exactly Horn Abbot's cost of production. Only by manufacturing and selling in volume could they make money. And this they were not doing. From the Montreal Toy Fair in February 1982 they expected several thousand orders. They came away with less than three hundred. Worse still, as Canadian stores did gradually sell their stocks and reorder, Horn Abbot, now virtually insolvent, could not produce new stocks.

A last ditch effort resulted in a $75,000 loan from a Canadian bank, enabling a further 20,000 games to be produced in May 1982.

However, although Haney and Abbott were certainly not 'doing things right' according to textbook business management theory, they had, often sub-consciously, been largely 'doing the right things'.

There is no doubt whatsoever that they were 'close to their customers'. Quite simply they described their target market as 'people like us', the so-called baby boomers. They thought that 'the people who made the Beatles rich will make us rich'. They decided that 'people like us' were sociable, often meeting with friends, frequently liberal and often mistrusting authority. To compile all the questions they went to Spain to be with 'people like us', to Nerja on the southern coast, which tends to be a refuge for expatriates and beach bums from all over the world. They compiled questions and tried out the game with 'people like us' on the beach in Nerja. They knew what made a good trivial pursuits question. It was 'things that got people going'. If questions provoked discussion, laughter, memories, they knew they were right for 'people like us'. Although Horn Abbot did not know about the problems being experienced by the board game companies they did know that there were an awful lot of 'people like us', in North America and all over the western world.

They were also effective in other ways. They made the packaging different to other board games, a high square box rather than a long flat one. The box was made to look expensive, which, along with its price would give the game an up-market image.

However, certain basic business skills are necessary to the success of any company. Luckily for Horn Abbot, America's biggest board game manufacturer, Selchow and Righter heard of the game. Hit very hard by Pac-man and its stable-mates, Selchow and Righter were desperate for something to revive the flagging fortunes of the board game market. Three directors of the company sat down and played the game in their office in September 1982. They knew it was right. Banking on a belief that parents were weary of the isolation of the video games and were keen for more social interaction, Selchow and Righter reached a deal enabling them to manufacture and market the game in the USA in return for a large advance and a 15% royalty on all sales.

Selchow and Righter continued to do the right things, especially on the promotional front. Despite having only a very small promotional budget ($40,000), they created a very high level of awareness of and interest in the game in the right places. They did this in two ways.

Firstly, in tiny envelopes, they mailed the buyers of retail stores, over three consecutive weeks. Each time they enclosed a small trivial pursuits look-alike question card with a good sample question. On the back with the answers was one simple message each week saying:

Week 1: 'Trivial Pursuit. A Canadian success story.'

Week 2: 'Official US introduction Toy Fair '83.'

Week 3: 'Now from Selchow and Righter.'

By the time of the Toy Fair most of the buyers were clamouring to see the game.

The second promotional initiative was even bolder, and perhaps even more effective. They took all the trivial pursuits cards containing a question about a living star and sent them to that person together with a letter and a complimentary game. Larry Hagman is reported to have replied that he'd always known he was trivial, but not that he would become famous for it. In Hollywood the game took off. All the stars were giving Trivial Pursuit parties, including the cast of the sixties nostalgia film 'The Big Chill', as a result of which the game received a lot of free media attention. As we will see in Chapter 7, opinion leaders can be crucial to the success of any new product.

In 1983 sales totalled $40 million in the USA and slightly more in Canada. Baby Boomer, Young Players, Genus II, Silver Screen and Sports editions followed as did the game's launch in a further twenty one countries in 1984 and 1985, often with specially written questions to suit the culture of the country concerned. In 1984 fourty million games were sold around the world, to all kinds of buyers. There is no doubt that the game took off initially because it met the needs of 'people like us', but it required the commercial acumen of Selchow and Righter to make it succeed in the marketplace.

Conclusion

Marketing therefore is all about winning and keeping satisfied customers. Firms maximise their chances of achieving this by being close to their customers. The closer they are the more they understand their needs, preferences, likes and dislikes. Being outward looking and close to their customers should enable them to come up with the right product for the right market, just like Trivial Pursuit. The company must also be sure to organise itself to continue to deliver satisfaction to customers, and very importantly to tell everybody that they have the new product or service. In the late twentieth century nobody can afford to sit in a wood and wait for the world to beat a path to their door.

Assignment

Doing the Right Things

You are a member of a consortium which intends to invest in a new or established business. You recognise the importance of marketing in contributing to a company's success.

Task

Choose any well known company which in your opinion has got its marketing right. Prepare an informal report for the members of your consortium in which describe the company, its products and why you think that it is so good at marketing.

Chapter 2
Analysing Markets

Introduction

Analysing markets is the first step in the marketing process. In chapter one we spoke of the importance of the company and its staff being outward looking, because all the firm's activities and priorities must derive from the market place and from customers. If we accept that the objective of the marketer is 'to identify a group of potential customers who have an unsatisfied need which could be filled by our company', it is easy to see the importance of the analysis stage. It is so important that people in marketing jobs will often spend a considerable proportion of their time on this task.

Earlier we noted that authors such as Peters and Waterman tend to agree that successful companies are close to their customers. They understand their markets and the way in which they operate. Apart from some small businesses which are naturally close to their customers, and therefore have a very good understanding of them, firms cannot usually take this knowledge of their markets for granted. They have to develop and maintain this understanding through painstaking and continuous analysis. This chapter will examine the whole concept of analysing markets. It is a large area of study which needs to be broken down into a number of component parts because there are many factors that lead to a comprehensive understanding of a company's markets. Marketers ideally need to understand all features of their markets which may have impact on the success of their company. In fact, we can define marketing analysis as follows:

'The gathering and analysis of information concerning all the forces and institutions outside the firm which may be relevant to its present and future activities.'

This could be a virtually endless task, but broadly speaking there are three main aspects of analysing markets. Firstly the firm must analyse the general environment in which it operates. Secondly it must have a detailed knowledge of the way the market itself works and thirdly it must understand its customers. We will deal with each of these aspects.

2.1 Understanding the environment

We live in a constantly changing world, and as time goes by the pace of change is accelerating. From time to time major events change things suddenly and completely. Two world wars, the 1930's Depression and most recently the oil crisis of 1974 would be examples of such far reaching changes. On the whole though, firms are faced with a succession of small events and developments which are gradually and continuously changing the environment in which they must operate. Organisations must understand all outside forces which could have an effect upon their operations. We can group these outside forces into four categories, neatly summarised by the acronym 'PEST'. They are:

1. Political factors.

2. Economic factors.

3. Social factors.

4. Technological factors.

The marketer needs to be aware of the following.

2.1.1 Understanding the political environment

The basic operating conditions and business climate in every country are determined by its political system. The way business can behave in an advanced western democracy is very different to the way it must behave within the eastern bloc countries, and different again to the political climate it would have to face in an undeveloped third world country. Unfavourable political conditions might make it virtually impossible for a company to make money in some countries. Organisations must therefore both understand the current political environment and attempt to forecast future political developments which may affect the running of their business.

There are three aspects of the political environment which could affect a company's ability to carry out its business: the attitude of the government towards business activity, legal controls on business activity and the influence of pressure groups.

(a) Government's attitude towards business activity

This can be a fundamental factor in the profitability of most companies. Some people would argue that the Thatcher government of the 1980's created a more favourable operating climate for business activity in Britain than at any time since at least the 1950's. Lower corporate taxation, fewer government controls, financial help with consultancy and new technology and privatisation all opened new opportunities for business activity.

In other countries government attitudes towards profit making activities may be quite different. Communist countries, for example, will be much less sympathetic towards western profit motives. They will usually trade with western firms only on their terms and only for items which they need and approve.

Some countries are accused of 'economic nationalism', over-protecting their own industries against foreign competition. In such countries the government's objective often appears to outsiders to be to make life as difficult as possible for foreign businesses. This can lead to the kind of administrative harassment which makes it very difficult for a company to trade in that country.

An example would be the Japanese insistence that Trebor 'Sherbet Lemons' must be made in a less bright yellow, not because of any health hazard of the yellow colouring but because of its 'potentially harmful effect on the eyesight'. Trebor's sales to Japan were only £250,000 per annum, and with such problems it made them wonder whether it was worth the effort. Maybe this was exactly the effect the Japanese wished to achieve.

(Source: 'Japan's One Way Traffic', *Sunday Times*, 12/5/85.)

It should be stressed that a company has no inherent right to operate in an overseas market. Economic nationalism may be irritating to companies but it is a common political factor which they must contend with in their planning.

Political instability is another problem which businesses have to contend with in some countries which can be subject to sudden changes of regime, often with one dictator replacing another. Dictatorships can be unpredictable in themselves and wars or civil war can also flare up playing havoc with business. In general, if political stability cannot reasonably be relied upon for the duration of a business project in a particular country it would be prudent not to proceed. A clear example of political instability affecting business confidence could be seen in Hong Kong in the early 1980's. With Britain in negotiation with China over the arrangements for the return of the colony in 1997 many Hong Kong companies were worried about the Chinese Government's attitude to business. They were concerned that the free market might come to an end and be replaced by the centralised, socialist economic system of China. Long term business investment in Hong Kong fell dramatically. With the signing of a satisfactory agreement by Britain and China in September 1984 these fears were largely allayed and economic activity in Hong Kong returned to normal.

(b) Legal controls on business activity

Legislation can affect business life. In Britain the Sunday trading laws have made it impossible for many of the retailers who would like to open for business on Sundays to do so. Cigarette manufacturers have found their freedom to advertise progressively curtailed. Brewers and pubs have had to adjust to the effects of drink driving legislation.

Opportunities can arise from legislation. When the income tax regulations on company cars were changed, Ford saw the opportunity to introduce new 1.4 litre engine to offer motorists the largest permissible engine size in the bottom tax band and a 1.8 litre engine to do the same in the middle tax band. New health and safety regulations presented an opportunity to producers of safety equipment which many companies would now have to use.

Legal constraints do not have to be formal regulations. They may be unwritten 'gentlemen's agreements' such as the informal arrangement between Britain and Japan that imports of Japanese cars into the U.K. will be kept to 10% of new vehicle registrations. The opening of the Nissan factory in the North East of England and the arrangement which enables Rover to manufacture Honda cars in the U.K. are two examples of Japanese companies reacting to their political environment and finding new ways to sell more cars in Britain.

Product liability laws can vary extensively between different countries with punitive settlements against manufacturers of defective products common in the U.S.A. In general, product liability regulations are being tightened everywhere including the U.K., for example, the Consumer Protection Act, 1987.

For companies involved in international marketing the array of regulations in different countries can be bewildering. Different legal requirements for the same product sold in different countries may apply to packaging, labelling, trade marks, arrangements with retailers, wholesalers or sub-contract manufacturers, pricing, advertising, sales promotion and many more matters. It is one of the chief objectives of the 'Single European Market', to stimulate business by overcoming such constraints to trade within the European Community by 1992.

All of these factors are fundamental to a company's marketing strategy so a thorough knowledge of the legal environment of each country in which it operates is an essential part of marketing planning.

(c) The influence of pressure groups

The influence of pressure groups can often lead to the introduction of the kind of legal constraints mentioned in the previous section. ASH and other anti-smoking pressure groups were instrumental in bringing about the tightening of restrictions on TV advertising of cigarettes in the U.K. The Society of Motor Manufacturers was very active in advocating measures to stop further Japanese penetration of the British car market. It was the influence of pressure groups in the U.S.A that was largely responsible for their very tough product liability laws. (See Chapter 16 for more details).

Many pressure groups are currently seeking to persuade governments to impose further legal constraints on business activities of various kinds. Ecological pressure groups such as Greenpeace are trying to curb any business activities that might have an adverse effect on the natural environment. Ecological pressure groups in general would like to see regulations to reduce the lead content in petrol; the Government has already responded by introducing tax advantages on lead free petrol, but the pressure groups see this as only a start since most petrol sold still contains lead. They would like to see the banning of the manufacture of aerosols which are harmful to the ozone layer. Some companies such as Johnsons, have already responded by investing in much more expensive aerosol manufacturing plant which does not have this harmful effect. Some people would like to prevent the sale of drinks in disposable glass bottles and we already have a growing number of bottle banks in all parts of the country. They would also like to see the end of nuclear power, and opinion does indeed seem to be turning slowly against it in the U.K.

Monitoring the activities of pressure groups can be a very good way for companies to predict future legal constraints. Pressure groups which attract a high level of popular support will often force governments to introduce legislation in support of their cause sooner or later.

2.1.2 The economic environment

As indicated in section 2.2.1 the economic environment within a country will often be directly influenced by the political attitude of its government. However, national economies are becoming increasingly dependent upon world economic trends and marketers need to be alert to all the economic factors which might influence their business.

In analysing investment potential in any particular country the marketer will need to be fully aware of the following economic factors.

(a) Income levels

Statistics about the size of the economies of different countries are readily available and are usually expressed in terms of GDP or GNP. GDP (Gross Domestic Product) refers to the value of goods produced within the country and GNP (Gross National Product) to the value of domestically produced goods plus the country's overseas earnings. GNP therefore describes most closely the country's national income.

In general one would expect more business opportunities in a country with a high national income than in one with a low GNP. However it may not be so simple. A country with a very large population, like India for example, might have a high GNP but may not be a rich country. Other countries, like the Gulf States, could be extremely rich, but would have a relatively low GNP due to their very small size.

A more accurate measure therefore of a country's wealth would be its 'per capita' income which is its national income divided by its population. This gives a rough indication of that country's standard of living. A typical Gulf State might have a per capita income of around $20,000 per annum, whereas some African countries would struggle to exceed $100 per annum. Most western economies have per capita incomes of around $10,000 per annum, with the US in the lead and Britain lagging some way behind the wealthier European countries such as Switzerland, West Germany, Sweden or Austria.

The marketer's first step in his economic analysis therefore is to ascertain the wealth of the country, and the most accurate indicator for this is per capita income.

(b) Growth rates

Some countries, for example Brazil, have shown rapid growth rates over recent years. Others, such as Britain until recently have had a much less satisfactory growth records. At any given level of national wealth it is clearly preferable to invest in a high growth rather than a low growth economy.

(c) Inflation

Inflation erodes purchasing power and causes other severe problems for marketers in areas such as pricing and estimating demand accurately. At times of high inflation people feel worse off. They may spend less or trade down. For example, it is possible that the high inflation of the 1970's in Britain contributed to the move away from branded groceries towards cheaper own label products.

(d) Purchasing power

What the marketer is really interested in is the purchasing power of his potential customers. Wage levels, price levels, the rates of taxation and inflation can all affect the amount of money that individuals and companies have to spend.

There are two kinds of purchasing power that the marketer should be interested in. Firstly, 'disposable income' describes the amount of money that people have left after deductions such as tax and National Insurance contributions. This is more useful than general measures such as per capita income, but may still not describe the amount of money people actually have to spend. A better indicator of spending power is 'discretionary income' which describes the amount of money people have left over to spend as they choose after they have covered essential expenditure (housing, food, basic clothing etc). An apparently affluent family in the south east may not have as much discretionary income as a northern family with a lower disposable income because of the much higher housing costs in the south east.

(e) Distribution of income

Marketers still need more precise economic information. So far all figures have referred to 'averages'. Such averaged figures can hide a wide variety of income levels. The very rich, the middle class and the very poor in India will represent three totally different markets. With the importance of segmentation in marketing planning (see Chapter 3) it is vital that marketers have a detailed economic picture.

They will therefore want to know how the country's wealth is distributed. For example, Sweden has a higher per capita income than the U.K. and it is much more evenly distributed, with few very poor or very rich and a very large comfortable middle income bracket. Britain's lower national income is distributed much less evenly, with a much larger population of poor people, a smaller middle class and a much larger percentage of rich people. Although there are quite a number of countries with a higher 'per capita' income than Britain, the British market is the third best market for BMW cars after the US and West Germany. Some very poor countries can be surprisingly good markets for luxury products because although the large majority of the population is very poor, the ruling elite may be extremely wealthy. Some African countries for example have been very good markets for Mercedes cars and whisky.

(f) Consumption patterns

Even now the marketer may not have a sufficiently accurate picture. Although he may have established the level of spending power of different classes of the population, he still cannot be sure that there will be a market for his type of product. Sales patterns for some products may deviate from expectations. Cultural factors may also influence spending. Britain for example has a higher level of home video penetration than other European countries. This could not be predicted from any income statistics for there are other European countries which have higher levels of discretionary income, and one would therefore expect them to spend more on expensive consumer durables. The British, however, are particularly home oriented and spend more of their leisure time at home.

Another example to illustrate different consumption patterns would be the relative levels of vacuum cleaner ownership in Britain and Italy. Over three quarters of British homes have a vacuum cleaner, whereas less than one third of Italian homes possess one. The Italians do not have a lower per capita income than the British, nor are they more dirty. In fact they have fewer carpets in their homes.

2.1.3 The social environment

As suggested in the last paragraph, the potential of a market for a particular product cannot be estimated solely from straight economic data. Other behavioural factors, often deeply engrained in the culture of a community can often distort seemingly clear economic indicators. We can analyse the social environment in two parts. Firstly we will look at demographic trends, which are factual, often detailed and always very informative for the marketer. The social picture cannot be complete however without looking at the behavioural aspects of society, which are often cultural and usually much less clear cut.

(a) The social environment - demographic aspects

Demography is the study of populations. This is of great relevance to the marketer since people are the end result of most of his activities. Ultimately the marketer is interested in people buying his product or service in sufficient volumes to make his business profitable. The demographic make-up of the population will help him to work out whether he is likely to achieve this objective. There are five main demographic factors of interest to the marketer.

(i) Population size

The sheer size of the population may be of more relevance to some products than to others. For luxury goods consumed by only a wealthy élite, total population size will be of little relevance, but will be much more important for basic goods bought by a large percentage of the population.

(ii) Population growth

For basic products, strong population growth means an inevitably increasing potential market.

(iii) Geographical distribution

The marketer needs to know where the people are and whether the market is densely or sparsely populated. A densely populated market such as Singapore is easier and less costly to penetrate than a more sparsely populated area such as neighbouring Malaysia.

(iv) Age distribution

Since different age groups often buy various goods and services, the age distribution of the population is of great relevance to marketing planning. In Britain a number of demographic trends are currently apparent. Since the birth rate fell from the mid

1960's the youth market is declining. This will have adverse repercussions for companies which rely heavily on that market e.g. pop records, teenage magazines, young fashion shops. The next generation, the 25 - 45 year olds, often known as the baby boomers since they were born in the years of high birth rate after the Second World War, will be a large market. With rising income levels this is resulting in a move up-market, especially evident in retailing. Chains like Next, Richards and Principles have been the growth areas in women's clothing. The other demographic group showing strong growth is retired people. In particular a new, younger, more affluent retired group is emerging, keen to spend money, especially on leisure. Activities from gardening to foreign holidays represent significant market opportunities here.

(v) Changing family patterns

The typical family is no more. Mr. and Mrs. Average, both in their first marriage, with two kids, the husband at work and the wife at home, now represent less than 4% of all families. Divorces are increasingly common as are single parent families, all of which means that the number of households is increasing at a faster rate than the population. Thus, items such as fridges which are purchased by households rather than individuals have more potential sales growth than would be apparent from the bare population statistics. The huge growth in the working women population has revolutionised many markets - the growth in convenience food and labour-saving appliances being obvious examples.

(b) The social environment - behavioural aspects

As indicated earlier, marketing is a behavioural discipline. It is all about people and the way they behave when purchasing goods and services. Individual buying behaviour will be examined in section 2.4 but there are likely to be certain behavioural characteristics which are common to large sections of a community. It is these general cultural factors which the marketer seeking to compare the potential of two markets (e.g. two countries) would consider at this stage. Many factors could be relevant here. We will highlight some of them.

(i) Core cultural values

People grow up in a society which shapes their basic beliefs and values. Core cultural values are passed on from parents to children and are reinforced by the major institutions of society such as school, church and government. Marketers would be wise not to attempt to override core cultural values. Philip Kotler gives the example of the topless dress which attacks a core cultural value and would therefore be unlikely to succeed commercially, whereas a very revealing low cut or see through dress does not quite breach that core value and may therefore succeed. In other countries, such as those in the Moslem world, core cultural values demand much greater female modesty, and an appropriate stance must once again be taken by marketers.

(ii) Social trends

Any community will also have a large variety of secondary cultural or social values. These may be attitudes, beliefs or trends which are less firmly adhered to than the core cultural values, indeed, they may be accepted only by certain sections of the community. Current examples in the U.K. would be physical fitness and healthy eating, both clear national trends, both followed more by some sections of society than by others but both affording considerable marketing opportunities.

(iii) Aesthetic values

A marketer needs to know what a society rates as attractive and unattractive in terms of design, styling, fashion and colour. Early Japanese cars for example suffered in European markets because their styling was geared to American tastes. This resulted in a brash, chromy image which they have struggled to remove ever since.

2.1.4 The Technological Environment

Technology is changing continuously and at an ever increasing rate. You have only to think of just a few of the major inventions which have occurred in the twentieth century such as electric lighting, radio, television, photocopying, X-rays, life support machines, synthetic fibres, plastics, electronic circuits and the computer. An organisation that does not keep up with relevant technological advances will be doomed to failure, sooner or later. As far as the technological environment is concerned the marketer should be concerned with four main factors in his planning.

(a) New processes

New ways of doing things are being constantly fuelled by technological innovations. One has only to think of cash dispensers outside banks, EPOS tills in supermarkets (the tills which record the price of each item simply by reading the bar code), flexible manufacturing systems which enable many of the operations involved in building a car to be performed automatically by robots. The firm has to keep up with these changes. If it does not and its competitors adopt them it will soon become uncompetitive. Equally, if it does not keep up with new technology it may not be able to meet the needs of its customers. The manufacturer of shop tills which could not supply the new EPOS tills would soon find itself losing customers. The British washing machine industry suffered a major setback in the 1970's because it placed too much reliance on the continuing popularity of the twin tub, when foreign manufacturers were putting more effort into the difficult task of developing new automatic washing machines.

(b) New materials

Carbon fibres, graphite, and kevlar are just three of the new high performance materials which have come to prominence in recent years. They are now widely used in the manufacture of sporting equipment from squash rackets to racing cars, from fishing rods to catamarans. Any manufacturer of high performance sporting goods who had not adapted to these new materials would find sales falling dramatically. The customers demand them.

(c) Generic replacements

A generic product is a product class. Coffee is a generic product, Nescafé is not, it is a particular brand of coffee. From time to time a technological innovation will make a generic product (and obviously all the specific products within that class) obsolete. Cassette recorders took over from reel to reel tape recorders. Calculators made slide rules obsolete. Drawing office equipment is gradually being replaced by computer aided design.

The American marketing professor, Theodore Levitt, has explained why this happens. Nobody, says Levitt, buys drills. Customers buy holes. It is not the drill itself which they value but its hole making capabilities because it is the holes for which they have a need. If a new, more cost effective method of making holes were developed (lasers perhaps) customers would soon abandon the traditional steel twist drill and turn to the new hole making method. If drill manufacturers could not supply the new hole makers they would soon find themselves without a business. As Levitt says, customers do not buy products, they buy the service which that product performs for them. This is how manufacturers should think of their products, in terms of the customer need which they meet. Washing machine buyers are not actually buying a white lump of metal but the ability to wash their clothes in the most easy, labour saving way possible. If the British washing machine manufacturers had thought of their product in this way the importance of investing in the development of the automatic machine would have been self evident.

(d) Material culture

It is vital therefore to keep up with new technology otherwise the company could find its products made obsolete at any time. However, this does not necessarily mean that companies always have to adopt the latest technology for all their products to all their markets. The level of technology must be suited to the technological development of each market. The first home computers for example could not have been successful in a society where households did not already possess a television and a cassette recorder. As well as material infrastructure, societies need a certain level of technological understanding to use and maintain complex technical products. Third world countries have often been littered with abandoned products (for example vehicles) which cannot be maintained due to lack of know how or spare parts. Thus a seemingly obsolete product may find a buoyant market in some countries. Raleigh for example sold bicycles very successfully to third world countries long after its sales had declined seriously in the U.K.

As you can now see, analysing information on all the forces and institutions which make up the external environment and can affect the firm is a major task. Equally, you can also see the importance of a close understanding of this wider environment. If the marketer is to identify promising marketing opportunities he must gradually build up a kind of jigsaw picture of the firm's operating environment. We have now examined the first four pieces. At the moment the jigsaw resembles the diagram below.

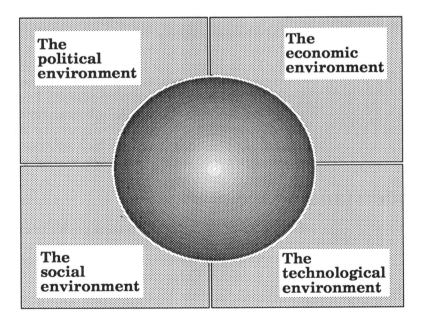

Figure 2.1 The firm's wider environment.

Some organisations specialise in the gathering and analysis of environmental data. They produce reports and often make forecasts, all of which can be very interesting to the marketer. One such organisation is the Henley Centre for Forecasting. To illustrate the value of environmental analysis two of the Centre's recent forecasts for future market trends, the growth of the 'Connoisseur Consumer' and the 'Cellular Household' are included below.

The Connoisseur Consumer

As markets become more competitive consumers are faced with more and more choice. Ford, for example, may have only four basic alternative car models in the U.K. (Fiesta, Escort, Sierra and Granada) but the company actually sells over one hundred different variations of those four basic cars. They have to, because customers demand choice. They want to be able to buy exactly the combination of features which they prefer. Gone are the mass production days of the Model T Ford, all identical and in black. Consumers now want to be different, they want to express individuality. They take pride in shopping around, comparing different brands, and often selecting a little heard of brand which may express their individuality and perhaps also their skill as a buyer. Organisations will have to cater for these needs. They will have to provide a wide range of choice, especially with items like leisure or sporting goods. This will provide opportunities for small firms to exploit market niches (see Chapter 3), and may see the market share of leading brands being gradually eroded.

The Cellular Household

Families are tending to spend less time together as a unit. Mother, father and children are increasingly likely to be 'doing their own thing'. They no longer want to conform to set patterns laid down by the family or by society at large. The penetration of videos allows people to watch their favourite TV programmes at a time which suits them. The adoption of microwaves allows them to eat their meal at a time that suits them, maybe not with the family but upstairs in their bedroom watching a recording of the previous evening's TV programme. Many households now have two or even three TV's. Products which can meet the needs of this independent 'self- service' lifestyle will be successful. As well as the video and the microwave, products currently meeting the needs of the cellular household include wine boxes, personal stereos, convenience meals and takeaway food.

Marketers planning their future strategy would be well advised to take considerable notice of the kind of environmental trends predicted by organisations such as the Henley Centre for Forecasting. However, although the wider environment is very important most marketers will be even more concerned about the factors which govern activity in their own particular markets. If you sell dish washers or running shoes the concepts of the cellular household and the connoisseur consumer will be of extreme interest, but there will also be many more forces and organisations specific to your own market which will need very careful analysis. It is to the understanding of particular markets that we must now turn our attention.

2.2 Understanding the market

Some authors refer to the market environment as the 'task environment'. Understanding this task environment involves an analysis of six main factors: 1. Market structure and performance 2. Competitive forces 3. Intermediaries 4. Suppliers 5. Other publics 6. Customers

Customers are so important that they require a more in depth analysis which we will leave to section 2.4. The remaining five aspects of the market environment will be examined in this section.

2.2.1 Market structure and performance

According to Kotler, a market is:

'A collection of individuals and organisations who are actual or potential buyers of a product or service.'

Market structure concerns the make-up of markets and tends to involve factors which change slowly over time. Market performance covers the more dynamic aspects of markets. There are a number of important factors concerning the market itself which must be analysed. These are buyers, purchases, market size, market potential, market growth, barriers to entry.

2.2.2 Buyers

The historical view of a market was that of a physical space in which buyers and sellers could meet to buy and sell goods and services. Economists have basically kept the same definition of markets but see this market place activity in its abstract form. They see markets as involving all the potential buyers and sellers of a particular good or service and regard the economic exchange process as the essential activity within that arena. The marketing discipline limits its definition to the buying side of these transactions. The market for instant custard refers to all those consumers who buy instant custard. The organisations which sell instant custard will be referred to as 'the industry' or 'the competition'.

As far as marketers are concerned there are two basic types of market - consumer markets organisational markets.

Consumer markets are made up of individuals who buy items for personal or domestic consumption. They typically buy from middlemen such as retailers and transactions are of a low value. A £5,000 purchase (e.g. a car) is a highly important and very infrequent transaction for most buyers in consumer markets.

Organisational markets can be further split into industrial markets, where buyers purchase goods and services to use in the production of other goods or services; reseller markets where organisations such as shops buy goods for resale, and government markets where public sector organisations buy goods and services which they consume in the provision of state services. For most organisational buyers £5,000 will represent a relatively small transaction. Orders worth millions of pounds frequently occur in organisational markets.

2.2.3 Purchases

Buyers, by definition, must be buying something. This 'something' is a purchase. Markets can be classified according to the type of purchases being made. There are two different methods of classifying markets according to the nature of the purchases made. The first method is based on the tangibility of the purchases and can be divided into three sections:

(a) Durables

These are tangible goods, which are expected to last for a long time in use, at least for over a year. Furniture and tools would be examples.

(b) Non-durables

These are tangible goods which are normally used up quickly, after one or a few uses. Food and batteries would be examples.

(c) Services

These are intangible items such as activities, manual or intellectual forms of assistance or even ideas. They cannot be touched or stored but they do offer benefits to buyers. Hair dressing, decorating, education and advertising are all services.

The second method is based on the way in which buyers make such purchases and can also be divided into three categories:

(i) Convenience goods

Usually purchased on a regular basis, often of relatively low value, purchases of convenience goods are made with very little thought or pre-planning. They are usually habitual purchases but may also be made on impulse. Basic foodstuffs, sweets, beer and newspapers would all come into this category.

(ii) Shopping goods

These purchases require more consideration. Buyers will often 'shop around' comparing competing brands with the objective of obtaining the best value for their money. They will also include high visibility items, often called 'conspicuous purchases' which may affect the way they are viewed by other people, and whose purchase therefore involves particular care. Examples of shopping goods would be clothes, furniture, holidays and perhaps some special food purchases such as wine.

(iii) Speciality goods

These purchases have the same attributes as shopping goods but are also special interest purchases, typical of the behaviour of the 'conoisseur consumer'. For these purchases consumers will be prepared to go out of their way to buy exactly what they want. They will be more knowledgeable about these goods and the relative attributes of competing brands and they will often want to buy the best they can afford rather than going for value for money. Speciality goods include cameras, hi- fi and sporting equipment.

As you can see, there is no set way of defining a market. Firms will often develop their own definition based partly on the kind of product being sold and partly on the typical target customer. Thus as far as Club 18 - 30 is concerned their market would be defined as 'foreign package holidays (product) for young adults (buyer)'.

Market analysis, however, will often concentrate on the more dynamic aspects of markets such as those outlined below.

2.2.4 Market size

For common consumer goods and services in western markets, market size figures, expressed in value or volume terms, are usually quite easy to find in published form. For obscure goods, many industrial goods and virtually all products in less developed countries, market size statistics are much more difficult to come by. These figures are essential however for planning purposes. If the size of the market is known, and the company believes it can secure a percentage share of that market then sales can be forecasted. Therefore, if market size information is not readily available it must be estimated using primary research techniques (see Chapter 4).

2.2.5 Market potential

Market size refers to the existing total of purchases of that product type, but as our original definition indicated, marketers regard markets as including all potential future buyers as well as existing buyers. The potential U.K. market for domestic dish washers includes every household, but the existing market size is still only a small proportion of its potential.

In theory, a market can exist when not a single sale has been made. This is neatly illustrated by a common marketing story concerning two shoe salesmen. The first was sent by his company to explore the prospects for exporting shoes to Mars. Following his visit he returned very depressed reporting that there was no market because nobody wore shoes. Just to make sure the company also sent the second salesman to investigate. He returned very excited saying that the potential market was enormous because nobody had any shoes! Of course, to discover the real answer the company would have to ascertain whether the Martians knew all about shoes but had rejected them or were ignorant of the whole concept of shoes. However, the story illustrates very well the difference between existing and potential market size.

2.2.6 Market growth

If potential is greater than existing market size the marketer would like to know how quickly the market is likely to grow towards that potential. Marketers always seek high growth markets because they are often more profitable. In low growth, static or declining markets, competition tends to be very fierce with sellers often resorting to extreme tactics such as large price cuts. This is often felt necessary as the only way in which companies can increase their sales is to take business from competitors. In high growth markets it is much easier for suppliers to meet their growth targets. a company seeking an annual growth in sales of 10% operating in a market with a growth rate of 10% needs to perform only at the industry average to achieve its objectives. It does not need to take business from competitors but can rely on the fact that the market is getting bigger. In the early days of personal computers when the market was showing rapid growth many British manufacturers performed extremely well. But as market size began to approach market potential, growth slowed and competition intensified. Many smaller manufacturers went out of business and even the most famous such as Sinclair and Acorn experienced extreme difficulties.

2.2.7 Barriers to entry

Some markets are made artificially less attractive because governments erect barriers to entry against foreign suppliers. Usually in the form of tariff barriers (import duties) they can also take the form of administrative or safety procedures which are difficult and expensive to conform to. Barriers to entry can also be commercial. In the washing powder market, for example, the two dominating suppliers, Lever Bros. and Proctor and Gamble try to make it very difficult for new competitors to enter the market. Each produces a wide range of similar brands, filling the supermarket shelves and making it very difficult for a new entrant to find an opening. By maintaining extremely high advertising expenditures they make the promotion of any new competing product extremely expensive.

2.3 Competitive forces

Amongst the main factors affecting any business are the activities of its competitors. Michael Porter defines competitors as:

'the group of firms producing products that are close substitutes for each other.'

In fact we can identify three levels of competition:- direct competition, indirect competition, need competition.

2.3.1 Direct Competition

Consumers purchasing virtually any product or service will usually have the opportunity of choosing between the offerings of a number of competing suppliers. A person in the market for a small family car may be choosing between direct competitors such as a new Ford Escort, Austin Maestro, Vauxhall Astra, Peugeot 309 and other cars of a similar size. People who want their house painted may seek quotations from several different painters and decorators.

2.3.2 Indirect Competition

Sometimes, however, consumers can examine alternative ways of meeting the same need. An elderly lady considering the purchase of a new car may decide that since she does not make many long journeys she will continue running her old car and use the train for long journeys. Alternatively she might decide that it would be more economical and less trouble to cease owning a car altogether and rely on a combination of bus, taxi and hire cars to meet her travel needs. a couple whose house needs painting could decide to do it themselves rather than employ a professional painter.

2.3.3 Need Competition

A third possibility is that the consumer may choose to leave that particular need unsatisfied for the time being. Competition can occur between needs as well as between methods of meeting a particular need. The potential car buyer may decide to buy new furniture instead, and the couple whose house needs painting may decide to neglect their property and have a better summer holiday instead.

Competition therefore is anything which could prompt a potential buyer to spend their money elsewhere.

Balancing threats and opportunities

Businesses do not necessarily make it their priority to avoid competition. It is quite common in large cities to see competing shops clustered together in the same location. a certain street will become known as the place to go to buy a stereo because it is filled with one stereo shop after another. a second street may be populated with Greek restaurants, another with fashion shops. Perhaps the owners of these businesses regard indirect or need competition as a greater threat.

In analysing market opportunities a balance must be struck between market opportunities and competitive threats. In an ideal world one would hope to find an unexploited market with unlimited growth potential and no competition whatsoever. In the real world it is likely that the greater the market opportunity the more intense will be the competition, because, naturally, many firms are attracted by market opportunities. The shrewd marketer will therefore look not just for a good market opportunity but for one where the level of competition is not excessive.

2.4 Intermediaries

In many markets, intermediaries such as retailers, wholesalers or agents are necessary to get the product to its final consumers (see Chapter 9 for a thorough discussion of the role of distributors). In foreign markets use of middlemen will almost certainly be necessary.

A vital part of analysing market opportunities is ensuring that the distribution network will be adequate to support the forecasted level of sales in that market. In some less developed countries the economic infrastructure may make this very uncertain.

Distributors' margins also need to be taken into account. In Japan some imported products can end up costing almost twice as much as in their home markets largely because of high distribution costs.

2.5 Suppliers

If products are to be manufactured in a market rather than imported, the chain of supply will be important. Suppliers can affect the company's marketing operation in several ways. They can affect the quality of the product. Jaguar cars had developed a very bad reputation for quality by the end of the 1970's. When the company made a determined effort to improve matters under the management of John Egan it discovered that although Jaguar's own quality control was poor, the majority of quality problems were actually caused by sub-standard components obtained from outside suppliers.

Suppliers can also cause pricing problems, particularly if the company is dependent on one or a very small number of suppliers and of course they can affect production if their deliveries prove unreliable.

2.6 Other publics

A 'public' is any group that has an actual or a potential interest in or impact on a company's ability to achieve its objectives. The marketer should therefore be aware of the possible impact of medi publics (newspapers, TV, advertising agencies), financial publics, especially shareholders, government publics such as safety inspectors, pressure groups and the general public, since a good public image is always to the company's advantage. For example, pressure groups such as Friends of the Earth are currently campaigning about the unwelcome ecological effects caused by the destruction of tropical rain forests in countries like Brazil and Indonesia. They have produced a 'Good Wood Guide' which outlines the sources of timber which they believe to be produced in an ecologically responsible manner. The guide also highlights the manufacturers and retailers who are using or stocking this 'approved' wood. This type of pressure group activity can exert a significant influence on the market environment. Buyers, competitors, intermediaries and suppliers may modify their views over a period of time.

The market analysis jigsaw has become a little more complete with the examination of the organisation's market (or task) environment. The diagram below summarises this environment.

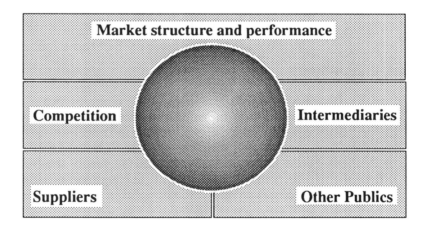

Figure 2.2 The organisation's market environment.

In identifying market opportunities therefore, the marketer must ensure that the market is large enough, can sustain adequate growth, is not too competitive and that the organisation's marketing effort is not likely to be harmed by intermediaries, suppliers or any other public. However, we did stress that markets are about people, buyers and potential buyers to be specific. If the marketer's objective is to identify a group of buyers who have an unsatisfied need which could be filled by a product from his company, then he must know considerably more about these buyers and potential buyers. It is to this are that we must therefore now turn our attention.

2.7 Understanding Customers

Developing a very close understanding of customers lies at the heart of the marketer's work. Marketing is all about meeting their needs for goods and services so marketers must acquire as much knowledge as possible about all aspects of consumers' needs for their organisation's goods or services.

As indicated in the previous section markets fall into the two broad categories of consumer and organisational markets. The customers in these two kinds of market can be very different as can their buying behaviour. We will therefore examine each in turn.

Understanding buyers in consumer markets.

According to Kotler a consumer market is:

' *collection of all the individuals and households who buy or acquire goods or services for personal consumption'.*

In order to fully understand customers the marketer needs to be able to answer four straight-forward questions.

Who buys?

What do they buy?

How do they buy?

How do they make their buying decisions?

We will try to answer each of these four questions in turn.

2.7.1 Who buys?

A detailed knowledge of the type or types of consumer who buy the organisation's products is essential to marketers. They will want to know all about their age, sex, family position, occupation, income, interests and activities. Marketers also need to acquire information about their home and the neighbourhood in which it is found, the kind of newspapers and magazines they read, the car they drive, in fact, all about their lifestyle in general. Through the possession of such detailed knowledge marketers can match the benefits offered by their product or service to the right group of consumers. In order to match their product accurately enough marketers will often divide the total buying population into much smaller groups of consumers. These small groups are known as 'segments' and might include all consumers in a certain age group, a certain income band or with a similar lifestyle. Many people believe that this process of matching the product or service very accurately to segments of the market lies at the heart of marketing success. The whole process of segmentation will be examined in much more detail in Chapter 3.

2.7.2 What do they buy?

This question is a logical development of the first. If the aim of marketing is to try to match the organisation's product with the right market segment then marketers must know exactly which products are currently bought by those consumers. In fact, the 'what' should refer broadly to the whole marketing mix since the benefits sought by consumers may lie in the non-product areas of the marketing mix.

This is one of the reasons why consumer marketers find market share figures so important. Market share figures provide the basis for answering this question. It is important to know whether buyers prefer an Escort, Maestro, Astra, Golf or Tipo. For most common consumer products companies will study share statistics on a monthly basis. They will look for the effects of quite small modifications in the marketing mix such as a new sales promotion as well as major developments such as the introduction of a new model.

Marketers do however need much more detailed information on exactly what customers buy. The car manufacturer might hold a number of clinics in different regions with their own and competitors' models on hand. Consumers, typical of those who make up the Escort buying segment, will be invited to view and test drive cars, to share some refreshments, perhaps see a company video, but above all to answer some detailed questions. With the cars there in front of them, they can be asked exactly what they like and dislike about each one. The smallest details will be covered, such as the clarity of the stereo, the ease of use of the switches, the fabric on the seats. As a result of such clinics marketers can rank consumers' priorities for different features and see how well their own models meet these needs compared to their competitors' models.

The marketers ultimate objective is not to build the world's best car but to produce a model which most closely matches 'what consumers want to buy'.

2.7.3 How do they buy?

This question is again a logical development of the previous one. It is concerned with the 'place' element of the marketing mix in its broadest sense and in particular with the way that people behave when they are buying the product or service. There are four main questions that the marketer will want to be able to answer here.

> Where do they buy?
>
> When do they buy?
>
> How often do they buy?
>
> How loyally do they buy?

(a) Where do they buy?

Some goods, such as most groceries, are bought at huge superstores. Some, like bread, meat and fresh vegetables at local shops. Some, such as fashion clothing or cameras are bought in specialist stores. Some, like soft drinks, are bought almost anywhere that is convenient, from the newsagent's to the railway station, from the fish and chip shop to the petrol station.

There are certain products that people like to choose at home. Leisure purchases often come into this category. Some people like to spend hours studying the seed catalogue before buying next years seeds for their garden. For products like this, people enjoy the actual process of buying. The way they are sold must therefore cater to this need, so seed companies usually provide interesting, detailed catalogues whilst sailboard manufacturers will produce exciting brochures full of dramatic photographs.

(b) When do they buy?

There are two aspects to this question. Firstly, there is the time of day or week when products are bought. Milk and newspapers, for example, are required early in the morning. Supermarkets have discovered that more and more people like to do their grocery shopping in the early evening after work, so most are now open until eight o'clock. Petrol stations have discovered that there is a range of basic essential items that households can run out of at any time and need to buy urgently. Many have therefore opened small convenience stores since their site is already open for business for petrol for long hours.

The second aspect for less frequently purchased items is the time of year. Fireworks are purchased mainly once a year, though the date of the annual order placed by retailers will be long before November. There is also a growing segment of that market which purchases fireworks all the year round for use at wedding receptions, parties and other functions.

(c) How often do they buy?

Frequency of purchase is very important to the marketer. The less frequently a product is purchased the more likely it is to be a significant act for the buyer, who therefore gives the whole buying process more thought. Very often marketers will divide buyers into heavy, medium and light users. Light users of the same product may buy in a different way from heavy users. A heavy magazine buyer, for example, will probably have a regular weekly order for a particular magazine, or several magazines, and will tend to stick to the same titles. An occasional magazine buyer, who buys a magazine to read on a long train journey perhaps, is likely to take much more care over the purchase of that magazine, flicking through several titles and inspecting the contents before making his decision. This leads into our fourth question.

(d) How loyally do people buy?

Some products command a very high degree of brand loyalty. National newspapers are a good example. The higher the buyers' level of loyalty the more difficult it is to break into a market. Eddie Shah discovered this with his *Today* newspaper, which did not reach the level of sales he predicted. Even now, long after Shah's departure the circulation of *Today* is well below its main rivals such as the *Express* and *Mail*. In general magazines have a less loyal following, with many chosen at the newsagent's or newstand by buyers who are sometimes in a rush and who often choose a different title each time. This different buyer behaviour is reflected in the much greater number of launches of new magazines.

2.7.4 How do they make their buying decisions?

Understanding the way in which consumers make their decision to purchase a product or service is a vital part of the marketing manager's job. As we will see, this can be a long and complicated process, and the organisation will need to apply the right information, publicity and persuasion at the right time if it is to influence consumers' decision making processes.

The basic steps in this decision making process are shown in the diagram below.

Figure 2.3 The purchase decision making process.

Each one of these steps can involve a number of factors of relevance to the marketer, so we will examine each in more detail.

(a) Felt need

We constantly experience needs of all kinds from basic needs for warmth and food, called 'biogenic needs', to more sophisticated needs for job satisfaction and social status, termed 'psychogenic needs'. Before the purchase decision making process can begin the consumer must first become aware of the existence of a need. This is sometimes called 'problem recognition'. Once the consumer has perceived this 'felt need' he will be motivated towards the satisfaction of that need.

A need can be aroused through internal or external stimuli. Hunger pangs may originate purely internally if a long time has elapsed since eating, or they may be triggered by external stimuli such as walking past a fish and chip shop. The marketer can aim to stimulate needs through means such as advertising. In the late 1970's people did not know that they needed video recorders until advertising pointed out their existence and their benefits.

Once a person is aware of a need it becomes a 'drive', so-called because the individual feels a drive or an urge to satisfy that need. Marketers must understand the kind of drives that lead a consumer to choose their product offering. Some cars may be bought to satisfy a need for basic transportation, some to satisfy a need for status, and others to satisfy a need for excitement. The nature of the felt need should exert a significant influence on the kind of marketing communications developed by suppliers.

(b) Information search

Having become aware of the need or problem, the individual sets about solving it. Sometimes a problem is solved immediately. Hunger is felt and a biscuit may be eaten. Sometimes however the problem is greater and a process of seeking information of relevance to the solution of the problem begins.

The first source of information consulted by most people is the memory. If I need a new exhaust pipe for my car, my first thought will almost certainly be towards my solution of this problem the last time it arose. Where did I have the new exhaust pipe fitted last time? Was it O.K., was the service efficient, was it reasonably priced? If my memory is favourable, that may be the end of it. I may skip the evaluation stage, make a decision to return to the same place and get the car booked in.

Often however the information search will be more lengthy. I may not be entirely satisfied that the information stored in my memory is adequate to enable me to make the best decision on this matter. If so, I must turn to external sources of information. As a minimum search I may ring up another two or three exhaust centres simply to find out some prices. But what if it is my first car and I have never had to replace an exhaust pipe before?

I may consult up to three kinds of external sources of information. Firstly, I might use personal sources of information such as a friend, next door neighbour or relative who might have much more experience of this kind of purchase and could give me good advice. Secondly, I might consult public sources of information. These are objective sources not connected with the manufacturer, such as the Yellow Pages or Thomsons Directory. For some products there may be buyers' guides published, or one might consult a magazine such as *Which?* to find a good comparison of alternative products. The third possibility would be to rely on commercial sources of information, which in this case would consist mainly of exhaust centres' advertising in the local press. I could ring up several centres and ask for full details of their service, the kind of exhaust they would fit, the length of guarantee with the product and the price.

The decision making process covered so far can be demonstrated in the diagram below.

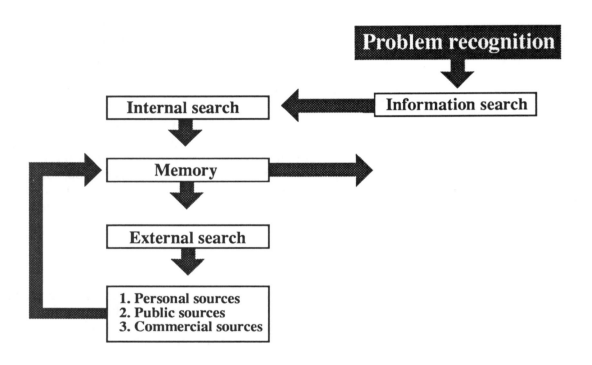

Figure 2.4 Problem solving: the search for information.

A new exhaust pipe is not a major purchase and its urgency must necessarily put a time limit on the information search stage. Some products, however, represent a big step for buyers to take. In their concern to make a good decision they may spend a considerable time at the information search stage. They will not be actively seeking information the whole time but they will be in a state of 'heightened attention'. In other words they will be alert to any information concerning that felt need whether it arises in advertisements, articles or casual conversation.

Knowledge of the sources of information generally consulted by buyers of their product is very useful to marketers. They must make great efforts to ensure that information concerning their products is available from those sources. It would be foolish, for example if the exhaust centre did not invest in an eye catching display advert in Yellow Pages which is likely to be the first source of information consulted by many buyers of replacement exhaust pipes.

(c) Evaluation

By this time a number of alternative ways of meeting the felt need should become evident. These alternatives must therefore be evaluated which involves determining how well each alternative meets the felt need. Sometimes deep rooted beliefs can affect this process. Cultural factors often influence attitudes and behaviour, as discussed earlier in this chapter. Prejudices may rule out some of the alternatives. Some people, for example, prefer not to buy foreign cars. However usually, people try to make an objective comparison of different alternatives. Each alternative will offer definite benefits but probably some drawbacks too. For more important purchases buyers will attempt to weigh the benefits and drawbacks of each alternative against each other. Buyers might even draw up lists to help them with their evaluation. For most purchases however, the time for evaluation is limited. Many decisions, for example are made whilst walking round the supermarket. In this situation most of the alternatives are quickly eliminated and the comparison of perhaps two alternatives will be made a little more carefully. Buyers therefore can arrive at product preferences in different ways. In fact the same individual might arrive at product preferences in different ways for different product classes. Careful research must therefore be undertaken by the marketer to establish buyers' methods of evaluation for his particular product.

(d) Decision

Having weighed up the alternatives a decision will be made. Even then, this decision may still be little more than an 'intention to purchase'. Unless the buyer is in the shop handing over cash for the item or on the telephone placing an order, the decision is usually a stage which precedes the purchase by some time. For some expensive items the decision in principle to buy and the choice of one of the alternatives could precede the actual purchase by a lengthy period, perhaps several months.

This is a problem for the marketer because research studies show that stated intention to purchase is almost always significantly higher than the subsequent level of actual purchases. Several factors can interfere with the decision. Firstly, unfavourable attitudes of friends or family might weaken a prospective buyer's resolve. The man who has firmly resolved, in the company of male colleagues at work, to buy an expensive set of new golf clubs, may never quite get round to making the purchase if his wife's opposition is sufficiently intense. Secondly, unforeseen factors such as redundancy, or an unexpected expense such as a car breakdown may force the postponement of a purchase. The more expensive the item and the more it falls into the luxury category, the larger and less certain will be the step from decision to purchase.

An additional factor at this stage is the level of risk the consumer associates with the purchase. The level will be higher for expensive items, usually items where the buyer's product knowledge is poor and he or she has consequently found it difficult to evaluate the alternatives. Conspicuous purchases, which may affect the buyer's credibility in the eyes of others, also tend to be associated with a high level of risk. Some individuals of course are more prone to uncertainty than others, but virtually everyone will be uncertain about some purchases.

The marketer must take all possible steps to reduce any unecessary delay or uncertainty in a buyers' decision making process. The provision of sufficient, clear product information is one method. Another method is to promote special short term offers to give people an additional incentive to act. Marketers also try to build up the strength of their brand image, because well known brands in which consumers have confidence are less likely to be seen as risky purchases than are little known brands from companies with no track record.

(e) Outcomes

Of those decision makers who do carry out their intention to purchase, some will be totally satisfied with the product and others less so. Whatever the outcome, the buyer is likely to remember this level of satisfaction and for all but the most trivial purchases this memory is likely to be influential in subsequent similar decision making situations.

Some purchases, particularly important and expensive ones, tend to result in a great deal of subsequent reappraisal by buyers. Leon Festinger has coined the term 'cognitive dissonance' to describe these second thoughts. This refers to the doubts that can be felt by the consumer when they realise that some of the unchosen alternatives also have desirable attributes. In fact their state of 'heightened attention' is often increased after a purchase. Promotional material will be noticed, other competing products inspected and their owners possibly questioned. It is as though buyers are trying to convince themselves that they were smart enough to have made a good decision.

In this situation it is wise for marketers to do all they can to reinforce consumers' confidence in their choice. Some advertising for inherently high risk purchasers such as cars is aimed very much at recent purchasers, showing perhaps satisfied buyers with their new car. Supportive communications can also be sent through the post or reassuring telephone calls made. This is particularly important in view of the messages that these buyers can pass on to other potential buyers when they are at the stage of evaluating alternatives.

Post-purchase outcomes therefore are important in that they feed back into the decision making processes of future purchases. The diagram of the complete process is shown on the next page.

2.7.5 The complexity of purchase

As suggested throughout this analysis of consumer buying behaviour, the process will not be the same for all purchases. Quite simply, some purchases are much more important than others and although we cannot put all buying categories neatly into boxes, we can attach lables to broad bands of purchases according to their complexity.

(a) High involvement purchases

This describes the most difficult type of purchase facing the consumer. It may involve an unfamiliar product class, with which the buyer has no previous experience. This lack of experience reduces the buyer's confidence in his own ability to evaluate the alternatives even though he may have undertaken a very thorough information search. Kotler describes this as a state of 'extensive problem solving' and points out that those marketers most able to help such buyers with their decision making will improve their chances of making a sale. They will do this by helping to educate buyers about the product class, thus making it easier for the buyer to learn product attributes and benefits, and by reinforcing their own brand's high standing within the product class in the hope of reducing buyer uncertainty.

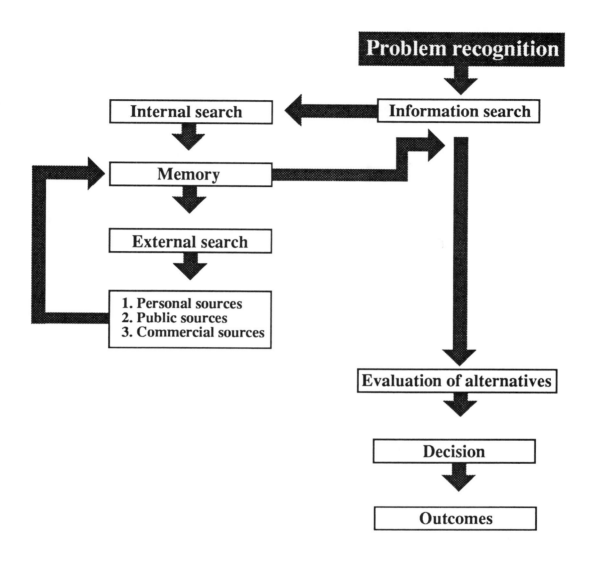

Figure 2.5 The consumer buying behaviour process

(b) Low involvement purchases

At the other extreme, some purchases are so common that little or no conscious thought is given to the buying decision making process. Most habitual purchases such as the commuter grabbing his newspaper at the newstand on his way to the morning train or the smoker buying cigarettes, would come into this category. Kotler describes this simplest type of buyer behaviour as 'routinised response' behaviour.

In this situation virtually all the steps in the buying decision process could be missed out by consumers. They could move straight from felt need to purchase with no thought being given to the interim stages or the outcome unless something untoward occurred such as their normal newspaper being unavailable.

In this situation it is relatively easy for sellers to retain the loyalty of existing customers but very difficult for new entrants to the market place to break these habits.

Of course most buyer behaviour does not fall into either of these extreme categories. Most purchases are of more or less familiar products, but since buyers' knowledge is rarely complete and new or modified products are continuously being introduced, a certain amount of information gathering and evaluation usually takes place, which Kotler would call 'limited problem solving'. In these circumstances the buyer would go through most of the steps in the consumer buying behaviour process but would do so very quickly.

2.7.6 Understanding buyers in organisational markets

Since the understanding of customers lies at the heart of the analysis of markets it is necessary to look separately at individual consumers and at organisational customers because their purchasing behaviour will often show significant differences.

Firstly we must define what we mean by organisational markets. Organisational markets are:

> *'markets where the customers are businesses or other organisations that purchase goods and services to be used directly or indirectly in the production of other goods and services or to be resold.'*

The marketer analysing buyer behaviour in organisational markets must still be able to answer the same basic questions that we examined for consumer buyer behaviour. We will therefore follow the same format in this section.

2.7.7 Who buys?

If a company is selling to other organisations, it still needs to be close to its customers. Firstly, it needs to know all about them as organisations. Are they large or small, public sector or private sector, manufacturers or distributors? Organisational markets should be segmented just as consumer markets should.

Secondly, marketers need to know about the relevant individuals who work within the organisations that they sell to. However large a company or a government authority, it is people who make enquiries, do any negotiating and place orders. In organisations of any size a number of individuals will be involved in the purchase decision. This group of people is known as a 'decision making unit' (DMU). It can be a formal committee but more usually it is an informal group of people each with a different involvement in making the purchase.

The kind of people involved in the DMU can vary from one organisation to another but one would expect to see some or all of the following. Apart from the smallest companies there will be a buyer, or purchasing manager who is in charge of all the administrative aspects of purchasing. Specialists are also likely to be involved. If equipment for the factory floor is to be bought, the production manager would be influential, if a new computer for the office is under consideration the data processing manager would be important. These managers might also include in the decision making members of their department who are going to use the product. People from finance will be involved when it comes to paying, or if the sum is large they may have to approve it. For important purchases senior management, even the whole board of directors might be involved.

The exact make-up of a DMU cannot be predicted from one company to another. What is certain is that several people are almost always involved. It is most unusual for only one person to be involved in the buying process as shown in the diagram below.

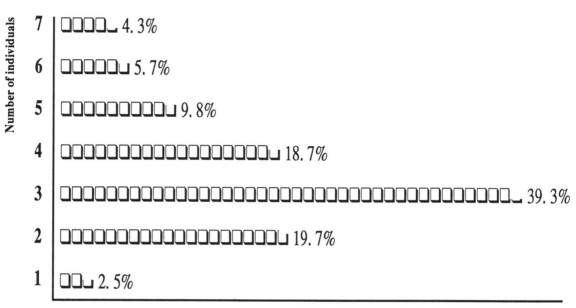

Figure 2.6 Number of people influencing the purchase decision.

Of course, the larger the organisation the more people tend to be involved in the DMU as shown in the table below.

Company size (employees)	Average number influencing the buying decision.
Below 200	3.43
200-400	4.85
400-1,000	5.81
Over 1,000	6.50

Figure 2.7 Average DMU size by company size.

Given that the individuals and job titles which make up the DMU will vary from one company to another, an alternative way of analysing the composition is to look at the roles of its members, in other words to look at the task they perform in the buying process rather than at their official job title. Developed by Frederick Webster and Yoram Wind and later modified by Thomas Bonoma we can list these buying roles as follows:

INITIATOR

USER

INFLUENCER

PURCHASER

DECISION MAKER

GATEKEEPER

Figure 2.8 Individual buying roles within the DMU.

(a) Initiator

As we saw in our analysis of consumer buying behaviour, all purchases have to start somewhere. Although organisations may experience a state akin to 'felt need' (for example, stocks of a regularly purchased material are running low), Thomas Bonoma has pointed out that most major purchases will arise as a result of a suggestion from someone. This initiator could be an employee who sees possibilities for improved efficiency, it could be a senior manager or it could be someone outside the company such as a consultant or a specifier. Architects are often the specifiers for new buildings - they draw up the specifications. Thus the purchases made by the builder will often be initiated by the architect who specifies what materials he must use. Marketers need to understand the role of specifiers because it could well be that their marketing communications need to be directed towards specifiers as much as towards the organisation which is actually placing the order.

(b) User

Users are the individuals who will be using the equipment, materials or service that is to be purchased. Users could come from any level of the organisation's hierarchy, and the extent of their involvement will depend partly on their seniority and partly on the company's attitude to involving employees in its decision making processes. Most often users are relatively low in status and influence but they can sometimes have a critical effect at certain stages of some industrial purchases. For example, if the skilled manual workers in a plastic moulding factory insist that a new material is difficult to work or performs less well than existing materials this may be enough to ensure that the material is not considered for purchase by more senior staff.

(c) Influencer

Influencers affect the purchase decision by supplying information for the evaluation of alternatives or by setting buying specifications. Often technical staff such as engineers or quality controllers exert a significant influence on industrial purchase decisions because they have the specialist knowledge that more senior management may lack. They can certainly be important enough to stop a sale proceeding and can often be sufficiently powerful to sway decision makers to their preferred choice. For more expensive purchases, the finance department will exert a similar level of influence. Marketers must therefore identify possible influencers and be sure to supply them with sufficient information about their products.

(d) Purchaser

The purchaser is usually the individual with formal authority for selecting a supplier and implementing all the procedures that result in placing the order. However, in some instances buyers will not even be influencers let alone deciders, but will merely carry out the administrative functions involved in the purchase. Although marketers must be aware of the purchasing manager's role and priorities they must not make the mistake of assuming that the buyer is the most important person to influence.

(e) Decision makers

Decision makers are the individuals who are most influential in the making of the purchase decision. It may be an individual or a committee. For major purchases the decision maker will be from senior management, but in many organisational purchases, the identification of the decision maker is the most difficult task facing suppliers.

(f) Gatekeepers

Gatekeepers are said to control the flow of information through an organisation. They could be secretaries, mail room managers, purchasing officers. They could be anyone with responsibility for distributing printed information (such as mailshots, trade journals or letters) or with the ability to direct incoming telephone calls. They may stop suppliers' sales literature from reaching certain members of the DMU, or prevent sales representatives from making appointments with certain staff and can therefore exert a powerful influence over suppliers' marketing.

The DMU therefore is a complex animal which may vary in its composition from one organisation to another. The buying roles do however help marketers to identify the kind of individuals to which they must appeal within organisations. Since these individuals will have different roles and therefore different priorities, Peter Chisnall has suggested that 'the shrewd marketer will segment his promotional campaign so that different appeals are made to various specialists taking part in the purchase of his products.'

2.8 What do they buy?

Compared with most consumer products ,organisational products tend to be more complex and more costly. Items such as large production machinery, mainframe computers, forklift trucks and office heating systems would all be examples of capital equipment, infrequently purchased at great expense. Unlike typical consumer purchase, they are often the subject of long deliberation, and the negotiations which lead to a sale can continue for months,even for years. However, organisations also have to buy simple components, paper for the office, cleaning services and fuel for their vehicles. The American authors Reeder, Brierty and Reeder have classified industrial purchases as follows.

MATERIALS AND PARTS	CAPITAL ITEMS	SUPPLIES AND SERVICES
Raw Materials, manufactured materials and parts.	Installations, accessories and equipment.	Supplies and Business Services.

Figure 2.9 Classifying industrial products.

(Source: *'Industrial Marketing'* by Reeder, Brierty and Reeder.)

2.8.1 Materials and parts

Raw materials such as agricultural produce or coal normally enter the production process with little or no alteration. Materials may be used up in the manufacturing process, such as coal purchased by the Central Electricity Generating Board, or they may be turned into other products, for example, apples purchased by Bulmers.

Manufactured materials such as nylon or polyester have been processed once before entering the manufacturing process. Component parts such as switches, seals or printed circuit boards have already been manufactured by one company before being assembled into a final product.

Although there are differences, all products in this category are directly used up in the manufacture of other goods or services.

2.8.2 Capital items

Capital items become part of the production process. They are not used up although they do wear out over time. Installations are major items which represent a long term investment such as a new factory processing plant or office block. Equipment such as an advanced new computer aided manufacturing system or a combined harvester for a farm can also be a major investment, or may be much smaller and less costly. Often termed 'accessories' such equipment could include hand tools, small power tools and compressors.

2.8.3 Supplies and services

Some purchases neither become part of the finished product nor part of the production process but support the operation of the organisation. Supplies such as cleaning compounds and office paper and services such as contract cleaning or market research could all come into this category.

Organisational markets can often be more usefully defined in terms of 'what they buy' than in terms of the kind of company or individual who does the buying. This is particularly true of markets for general supplies, products and services. Photocopiers for example will be bought by almost all organisations above a certain size. The supplier of photocopiers can more usefully define the copier market in terms of the type of copiers required rather than the type of company buying. Indeed a given company may be in different photocopier markets. A large engineering company for example will require some very large, sophisticated photocopiers capable of copying large, complex engineering drawings with perfect clarity. It will also require basic photocopiers for the offices. As far as the suppliers are concerned, these are two different markets.

As with consumer markets it is important to define 'what customers buy' in terms of the whole marketing mix. Do companies want a very high quality product for which they will pay a high price or do they want a bargain basement product? Do they need a lot of information to help them buy or are they already familiar with this product? Organisational markets can often be best segmented according to these kind of needs.

It is particularly important in industrial markets to remember Levitt's story about drills and holes. Marketers should define products in terms of the service they provide for customers. It will be as a result of finding new ways to meet customers' needs more efficiently rather than simply modifying existing products that new organisational markets are likely to be opened up.

2.9 How do they buy?

The average organisational buyer is a much more sophisticated animal than the typical consumer market buyer. Organisational buyers tend to be very knowledgeable about the technical attributes of the products they buy, they probably have a good grasp of the range of prices in the market and they are likely to be accomplished and determined negotiators.

They may employ sophisticated buying techniques such as JIT, QA, vendor rating or value analysis. JIT, now spreading to this country from Japan, involves the supplier delivering the goods 'just in time' for their inclusion in the customer's manufacturing process. Components may be delivered right to the beginning of the customer's production line, which greatly reduces the manufacturer's stock holding costs but makes the supplier's role much more difficult and demanding. Quality assurance (QA) also places greater demands on the supplier. In Britain, companies which have quality systems approved to British Standard 5750 have to check that the suppliers of all materials or components they purchase are able to consistently meet strict quality standards. Increasingly organisational buyers are evaluating and rating their suppliers according to formal vendor rating systems. This involves monitoring their performance over a period of time and awarding scores in areas such as quality, delivery, reliability and price. Suppliers who do not meet expectations (for example, a delivery date missed) may find themselves removed from the approved list of suppliers. Value analysis is an engineering technique which enables organisations to appraise the cost effectiveness of all manufactured products. Such analysis will often discover that a component could be made more cheaply than the price quoted by a supplier, or that a completely different material could be used, or that less material could be used if the design were modified.

All these techniques have one thing in common. They make the organisation a more efficient producer, but they also force the organisation's suppliers to become more efficient too. In analysing market opportunities companies must pay particular attention to the sophistication of buyers. If they do not feel they are sufficiently professional or developed to meet the demands of the strictest buyers it may be wiser to look for less demanding markets.

The factors examined under this question in the consumer marketing section also have relevance to organisational markets. It is true that organisations are much more likely than individual consumers to purchase directly from the original manufacturer but many purchases are also made through middlemen. In their analysis, marketers must identify how best to reach organisational markets. If the product tends to be sold direct, an efficient sales force will be required. If the product tends to be bought through middlemen, as is the case with most supplies and many components, a suitable network of distributors will need to be found.

2.10 How do they make their buying decisions?

As with consumer purchases, all writers agree that industrial buying decisions also go through a sequence but whereas in consumer buying most or all of the steps occur within the mind of the individual buyer, the organisational buying decision process usually involves discussions between different members of the DMU. The organisational buying decision process has six main steps as shown in the diagram below.

2.10.1 Need recognition

As with consumers, the first stage in the process is the recognition of a need. This state of affairs could be the result of internal events such as the breakdown of a machine or the regular need to order materials. On the other hand the need could be recognised as a result of external stimuli such as the suggestion of an outside consultant or the marketing communications of potential suppliers, either of which could demonstrate opportunities for improving the organisation's performance.

2.10.2 Determination of product specifications

Having recognised a need, internal discussion usually takes place with the objective of generating alternative solutions to the problem. For major purchases, quite a few people could be involved at this stage. As a result of these deliberations, the DMU will reach a consensus on the best way to meet the need. Suitably qualified personnel will then draw up a detailed specification for the product or service required.

NEED RECOGNITION

DETERMINATION OF PRODUCT SPECIFICATIONS

INFORMATION SEARCH

EVALUATION OF POTENTIAL SUPPLIERS

NEGOTIATION OF PURCHASE ORDER

EVALUATION OF PRODUCT AND SUPPLIER PERFORMANCE

Figure 2.10   The organisational buying decision process.

2.10.3 Information search

The next step is to identify and approach potential suppliers. Some buyers may have formal procedures for identifying suppliers but many will simply contact those who spring to mind with most prominence or which are easiest to identify. If there is a large number of potential suppliers a brief initial appraisal of them may follow, perhaps based just on their firm's literature, after which a short list of three or four may be drawn up.

2.10.4 Evaluation of suppliers

Extensive discussions may be held with this small number of potential suppliers as the buyer tries to get to know them as companies and to understand the relative benefits of their product offerings. The suppliers will probably then be requested to submit a formal quotation. Evaluation will be based partly on that quotation, partly on objective analysis of their respective product offerings and partly on subjective feelings about their likely performance as suppliers. (If the buyer has done business with a supplier in the past, this last factor will be more objective, based on their actual performance as a supplier.)

2.10.5 Negotiation of a purchase order

Once the supplier has been selected there may still be many details to work out such as delivery dates, terms of payment, or penalty clauses and extensive negotiations may take place before a purchase order is finally placed. For some complex organisational purchases the purchase order itself can be a very lengthy legal document.

2.10.6 Evaluation of product and supplier performance

As suggested in point 2.9, many organisational buyers have formal procedures for evaluating suppliers. In many routine areas of purchasing, some kind of performance review is the most important factor in determining the choice of future suppliers.

As we will see in point 2.11, not all organisational purchases go through all the same steps but the stages outlined above do represent a common pattern that will apply to many purchases. Marketers should try to understand the exact process that each of their major customers goes through and be alert to any way of influencing that process at each stage with their marketing communications. In general the higher up the decision sequence they can begin to build a relationship with suppliers the more likely they are to influence the final outcome. Involvement at the outset would give the supplier the opportunity to try to shape the specification in a form appropriate to his own company's strengths. Suppliers must also be aware of customers' sources of information if they are to ensure that they will be identified at the information search stage. The company that does not promote itself thoroughly in organisational markets may never be given an opportunity to submit a proposal however good its product or service.

2.11 The complexity of the purchase decision

Organisational markets also have their high and low involvement purchases, but they are referred to as 'new task' purchases and 'straight rebuys'. In fact, most textbooks split the organisational buying situation into three basic types, the 'new task', the 'modified rebuy' and the 'straight rebuy'. We will look briefly at each one.

2.11.1 New task

The new task purchasing situation is outside the buyer's past experience. Therefore buyer uncertainty over the outcome of the purchase is at its height. They are involved in 'extensive problem solving' and will require a lot of information to make their decision. The DMU is likely to be at its largest, the decision making process its longest and the final decision maker a member of senior management.

The marketer needs to be aware of this complex situation and should tailor marketing strategies and communications to different stages of the decision process and to different members of the DMU who may have differing priorities. The marketer must always be prepared to provide extensive information and above all must build a relationship with customers to reduce their level of uncertainty in the face of this high risk purchase.

Usually associated with large capital items, a new task purchase can apply to any product or service not previously experienced. Any company computerising for the first time is in a new task situation whether it is buying a mainframe computer for over £100,000 or a desk top micro for £500. Equally a company using a new material (such as plastic rather than steel for a component) is involved in a new task purchase.

2.11.2 Modified rebuy

A modified rebuy is a purchase not totally outside the experience of the buyers but also not totally within it. In the modified rebuy situation participants in the DMU feel that significant benefits may be derived from seeking new information and re-evaluating their alternatives.

Modified rebuy decision making can be described as 'limited problem solving'. Although members of the DMU have considerable experience of buying this type of product, some change in the supply environment (such as a technological advance or a marketing initiative from a supplier) has made the organisation uncertain as to which supplier best meets its needs. However a fairly straight forward information search and reappraisal of suppliers usually results in a relatively quick decision in the modified rebuy situation.

2.11.3 Straight rebuy

In a straight rebuy situation buyers have extensive experience of purchasing the product or service. They have considerable knowledge of the market for such products and substantial information on most if not all suppliers and the products they offer. These routine purchasing decisions are most likely to be handled by the purchasing department with little or no involvement from other departments. The DMU may be very small and the decision taken very quickly. As long as past purchases of the product in question have remained satisfactory buyers will often seek no new information but will simply reorder the product when necessary from the same supplier. In fact, in some companies straight rebuys have become so systematic that a computer reorders automatically when stocks of the product fall to a certain predetermined level.

In the straight rebuy situation the existing supplier, (often called the 'in-supplier') holds all the marketing advantages. Already known and approved by the purchasing company, already supplying adequate products in a satisfactory manner 'in-suppliers' need do no better than maintain their existing level of performance. Buyers like this situation because it holds very little uncertainty. Any change would be likely to increase the level of uncertainty.

The 'out-suppliers' (firms with which the organisation is not currently doing business) hold all the marketing disadvantages. To make the buyer reconsider they must disturb the equilibrium, which may not be easy. a new product would have to be a significant improvement over the product of the 'in-supplier'. a price cut would have to be quite large before many buyers would consider changing to an 'out-supplier'. 'Out-suppliers' ' objective, however, is to move the buying situation into the modified rebuy category.

Conclusion

If marketers are to identify the best opportunities, well suited to the strengths of their organisation, their analysis must be wide ranging indeed. They must scan the organisation's wider environment and understand the trends, with their resultant opportunities and threats, in the political environment, the economic environment, the social environment and the technological environment. They must be very close to the firm's own market environment, understanding its structure and performance. They need a deep knowledge of competitors and of the way in which their own business can be affected by other organisations such as distributors, suppliers, advertising agencies or financial institutions. Very importantly they must know and understand their customers, who they are, what and how they buy. The customer, and the customer's needs lie at the heart of the marketing philosophy and at the centre of any analysis of market opportunities. The diagram below shows the areas that have been described in this chapter, starting with the firm's wider environment and working towards the customer at the centre.

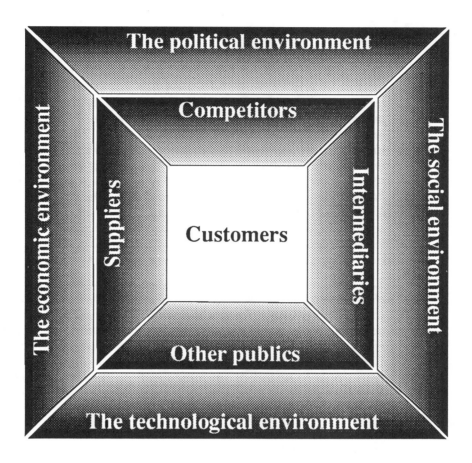

Figure 2.11 Analysing marketing opportunities.

Analysing and understanding customers can be the most difficult task of all because their needs and behaviour can change very quickly. The task of understanding customers is therefore even greater than the areas covered in this chapter. Marketers will seek to build an intimate knowledge of customers which will enable them to divide their market into groups or segments, each containing consumers with slightly different characteristics and requirements. This enables marketers to tailor their marketing mix more precisely to the needs of customers. As we pointed out in Chapter 1, it is this matching process that lies at the heart of the marketing concept. The next chapter will examine how markets are segmented.

Assignment   Downtown United F.C.

The board of Downtown United F.C. were about to commence a very difficult meeting. A very unsuccessful season had just ended. The proud club, once recognised as the most successful in the country had just spent the whole season propping up the second division. During the course of the season three different managers had failed to revive the team's fortunes. The average home gate had slumped to around 4,000 and as a result the club's financial record had been only slightly less disastrous than its performance on the field. It looked as though some of the club's best players would have to be sold over the summer just to balance the books. In the third division the club would also receive a lower share of the new deal the Football League was due to make with the TV companies, and its own team sponsorship agreement, also up for renewal would be less attractive with the team entertaining Mansfield and Port Vale rather than Manchester City and Leeds United.

The meeting was less stormy than expected. Two directors resigned and the chairman stepped down. Howard Grant was voted chairman. Noisy and sometimes aggressive Howard 'the mouth' Grant had not always been popular with other board members, but he was a good businessman, and this, the board realised, was what Downtown United now needed more than anything else. The new chairman's opening remarks did much to lift morale. He insisted that there would be no talk of any more sackings. The current manager could not have been expected to resurrect a team that was virtually relegated before he took over.

The chairman's talk was about future hope rather than past disappointments. He referred to some clubs which were thriving despite their location in small towns and their position in the lower divisions. He spoke of sports clubs with squash courts and social activities, of lower division teams with artificial pitches which were being successfully hired out seven days a week. He spoke of clubs with very profitable hospitality businesses where the luxury of the box and the quality of the catering and the service can be more important than the standard of the football. He spoke of local advertising and sponsorship opportunities and of initiatives taken by some teams to raise gates, such as promoting match day activities and facilities to attract families. He spoke of opportunities in the public sector including the Government's new training initiative for the unemployed which some football clubs were getting involved in. The chairman insisted that the club faced a wealth of marketing opportunities. And, he insisted, they would identify the best and exploit them. Business success would lead to profitability, and profits, he pointed out would help to rebuild the team.

Howard Grant had turned on its head the club's previous approach to running its affairs. It had always been assumed that the way to profits was a winning team. Success on the pitch would bring in the fans. Good gates would lead to profits which could strengthen the team. The team was everything.

This guiding philosophy was about to end. The team's success was of course the most important long term objective, but making the club profitable was to be the first essential step. Howard the Mouth announced that Downtown United F.C. would appoint a Commercial Manager. The Team Manager would manage the club's football activities, the Commercial Manager would manage its business activities. Not all the board members were sure about this, but no real objections were made.

Within three weeks, Howard Grant, who was not a time waster, was interviewing candidates for the new job. He appointed Howard Ratcliffe, a dynamic thirty six year old graduate in economics, who had an extremely good track record in marketing and, in his younger days had been a very promising right back for his university team.

Still not wanting to waste time Howard Grant instructed his new Commercial Manager to give him a full written report of the club's marketing opportunities within one month of taking up his post.

This was a demanding, possibly unrealistic task. Howard however had plenty of contacts including one Anton Shari, an even more tenacious full back from Howard's university days who had since pursued a brilliant cosmopolitan career, including a spell as marketing manager of an American baseball team. He now lectured in marketing analysis and planning at a top British business school.

Task

Following a phone call from Howard, Anton was happy to give him what advice he could. They agreed to get together for a day during which Anton would explain the kind of steps he would take to identify and analyse the marketing opportunities facing Downtown United together with a few recommendations for action gleaned from his own past experience.

In the role of Anton Shari outline the points that Anton should cover with Howard Ratcliffe about marketing analysis together with any useful recommendations that he might make.

Chapter 3
Market Segmentation

Introduction

We said in the first chapter that marketing is all about meeting the needs of customers, and that these needs are not usually covered by the product alone but by a marketing mix, a whole package of benefits offered by the seller. In Chapter Two we stressed the importance to all companies of a detailed understanding of their customers in terms of who they are, how they satisfy their needs and how they make buying decisions. Hints were also made in Chapter Two that not all customers are the same in terms of what, how and why they buy. It is recognition of this fact that customers do differ from one another in many ways, which forms the basis of the concept of market segmentation. To give one simple example, a poor 65 year old married lady is a different person to a very wealthy unmarried 22 year old man. They will buy different products and services, they will have different priorities and they will have different lifestyles. Quite simply they have different needs and it would not be possible for marketers of the vast majority of products to treat them in the same way. The logic of the marketing philosophy dictates that if the purpose of marketing is to meet customers' needs, and some customers' needs differ, then the marketer must do different things to meet those needs. Customers' needs cannot all be met by the same product sold in the same way. The 65 year old lady and the 22 year old man are in different market segments. We will define a market segment in the words of two American writers, Yoram Wind and Richard Cardozo as follows: a market segment is: 'A group of present or potential customers with some common characteristic which is relevant in explaining and predicting their response to a supplier's marketing stimuli.' *This definition covers the essential characteristics of segmentation. Market segments are groups of customers who have something in common. Customers within segments will be similar to each other, customers in different segments will be dissimilar to each other. However, the method by which the marketer divides the market into segments is extremely important. One method might be to divide the population into groups according to hair colour. We might end up with people with black hair, people with fair hair, people with red hair and people with no hair. This would be a perfectly valid method of classifying people into groups whose members were similar to each other and dissimilar from members of other groups. But what use would it be to the marketer of frozen peas, designer jeans, gloss paint or domestic electrical services? Very little. The most important aspect of market segmentation is the choice of criteria used to divide customers into groups. As Wind and Cardozo point out these criteria must be relevant to the customers' needs and / or their behaviour in the market concerned.*

3.1 Criteria for market segmentation

Choosing the right criteria is a critical task for marketers. They are often faced with many alternative ways of grouping customers. This section will examine the more common criteria used to segment markets. You will see that the methods relate closely to the different aspects of understanding customers outlined in Chapter 2.4.

3.1.1 Demographic segmentation

This is similar to asking the question 'who buys?' We want to know who these people are and we want to know all about them so that we can divide them into groups. There are a number of demographic criteria which may be of relevance to different markets.

(a) Age

Segmenting customers according to age bands is very common. Children are clearly different to retired people but quite narrow age bands can help to describe variations in purchasing behaviour for some products. Take the following female fashion chains:

Chelsea Girl, Miss Selfridge, Top Girl, Etam, Dorothy Perkins, Principles, Richards and Next.

Each is aimed at a slightly older age band than the previous one, starting with teenage girls and ending with women in their thirties and forties. The age bands overlap, but the steps in the age segments catered for are not large.

(b) Sex

Sex is a relevant segmentation criterion for many markets. Some products, like the fashions in Top Girl, are aimed exclusively at one sex. Many other products, like beer, are aimed primarily at one sex. It is not likely that sex will be used as a criterion on its own. It is more usual for it to be used in conjunction with other criteria to describe the members of a segment. The practice of using more than one variable to segment markets is very common. 'Next', for example, might be aiming at a segment of 30 - 45 year old women; two variables used to define the segment.

In fact, Next is much more likely to have used at least three variables, with the third criterion referring to the customers' spending power. 'Next' is not aimed at women with very little money to spend.

(c) Income

For many products income levels can be a sure discriminator. Products like dish washers, video cameras and holidays to the Caribbean are not likely to be bought by consumers with very low levels of income. Even within a product class, top of the range and bargain basement versions will often be designed to appeal to buyers with differing income levels. An Escort XR3i is aimed at a more affluent buyer than an Escort Popular. This can also be the case with everyday products. Nescafe Gold Blend coffee is targeted at a more affluent consumer than a basic own label instant coffee which will usually be less than half the price. (N.B. As already suggested, and as we will also see later, most products, including the coffee, will also be liable to additional segmentation criteria.) The discriminatory value of income levels should be clear to see. It is important however to emphasise, as explained in Chapter 2.2.2, that it is consumers' level of discretionary income which is of relevance to marketers of most products.

(d) Level of education

Sometimes, the age at which people left full time education is used as a segmentation variable. This criterion has obvious value with products requiring a certain level of intellectual application, such as books, but has also been found to influence other products as well. For example, research has shown that people with degrees are more likely to make an objective analysis of value for money when buying groceries and often buy own label products rather than more expensive branded equivalents. People with lower levels of education often opt for the 'safety' of the well known brand, even though their income may be lower. As you can see, segmentation is a complex issue. Will the well educated, affluent coffee consumer buy own label or Gold Blend? To answer this question the marketer will need to understand consumers very well and to segment the market according to several variables.

(e) Social class

Segmentation by social class is used very frequently by consumer marketers in the U.K. It will often be used instead of the income and educational variable since it incorporates aspects of both, together with additional sociological concepts about dividing people into groups. There are a number of methods of dividing the British population into social classes, most of which are broadly similar. The method most commonly used by marketers is that devised by the National Readership Survey (NRS). It was developed in the years after the Second World War to classify readers of national newspapers and magazines but has since been applied to most consumer goods and services. NRS break the British people down into six social classes as follows.

A: Upper Middle Class

Forming 3% of the population, social class A covers higher managerial , administrative and professional occupations. The head of the household will be a successful business or professional person or may have considerable inherited wealth. They would normally live in expensive detached houses in provincial areas or, if in London, in expensive flats or town houses in the better parts of town. Social class A occupations include barristers, bishops, brain surgeons and top businessmen and women.

B: Middle Class

Defined as intermediate managerial administrative or professional occupations, social class B covers people who are quite senior but not at the top of their profession and could include younger people, destined for social class a who have not yet climbed so far up their career ladder. They are well off but their lifestyle is respectable rather than rich or luxurious.

Ten percent of Britons are in this class including most people in management and 'teachers over 28 years of age'!

C1: Lower Middle Class

Covering supervisory, clerical and junior managerial positions, often called white collar jobs, the lower middle class will often be significantly less affluent than classes a and B and includes 24% of the population. Teachers under 28 years of age, most nurses and many civil servants would be in social class C1.

C2: Skilled working class

The largest class with 30% of the population, it consists mainly of skilled workers. Tending to be of lower educational attainment and status than social class C1, they can nevertheless often be higher earners. Print workers, fitters, electricians and plumbers would be classified as skilled working class.

D: Working class

Consisting entirely of manual workers, semi-skilled or unskilled, this class includes assembly line workers and farm workers and unskilled workers in service industries.

E: Those at the lowest levels of subsistence

Social class E is made up largely of the unemployed and the poorest pensioners. Together, social classes D and E comprise one third of the population.

One can criticise the NRS method of segmentation for several reasons. Firstly, society is much less stable and many purchases are less class based than forty years ago when the NRS system was first developed. Secondly, the pace of social change is increasing and the accuracy of the classification can be seriously weakened by factors such as changing unemployment levels and work patterns. Thirdly, households are classified by NRS according to the occupation of the head of the household, who is considered to be male. The occupation of a female would be used only in the case of households with no male. Changes in society have made this unrealistic. Increasingly family prosperity is based on the joint earning power of husband and wife. More and more women are now earning more than their male partners. Fourthly, it is argued, the class system is gradually breaking down. Labels of status and success are changing. We will examine these matters when we look at lifestyle segmentation.

(f) Family life cycle

Another demographically based variable is the stage that consumers have reached in their family development. There is no denying that two married couples with identical jobs and income levels, one with four children and the other childless will exhibit significant differences in their spending patterns. On the other hand couples of different ages, e.g. 45 and 25 years old could have children of similar ages. For many types of purchase, e.g. groceries, marketers can more usefully place these two families in the same segment rather than in different segments according to age bands. Family life cycle segments might include young single people, young couples with no children, families with young children, families with older children, middle aged couples with no children or whose children now live away from home, retired couples, retired single people.

3.1.2 Geographic segmentation

This segmentation variable is of obvious value in international marketing but even within countries can be essential. In a large country with a high population such as the USA, needs and purchasing behaviour can show significant regional variations. Even in a small country like the U.K., the same can be true. If one were to analyse consumption patterns of whisky, beer and wine, significant regional variations would be found between Scotland, the North of England and the South East of England. Increasingly marketers are making distinctions between affluent and poor areas. This is not necessarily regional but can be applied to much smaller geographic areas (see geo-demographic segmentation).

Traditionally however, geographic segmentation in Britain has been regionally based. The most important reason for this is that advertising can be accurately targeted in this way if TV regions are used as the segmentation base. Therefore the geographical regions of Great Britain often have TV reception areas as their boundaries. Details of these regions can be found in Chapter 11.

3.1.3 Benefit segmentation

This refers to the question 'what do they buy?', but, true to the outward looking marketing philosophy 'what customers buy' should not be viewed in terms of drills but in terms of holes. Many markets can be segmented in terms of benefits sought by customers. Car buyers may be looking primarily for reliability, high mileage to the gallon, speed, interior comfort or exterior appearance. There are said to be five main segments in the toothpaste market. Some buy for cosmetic reasons; they want white shining teeth. Secondly, there are those who buy strong toothpaste to avoid bad breath. A third segment buys mainly for medical reasons, to prevent tooth decay.

Fourthly, there are those, buying for mainly children who buy for the flavour and finally, there is the price conscious segment. Shampoo is often sold on a benefits basis - good for greasy or dry hair, good for daily washing, good for fighting dandruff.

3.1.4 Behaviour segmentation

How people buy can also offer many good opportunities for market segmentation. Some of the specific variables which can be used here were referred to in Chapter 2.4 such as frequency of purchase, customers' level of loyalty' to a particular brand or their preference for shopping from home, in large superstores or at small local shops. Markets for products such as cigarettes and alcoholic drinks will often be segmented according to heavy, medium and light users.

3.1.5 Geo-demographic segmentation

The criticism of the social class based, NRS method of segmentation, which until comparatively recently was almost universally used and accepted by consumer marketers, has prompted a search for more accurate methods of segmentation which should be more reliable predictors of buying behaviour.

Amongst the most successful of the new methods are those which seek to combine geographic and demographic principles of segmentation. The most well known of these new methods is ACORN which stands for 'A Classification Of Residential Neighbourhoods'. Developed by Richard Webber in the late 1970's and based on detailed information from the 1971 census (later updated from the 1981 data), ACORN classifies households according to the neighbourhood in which they are found. The underlying philosophy of ACORN (and other geo-demographic methods of segmentation) is that certain types of neighbourhood will not only display similar housing but also will have residents with similar demographic and social characteristics who will share common lifestyles and will tend to display similar purchasing behaviour.

Based initially on the 120,000 census enumeration districts (each of which contains around 150 households) and more recently linked with the one and a quarter million post codes (each of which can cover as little as one side of one street), the geographical areas covered by ACORN are very small precise units. From analysing the inhabitants of a sample of these districts Webber found that they shared many characteristics, such as age, income, race and family structure. From these districts 38 precise neighbourhood types were identified and they have been consolidated into the 11 ACORN types now in common use. They are:

A: Agricultural areas 3.3% of households

B: Modern family housing, higher incomes 14.8%

C: Older housing of intermediate status 18.7%

D: Poor quality older terraced housing 4.6%

E: Better off council estates 12.2%

F: Less well off council estates 10.4%

G: Poorest council estates 6.8%

H: Multi-racial areas 3.5%

I: High status non-family areas 4.9%

J: Affluent suburban housing 18.9%

K: Better off retirement areas 4.8%

Supplemented by other research data such as tracking studies (see Chapter 4) ACORN has been used to segment markets for many specific products such as food, domestic appliances, financial services and cars. Its great advantage is its practicality.

In the age of computers and with the growth of direct mail, its link with postal codes makes it a very usable method of segmentation enabling potential buyers to be targeted in a very precise way. ACORN data have also been used in shop location decisions since the percentage of ACORN household types in the catchment are of a potential retail location could predict the level of store traffic.

The main criticism of all forms of geo-demographic segmentation is that they are not always reliable predictors of purchasing behaviour for specific products. It is said that the chain leading from ACORN types to the purchase of individual products is too long. One must assume that people living in areas of similar housing share similar demographic, income and lifestyle characteristics and that, as a result, they will tend to purchase similar products. It may be unrealistic to expect that any general method of segmentation can encompass common characteristics across such a wide spread of variables.

3.1.6 Lifestyle segmentation

The lifestyle concept was developed originally by the Leo Burnett advertising agency in conjunction with the University of Chicago.

It covers peoples' day to day habits, work patterns, leisure interests, attitudes and values. Lifestyle segments would be based on distinctive ways of living and social values portrayed by certain types of people. In fact the lifestyle concept is sometimes, more accurately, referred to as values and lifestyles.

An example of lifestyle segmentation would be the Social Value Groups identified by the Applied Futures Unit within the market research company Taylor Nelson. Based on a continuous survey of 2,000 adults per annum which has been running since 1973, Applied Futures has identified three broad social value groups; the 'sustenance driven groups', the 'outer directed groups' and the 'inner directed groups'. These three groups can be further divided into seven social value segments as follows.

(a) Sustenance driven groups

(i) 'Aimless'

Comprising 5% of the population, often young and often unemployed, this group lives from day to day, often motived by short term pleasure of 'kicks'. Often anti-authority and sometimes violent (for example, football hooligans) many end up as gamblers and petty criminals.

(ii) 'Survivors'

Often displaying traditional working class values, they are hard working, conservative, cheerful and have a strong community spirit. Motives are usually short term and they still make up 16% of the population though their numbers are declining slowly.

(b) Outer directed groups

(iii) 'Belongers'

Really on the borderline between the sustainers and the outer directed group, 'belongers' comprise 18% of the population. They are conservative in nature and seek a quiet family life. The family is rated very highly and considerable sacrifices will be made on its behalf. Belongers have longer term horizons, often avoiding short term pleasures. They are more likely to be savers and house owners, are law abiding and traditional and are concerned to be seen in this way by others.

(iv)'Conspicuous consumers'

Also very concerned with the views of other people and also conservative and pro-authority, this group has more short term objectives than the belongers. They are very materialistic, buyers of the latest household gadgets and are particularly keen on highly visible products which may display their affluence to friends, relatives and neighbours. The largest single group, 19% of the population, it is still growing slowly.

(c) Inner directed groups

(v) 'Social resisters'

These are the caring people whose motives are fairness and quality of life. They are likely to be concerned with social issues such as peace, disarmament, ecology, overseas aid and community politics. They may be dogmatic and moralistic. Often characterised as the sandals and fibre brigade they currently represent 11% of the population.

(vi) 'Experimentalists'

Representing 14% of the population their motivation is pleasure. Materialistic, in favour of new products and developments they are also highly individualistic often rejecting traditional authority and established norms, thus representing a powerful force for change.

(vii) 'Self explorers'

Sixteen percent of the population, they are motivated by self expression and self realisation. Sharing some of the social concerns of the social resister without following their passion for non-conformity, and agreeing with the experimentalists' passion for individualism, without their emphasis on materialism. Of all the social value groups, the self explorers are the most broad minded, are the most likely to be problem solvers and have the most ability to take decisions and act in an independent way. The group is growing slowly.

It is held that such values and lifestyle information can be a particularly relevant to purchasing behaviour for specific products. The four tenuous links in the geo-demographic chain have now been reduced to two closely connected variables, lifestyle and buying behaviour.

The same market research company, Taylor Nelson, has also been responsible for market research for Volkswagen into the lifestyles of car buyers in the U.K. Their lifestyle segments were based on a continuum labelled 'Flight' or 'Fight' along which six lifestyle segments were placed as follows.

(FRIGHTENED)   (Flight)

(SUNDAY DRIVER)

(SMALL IS BEAUTIFUL)

(CAR DISINTERESTED)

(PRO-AM)

(BOY RACER)   (Fight)

As well as general lifestyle and attitudes, each group is also defined in terms of driving related characteristics. The group descriptions which were the result of qualitative research are as follows.

Frightened

This is the most extreme of the flight typologies and accounts for 15% of all new car buyers. Their primary characteristic is a lack of confidence in their driving ability to the extent that they would not drive at all if they had their choice. People in this group also tend to be more inward looking introverted characters.

It is important to realise that this group is almost equally split between men and women but their characteristics are different. Men are older, and it seems likely they have grown up in traffic conditions far removed from today's fast moving and congested situations. Women are younger, married, with family responsibilities, and it is clear that their fear stems from this concern about children linked to their lack of confidence in their driving ability.

In addressing this group, the most important point will be reassurance. Safety and reliability will be the two key attributes for any car purchased by this group. Technology which makes driving easier and reduces strain will also be attractive, but they are not technocrats and technology will need to be user friendly.

Sunday Driver

This is an almost entirely male group, very introverted and uses the car less frequently than other groups. They are working men but are likely to be public transport commuters on weekdays and closely fit the stereotype view of the 'Sunday driver'. They tend to be about average in terms of driving confidence and mechanical knowledge.

Their most important reason for choosing a car is value for money. Characterisation (using people in advertising that the Sunday drivers can associate with) will be important, thus, inward looking average types should be used as opposed to young, brash people in social situations. Sunday drivers are more likely to be working in planning and thinking occupations rather than in extrovert based ones such as sales.

Small is beautiful

The primary rationale for this typology is a preference for small cars. They buy smaller cars not from economic necessity but from choice and are therefore less likely than other groups to trade up. This is the largest group comprising 21% of new car buyers. They are not very confident and their preference for a small car doubtless stems from this together with the need to feel in control for manoeuvring and parking.

Two thirds of this group are female but the two sexes have different demographic characteristics. Men are older, probably C1 and mainly without children in the household. Women are younger, mainly AB and with children. Reliability and ease of handling, particularly ease of parking, are their main priorities. Running costs and fuel consumption are important though secondary issues.

Car disinterested

This typology is basically negative with regard to cars and all aspects of motoring. They are not at all mechanically minded and do not regard the vehicle as a status symbol. Although they may use the car often they see it only as a means of getting from A to B. They are the second largest group comprising 18% of new car buyers. Slightly over half are female, mainly middle aged and very AB. Males tend to be rather older.

Deciding a promotional strategy to appeal to this group will be a real test of creative ability since the typology is completely disinterested in cars and driving. Nevertheless they are often heavy users of the car and it plays an important if not very glamorous role in their lives. The key would appear to lie in devising situations where the car plays a vital but back seat role.

Pro-Am

This typology is the antithesis of the previous one. Its members are interested in all aspects of cars and driving. They read the motoring press, advise others about cars and engines and have a secret desire to be racing or rally drivers. The group comprises 16% of new car buyers.

This group is made up almost entirely of men in the 25 - 54 age range and it has the lowest proportion of AB's. They are not high flyers, tending to work in skilled manual, clerical or junior to middle management positions. Advertising strategies should stress engineering excellence. Reliability and safety are important and can be addressed in a fairly technical manner, and cars can be performance related but not flashy since exterior shape and styling are less important to this group than engineering. Advertising characters should feature C1/C2 men.

Boy racers

This last typology comprises 17% of new car buyers and is the extreme 'flight' group. Its members are aggressive drivers, very status conscious and see the car as a status (and male sexual) symbol. They like large flashy cars, preferably out of the ordinary. Whilst the group is male oriented, just over a third (37%) are female (girl racers). They have the youngest age profile of any group, are very AB and could be said to typify the 'Yuppie' population. They are mainly interested in outward appearance and this, together with the correct characterisation will be the main advertising strategy. Characters should be young, professional and part of the 'in-scene'.

To be of real value such typologies have to be linked to the company's brands and must give more general lifestyle details such as leisure interests and social values. These were in fact provided by Taylor Nelson, in their report to Volkswagen which ran into many tens of pages. Some of these additional details can be found in Chapter 10 of this book.

The Taylor Nelson information does highlight several important aspects of lifestyle segmentation. Firstly it is at its most useful when linked directly to specific brands marketed by the company. Different product groups will be faced with different market segments filled with different people leading different lives and sharing different values. General values and lifestyle descriptors, however accurate they may be sociologically, cannot be applied indiscriminately to all product classes. Their labels can be used to help describe behaviour but cannot be expected to paint the whole picture.

Secondly segmentation is used to help marketers develop all aspects of their marketing mix. Volkswagen commissions such research entirely for advertising purposes since, as a distributor of imported vehicles it has little control over the product design and development process. However, this information is very useful for advertising purposes. If customers are to take notice of advertising they must relate to it, and such segmentation, with its emphasis on characterisation is of great help to the creative work of the agency.

Thirdly, the very nature of the strengths of lifestyle segmentation is the root cause of its main weakness. Being product specific is excellent for accuracy in segmenting that particular market, but this exclusiveness makes it much less convenient as a marketing tool. Generalised segmentation variables such as age, NRS social classes or ACORN go into great detail about their groups, including their occupations, income levels, TV viewing habits, reading habits and a whole host of additional information. This makes it easy for the marketer to target his communications through appropriate media. Product specific market segmentation does not. It requires further research to discover the readership and TV viewing habits of 'Sunday drivers', 'boy racers' and 'small is beautiful' car buyers. Product specific lifestyle segmentation is accurate but difficult and costly to obtain and use, whereas general demographic and geo-demographic segmentation variables are less accurate when applied to specific products but much easier and cheaper to obtain and use. It is a dilemma still unresolved in the marketing world.

3.2 Targeting

Although segmentation is of great value when it comes to communication with markets, we must return to our statement in the opening chapter of this book. Marketers' chief objective is to locate a group of customers who have an unsatisfied need which could be met by their company. Segmentation helps them to move towards this objective because it enables them to analyse and describe customers' needs in more detail. To attain their objective they must take the next step of identifying that particular group or segment which has an appropriate need which could be met by their company. This is back to the matching concept. The marketer will try to match the strengths of the company and its products with the market segment or segments exhibiting the most suitable needs and priorities. This is the process of targeting which is the next logical step after segmentation.

3.2.1 Targeting strategies

When selecting the most appropriate segments to target, the marketer has three broad strategies to choose from. These are shown in figure 3.1.

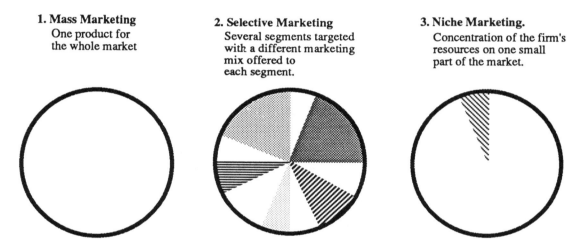

1. Mass Marketing
One product for
the whole market

2. Selective Marketing
Several segments targeted
with a different marketing
mix offered to
each segment.

3. Niche Marketing.
Concentration of the firm's
resources on one small
part of the market.

Figure 3.1 Three broad targeting strategies

(a) Mass marketing

Sometimes called undifferentiated marketing this involves selling one product to the entire market, or at least to a very large proportion of it. Well known examples in the past have been the Model T Ford and Coca Cola. Mass marketing has to focus on what is similar in the needs of customers rather than on what is different and must develop a product and marketing programme that aims to appeal to most buyers.

Mass marketing has some major advantages for the supplier. The economies of scale afforded by mass production, distribution in bulk and global advertising help to make the organisation more efficient, enabling it to reduce its costs and become more price competitive.

The whole marketing concept, however, has been built mainly upon the rejection of this inward looking, production oriented philosophy. General Motors won market leadership from Ford by abandoning the undifferentiated approach and offering customers choice, even though it increased G.M.'s costs, forcing them to raise prices. The customers paid. They were prepared to pay for choice. Coca Cola has also now abandoned its undifferentiated approach, offering diet Coke, caffeine free Coke and flavoured Cokes to meet the needs of different market segments.

(b) Selective marketing

A selective marketing strategy will be followed by most medium and large sized companies. It involves covering several or even all the segments of the market, but in contrast to mass marketing will offer a different marketing mix carefully designed to meet the needs of each segment served. Most of the large car manufacturers sell a range of models designed to cover most market segments.

(c) Niche marketing

Often most suited to the strengths of small companies, niche marketing involves concentrating the organisation's resources on just one small segment, or, at most a small number of tiny segments. These small segments are called 'niches'. Such a strategy makes a lot of sense for small companies for two reasons. Firstly, they can concentrate their limited resources on being one of the best suppliers in a precise market. This is a feasible objective for a small company. If a small company spreads its resources too thinly across many segments it will probably perform poorly in all areas. a large share of a niche market will probably be worth more to the small firm than a tiny share of a much larger market.

Secondly, many niches are ignored by large companies because they are not considered to represent a sufficiently worthwhile opportunity (see 3.3.2). The small company may therefore find that it faces less competition from large companies in carefully chosen niche markets. Morgan Cars has been extremely successful with its niche marketing strategy. Morgan faces no direct competition from large companies because that market segment is much too small for a large company such as Ford or Rover to even contemplate.

3.2.2 Qualifying segments

In following one of the targeting strategies outlined above and choosing one or more segments to serve, the organisation must have a way of qualifying segments. In other words it must be able to assess their validity as a market segment and their suitability as a target market. In qualifying market segments, the organisation must ensure that each displays certain essential characteristics. Market segments must be: identifiable, measurable, viable, accessible and relevant.

(a) Identifiable

To be valid a segment must be a distinct part of the market, clearly different from other segments in that market and containing customers who share one or more clearly identifiable characteristic in common.

(b) Measurable

To compare one segment against another, it must be possible to define the segment in a quantifiable way. It is no good defining a segment as 'those British people interested in holidays to Thailand' if we do not know how many people are interested in such holidays and whether they are sufficiently interested to pay the appropriate price.

(c) Viable

If segments are not measurable, it is not possible to assess their viability. There would be no point investing money in a business selling holidays to Thailand if that segment was not viable due to insufficient demand. Viability can mean different things to different companies. As suggested earlier a very small niche can offer a viable opportunity to a small company, but larger companies usually require a much higher level of potential sales to make a segment viable for them.

(d) Accessible

We have said that the organisation will develop a distinct marketing mix for each segment it targets. For this to succeed the segment must be accessible or reachable. The organisation must be able to reach customers with its products. Can it sell direct through mail order, a factory shop, its own high street shops, or through sales representatives who take orders? If not, can it reach customers through middlemen such as wholesalers, retailers or agents (see Chapter 9). It may seem unlikely that a market cannot be reached through one of these channels. In a developed country like England this may be true but in less developed countries such as Thailand or Nepal or Angola the economic infrastructure may be so poor that they may not, in reality, be sufficiently accessible for some products. Even in the U.K. the question must be posed. Distributors may require too much margin to make their use profitable for a manufacturer. If so, one has to assess very carefully whether consumer markets in particular can be reached directly.

A second aspect of accessibility is whether segments can be reached with the organisation's marketing communications. If the marketing mix is to be different for different segments the promotional messages sent to segments must also be different. The organisation must ask if the customers in a segment can be reached exclusively with distinct promotional messages, or will communications sent for segment a also reach segments B, C and D? As suggested in 3.1.6, this is the main weakness of generalised methods of lifestyle segmentation. Because 'Sunday drivers', 'car disinterested', 'frightened' and 'small is beautiful' car buyers have overlapping rather than distinct media habits (e.g. readership of national newspapers and magazines) it is virtually impossible to reach a specific segment with a specific message without also broadcasting that message to other segments.

(e) Relevance

Finally, segments should be appropriate to the organisation's resources, its strengths and its overall objectives. At the beginning of this chapter we said that the common characteristics shared by customers in a particular segment should be relevant in explaining and predicting their buying behaviour. If segments are defined in this way then it is not difficult to judge their relevance to an organisation's activities. As we said in Chapter 1, the organisation has to match buyers' needs and priorities with its own marketing mix.

3.3 Market positioning

Having targeted one or more segments does not conclude the process. Even within a carefully defined market segment all buyers will not be identical. Competing products will not be identical. The organisation must therefore decide how it will position its product offering within each targeted segment. We can define market positioning quite simply as the way the product is viewed by customers relative to competing products in the same market segment. Marketers must seek to match the attributes of their product (and buyers' perceptions of those attributes) with the needs and priorities of customers in that segment.

Market positioning is a very important concept because it relates to the way in which people absorb and store information. Consumers are faced with much more information about products and services than they can possibly absorb. Many studies have shown that consumers do not make use of much of the information provided for them when making product choice decisions. For example, a study by Jacoby, Chestnut and Silberman in the US showed that the vast majority of consumers did not consult or even understand the nutritional information provided on the labels of food products when making their purchase choices. In fact there is evidence for a whole range of purchases, including high involvement decisions such as car buying, that consumers do not laboriously go through the whole process described in Chapter 2.4, but take plenty of short cuts. They often form rather superficial images of competing products, which is why market positioning is so important.

People do not, therefore, absorb and retain in their memory all the information to which they are exposed. As far as products are concerned they tend to organise them into little boxes which can be conveniently stored in a compartment in the mind. Each product box is that consumer's image or perception of that product, its attributes and benefits. Once that box is in its compartment, the consumer will be reluctant to change the contents of the box so the marketer must get it right first time. Market positioning is all about getting the box right.

Many companies have found that the best way to position their product is not to try to stress all its attributes and benefits because the consumer's mental box is just not big enough to take them all in. If consumers are to form a strong image of the product certain key attributes must be stressed. Crest toothpaste was a successful new product launch in a fiercely competitive market because it stressed just one key benefit, the reduction of tooth decay.

To position its product within a market segment the company must first analyse the market to discover the key attributes used to form consumers' product images. Beer is a good example of a product which needs to be carefully positioned in the market. Assume that market research has been carried out which has identified that the two key attributes on which consumers rate beer are its strength and its flavour and that flavour usually relates to the bitterness or sweetness of the beer. This enables the marketer to discover the market position of all the main competing products in that segment by asking customers to rate each brand of beer according to strength and flavour. The customer may be asked to rate each on a ten point scale. The results can then be plotted on a scatter diagram where the position of each response can be accurately marked. So if the first respondent thinks that beer a is strong (8/10) and quite sweet (7/10); beer B is quite weak (4/10) and rather bitter (3/10) and beer C is very strong (9/10) and not really sweet or bitter (5/10), his responses would be plotted as in fig 3.2.

The first respondent's perceptions may or may not be typical, but asking the same questions to many more people will result in a scatter diagram which is covered with crosses, as shown in Figure 3.3. The crosses however will almost certainly cluster into certain areas for products A, B and C, enabling the marketer to define the product position of each. Sophisticated computer analysis enables very large numbers of responses to be handled efficiently and the responses for each product to be consolidated into clear product positions as shown by Figure 3.4. These positions represent the boxes stored in the relevant compartment in the consumers' minds. The size of the circle can be used to represent the level of sales of each product. One more piece of information completes the picture. Respondents should also be asked about the attributes of the ideal beer. These can be plotted in the same way. The position of the ideal beer may coincide with one of the existing products on the market or it might, as in this case occupy a slightly different position to any existing product.

The task of the marketer is now clear. The best position for the new product must be determined. If working with an existing product the marketer will be constrained by its physical properties. One cannot suddenly make a weak beer strong or a bitter one sweet, but by slight product modifications and careful marketing communications it may be possible to reposition an existing product slightly closer to the ideal position.

Marketers developing a new product will have no such constraints placed on their choices. If they are very lucky the survey will have revealed an 'ideal' position not occupied by any existing product. If so, the objective of locating a group of customers with an unsatisfied need will have been achieved. However, in reality in today's very competitive markets the product positioning map will probably not

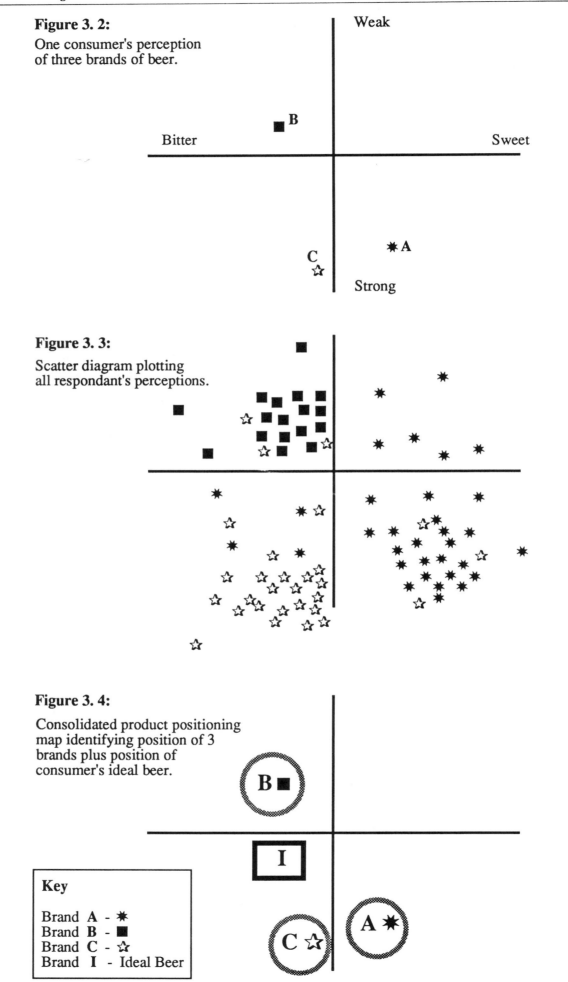

Figure 3. 2:
One consumer's perception of three brands of beer.

Figure 3. 3:
Scatter diagram plotting all respondant's perceptions.

Figure 3. 4:
Consolidated product positioning map identifying position of 3 brands plus position of consumer's ideal beer.

Key

Brand **A** - ✳
Brand **B** - ■
Brand **C** - ☆
Brand **I** - Ideal Beer

reveal such an obvious opportunity. The ideal product may be close to or identical to an existing or several existing products. If so the marketer has two basic choices.

Firstly one could introduce a 'me too product, close to the ideal position, thus replicating the attributes of existing products occupying a similar position. Amstrad introduced its PC 1512 range of personal computers as a 'me too' product range. They were deliberately positioned as closely as possible to the market leading IBM PC range, but they were significantly cheaper. This 'me too' strategy, coupled with the additional benefit of low cost, enabled Amstrad to win market leadership in volume terms in that segment.

On the other hand the marketer could move into a gap on the product positioning map, introducing a product bearing little similarity to any of the existing leading products. 7-Up became the third best selling soft drink in the USA when it was positioned as the 'un-cola', away from the head to head competition of Coke and Pepsi and promoted as the clear, smooth, thirst quenching, different drink.

Marketers must choose between these alternative positioning strategies with care. Amstrad were successful, but many 'me-too' products fail miserably, even if they are cheaper because if benefits are identical, consumers tend to opt for the safer, better known brands.

A new product with a difference like 7-Up will stand much more chance of being noticed in crowded consumer markets. The risks however are much greater. In the 'me too' position the demand for such a product is proven. In the gap it is not. The opportunity in the gap could be immense or it could be non-existent. Through market research and product testing marketers will, of course, try to ascertain that there is a sufficient level of demand for a new and different product. 7-Up was extensively tested to get the taste just how consumers wanted it, and the market extensively researched to satisfy the company that consumers would buy it as well as like it. Even so, there are many examples of new consumer products which have followed all the rules of new product development still failing in the market place (see Chapter 7). Moving into the gap will always be risky, but as with many business opportunities high risk can also mean high rewards for those who are successful.

The company's market positioning decisions will determine who its main competitors will be. The matching process must therefore be strictly adhered to. The company must match its main differential strengths to relevant market opportunities. It must choose market positions where its relevant strengths will be better than the strengths which the competition can bring to bear. This enabled Amstrad to be successful with its 'me-too' computer. If the company cannot find a viable market position where it can be better than the competition it must choose one where it can be different from the competition, as in the 7-Up example.

Assignment   'SMILE'

AB Chemicals Ltd. manufacture a range of cosmetics and also have a strong pharmaceutical division. Their drugs and cosmetics were well thought of and tended to occupy profitable market positions at the high quality end of both markets. The company had an excellent reputation for research and development, having made several well publicised advances in the pharmaceutical field.

For some time the company had been looking to diversify and saw the toiletries market as a promising opportunity. The market was close to its present businesses, required similar research capabilities and its products were often bought at the same outlets, (chemists shops) as AB's existing product ranges, although supermarket sales were much more important in the toiletries market.

As part of these diversification moves some of the company's R & D staff had been working on the development of a new toothpaste. After six months work they confidently announced that not only had they completed their work but they had developed a toothpaste which cleaned teeth better than any existing product on the market. This could be proved by clinical tests and was due to the inclusion of some new ingredients not used by other manufacturers.

Very optimistic about the prospects of the new toothpaste the board gave approval for the marketing department to go ahead with plans for commercialisation, including packaging design, choice of brand name, selection of distributors and the development of an advertising and publicity campaign.

The brand name chosen for the new product was 'Smile', which everyone agreed was a wonderful name for a toothpaste. Tube and carton design were very impressive, emphasising pleasing pastel colours. It was decided to distribute the product through the company's existing network of pharmaceutical wholesalers and retailers since it would be economical for all the company's products to continue to be sold through the same channels. The marketing department also wished to charge a premium price for the new product, partly to sustain the company's general image as a high quality high price supplier and partly because the improved teeth cleaning properties of 'Smile' should make it appear to be good value for money even at the higher price. It was felt that the premium pricing policy was also consistent with the use of existing distributors rather than supermarkets since the latter would almost certainly want to exert downward pressure on AB's price. The advertising campaign was expected to make a big impact. A well known female pop star had been employed to (literally) sing the praises of 'Smile' in the noisy way common to many current TV adverts. AB Chemicals was a company with considerable resources and a large advertising budget had been allocated, so that TV and national press advertising for 'Smile' for the first three months after its launch would match the rate spent on the present leading brand. A small PR company had also been hired to generate publicity for 'Smile' and to explain its dental advantages, especially in the more serious medical and scientific journals.

The launch proceeded as planned. The pharmacy outlets were well stocked and the television advertising made a good impact. Sales however were disappointingly slow. Three months after the launch some retailers were pressing AB to accept returns of unsold cartons of 'Smile'.

Perplexed as well as disappointed, AB commissioned an outside market research agency to find out what had gone wrong. After interviewing a sample of two hundred and fifty consumers the agency produced its report. The responses can be well summarised by the few quotes given below:

'The toothpaste I usually buy tastes very nice. Smile tastes awful.'

'Oh yes, I have seen the adverts with Tracey Thingey, but I haven't ever noticed Smile on sale in my supermarket.'

'There's nothing wrong with my current toothpaste. What's the point in changing?'

'I'm not prepared to pay that much for any toothpaste. It can't possibly be that much better.'

'I'm not interested in gimmicky new toothpastes. I brush my teeth to prevent decay so I always buy 'Dental paste X' which is well known for its teeth cleaning properties.'

'I like a good strong toothpaste which makes your teeth and mouth feel really clean. Smile doesn't really leave that clean feeling in your mouth.'

Task

In order to try to rescue the 'Smile' brand before it was too late, AB Chemicals called in a marketing consultant. As the marketing consultant, write a short report to the Managing Director in which you:

(a) Identify any mistakes made by AB Chemicals in its marketing of the new product.

and

(b) Advise on the importance of segmentation, targeting and positioning, which, if adopted, could help AB Chemicals to relaunch the product more successfully.

Chapter 4
Marketing Research

Introduction

In the first three chapters of this book we have looked at the marketing process starting with the idea that the marketer's objective is to locate and target a group of customers with an unsatisfied need which could be met by his or her company. We have seen in Chapters 2 and 3 how marketers will seek to achieve this objective through a careful analysis of the firm's general operating environment, its markets and its customers. They also endeavour to accumulate as much information as possible about those customers in order to segment their markets and target their product more accurately. Now it is necessary to explain how marketers use marketing research to gather all this information.

As we have seen, information is very important to marketers and a company's marketing success may well depend on how good it is at gathering and analysing relevant information. Marketing research is in fact about gathering and analysing relevant information.

We can define marketing research as:

'The use of scientific methods to collect information relevant to the marketing of products or services.'

According to Margaret Crimp marketing research has two basic purposes:

To reduce uncertainty when plans are being made. This could refer to the whole marketing plan or just to small parts of that plan such as the advertising programme and to monitor performance after plans have been put into operation.

Note the use of the term 'marketing research'. Strictly speaking market research refers only to research into markets whereas marketing research, the more accurate term, refers to research into any aspect of the marketing process. As we said in Chapter 2, marketing analysis involved 'the gathering and analysis of information concerning all the forces and institutions outside the firm which may be relevant to its present and future activities.' In theory marketing research could be equally broad, but in practice it is usually concerned with the gathering and analysis of much more precise information about markets, customers' needs, attitudes, buying behaviour and their response to sellers' marketing communications.

In very general terms there are three sources of the information which the marketing researcher may have to gather. Firstly the researcher could look within the company at information which already exists there. These are internal sources of information. The next step, which usually involves more work and more cost, is to look outside the company to external sources of information which do already exist, perhaps in the form of a published market report or government statistics. These are secondary sources of information. The third and most expensive step of all is to look for information which does not already exist in any retrievable form. This information has to be gathered from consumers and usually involves asking questions to find out the desired facts or opinions. These are primary sources of information. We will now examine, in turn, each of these three possible ways of gathering information.

4.1 Internal sources of information

Most companies are awash with information. But as Kotler says, *'marketers rarely have all the information they need and rarely need all the information they have.'* The secret is to make the most of in-company opportunities for gathering information and to organise that internal information efficiently once it exists. There are four main sources of information within the company.

4.1.1 Stored information on paper

As most people who have worked in an office know, companies tend to be bursting at the seams with filing cabinets, all stuffed full of information. Much of it will be old and therefore useless, especially in fast changing market environments. Another common problem is that nobody knows where to find anything. To be of any use stored information must be capable of quick retrieval. Time must therefore be spent purging filing cabinets on a regular basis of old or irrelevant items and an efficient indexing system must be in operation.

However, if it is handled efficiently, an internal store of marketing information is well worth building up. Such a system might include:

1. Summaries of past sales figures broken down by company size, market segment or any other relevant variables.

2. Prospect files, which are basically records of opportunities which the company has not yet succeeded in exploiting.

3. Competitor information including their brochures and any other useful company or product information.

4. Clippings from trade journals or the business press of relevance to the firm's markets or operating environment.

5. Copies of information previously acquired from external sources, provided it is still valid.

4.1.2 Information in the computer

Computers have made the task of storing, analysing and retrieving marketing information much easier. Apart from taking up much less space to store vast quantities of information computers can help the marketer to make use of stored information in two main ways.

1. Computers can process large quantities of information very quickly. This enables the marketer to analyse information on a continuous basis. Shops can discuss their previous week's sales figures first thing on Monday morning because between Saturday evening and Monday morning the computer can be programmed to receive data via the telephone network from however many branches the retailer has, collate and analyse that data and produce a summarised print out of the main analyses required by management. This helps marketers to keep in close contact with what is happening in their markets.

2. Computers can search for information very quickly. a mail order company may have files on 100,000 customers and 200,000 prospects containing detailed records of their past purchases and known interests. It has a new offer on garden furniture and wishes to identify those customers who may be potential purchasers. This task, virtually impossible manually, becomes perfectly straight forward with the right computer system. In fact it is being done all the time by companies in consumer markets, especially those making extensive use of direct mail. And they are doing it in much larger numbers. In 1982 it was reported in the marketing press that CACI International (owners of the ACORN segmentation system) had reached an agreement with CCN Systems (part of the Great Universal Stores Group) to provide a

joint service selling mailing lists from the CCN database, segmented by ACORN. Two major customers were to be the AA and American Express. Hardly surprising - CCN has details of 18 million people in its computers!

4.1.3 The sales force

Most companies employ sales people. Some may work in shops and sell to customers over the counter, some, mainly in business to business markets, others, drive around in cars and visit customers. Some sales people work in offices and take enquiries and orders over the telephone. All of these people are close to customers, especially the sales representative who is visiting customers on their premises or in their home. It has been said that the sales force is the company's eyes and ears in the market place. Sales people should be encouraged to report back any interesting information they have gleaned about customers or activity in the market place. If the organisation has a formal method of gathering the information in the minds of the sales people much useful information can be recorded.

4.1.4 Other staff

Sales staff are not the only people who have contact with customers. Service engineers, delivery men, senior management, quality control staff, R & D staff might all have to make visits to customers. Very often people such as service engineers and technical staff will have much more useful conversations with customers than will sales staff. They can learn about customers' needs, their problems, their current activities and future purchases. This is all potentially valuable information which should not be wasted.

4.2 Secondary sources of information

Usually, internal sources of information will not tell marketers all they need to know. Their next step is to look for relevant information which has already been gathered by other organisations outside the company and is available for purchase or hire or maybe freely available through libraries. There is a wealth of information available to the marketer from secondary sources. We will look very briefly at some of the more commonly used examples.

4.2.1 Information about markets

Information is big business and many companies make very handsome profits by gathering information about markets, compiling it into reports and selling them to anyone who wants to buy them. They can often be read in large public or college libraries. The government also produces statistics and information on markets which can also be bought or consulted in the main libraries. Listed below are some of the more common sources of market information.

(a) Mintel Reports

Mintel produce a monthly journal containing about six reports on markets of interest. They are almost always consumer markets. Figure 4.1 shows their variety and volume.

INDEX

The following index is a guide to all Mintel reports appearing in Market Intelligence (those specified by month and year only), Leisure Intelligence, Retail Intelligence, Personal Finance Intelligence (PFI), and Mintel Special reports since 1985.

Further information on reports and services can be obtained from Mintel Publications by telephoning 01-836 1814 or 01-379 3536. From outside United Kingdom dial international prefix plus 44-1-379 3536. Sales HOTLINE 01-240 8111

SUBJECT	MONTH	YEAR
Accessories, car	October	1988
Accessories, car (Car After Market)	Special	1987
Accidents, road (The Driver)	Special	1988
Accommodation, UK holiday	Leisure Vol 3	1988
Additives (Additives and Ingredients)	Special	1987
Adhesives, wallpaper	November	1987
Adhesives & sealants (DIY)	Special	1986
Advertising agencies (The Marketing Services Business)	Special	1987
Advertising, poster	May	1986
Advertising, retail	Retail Vol 1	1988
Adult board games	Leisure Vol 1	1987
After dinner drinks	December	1988
After-shave (men's toiletries)	April	1988
After-shave (Bodycare)	Special	1988
Air fresheners & insecticides	July	1988
Airport & duty free shops	Retail Spring	1986
Alarms (home protection)	September	1988
Alarms, car (car accessories)	October	1988
Alcoholic drinks (drinking out)	Leisure Vol 1	1989
Alcoholic drinks	Special	1988
Alcoholic drinks	Retail Vol 4	1987
Ales, stout &	March	1989
Alternative investments	PFI Issue 4	1986
Alternative credit	PFI Issue 6	1986
Alternatives non-store (Non-store Alternatives	Special	1987
Aluminium foil (kitchen wraps)	September	1987
Amenities, housing (Homes & Housing)	Special	1988
Analgesics	March	1989
Angling	Leisure Issue 15	1986
Answering machines (Telecommunications)	Special	1987
Anti-freeze (car care products)	August	1988
Anti-freeze (Car After Market)	Special	1987
Aperitifs (Alcoholic Drinks)	Special	1988
Aquaria	Leisure Vol 1	1988
Artificial sweeteners, sugar and	February	1989
Artificial sweeteners (Health, Diet & Today's Consumer)	Special	1988
Arts, sponsorship (Sponsorship)	Special	1988
ATMs	PFI Vol 2	1988
Audio equipment (Leisure Electronics)	Special	1985
Audio systems - a mass market?	Leisure Vol 3	1988
Audio Visual Markets	Special	1988
Audio visual software	Leisure Vol 1	1988
Automatic vending	Retail Vol 2	1988
Baby and pre-school clothing	July	1988
Baby market	Special	1985
Baby toiletries	August	1986
Bacon and fresh meat	September	1988
Bakers (specialist food retailers)	Retail Vol 3	1988
Baking, home	October	1987
Bank accounts	PFI Vol 4	1987
Banking	November	1987

Bank lending	PFI Vol 1	1987
Banking, electronic developments	Special	1987
Banks, competition and the	PFI Vol 5	1987
Baths & showers	January	1988
Bath & shower products	February	1988
Bath & shower products (Bodycare)	Special	1988
Batteries, car (Car After Market)	Special	1987
Batteries & torches	October	1986
Bed linen (household textiles)	January	1989
Bed linen, blankets and	April	1987
Bedding plants (garden stock)	April	1988
Bedroom furniture	November	1988
Beds & mattresses	April	1989
Beef (fresh meat and bacon)	September	1988
Beef extracts (savoury spreads)	February	1989
Beer (Alcoholic Drinks)	Special	1988
Beer (On Trade and Off Trade)	Special	1986
Beers (ales & stout)	March	1989
Betting	March	1985
Betting (the gambler)	Leisure Vol 3	1988
Beverages, hot	December	1987
Bicycles	October	1987
Bingo (the gambler)	Leisure Vol 3	1988
Biscuits & cakes	May	1988
Biscuits (Snacking - an Eating Revolution)	Special	1987
Blankets (household textiles)	January	1989
Blankets, electric	February	1985
Blankets & bed linen	April	1987
Blinds, curtains and accessories	September	1987
Board games, adult	Leisure Vol 1	1987
Boats & boating	Leisure Issue 16	1986
Books (leisure paperbacks)	June	1986
Book retailing	Retail Vol 1	1989
Bottled sauces	May	1986
Bottled waters (Soft Drinks)	Special	1986
Brake parts (Car After Market)	Special	1987
Brandy (dark spirits)	August	1987
Brandy (Alcoholic Drinks)	Special	1988
Bread	November	1988
Bread (Health, Diet & Today's Consumer)	Special	1988
Bread (Snacking - an Eating Revolution)	Special	1987
Bread alternatives	April	1988
Breakfast cereals	April	1987
Breakfast cereals (Health, Diet & Today's Consumer)	Special	1988
Brewers (On Trade Revolution)	Special	1988
Brewing, home	Leisure Vol 4	1987
British Lifestyles 1987	Special	1988
British Sportsman	Special	1986
Broadcast, sponsorship (Sponsorship)	Special	1988
Brokers, insurance	PFI Vol 3	1987
Builders (Homes & Housing)	Special	1988
Building societies after deregulation	PFI Vol 4	1987
Building society savings	PFI Issue 1	1985
Bulbs, seeds and plants (Gardener)	Special	1988

Figure 4.1 The large scope and volume of Mintel reports.

Monthly Mintel reports are about ten to twenty pages long and give the kind of basic information that marketers need for a quick preliminary scan of the market, such as: market size, projected growth, main competitors, market share of main products, advertising spend of main brands and any other significant trends.

Mintel also produce special reports, covering similar topics in much greater depth, perhaps two or three hundred pages long on one specific market, e.g. the wine market in the U.K. Other special compilations such as retailing reports or marketing in Europe reports are also published from time to time. Many companies subscribe to the regular monthly reports and the special reports are sold individually. Copies can also be found in the main business libraries.

(b) Euromonitor reports

Operating in a very similar way to Mintel with monthly compilations and special reports, the Euromonitor further broadens the range of up to date market reports available to the marketer.

(c) Other consumer market reports

Similar again, but concentrating entirely on retail marketing, Retail Business is another monthly publication. Many organisations also produce a much smaller volume of very specialist reports. In the food sector for example, organisations like the Leatherhead Food Research Association, the Food Policy Research unit at Bradford University and the Institute of Grocery Distribution all publish reports such as 'Low calorie foods in the U.K.', 'Ethnic foods in the U.K.', or 'Talking about healthy eating'.

(d) Key Note Reports

Key Note differ in that they produce reports for business to business markets. They do not have a regular monthly edition but cover a range of business markets and update the reports on a regular basis. Around 75 pages long they provide a fairly detailed introduction to markets.

A list of markets covered by Key Note publications is shown in Figure 4.2 .

e) Other business to business reports

There is quite a wide range of reports available to the researcher of business to business markets but since they are often published in very small quantities by a large number of different companies they are more difficult to locate. They also tend to be very expensive. There are a number of common ones. Frost and Sullivan publish quite a large number of reports and the ICC Financial Ratio tables which contain a mass of financial information on company performance are published on a sector by sector basis for industrial markets. Luckily for the researcher there are some guides to this information. One of the best is a small but rather thick book entitled Marketsearch which is a directory of published market research reports containing around 12,000 entries, all less than five years old. Keeping up with modern technology, the company also offers a 'Marketsearch Hot Line' service. The use of such a manual is essential for the market researcher who needs to study a specific market in depth.

Key Note Reports Currently Available £155 each

AGRICULTURE

Agricultural Machinery
Animal Feedstuffs
Battery Farming
Fertilizers
Pesticides
Veterinary Products

CHEMICALS & ALLIED INDUSTRIES

Adhesives
Biotechnology Products
Chemical Industry
Cosmetics
Dry Batteries
Hair Care Products
Prescribed Pharmaceuticals
OTC Pharmaceuticals
Plastics Processing
Rubber Mfrs and Processors
Soaps and Detergents
Toiletries

CLOTHING & PERSONAL GOODS

Baby Products
Clothing Manufacturers
Fibres
Footwear
Jewellery
Leathergoods & Accessories
Personal Protection Equipment
Sports Clothing & Footwear
Women's Fashions

CONSTRUCTION & HOME IMPROVEMENTS

Baths & Sanitaryware
Bricks & Tiles
Building Contracting
Builders' Merchants
Building Materials
Civil Engineering
DIY
Domestic Heating
Fitted Kitchens
Garden Equipment
Heating, Ventilating & Air Conditioning
Housebuilding
Insulation Products
Paints & Varnishes
Self Assembly Furniture
Timber & Joinery
Wallcoverings
Windows & Doors

DRINKS & TOBACCO

After Dinner Drinks
Aperitifs
Breweries
Cider
Cigarettes & Tobacco
Distillers (Whisky)
Distillers (White Spirits)
Fruit Juices & Health Drinks
Home Brewing & Wine Making
Hot Drinks
Public Houses
Soft Drinks (Carbonated & Concentrated)
The Off-Licence Trade
Wine

ELECTRICAL ELECTRONICS

Domestic Electrical Wiring Accessories
Electronic Component Manufacturers
Electronic Component Distributors
Electronic Medical Equipment
Home Computers/Software
Lighting Equipment
Medical Equipment
Microcomputers
On-line Databases
Printed Circuits
Scientific Instruments
Telecommunications
Videotex (Teletex/Viewdata)

ENGINEERING & HEAVY INDUSTRIES

Aerospace
Defence Equipment
Industrial Fasteners
Industrial Pumps
Industrial Robots
Industrial Valves
Machine Tools
Mechanical Handling
Plant Hire
Scrap Metal Processing
Steel Stockholders

FINANCE & BUSINESS SERVICES

Advertising Agents
Building Societies
Credit Cards
Debt Collecting & Factoring
Direct Marketing
Employment Agencies
Equipment Leasing
Estate Agents
Finance Houses
Franchising
Industrial Development Areas
Insurance Brokers
Insurance Companies
Market Research Industry
PR Consultancies
Retail Banking
Stockbrokers
UK Financial Markets (Deregulation Restructuring Prospects)

FOOD

Bread Bakers
Breakfast Cereals
Canned Foods
Chilled Foods
Confectionery
Contract Catering
Ethnic Foods
Fast Food Outlets
Flour Confectionery
Food Flavourings & Ingredients
Frozen Foods
Fruit & Vegetables
Health Foods
Meat & Meat Products
Milk & Dairy Products
Pet Foods
Slimming Products
Sauces & Spreads
Snack Foods

HOUSEHOLD GOODS

Audio Visual Market
Carpets
China & Earthenware
Cutlery
Furniture & Bedding
Glassware
Holloware
Home Furnishings
Household Appliances (White Goods)
Household Cleaning Products
Small Domestic Electrical Appliances

OFFICE EQUIPMENT

Micrographics
Office Furniture
Office Software
Photocopiers
Stationery (Personal & Office)
Word Processors

PACKAGING PRINTING PUBLISHING

Book Publishing
Booksellers
Business Press
Commercial Printing
Consumer Magazines
Disposable Tissue Products
Greetings Cards
Newspapers
Packaging (Glass)
Packaging (Metals & Aerosols)
Packaging (Paper & Board)
Packaging (Plastics)
Paper & Board Manufacturers
Printing Inks
Women's Magazines

RETAILING

Cash & Carry Outlets
Confectioners Tobacconists Newsagents
Convenience Stores
Department Stores
Electrical Goods Retailing
Fish Retailing
Food Retailing
Freezer Centres
Horticultural Retailing
Mail Order
Mens Clothing Retailers
Mixed Retail Businesses
New Trends in Retailing
Own Brands
Retail Chemists
Specialist Food Retailing
Supermarkets & Superstores
Vending Machines

TRANSPORT & MOTOR GOODS

Autoparts
Bicycles
Commercial Vehicles
Freight Forwarders
Motorcycles
Motor Distributors
Road Haulage
Vehicle Leasing & Hire

TRAVEL & LEISURE

Airlines
Betting & Gaming
Business Travel
Cable T.V./DBS Services
Camping & Caravanning
Cinemas & Theatres
Commercial Radio
Commercial T.V.
Cross Channel Ferries
Football Clubs
Health & Fitness Equipment
Hotels
Photography
Records & Tapes
Restaurants
Sports Equipment
Tourism in the UK
Toys & Games
Travel Agents & Overseas Tour Operators
UK Airports
Video Software

OTHER GOODS & SERVICES

Charities
Contract Cleaning
Fire Protection Equipment
Giftware
Laboratory Equipment
Ophthalmic Goods & Services
Private Health Care
Security
Shopfitters

MARKET REVIEWS (upto £295)

UK Catering Market
Computers, Hardware, Software, Services
Personal Finance and Savings in the UK
UK Drinking Habits
UK DIY & Home Improvements
UK Food Market (Trends & Prospects)
UK Leisure and Recreation
UK Sports Market
Retailing in the UK
UK Defence Industry

EUROVIEWS £365

Retail Food Markets in Europe
European Drinking Habits
Telecommunications in Europe

SPECIAL TITLES

Guide to Marketing Research £58

Guide to Official Business Statistics £58

Figure 4.2 Key Note reports.

To give an example of the range and cost of reports which may be available, the following reports might be of relevance to any company which manufactures wood products and requires basic information on market opportunities.

PUBLISHED REPORTS OF RELEVANCE TO THE WOODWORKING INDUSTRY.

All of these reports date from 1986, 1987 or 1988.

Key Note Reports £155

Self assembly furniture, Office furniture, Housebuilding, Timber merchants, Windows and doors Garden equipment.

ICC Business Ratio Reports £155

Timber merchants

Mintel Special Reports £495

DIY Gardening, The Kitchen, Furniture and furnishings, Furniture, self assembly Hardware and home improvements.

Mintel Reports £145

Furniture. Kitchens, fitted Houses.

Euromonitor Reports £50

Garden furniture, Fitted Kitchens.

Euromonitor Special Report £220

Hard furnishings: current trends in the U.K. market place.

Retail Business Reports £45

DIY: wood and carpentry DIY: materials DIY: retail chain stores DIY: market overview and distribution Furniture, self assembly Gardening products part 4: furniture, bar-b-ques and buildings, Refurbishment of retail outlets.

Business and Research Associates Reports £200

Review of the domestic UK furniture industry UK market for kitchen furniture UK market for dining and occasional furniture

Datagroup Reports £1,295

Hardwood veneer and plywood, Western Europe Softwood veneer and plywood, Western Europe Wood kitchen cabinets Millwork (i.e. windows and doors etc.) Sawmills Hardwood dimension and flooring Logging Structural wood members Furnishings, home Furnishings, office.

Industrial Market Research Ltd.

Private office refurbishment: current and future Market prospects.

MSI Database £35

Wood care products.

The Food and Agriculture Organisation £4

Forest products: world outlook 1985 - 2000. This report includes projections of production and consumption including: sawn wood, wood based panels, paper products, wood and total industrial round wood input. (Available from: HMSO Books).

As you can see, the market researcher is often faced with a large volume of published secondary source material of relevance to his business. Though many of the reports are not cheap, they will still represent a cost effective way for many companies to acquire general descriptive information about markets.

(f) Government statistics

There is an almost equally large and bewildering range of government statistics available to the marketer. The best place to start is the free guide from the CSO (Central Statistical Office) entitled, *Government Statistics: A Brief Guide to Sources*. Each Government department prepares its own statistics and the small guide lists the most important statistics by subject and shows which departments are responsible for the statistics. A much larger *Guide to Official Statistics*, costing around £22 is also available, covering all government and many non-government sources of data. There are many CSO publications which could be of interest to marketers, so we will just look briefly at some of the more commonly used.

Business Monitors, published quarterly, give up to date information on market size for a vast range of highly precise markets. They contain details of exports, imports, price inflation and employment as well as detailed market statistics. Business monitors are broken down by SIC code. This stands for Standard Industrial Classification and as you can see from Figure 4.3 on the next page it is very detailed. Since it is the Government's official method for classifying markets it has been widely adopted by industry at large and will therefore be referred to frequently by the marketer.

The chief source for all information on social trends is the official census carried out every ten years (the next one is in 1991). The Office of Population, Censuses and Surveys issues many useful publications based on the census returns. The office is also responsible for two continuous surveys, the Family Expenditure Survey and the General Household Survey, both of which furnish very useful information for the marketer.

(g) Audits

Retail audits record sales to consumers through a sample of retail outlets, usually at two monthly intervals. Though retail audits have existed for many years, the spread of EPOS (electronic point of sale) tills has greatly facilitated the task of data collection. Two companies, A.C. Nielsen and Retail Audits are the most well known in this field. They collect data of retail sales typically of goods sold through supermarkets or major retail chains, and sell the figures, usually on a product by product basis to anyone who wants to buy them. Both retailers and manufacturers find such detailed up to date tracking of sales extremely useful. It enables them to work out matters such as market shares, the performance of new products, the effect of a price change, a sales promotion or a new advertising campaign. It offers a continuous monitor of their performance in the market place. Many of the published reports outlined in section (a) have to use sources such as these for their raw data.

(h) Panels

Panels are groups of consumers who record their purchases, their media habits and/or their attitudes in a regularly kept diary. The diary will be very easy to keep, a matter of ticking boxes mainly.

The purpose of panels is not to provide information about the volume of purchases on a macro level, a task performed more efficiently and reliably by retail audits, but to link specific purchases to other variables at the micro level. The micro level could be the individual or the household. The diary data enables the research company to link purchases with such variables as buyers' demographic details, neighbourhood location, social status, occupation and level of income, personal interests and media habits. As we know from Chapters 2 and 3, for the purposes of segmentation and targeting such information is invaluable. Panel data can also be used to monitor changes in the behaviour of people over a period of time.

DIVISION 0: AGRICULTURE, FORESTRY AND FISHING

01000 Agriculture and horticulture (general)
01001 Arable farming and livestock production
01002 Horticulture
01003 Agricultural and horticultural services
02000 Forestry
03000 Fishing (general)
03001 Commercial sea fishing
03002 Commercial fishing in inland waters

DIVISION 1: ENERGY AND WATER SUPPLY INDUSTRIES

11100 Coal extraction and manufacture of solid fuels (general)
11130 Deep coal mines
11140 Opencast coal working
11150 Manufacture of solid fuels
12001 Colliery coke ovens
12002 Iron and steel industry coke ovens
12003 Other coke ovens
12004 Low temperature carbonisation plants
13000 Extraction of mineral oil and natural gas
14010 Mineral oil refining
14020 Other treatment of petroleum products (excluding petrochemical manufacture)
15200 Nuclear fuel production
16101 Public electricity supply
16102 Other electricity generating, separately identifiable
16200 Public gas supply
16300 Production and distribution of other forms of energy
17000 Water supply industry

DIVISION 2: EXTRACTION OF MINERALS AND ORES OTHER THAN FUELS; MANUFACTURE OF METALS, MINERAL PRODUCTS AND CHEMICALS

21000 Extraction and preparation of metalliferous ores
22100 Iron and steel industry
22200 Steel tube manufacturing
22340 Drawing and manufacture of steel wire and steel wire products
22350 Other drawing, cold rolling and cold forming of steel
22450 Aluminium and aluminium alloys industry (general)
22451 Primary and secondary aluminium and aluminium alloys unwrought
22452 Rolled, drawn, extruded and other semi-manufactured aluminium products
22460 Copper, brass and other copper alloys (general)
22461 Primary and secondary copper and copper based alloys unwrought
22462 Rolled, drawn, extruded and other semi-manufactured copper and copper alloy products
22470 Other non-ferrous metals and their alloys
22471 Other base non-ferrous metals
22472 Precious metals
23100 General or unspecified quarrying
23101 Slate quarrying and mining
23102 Stone quarrying and mining
23103 Chalk quarrying and mining
23104 Extraction and dredging of sand, pebbles and gravel
23105 Gypsum quarrying and mining
23106 Extraction of clay, kaolin and marl
23300 Salt extraction and refining
23960 Extraction other minerals not elsewhere specified
24100 Manufacture of structural clay products
24200 Manufacture of cement, lime and plaster
24360 Manufacture of ready mixed concrete
24370 Manufacture of other building products of concrete, cement or plastic
24400 Manufacture of asbestos goods
24501 Working of ground and processed minerals
24502 Working of slate products
24503 Working of building, ornamental and funerary stonework
24504 Working of other non-metallic mineral products
24600 Manufacture of abrasive products
24700 Manufacture of glass and glassware (general)
24710 Manufacture of flat glass (general)
24711 Manufacture of flat glass not further worked
24712 Manufacture of flat glass further worked
24780 Manufacture of glass containers
24791 Manufacture of domestic and ornamental glassware

24792 Manufacture of glass envelopes and illuminating glassware
24793 Manufacture of glass tubing and scientific glassware
24794 Manufacture of glass fibre and glass fibre products
24795 Manufacture of other glass products
24810 Manufacture of refractory goods
24891 Manufacture of glazed earthenware tiles
24892 Manufacture of ceramic sanitary ware
24893 Manufacture of domestic china and other pottery
24894 Manufacture of other ceramic goods
25000 General chemical manufacture
25100 Manufacture of basic industrial chemicals
25110 Manufacture of inorganic chemicals except industrial gases
25120 Manufacture of basic organic chemicals except specialised pharmaceutical chemicals
25130 Manufacture of fertilisers
25140 Manufacture of synthetic resins and plastic materials
25150 Manufacture of synthetic rubber
25160 Manufacture of dye stuffs and pigments
25500 Manufacture of paints, varnishes and printing ink (general)
25510 Manufacture of paints, varnishes and printers' fillings
25520 Manufacture of printing ink
25600 Manufacture of specialised chemical products mainly for industrial and agricultural purposes
25620 Manufacture of formulised adhesives and sealants
25630 Chemical treatment of oils and fats
25640 Manufacture of essential oils and flavouring materials
25650 Manufacture of explosives
25670 Manufacture of miscellaneous chemical products for industrial and general agricultural use
25680 Manufacture of formulated pesticides
25690 Manufacture of adhesive film and foil
25700 Manufacture of pharmaceutical products
25800 Manufacture of soap and toilet preparations (general)
25810 Manufacture of soap and synthetic detergents
25820 Manufacture of perfumes, cosmetics and toilet preparations
25910 Manufacture of photographic materials and chemicals
25990 Manufacture of domestic and office chemical products not elsewhere specified
26000 Manufacture of man-made fibres

DIVISION 3: METAL GOODS, ENGINEERING AND VEHICLES INDUSTRIES

31100 Foundries (general)
31110 Ferrous metal foundries
31120 Non-ferrous metal foundries
31200 Forging, pressing and stamping
31371 Manufacture of bolts, nuts, screws, washers, rivets etc.
31372 Manufacture of springs
31373 Manufacture of non-precision chains
31380 Heat and surface treatment of metals including sintering
31420 Manufacture of metal doors, windows etc.
31610 Manufacture of hand tools and implements (general)
31611 Manufacture of agricultural hand tools
31612 Manufacture of other hand tools
31621 Manufacture of cutlery, spoons, forks and similar tableware
31622 Manufacture of razors and razor blades
31630 Manufacture of metal storage vessels (mainly non-industrial)
31641 Manufacture of metal cans and boxes
31642 Manufacture of metal kegs, drums and barrels
31643 Manufacture of metallic closures
31644 Manufacture of foil packaging products of metal
31645 Manufacture of other packaging products of metal
31650 Manufacture of domestic heating and cooking appliances (non-electrical)
31661 Manufacture of metal furniture
31662 Manufacture of safes
31670 Manufacture of domestic and similar utensils of metal
31691 Manufacture of locks etc.
31692 Manufacture of needles, pins and other metal smallwares
31693 Manufacture of base metal fittings and mountings for furniture, builders' joinery, leather and travel goods not elsewhere specified
31694 Manufacture of miscellaneous finished metal products
32040 Fabricated constructional steelwork (general)
32041 Fabricated constructional steelwork for buildings
32042 Fabricated constructional steelwork for civil engineering works

Figure 4.3 Standard Industrial Classification (SIC codes).

AGB (Audits of Great Britain Ltd.) produce a large variety of panel data including the AGB Home Audit for household durables, the Personal Purchases Index for a range of consumer products and specialist records such as purchases of toiletries and cosmetics. Their Attwood Consumer Panel and Television Consumer Audit (TCA) delve into attitudes, lifestyle and media habits.

Other panels refer exclusively to media. The BARB (Broadcasters Audience Research Board) Audience Measurement Service is designed to monitor how many people are watching each TV station at all times of the day. Based on a sample of 3,000 households, data is collected automatically by means of a device plugged to the TV set which continuously records whether the set is on, and if so which station it is tuned to. Since there can be more than one individual watching, a second push button device enables each member of the household to 'clock into and out of' TV viewing simply by pressing the appropriate button. Audience statistics are published in great detail by BARB every week, and are the TV media planners bible (see Chapter 11).

Although not strictly speaking a panel, because it gathers information at specific times from different people, the Target Group Index (TGI) is very commonly used source of information about trends in consumer markets. Based on sample of 24,000 adults the survey covers 4,500 brands in 500 product and service sectors. The 70 page questionnaire also delves into consumers' media habits enabling TGI to link these two variables, which is of great value in the targeting of advertising and other marketing communications. TGI has also been linked with ACORN enabling more detailed comparisons to be made.

4.2.2 Information about media

Once again many sources could be listed under this heading but the main ones are as follows.

Benn's Media Directory

A source of general information Benn's includes brief details of many of the ways of sending promotional messages to customers, including TV and commercial radio companies, newspapers and magazines, posters or cinemas. it also gives details of other relevant organisations such as advertising agencies, direct mail houses etc.

Advertisers Annual

This publication goes into much more detail on advertising with fairly detailed comparisons of advertising agencies.

BRAD

Standing for British Rate and Data, it gives extensive details of all advertising media including virtually any publication which takes advertising, complete with costs and booking procedures.

MEAL

Media Expenditure Analysis Ltd. produce a detailed breakdown of the amount of money spent on advertising through all the main media across a wide range of product and service categories.

4.2.3 Information about companies

There is also a wealth of information about companies available to the market researcher. few of the most commonly used are outlined below.

Kompass

Produced in two volumes, the first gives details of products and services, listed by SIC code, and identifies suppliers. Volume two lists companies in alphabetical order and gives details of their activities, size, turnover and often even the names of their senior personnel.

Who Owns Whom

An annual publication which gives details of which subsidiary companies are owned by which parents.

Extel

A company information service which provides details from published accounts of all public companies and larger private companies.

McCarthy Information Ltd.

A clippings service which collects and files articles and information on companies and industries from leading business newspapers and journals. Copies of the latest information on specific companies and industries can be supplied.

Thus, for companies of any size, with a reasonable research budget it is possible to accumulate vast quantity of market information from published secondary sources. However, when using secondary data, marketers should pay particular attention to its suitability. There are many reasons why 'off the peg' information may not be appropriate. It may be too old. The sample from which the data was collected may not be exactly the same as the market segment being investigated by the researcher. The data provided may not quite answer the specific questions the researcher needs to answer. For such reasons, the researcher often needs to turn to primary sources of information.

4.3 Primary sources of information

To meet their specific research needs marketers often need to generate primary (first hand) information. There are four main methods of primary marketing research: observation, experimentation, survey and discussion groups.

We will look briefly at each method in turn.

4.3.1 Observation

Using this method an observer (or hidden camera) watches consumers, usually in the act of buying or choosing. It is most commonly used to observe consumer behaviour in stores, recording details like how consumers move through the store, whether they notice and stop at special in-store displays and probably most commonly, how they scan the shelves, since the shelf space and shelf location given to competing brands in supermarkets can often be significant factor in their sales.

With the help of special equipment (such as cameras which monitor eye movement), observation can also be used to monitor the way in which people read magazines or newspapers. This can be useful in suggesting areas within magazines, or areas within single page which are most commonly looked at. It can also identify the nature of the subject matter most noticed. Such research can help marketers to decide on the most cost effective sizes and positions for print advertisements and can give valuable feedback on the creative impact made by different ads on the same page.

The big advantage of observation is its objectivity. Actions are recorded in a factual manner and, the subjects' behaviour is normal and not affected by the pressures that may afflict survey responses (see 4.3.3). The disadvantage of observation stems from this very objectivity - it tells us what people do but not what makes them do it, so it is far from adequate to give marketers thorough understanding of their customers' behaviour.

4.3.2 Experimentation

Experimentation in any subject are involves the introduction of a stimulus into the environment, varying the stimulus and measuring the result. The results are normally measured on the basis of 'other things being equal', so the experimenter must try to eliminate or control any factors other than the variables being tested. In marketing, experimentation usually means changing some element of the marketing mix and measuring the change in customer behaviour. Examples might be testing two different adverts in controlled environment and measuring customer recall. Another example could be the introduction of well publicised price cut in one region and the monitoring of sales in that region compared to the rest of the country where the price had remained the same. Of course, the researcher cannot expect to exercise the level of control which would be found in clinical environment, such as that used for medical experiments, but information from the two main types of experimentation used by marketers can be very useful in helping them to predict consumer behaviour.

The first of these commonly used methods is the laboratory test where the experiment takes place in an artificial but fully controlled environment. An example would be tasting sessions for proposed new food products where consumers taste different products and are questioned about their reactions.

The second type of experiment is normal environment test where consumer reactions to tests carried out under normal market conditions are measured. Often referred to as 'test marketing' there are many possible examples. One example which enables real market tests to be carried out under very low risk conditions is the 'Mini-test Market' which is kind of consumer panel, but with a difference. In physical form it is large mobile shop fitted out like supermarket stocking 1,600 items. Anyone is at liberty to buy from it, but its objective is to call on a panel of named, card carrying shoppers. There are in fact two panels, northern one in Manchester and southern one in Southampton, each composed of 500 housewives. These panel members receive monthly colour magazine carrying editorial features and adverts, and have all their purchases from the mobile shop recorded. Companies planning to launch new products can use this limited experiment to identify potential flops before putting them on much more expensive test market launch (see Chapter 7).

Most experiments have 'test group' (or 'experimental group') and a 'control group'. Care must be taken to ensure that the characteristics of the two groups are as identical as possible. In the usual kind of 'before and after experiment', the first step is to measure the variable being tested, e.g. sales of 'Washing Powder X', in both test and control groups before the start of the experiment. Then one group, the test group, has the new stimulus applied, e.g. 'New Washing Powder X with Magic Whitening Ingredient Y'. In the other group, the control group, factors remain exactly as before, only old unmagic washing powder X is on sale. The difference in the change in sales between the test and control groups can then be attributed to the popularity, or unpopularity of the new powder. To be meaningful this experiment would have to last for number of customer purchase cycles because many consumers might try the new product initially, but only the level of repeat sales would be valid predictor of long term buyer behaviour.

Provided genuinely matched test and control groups can be used, experimentation can be a very useful predictor of purchase behaviour. The main problem for the marketer is whether consumers in this unreal situation (buying groceries from the mobile test lab) do behave in an identical way to their real life shopping behaviour. For example, because of the unusually high proportion of new products in the mobile lab, they may become tuned in to new products, and be more likely to buy them than normal consumers.

4.3.3 Survey

The survey is the most used method of data collection in marketing research. In theory there are two types of survey, the census and the sample. In practice, the census, which involves questioning everybody in the target market, is usually impractical except when numbers in the market are extremely low. Therefore, the sample survey, where a selection of respondents from a target market is used is by far the most common method. Of course, researchers should take care to ensure that their method of sampling produces sample which is as representative as possible of the total population. The first decision therefore to be made by the researchers is their method of sampling. There are two basic types of sample: random samples and non-random samples. We will look briefly at each in turn. There are three commonly employed methods of producing a random sample: simple random sampling; stratified random sampling and cluster sampling.

(a) Simple random sampling

Sometimes called probability sampling, the researcher starts with complete list (the population or sample frame) of the market or group to be surveyed. He or she then determines the size of sample required and chooses that sample from the complete list on a random basis, which means that each individual in the sample frame has the same likelihood of ending up in the sample. One way of achieving this would be to use computer to draw out names or numbers at random. Another method would be to draw systematic random sample as follows. Let's assume that in limited geographical are researcher had population of 10,000 in the sample frame. He or she wished to survey sample of 200. This would mean starting by dividing 10,000 by 200, giving an answer of 50. There are thus 200 equal groups containing 50 people in that population. One then chooses at random, number between 1 and 50; it might be 37. One can now identify the 37th, 87th, 137th, 187th, 237th etc. person on the list of 10,000 people. This would produce a systematic random sample of 200. Using statistical techniques the researcher can calculate the level of certainty with which results obtained from the random sample can be used to predict results for the total population of 10,000. The larger the sample the higher the degree of accuracy.

(b) Stratified random sampling

Random sampling can sometimes distort results in markets where some customers are more important than others. In this case stratified random sampling would be used. This involves the weighting of the sample on the basis of the importance of the various segments making up the market. Imagine that a company has 10,000 customers segmented as follows: 5,000 light users accounting for £5m. turnover, 3,000 medium users accounting for £20m. turnover, 2,000 heavy users accounting for £25m. turnover.

A randomly chosen sample of 200 would not be fully representative of the company's business. Since the heavy users account for half the company's turnover they should also make up half the sample, the medium users representing 40% of turnover should be 40% of the sample and the light users, although half the population only make up 10% of sales and should therefore form no more than 10% of the sample. Thus the 'strata' of the stratified sample would be: 100 heavy users randomly chosen from the heavy user population of 2,000, 80 medium users randomly chosen from the medium user population of 3,000, 20 light users randomly chosen from the light user population of 5,000.

(c) Cluster sampling

There is also third, less costly and very commonly used, way of producing random sample. Cluster sampling reduces the cost of the marketing research by concentrating the sampling in one or several representative areas. random sample drawn nationally would involve interviewing small numbers of respondents in scattered locations. For personal interviewing this would be time consuming and costly.

Random samples are therefore often drawn from small number of tightly defined locations (clusters) deemed to be typical of the target market in question. This method is considered to be of sufficient statistical accuracy for most commercial market research.

Non-random (non-probability) samples are quicker, easier and cheaper to carry out but they may not be as representative of the market as a whole, and statistical techniques cannot be legitimately used to apply levels of certainty to the results. The three main types of non-random sample are as follows:

(a) Convenience samples

This would involve gathering data from any convenient group, e.g. passers-by.

(b) Judgemental samples

Here respondents would be selected on the basis of the researcher's (or interviewer's) belief that they were representative of the target market being studied. The more knowledgeable the person who selects the respondents the more accurate it is likely to be.

(c) Quota samples

Quota controlled samples are frequently used by commercial marketing research agencies to minimise the cost of fieldwork. The research agency initially uses secondary sources to divide the population into groups. In the case of consumer research these groups will often be social class and / or age. The research agency then decides, on the basis of published statistics, on controlled quotas (or groups) of respondents for each interviewer in the field. For example the interviewer might be told to question 20 housewives aged 20 - 35, 15 housewives aged 36 - 50 and 25 housewives aged 51 and over. Using this method the agency can be certain that the quotas are an accurate reflection of the total population. However, there is no guarantee that the individuals within those age bands will represent an accurate sample of all housewives within that age band. The interviewer will simply question the first 20 housewives who agree to be interviewed in the 20 - 35 year old age band. This method is very commonly employed in commercial research simply because it is often considered to be the most cost effective way of producing data of sufficient accuracy.

Non-random samples can be perfectly satisfactory when statistical accuracy is not imperative such as in pilot studies to explore customers' general views on subject to aid in the design of full survey.

The range of sampling choices is illustrated in the diagram below.

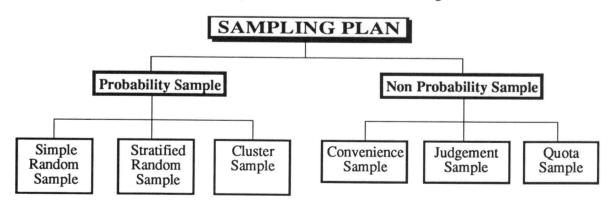

Figure 4.4 Sampling methods.

4.3.4 Administering the survey

The next decision to be taken is the method of administering the survey. We will look in turn at each of the three main methods: personal interviews; telephone interviews and postal questionnaires.

(a) Personal interviews

Personal interviews may be highly structured with the interviewer reading through list of questions, often with limited choice of set answers. This would lead to the collection of 'quantitative data'. These are data to which statistical techniques can be applied and from which specific conclusions can be drawn. For example, 20% of the target market finds new 'Washing Powder X' makes their whites whiter, or 47% of working women between the ages of 20 and 35 and from social classes A, B and C1 do not believe that any brand of washing powder has significantly superior whitening capabilities than any other.

On the other hand personal interviews can be much less structured, seemingly more like a conversation, with the interviewer working through list of topics but allowing the respondents to develop their views as they wish. This kind of interviewing produces 'qualitative' information where the emphasis is on insight, attitudes, explanation and depth of understanding. Although of great value in helping the marketer to get closer to his customers, conclusions cannot be justified statistically and projections cannot be made.

There are number of advantages of using personal interviews: much information can be obtained in great depth; the interviewer can explain exactly what is required; products, photographs or other stimuli can be used; the interviewer can also record observations; the interviewer can persuade people to agree to be questioned and relatively high response rates can usually be achieved.

There are however some disadvantages: they are usually expensive to administer; there is a danger of interviewer bias; some types of respondent may distort answers to please the interviewer or to avoid appearing foolish; some types of respondent, e.g. busy executives are reluctant to agree to lengthy personal interviews.

(b) Telephone interviews

Often used in business to business research and increasingly in consumer research, telephone interviews are quick and often very cost effective. They are particularly useful if cluster sampling is not acceptable. Telephone interviews must be short and to the point or the respondent may become irritated and discontinue the interview.

The main advantages of telephone interviews are: two way communication, enabling explanations to be made where necessary; they are quick and cost effective; national and international samples are possible; easy identification of respondents facilitates later recall if necessary; lack of eye contact reduces respondent embarrassment; the interviewer can key responses directly into a computer and response rates are quite good.

The main disadvantages of telephone surveys are: questions must be simple and total interview time is short; they are restricted to respondents with telephones and suitable only for target markets where the vast majority of buyers are telephone subscribers and some people regard telephone surveys as an invasion of their privacy and refuse to participate.

(c) Postal surveys

This involves mailing, or distributing door to door, a written questionnaire to sample of buyers for their completion at home or at work. Questionnaires must then be collected or the respondent left to post it back. Two methods are being increasingly used in an effort to boost responses. Firstly, an incentive may be offered to all respondents who complete and return the questionnaire. This may be small incentive for which all respondents qualify, e.g. £5 book token. This kind of incentive is popular in business to business research and is almost to be seen as recompense for the considerable amount of time that may be involved in the completion of some written questionnaires. Alternatively an attractive prize (e.g. colour TV and video recorder) may be offered to the first completed questionnaire drawn out of sack. This is popular for surveys requiring a large number of responses, usually in consumer markets.

A second way of increasing the response rate is to telephone all members of the sample beforehand to ask for their agreement to co-operate. The nature of the survey and any incentive involved can be explained. Those who refuse totally to participate need not be sent questionnaires. Those who agree will feel some obligation to complete the questionnaire and returns will thus be higher.

The advantages of postal questionnaires are: their very low cost; the lack of interviewer bias; total annonymity for respondents whose answers should thus be accurate; long, thought provoking or complex questions can be asked to suitable target audience; respondents who are reluctant to agree to personal or telephone interviews may be prepared to co-operate and diverse audiences can be reached.

The disadvantages of postal surveys are: questionnaires must be short unless sufficient incentive is offered; for many types of respondent the questions must be simple; without incentives response rates are very low; questions may be misinterpreted or missed; the meaning of questions cannot be explained and those who respond may not be typical of the whole sample.

4.3.5 Questionnaire design

Having made the decisions about sampling and the type of survey to be administered the researcher must design questionnaire. All methods of collecting data will require some kind of data collection form. The design of this data collection form should reflect both the survey method and the target group to which the questionnaire will be distributed.

There are number of types of question which may be asked.

(a) Closed questions

Closed questions give respondents fixed selection of answers to choose from. They are very popular with market researchers because they are the quickest and easiest to administer and analyse, offer the least scope for interviewer or respondent error and produce quantitative data. The interviewer (or respondent in self completion questionnaire) need only tick the relevant box.

Closed questions are frequently 'dichotomous', meaning that only two alternative answers are given. The following are dichotomous questions: Did you buy any soup yesterday? **YES/NO**   Do you agree that soup is nutritious? **YES/NO**

Sometimes more than two possible answers are given, as in the example below. Such questions are usually called multiple choice questions.   Which of these flavours of soup do you prefer?

TOMATO   OXTAIL   VEGETABLE   FISH

(b) Open questions

Sometimes the researcher does not want to lead the respondent in any way whatsoever, so an open question like the ones below would be used.

When do you serve soup?

Such a question may be useful if marketers suspect that consumption patterns are changing. Perhaps instead of the traditional starter to a three course lunch it is suspected that people are making soup as a snack in the evening or mid-morning. It was this kind of shifting behaviour that led to the introduction of 'cuppa soup'.

(c) Rating scales

Sometimes researchers need to quantify the strength of an answer. It may not be adequate to know which, from a list of four soups, was most liked by the respondents in the sample. It would almost certainly be more useful to know the degree of liking for each kind of soup. The two most commonly used rating scales are 'Likert scales' and 'semantic differential scales'. Likert scales are used to qualify the respondent's reaction to the question on a scale which goes through a range of degrees from one extreme to the other. For example: How much do you like tomato soup?

VERY MUCH   QUITE A LOT   NOT MUCH   NOT AT ALL.

A score can be given to each response, the final average score representing an overall preference rating for tomato flavoured soup. This rating can be compared with the scores given for the other three types of soup. Comparisons can also be made between ratings given by different groups of consumers, such as different social classes, which can help in the segmentation of markets.

Semantic differential scales measure the difference between words. The semantic differential scale presents the respondent with two contrasting attitudes and constructs a scale (known as an 'attitude battery') between these two opposing positions. A typical question, with the method of recording responses is shown in Figure 4.5.

Once a representative sample of consumers have completed the same attitude battery the results can be computed and a 'brand profile' drawn. If respondents are asked about more than one brand in the product class, profiles can be drawn and compared for all the competing brands. Such an analysis shows how one brand differs from another and can be useful in designing messages for advertising and other marketing communications.

Using a statistical technique known as 'multidimensional scaling' it is possible for brand profiles to be analysed by computer and a 'perceptual map' (market positioning map) to be produced. As explained in Chapter 3 this illustrates consumers' perceptions of competing brands. Results can be surprising, showing unexpected competitors for the product. In one market positioning exercise the closest competitor to lamb chops was identified as fish fingers. Below are examples of the kind of questions that might be asked.

Profiling Cuppa soup

Interviewer: 'I would like you to tell me what sort of people cuppa soup appeals to.' (Interviewer hands over semantic tick lists). 'This is done by putting a tick in ONE box on each line to show to whom cuppa soup appeals in your opinion. The nearer you tick to the statement on the left the more strongly you agree with that statement, the nearer you tick to the box on the right the more strongly you agree with that statement.

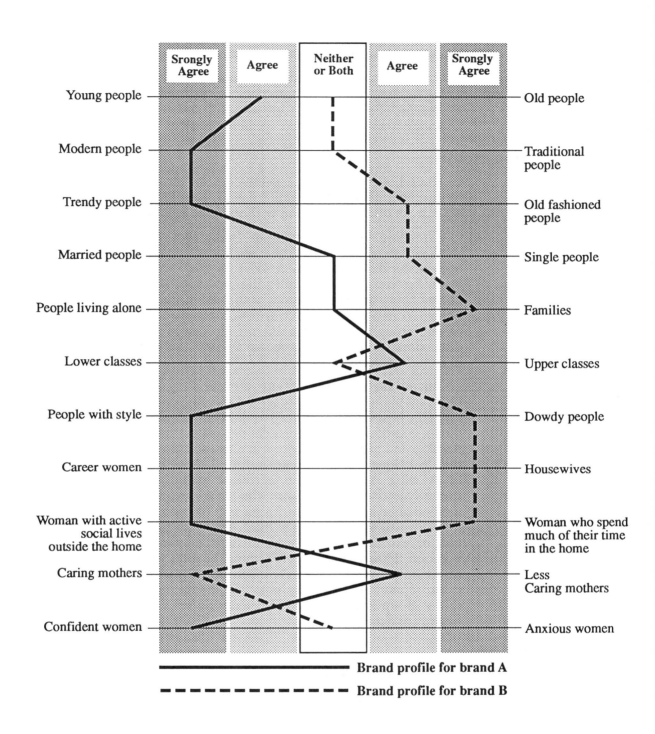

Figure 4.5 Semantic differential scales and brand mapping.

4.3.6 Analysis of data

Once the data has been collected the market researcher must be able to analyse it. As indicated in the previous section good questionnaire design will be an important factor in facilitating data analysis. There are many techniques used in the analysis of data collected in market research surveys. The explanation of statistical techniques does not however fall within the scope of this text although it is important to point out that the use of computers has made an immense contribution to the analysis of research data. Very large numbers of responses and very complex statistical analyses can be handled with ease by suitable computers. Using traditional manual methods they would have been time consuming at best and in many cases totally impractical. Perceptual mapping is just one example of the kind of sophisticated analysis that can be performed by computers.

Computers may be making data analysis easier, but having been analysed it still relies on human minds to draw conclusions from those results in order to present the research findings in the form of useful marketing information which provides an adequate basis for taking management decisions.

4.3.7 Discussion groups

In general, observation, experimentation and most types of survey will be best suited to the generation of quantitative data. Discussion groups and other types of group session are often the best way of developing more qualitative information.

Traditionally discussion groups (sometimes called focus groups) would involve small groups of consumers from the appropriate target market who sat round table and discussed a certain subject under the guidance of group leader. The discussions would be recorded and skilful group leader would be able to probe behind specific comments in an effort to understand the attitudes or thought process which lay behind them. Such discussions are often stimulated by group dynamics, the comment of one group member sparking off an idea in the mind of another. As result, discussions can be much more fruitful than the most unstructured of face to face personal interviews.

Increasingly, group sessions are adopting more complex psychological approaches in order to gain deeper insight into peoples' attitudes and values. In some cases the best way to elicit the required information from people is not to ask them direct question but to approach the matter indirectly allowing respondents to develop and express their views in a less self-conscious manner. In its early stages this technique was sometimes referred to as the 'friendly martian' method of questioning. A group (or an individual) might be asked how they would advise a friendly martian (who of course won't know anything about the subject) on the best method of heating his house. Faced with this task, respondents would go right back to basics, and would explain to the martian how one goes about making decision on heating, explaining in the process all their beliefs and attitudes. Faced with the direct question 'How did you decide upon the best method of heating your house?', respondents would usually take much more for granted and may even be less honest in their appraisal. It is on this basic 'friendly martian' principle that many of the more recent group techniques have been developed. Some commonly used group techniques are described below.

(a) Drawing pictures

'Thematic apperception' is based upon the assumption that it is easier and more accurate for people to describe their real feelings in pictures rather than words. In recently published book, 'Qualitative Market Research', Roy Langmaid and Wendy Gordon describe the results of survey into peoples' attitudes towards the TV companies in which the 50 respondents were asked to draw the four television stations as if they were people. BBC1 came out as rather old, dignified lady, with high neck blouse, tweeds, pearls and knitting on her lap. BBC2 was portrayed as serious academic man of middle age wearing corduroy jacket. ITV appeared as loud mouthed money grabbing yob and Channel 4 was split personality, wearing Walkman with opera plugged into one ear and rock music into the other. Such portraits paint clearer pictures of peoples' perceptions of the TV stations than could be elicited if people were asked to describe them in words.

In another example given, the manufacturer of Domestos bleach wanted to find out what people thought of the brand. Again respondents were asked to draw Domestos as person. One drew knight in shining armour. Another drew Mrs. Thatcher. The results apparently reassured Domestos about the accuracy of their brand image.

Sometimes however, marketers are less happy with the results. When similar research techniques were applied to Lucozade, people tended to draw sick child in bed. In an effort to strengthen Lucozade's brand image and to widen its market, Daley Thompson was brought in to star in the brand's advertising.

(b) Psychodrama

Sometimes called 'role play' or 'fantasy situations', respondents are asked to imagine that they are the product being discussed and to describe their feelings about being used or to act out the process of being used.

In recent psychodramatic exercises, groups of typical consumers of pain killers were asked to act out the process of a person's headache being cured by pain killer. In each group of three people one person had to be the sufferer, another had to be the pain and the third was to represent the pain killer. After brief discussion of how they would do it, most groups came out and showed the pain ruthlessly dominating the sufferer until the pain killer burst upon the scene and aggressively fought and subdued the pain, making the sufferer smile again. Some groups acted out different play. They still showed the pain dominating the sufferer but they showed the pain killer soothing the pain from the sufferer, being assertive but not violent. In the group discussions which followed the mimes, respondents were asked to put brand names to the two different types of pain killer which had been portrayed. The fighting pain killer presented people with no problem, many of the well known brand names being mentioned in this category. But the soothing pain killer was much more difficult, people finding it difficult or impossible to put a brand name to it. But, interestingly, there was a lot of support for the idea of soothing pain killer.

Had the researcher identified group of consumers with an unsatisfied need which could be met by one of his company's products? Yes he had! Before long Nurofen was being widely advertised as the pain killer which soothes away headaches.

Such projective techniques can uncover subconscious needs that might never be identified in any other way. However, their results must be interpreted with care. The group leader, or the respondents themselves, may misinterpret drawings or role play activities. Their conclusions therefore should be taken as ideas which, however good they may seem, should be further verified by more extensive, statistically valid research.

Conclusion

We have seen how the researcher usually has a wealth of information at his disposal both inside the company and outside it, in both secondary and primary form. Primary research techniques are many and varied from the very basic common sense approach to weird and wonderful psychological exercises. However, they all help the marketer to put together the jigsaw we have been describing in the last three chapters. It is marketing research that enables organisations to describe and segment markets, to understand buyers in those segments and to predict their likely responses to its marketing activities.

Assignment   The Questionnaire

The questionnaire shown is included with each Amstrad personal computer so that the company can build up a picture of its customer base.

TASK

Read through the questionnaire and answer the following questions.

1. On what basis will the survey help Amstrad to segment its market?

2. Which questions would be useful in helping Amstrad to develop its marketing mix and how would Amstrad be able to make use of that information?

3. Assume you are the market research manager for a company which manufactures hair dryers. Design a questionnaire to accompany your products.

4. Explain the purposes for which you will use the information provided by each question.

A

Registering your ownership : By filling in these details, you will help Amstrad and the Amstrad User Club to contact you, if necessary, about your purchase and about new products.

BRJ 01

Please give your name and address

1 ☐ Mr.   2 ☐ Mrs.   3 ☐ Ms.   4 ☐ Miss   5 Other title

First name | Initial | Surname

Address

Postcode

Date of Purchase
Day | Month | 1 9 | Year

3 Model | **CPC 464**

B

Please tell us about your purchase : Amstrad are keen to listen to their customers to learn about their changing needs. Your answers - and those of other customers - will be a great help to them.

Where was this product purchased? (Tick only ONE)

1 ☐ Don't know/received as a gift
2 ☐ Dixons
3 ☐ Currys
4 ☐ Rumbelows
5 ☐ Comet
6 ☐ Laskys
7 ☐ Other electrical multiple
8 ☐ Electricity Board showroom
9 ☐ Co-op
10 ☐ Independent electrical retailer
11 ☐ Department store
12 ☐ Argos
13 ☐ Mail order
14 ☐ Independent computer dealer
15 ☐ Television rental chain
16 ☐ Other

Price paid (to nearest £)   £ |__|__|__| : 00

Where did you first learn about this product? (Tick only ONE)

1 ☐ Received as a gift
2 ☐ Television advertisement
3 ☐ Newspaper advertisement
4 ☐ Magazine advertisement
5 ☐ From a friend
6 ☐ From a relative
7 ☐ In-store display
8 ☐ From a shop assistant
9 ☐ Mail order catalogue
10 ☐ News story/review
11 ☐ Other

Which TWO factors most influenced the selection of this product? (Tick no more than TWO)

1 ☐ Product design/appearance
2 ☐ Recommendation of salesperson
3 ☐ Recommendation of friend/relative
4 ☐ Price
5 ☐ Amstrad brand name
6 ☐ Ease of operation
7 ☐ Product features
8 ☐ Good value for money
9 ☐ Reputation for reliability
10 ☐ Other

8 **Was this Amstrad product (Tick only ONE)**

1 ☐ A first purchase of this type of product?
2 ☐ A replacement of an older Amstrad product?
3 ☐ A replacement of another brand (not Amstrad)?
4 ☐ An additional purchase to an Amstrad product already used?
5 ☐ An additional purchase to another brand already used (not Amstrad)?

9 **Which member(s) of your household were primarily responsible for the decision to purchase this product? (Tick only ONE)**

1 ☐ Joint decision between myself and my spouse
2 ☐ My spouse alone
3 ☐ Myself alone
4 ☐ Other adult household member(s)
5 ☐ Children
6 ☐ Received it as a gift from someone outside the household
7 ☐ Other

10 **Which ITV channel do you view most often? (Tick only ONE)**

1 ☐ Thames/London Weekend
2 ☐ Central
3 ☐ Granada
4 ☐ Yorkshire
5 ☐ HTV
6 ☐ TV South
7 ☐ Tyne Tees
8 ☐ Anglia
9 ☐ Grampian
10 ☐ TSW
11 ☐ Border
12 ☐ Scottish
13 ☐ Channel
14 ☐ Ulster

Please indicate if you or your family also watch regularly

1 ☐ TV AM
2 ☐ Channel 4
3 ☐ Through the night television
4 ☐ Cable television
5 ☐ Satellite television

C

Please tell us about yourself: Amstrad would also like to know more about you as a person - it helps when designing new products and planning advertising. Knowing more about you also helps Consumerlink and other respected organisations to ensure that, if you choose to receive information by post, it will interest you.

Is the person whose name appears above:

1 ☐ Male?   or   2 ☐ Female?

Date of birth of person whose name appears above:

Month | 1 9 | Year

Marital status:

1 ☐ Married
2 ☐ Widowed
3 ☐ Divorced/Separated
4 ☐ Single/never married

Occupation: | You | Spouse

	You	Spouse
Professional/senior management	1 ☐	1 ☐
Manager in business	2 ☐	2 ☐
Administrator/clerical	3 ☐	3 ☐
Manual	4 ☐	4 ☐
Housewife	5 ☐	5 ☐
Student	6 ☐	6 ☐
Retired	7 ☐	7 ☐
Other	8 ☐	8 ☐
Self-employed/business owner	9 ☐	9 ☐

Please indicate the ages of ALL children living at home:

☐ None
☐ Under 1
☐ 1 yr
☐ 2 yrs
☐ 3 yrs
☐ 4 yrs
☐ 5 yrs
☐ 6 yrs
☐ 7 yrs
☐ 8 yrs
☐ 9 yrs
☐ 10 yrs
☐ 11 yrs
☐ 12 yrs
☐ 13 yrs
☐ 14 yrs
☐ 15 yrs
☐ 16 yrs
☐ 17 yrs
☐ 18 yrs
☐ 19 & over

16 **Which group best describes your annual FAMILY income?**

1 ☐ Under £5,000 (Under £96 per week)
2 ☐ £5,000-7,499 (£96-144 p.w.)
3 ☐ £7,500-9,999 (£145-192 p.w.)
4 ☐ £10,000-12,499
5 ☐ £12,500-14,999
6 ☐ £15,000-17,499
7 ☐ £17,500-19,999
8 ☐ £20,000-22,499
9 ☐ £22,500-24,999
10 ☐ £25,000-29,999
11 ☐ £30,000-34,999
12 ☐ £35,000 and above

17 **Which of the following do you use regularly?**

1 ☐ American Express, Diners Club
2 ☐ Barclaycard, other Visa card, Access, other Master Card
3 ☐ Department store, shop, petrol, hotel credit card(s)
4 ☐ Bank cheque guarantee card
5 ☐ Airline club/frequent flyer programme
6 ☐ None of the above

18 **Thinking about your own home, do you:**

1 ☐ Own, or are buying, a house, flat or maisonette?
2 ☐ Rent a private house, flat or maisonette?
3 ☐ Rent a council house, flat or maisonette?
4 ☐ Live with parents/guardians?

19 **How long have you been at your present address?**

1 I only moved here |____| months ago,

OR

2 I've lived here for |____| years.

NOW PLEASE TURN OVER

20

To help us understand your leisure interests, please indicate the activities and interests which <u>you or your spouse</u> enjoy on a REGULAR basis :

01 ☐ Bicycle touring/racing	13 ☐ Crossword puzzles	25 ☐ Slimming	37 ☐ Theatre, cultural/arts events	49 ☐ Stocks and shares
02 ☐ Golf	14 ☐ Eating out	26 ☐ Fashion clothing	38 ☐ Religious activities	50 ☐ Unit trusts/investment progra
03 ☐ Jogging/physical fitness	15 ☐ Gardening	27 ☐ Model making	39 ☐ Caravanning/caravan camping	51 ☐ Cards, board games
04 ☐ Snow skiing	16 ☐ Grandchildren	28 ☐ Photography	40 ☐ Package holidays	52 ☐ Further education
05 ☐ Squash	17 ☐ Household pets	29 ☐ Science fiction	41 ☐ Foreign travel	53 ☐ Home computer games
06 ☐ Tennis	18 ☐ Motoring	30 ☐ Sewing/needlework/knitting	42 ☐ Charities/voluntary work	54 ☐ Personal computing
07 ☐ Bowls	19 ☐ Motorcycles	31 ☐ Stereo, records and tapes	43 ☐ National Trust	55 ☐ Science/new technology
08 ☐ Hiking/walking	20 ☐ Car maintenance	32 ☐ Book reading	44 ☐ Wildlife/environmental concerns 56	☐ Watching video films
09 ☐ Fishing	21 ☐ Do-it-yourself	33 ☐ Current affairs	45 ☐ Coin/stamp collecting	57 ☐ Watching sports on TV
10 ☐ Hunting/shooting	22 ☐ Doing the pools	34 ☐ Fine art/antiques	46 ☐ Collectibles/collections	58 ☐ Cigarette smoking
11 ☐ Motor/power boating	23 ☐ Going to the pub	35 ☐ Gourmet cooking/fine foods	47 ☐ Going to bingo	59 ☐ Pipe/cigar smoking
12 ☐ Sailing	24 ☐ Health foods	36 ☐ Wines	48 ☐ Shopping by catalogue	

21 From the list above, please indicate the numbers representing the three favourite activities for:

22 Do you have a car?

1 ☐ Yes   2 ☐ No

Make of car └┴┴┴┴┴┴┴┴┴┴┴┘
(e.g. Austin Rover, Vauxhall, Ford)

You: └┴┘ └┴┘ └┴┘

Is it:

3 ☐ Yours?   OR
4 ☐ A company car?

Model of car └┴┴┴┴┴┴┴┴┴┘
(e.g. Metro, Cavalier, Escort)

Your spouse: └┴┘ └┴┘ └┴┘

Year │1│9│ │ │ or letter └┘ of registration

Thank you for completing this questionnaire. We promise to take great care of the information you have provided. As mentioned before, Consumerlink offers you the chance to receive information from other respected organisations, about products and services that relate to your answers in part C. If you would prefer NOT to receive these details please tick here ☐ .

If you have any comments or questions about Amstrad, the Amstrad User Clu or the services of Consumerlink please write to :-

Amstrad plc.,
Brentwood House,
169 Kings Road,
Brentwood,
Essex, CM14 4EF.

Consumerlink Ltd.,
36 Broadway,
London,
SW1 OBH.

Figure 4.6 Amstrad market information card.

PART TWO THE MARKETING MIX

The first part of this book concentrated on the 'analysing' activities which the marketer must perform if he is to develop the right kind of strategy. We said that the marketer's objective was to identify a group of potential buyers with an unsatisfied need which could be met by his company. The marketer identifies such needs through marketing research, initially looking broadly at different aspects of his company's operating environment and progressively narrowing his field of analysis until he is studying the needs of individual consumers. By this time he will have segmented his market, dividing customers into groups which display similar needs and he will hope to have identified an unsatisfied (or poorly met) need in a particular market segment which his company can exploit.

Once the marketer turns his attention to meeting such a need he is moving away from analysis and planning and into the realm of 'doing', or implementation. If he is to compete successfully in the market segment he must meet customers' needs more closely than they are being met by any other supplier. Meeting customers' needs involves more than just selling them a suitable product. It involves 'giving them what they want' in the broadest sense of the term. Sir John Egan, Chairman of Jaguar has expressed it in this way:

'Business is about making money from satisfied customers. Without satisfied customers there can be no future for any commercial organisation.'

Customers usually want to satisfy a number of needs when they purchase a product. Very often these needs are fairly clear and relate almost entirrely to the product itself. For example, when people buy table salt, they want it to be dry, fine, white, free flowing and salty. But is that all they want? Surely they also want to buy it in a suitable container which will keep it dry and free flowing, with a hole of the right size in the top etc. In other words they are also interested in the packaging. Is that it? Not really, because as with most buyers of most products, they certainly do not want to pay more than a reasonable price for it. Anything else? Yes, because ideally they do not want to be put to too much inconvenience when they have to buy salt. Having to travel to a specialist salt shop on the edge of town or to send away to the Salt Mail Order Co. Ltd. would not be very convenient. Most people would much prefer to be able to buy salt at no extra inconvenience at the same time and in the same place as they buy their other groceries. In other words, they are interested in the availability and accessibility of the product.

And there can be more. The factors outlined above all covered very practical aspects of purchase which you would expect to concern most buyers of most products but there may also be less practical, more emotional criteria which can also affect the purchase decision. For example, what if one of the salt companies were sponsoring the British athletics team for the Olympic games, with a donation made for every carton top sent in. That could affect the consumer's purchase decision. More basic promotional offers such as an extra product free or money off incentives will also be very attractive to buyers of salt. Customers are also interested therefore in a host of factors which come under the heading of promotion.

In fact our buyer of salt is interested in the four P's:

Product Price Place Promotion.

If this mix of benefits is sought even by people making such a routine purchase as salt, how much more varied must be consumers' purchase criteria for many other products? It is safe to say that for virtually all purchases customers seek a mix of benefits, which we call the marketing mix, or the four P's. The following chapters of this book will examine in turn each element of the marketing mix.

Chapter 5
Products

Introduction

The product itself will almost always justify its position as the first and most important element of the marketing mix. Whereas a well designed, high quality product might sell quite well despite poor distribution or mediocre promotion, it is very unlikely that other elements of the marketing mix will ever make up for the drawbacks of a poorly designed, low quality product. Even an exceedingly low price will not usually overcome the disadvantages of a bad product, certainly not in the long run. In this chapter we will firstly examine exactly what we mean by this word 'product' and will then go on to look at the main areas of product management. The first area concerns overall management of the firm's range of products, because most companies will sell more than one product. Some suppliers of basic industrial products, or mail order companies can have thousands of products in their range. The way these products relate to each other and the priority given to different products can be extremely important. Secondly there is the subject of branding which is becoming increasingly important as companies try to make their products stand out from those of the competition. The takeover battle for Rowntree in 1988 which was eventually won by the Swiss firm Nestlé, made everybody even more conscious of the value of brands. The eventual takeover price valued Rowntree at approximately two billion more than its net asset value (the worth of its land, buildings, plant, machinery and stocks). This two billion of 'goodwill' can be partly ascribed to the value of the company as a going concern (i.e. its relationships with customers, suppliers and the workforce) but the bulk of this huge sum represented the value placed by Nestlé on Rowntree's brands, such as Kit Kat, Smarties, Yorkie and After Eight. Before looking at brands however, we must explore the nature of a 'product'.

5.1 What is a product?

A firm's product is whatever it sells. As far as marketers are concerned products do not have to be physical goods. A window cleaning service is a product just as much as a bucket, a ladder or a wash leather are products. Remember that people buy holes, not drills. They buy the service that products perform for them, so really, it helps to see all products as services rather than as physical goods.

Philip Kotler has developed an all embracing definition of a product. According to him a product is:

> '*Anything that can be offered to a market for attention, acquisition or consumption that might satisfy a want or a need. It includes physical objects, services, persons, places, organisations and ideas.*'

Of course, there must be much more to a product than the glib statement 'whatever we sell'. According to Theodore Levitt we should view the product at four levels:

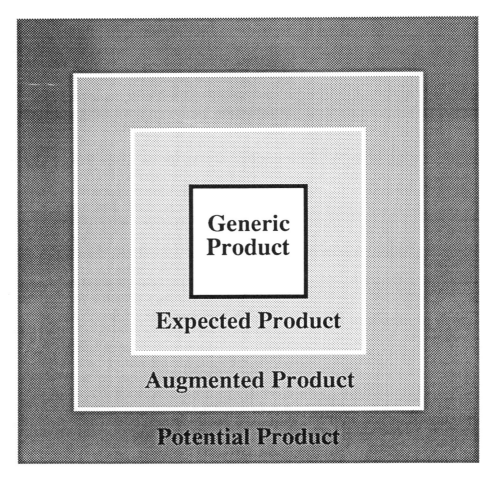

(Theodore Levitt, 1980)

Figure 5.1 The total product concept.

5.1.1 The generic product

The word 'generic' means type, so the generic product is quite simply the basic product type. At one time virtually all groceries were bought as generic products. Flour, tea, butter, would be weighed out by the grocer and placed in a plain wrapping. Although packaged, branded goods have taken over in the twentieth century, generic grocery products have made a certain comeback in recent years, with some supermarkets having bins containing generic products which can be scooped out, weighed and placed in a plain polythene bag by customers. Many health stores also sell generic products.

Kotler refers to this first product level as the core product or core benefit. What is the basic thing that people are buying? If it's drills, they are buying the ability to make holes, if it's a portable radio/cassette they are buying the ability to receive radio transmissions and listen to music.

5.1.2 The expected product

However, when people buy a radio / cassette, they don't just want any old box which will pick up broadcasts and produce a sound vaguely reminiscent of music. They expect additional things from a radio / cassette player. They expect a certain quality of sound, they expect stereo, they expect an FM wave band, they expect the controls to look sophisticated, they expect the choice of battery or mains operation and they seem to expect it to be very, very loud! These additional requirements for the expected product become the industry norm. Features that were once extras become standard, and radio/cassettes simply have to have them if they are to stand a chance of competing in that market. Any companies which fall behind on these expected features will certainly lose sales. Austin Rover for example has been very slow with the introduction of diesel engines, which has cost them sales at the heavy user, business end of the market. As time goes on, markets become more competitive and technology improves and consumers' expectations become ever higher. More and more standard features are constantly being added to the radio/cassette, the family car and virtually all other consumer durables.

5.1.3 The augmented product

In order to gain an advantage over the competition, suppliers are always trying to offer something over and above the expected product, since it may be that little something extra which clinches the sale over a rival product. The product can be augmented in major ways, by adding a second cassette to facilitate tape copying, for example. More usually however, the product is not augmented in such a tangible way. As shown in Figure 5.2, additional benefits become less tangible as one moves out from the core product. Any of the benefits mentioned in the diagram could be offered to augment the expected product. Design features and colour have recently been used to differentiate radio/cassettes. Instant credit is often available to would-be purchasers, likewise guarantees. Some electrical goods are offered with five year guarantees to offer an extra benefit over the competition. As far as suppliers are concerned, the augmented product has one problem. Today's augmented product becomes tomorrow's expected product. The dual cassette deck, initially a much sought after extra, has become a standard feature on most models within a few years. To overcome this problem, and to keep ahead of the competition, the marketer has to move to the potential product.

Figure 5. 2 The Concept of the Augmented Product

5.1.4 The potential product

According to Levitt the potential product includes 'everything that might be done to attract and hold customers'. Even for the most basic and mature of products, alert marketers can discover new ways of making their product more attractive to buyers. a good example is steel, a very mature product which one would expect to be very difficult to distinguish from its competitors. Not at all. In the 1980's suppliers of steel have used the concept of the potential product to offer new and valuable benefits to buyers. For example, Swedish steel maker Avesta AB has developed an 'improved machinability steel' which is actually easier to drill than normal stainless steel, so it causes less wear and tear to very expensive tools-a significant benefit to buyers. BSC Stainless in Sheffield now offer stainless steel sheet with a range of patterned finishes, which is opening up new uses for the material, such as exterior cladding for buildings. New benefits can be intangible too. Austin Trumann Steel in Manchester discovered that one of the most important priorities of steel buyers was totally reliable deliveries, so Austin Trumann now offer guaranteed deliveries with a self imposed financial penalty clause if they ever fail to meet their delivery schedules. These three suppliers of steel have one thing in common. They have added real value to their product in the eyes of suppliers. It is the role of marketing management to identify the best ways to add value, and, according to Levitt, the most successful companies in many markets are the ones whose marketing departments are most thorough in their identification of the potential product. If you sell soap, beer, banking services or fast food or any competitive product you have to be constantly looking towards the potential product. The results in the banking sector have been staggering over the last few years with the return of Saturday opening, goody bags for new student accounts, the spread of automatic cash dispensers, and the development of new types of bank account (such as the Midland Bank's Vector Account).

Successful companies will therefore manage their products very carefully. They will appreciate that customers buy holes rather than drills, and that some additional benefits must be provided to attract customers in competitive markets. Far sighted companies will therefore put much effort into research and development because the potential product is the one which will be a winner in tomorrow's markets.

5.2 A range of products

As we have seen in the preceding section products are continuously evolving to meet ever changing market needs. The potential product becomes the augmented product which in turn becomes the expected product. Companies dependent on one or a very restricted range of products are therefore always in a vulnerable position in today's rapidly changing environment.

5.2.1 Product life cycles

According to most marketing academics, it is due to these rapidly changing environments that all products are said to go through a 'life cycle'. All products have a beginning followed by a rapid or steady growth in sales, which eventually reach their peak. They may maintain this level of sales for some time, but sooner or later they will be adversely affected by changes in the environment, the market or technology and they will begin to decline, to be replaced by products more suited to the times.

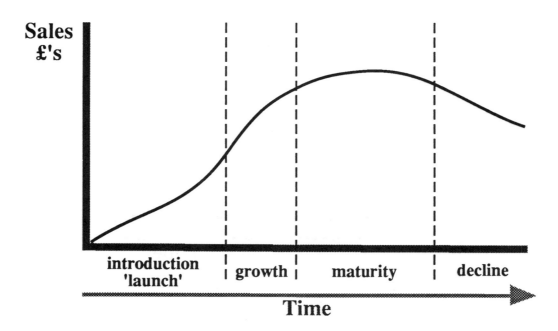

Figure 5.3 The product life cycle curve.

Although it is widely accepted that all products do follow a life cycle, the exact pattern and duration of the life cycle will differ for every product. The generic product bread is at the mature stage of an extremely long life cycle, but if we look at specific bread products we can see that the branded white sliced loaf which underwent rapid growth after the Second World War and was at its mature stage in the 1960's and most of the 1970's has now been in decline for several years. It has suffered from the move away from highly processed food towards more healthy, traditional, high fibre diets. Many of these high fibre, unsliced, bread products are currently at the growth stage of their life cycle.

Thus the time horizon, represented by the horizontal axis on the graph is of indeterminate length, as are the sales figures represented by the vertical axis. The shape of the curve will also vary. Some products may have a longer, flatter curve if their peak in sales follows very gradual growth over a long period of time. Other products typically exhibit much more rapid growth, and some an equally rapid decline. Examples of such product life cycle curves are shown in the two graphs below. Figure 5.4 shows a typical 'fashion' product life cycle. Most items of clothing now come into this category with two buying seasons per annum. Sales rise quickly each autumn for the winter fashions, followed by a short mature stage and an equally quick decline. By the end of the January sales very little additional business is done with the winter fashions which is why the summer clothes can appear in the shops whilst there is still snow on the ground. Although their life lasts longer (about five years on average) most individual car models show a similar life cycle pattern, with a strong rise in sales for their first year, a two to three year mature period and declining sales for their last year to eighteen months as buyers become rather tired of the model. In 1988 the Vauxhall Cavalier suffered seriously from this problem, partly because it began to look like an old model, and partly because buyers knew it was going to be replaced at the end of the year. Having dominated the medium car market for four years it saw its sales figures dramatically overtaken by the Ford Sierra.

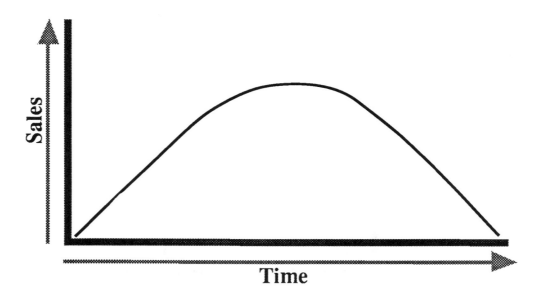

Figure 5.4 A 'fashion' product life cycle.

Fashion products may give their manufacturers the problem of having to produce a continuous stream of new designs, but the problem is predictable, it is in the nature of their business, so they have to plan accordingly. Life cycles of some products however are much less predictable. We call them 'fads'. Their sales can escalate dramatically, there can be shortages of the product as everyone clamours to buy, but for some reason the trend can subside as quickly as it grew, often leaving manufacturers and retailers with excessively high stocks. Skateboards are the most well known example of the 1980's. An even better example from thirty years ago was the 'hoola-hoop', a fad which unlike skateboards gripped everyone. Every household had to have its hoola hoop, and I'm sure some still survive in attics and garages, but the sales explosion lasted for only one summer. Sales of the records of many pop stars can also be seen as a 'fad' life cycle, their rise and fall in fortunes being almost as unpredictable as the skateboard and hoola hoop. The figure below shows a typical 'fad' life cycle with its steeply rising growth curve, the short or non-existent mature phase followed by an equally sudden decline.

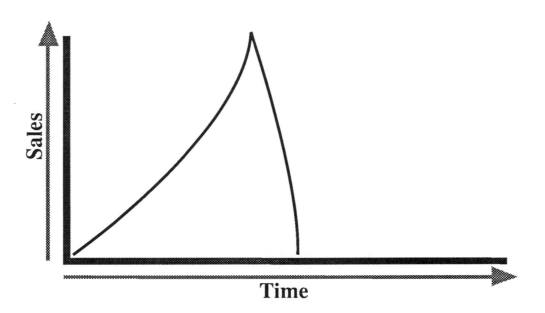

Figure 5.5 A 'fad' product life cycle.

5.2.2 Managing the product life cycle

In the simplest terms the marketer will have two objectives in the management of the product life cycle. He will want both axes to extend as far as possible. To be more specific, at the growth stage he will want sales to continue growing to their highest possible level, and at the mature stage he will want to continue at this plateau level for as long as possible before decline sets in. Let's examine the marketer's tactics at each stage of the life cycle.

(a) Introduction

This stage begins when the product is launched onto the market. It may already have undergone a long development stage (see Chapter 7), maybe including 'test marketing', but the product life cycle begins only when the product is fully launched on to the market. At first sales growth can be very slow, mainly because most people are hesitant about trying new ideas and new products. They prefer to watch other people try them first. In 1962 Everett Rogers produced his famous 'adoption of innovations' model which describes how people react to innovations.

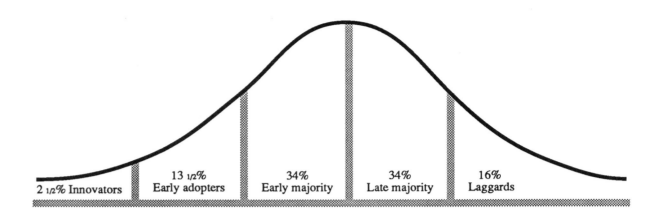

Figure 5.6 Everett Rogers' Innovation Adoption Model.

As can be seen from the diagram, Rogers states that genuine innovators who are prepared to take risks and like having new products simply because they are new are a very small proportion of the population, only 2.5%. Manufacturers therefore have to work very hard to push the sales of most new products beyond this group during the introductory stage of the product life cycle.

Moreover the manufacturer will almost certainly be losing money at this stage. His development costs may have been considerable, and the marketing costs at this introductory stage will also be very high. Advertising, direct mail, exhibitions and sales promotions are all communications techniques which may need to be used at this stage to generate awareness of the new product and to give consumers an incentive to try it. Distributors may have to be offered financial incentives to stock the product or to give it favourable shelf space and special display material may have to be produced for them. With low production volumes, costs will also be high, so it is most unlikely that the product will manage to reach break even point (see Chapter 8). Some genuinely innovative new products can be profitable at this stage because they are able to charge a very high price. They can afford to go for the top end of the market where the small group of 'innovators' will be prepared to pay handsomely for the status value of such a conspicuous purchase. The first CD players and the discs themselves would be good examples.

(b) Growth

The growth stage is the 'take-off' phase when the 'early adopters' begin to purchase the product. They are typically fashionable, successful and keen to be associated with new ideas and products as soon as it is clear that they are socially acceptable. They will be joined later in the growth stage by the 'early majority' who do want to be fashionable but are followers rather than leaders.

Sales will now be climbing rapidly. This will attract attention in the business world and new competitors will be attracted to the market. Their products may even have new features or be offered at a lower price. The Japanese company Brother is the world leader in portable electronic typewriters. When they launched the first electronic typewriter they had an eighteen month opportunity to exploit the market and build their position before they faced highly aggressive competition. As the market has matured this period has shortened. Now, when they introduce a new model they expect to have a 'window of opportunity' of only four weeks before a competitor comes out with a product which does the same things at a lower price or offers more benefits at the same price.

At the growth stage, whether it is four weeks or four years, prices are likely to remain quite high, although as competition begins to intensify, the first pressures on prices will be seen. Thus we can see price competition affecting growth products such as fax machines, car telephones, and to a lesser extent so far, compact discs. Manufacturers will continue to push hard with promotional activities at this stage, especially advertising designed to increase interest and build brand loyalty. Although marketing costs are still high they are now a much smaller proportion of the growing sales which helps to move the product into profitability.

(c) Maturity

Sales growth for all products slows down sooner or later as market penetration approaches its maximum. Products such as video recorders or microwave ovens have now reached their mature stage.

During the mature stage most remaining potential consumers will become customers. The 'late majority' tend to be sceptical and old fashioned but will change when the evidence is overwhelming. Such people would now buy an automatic washing machine but are most unlikely to have been converted to the concept of dish washers at the present time.

The maturity stage should last considerably longer than the introduction and growth stages, but competition will now be intense and this will be reflected in falling prices or frequent sales promotions seeking to add value in customers' eyes. Advertising and perhaps public relations activities such as sponsorship will continue but will be more defensive, concentrating on image and the encouragement of loyal customers. By now however, marketers may have to consider more tangible ways of supporting the stagnating sales of their brand. Their objective will be to prolong the mature stage and stave off the decline stage for as long as possible. Product modifications may therefore be made in the hope of giving the brand a new lease of life, as shown below.

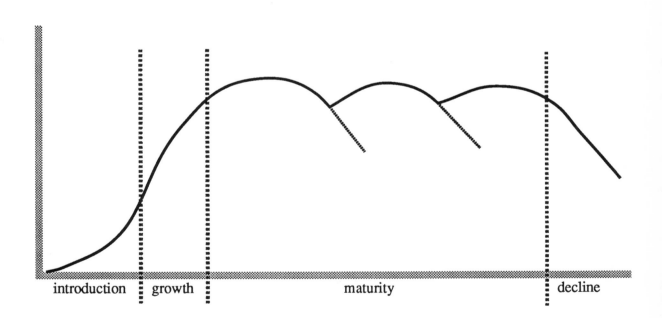

introduction   growth   maturity   decline

Figure 5.7 Extending the product life cycle.

This is a tactic particularly favoured by car manufacturers. During the early part of the mature stage product modifications can be purely cosmetic. Often called 'concept cars', a special model will be introduced with a number of extra features such as superior upholstery, sun roof, and perhaps an improved stereo as standard. Often they will have a special exterior appearance to increase their distinctiveness. In recent years we have seen Ford Escort, Sierra and Capri 'Lasers', all white

Vauxhall Nova, Astra and Cavalier 'Clubs', Mini 'Mayfairs' and 'Park Lanes' and many more concept cars. As the mature stage proceeds, such modifications may need to become more fundamental. a completely updated model may need to be introduced, probably retaining most of the mechanical parts of its predecessor but with a new external appearance. Ford have been masters of extending the product life cycle in this way, giving models a timely face lift before their sales began to decline. We saw five versions of the Ford Cortina, three Capris and we are currently on the Mark IV version of the Escort. Extending the product life cycle in this way can be much cheaper and less risky than launching a completely new product. Ford discovered this to its cost when it replaced the very successful Cortina with the Sierra. It was very unpopular at first, largely because of its different exterior appearance. Loyal Cortina buyers deserted in droves, mainly to the Cavalier, a more conventional looking car which had the option of a boot, and it was five years before the Sierra regained market leadership of a segment which the Cortina had dominated for a decade.

(d) Decline

All products eventually enter a stage of declining sales, perhaps because they have become obsolete due to changes in technology or fashion or simply because the competition has a rival product which offers much better value. Declining sales result in over capacity and a consequent temptation to cut prices simply to keep production lines going and employees in jobs. The remaining Ford Capris in the car showrooms in 1987 could be bought for very low prices. Small black and white televisions cost no more now than they did fifteen years ago, which means that in real terms they cost considerably less.

This fierce price competition hits profits with the result that manufacturers' first reaction is to make marketing economies elsewhere. Product modifications and development come to an end, advertising is cut or curtailed. Despite such economies the declining products may still be unprofitable as sales and prices continue to fall. As a result many suppliers will withdraw from the market. Some products simply disappear. Slide rules, for example, have been replaced by calculators. Some declining products can however offer good opportunities for companies which remain in the market, as there may be a long term demand, albeit at a lower level, from the 'laggards', who resist change and almost regard it as a matter of pride to be owners of untrendy products. New Morris Minors, Volkswagen Beetles and Citroen 2CV's are still manufactured under licence in various overseas countries and exported to Western Europe where each still has its very small but dedicated following.

5.2.3 Fifty years old and still growing

Fifty years ago in 1938 Swiss firm Nestlé invented instant coffee. The first tin of Nescafé was sold in Britain in 1939. Helped by wartime rationing of tea, instant coffee became firmly established as an alternative drink but it was still very much a minority taste, and even according to research, suffered from the fact that, like many other convenience foods at this time, it was associated with laziness.

This introductory period lasted at least fifteen years, with real growth not beginning until the 1950's. Whether it was the coffee bar boom, associating coffee with rock and roll and trendiness, reinforced by American films and TV programmes, or whether it was the fact that the product improved (Nescafé was made from 100% pure coffee for the first time), nobody really knows, but sales began to show much stronger growth. Maxwell House (produced by the American firm General Foods) appeared as the first significant competitor and Nestlé segmented the market for the first time with its introduction of the stronger Blend 37.

The 1960's saw further developments. Tins were gradually replaced by jars, a production process was developed which retained the coffee aroma - often seen as the product's best selling point, and the first freeze dried coffee granules were produced. Gold Blend, launched in 1965 was the first freeze dried product, and helped to open up a more up-market segment. By the end of the decade the total instant coffee market was worth fifty million a year.

By the 1970's, though still growing the market was beginning to show the signs of maturity. The supermarkets' own label products were now selling well and undercutting the main brands on price. Nestlé introduced Fine Blend, a mild coffee and Nescoré, a French style blend of coffee and chicory. Also, Nescafé was relaunched in granular form in its present packaging of a clear glass jar with brown top and the red Nescafé cup on the label.

A setback occurred in 1975 when a late frost destroyed most of the Brazilian crop resulting in a tenfold increase in the price of raw coffee. The knock-on effect saw a 4oz. jar of Nescafé rise from 39p. to £1.49, leading to a 15% slump in the market which did not recover until 1980.

By the mid 1980's the product is undeniably in its mature stage, even though the market has grown by 13% in volume terms during the decade, reaching sales worth 550 million in 1986. During that period Nescafé has increased its market share from 24% to 37% and with Gold Blend and Blend 37 enjoying around 7% between them, Nestlé has over half of the market. As a mature product Nescafé's success is based on two main platforms. Firstly it puts considerable effort into maintaining the highest possible quality standards and secondly it advertises continuously (Nescafé ads appear every single week of the year on TV, radio and in the press) and extensively to reinforce this image of high quality. The annual advertising budget for Nescafé alone exceeds 10 million pounds, making it the most advertised brand in the U.K. Gold Blend receives over 6 million pounds, and Nestlé's total instant coffee budget exceeds 20 million pounds which is as much as the total spent on advertising by all the other brands put together. The beans always figure prominently in the Nescafé ads to deliver the high quality, 100% pure coffee message, and to take advantage of consumers' attraction to the aroma of fresh coffee.

The continuing growth in the coffee market is now largely at the expense of tea. In the mid 1960's six times as much tea as coffee was drunk, but now the ratio is down to two to one. To narrow the gap further, Nestlé is concentrating on specific market segments. Firstly there is the breakfast time problem. The average Briton, it seems, still prefers to wake up to a cup of tea. Despite advertising aimed at breakfast time coffee drinking and sales promotions offering premiums such as the red Nescafé mug and matching egg cup it would appear that little headway has been made so far in changing the nation's habits. Perhaps the early morning cup of tea is a 'core cultural value'!

A second target segment is the youth market, which led to Nescafé's sponsorship of the first Network Chartshow on commercial radio. Special promotions linked to the chart show were run in the youth and pop music press and David Jensen took a Nescafé Chartshow tour to clubs and discos around the country. Nescafé Frappé (iced coffee) is another attempt to give the brand some style in the youth market, following also the trend from hot to cold drinks among young people.

The life cycle of instant coffee demonstrates very clearly how protracted the introductory stage of a product's life cycle can be. However, once the product has become accepted, growth can be swift. As growth slowed and the product began to reach maturity, competition became more intense, leading to the introduction of new types of instant coffee. Of course, brands such as Gold Blend and Nescafé Frappé will have their own life cycles which will almost certainly be shorter than the life cycle of the generic product. As the market matures further in the 1990's it will be interesting to see what changes of emphasis and perhaps relaunches are in store for Nescafé.

5.2.4 A basket of products

Perhaps the most valuable message of the product life cycle is to remind management that products, however successful they are today, do not go on for ever. The company must replace products which are reaching their decline stage with new products which can take their place. The risk of having 'all your eggs in one basket' is a generally accepted principle in all walks of life. People and businesses avoid this risk by giving themselves more than one option, companies usually having a range of products with the more successful ones making up for any losses incurred through under performing products.

Management writer Peter Drucker has linked this philosophy with the product life cycle concept and has suggested that the firm needs a range of products each at a different stage of its life cycle so that a succession of profitable products should always be on stream. Shown in Figure 5.8 below, Drucker labels this stream of products as today's breadwinners, tomorrow's breadwinners and yesterday's breadwinners. The profits from today's breadwinners must be used to finance the development of tomorrow's breadwinners which will be able to replace yesterday's breadwinners.

Analyse your Product Range in terms of:

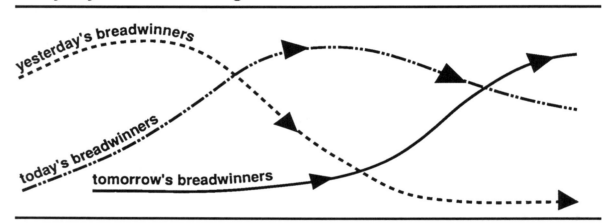

Figure 5. 8 Peter Drucker's Breadwinners.

The main problem with the product life cycle concept, and Drucker's breadwinners, is that it is very difficult in practice to know when your product has reached a certain stage. With the objective of helping marketers to tackle this practical problem, the Boston Consulting Group in the US developed an approach known as product portfolio analysis. The BCG theory works on the same principles as Drucker, but uses the analogy of stocks and shares. Serious investors on the stock market will try to cover their risk by investing in a portfolio of shares, so that they are cushioned from the full effects of unexpected sharp falls in an individual share price. Extending the same approach to products, a company is recommended to have a portfolio of products, the more successful ones financing the weaker ones.

BCG portfolio analysis, shown in Figure 5.9, does link in strongly with the product life cycle. Proceeding round the diagram in an anti-clockwise direction, equivalent to the introduction stage are problem children, aptly named since many new product launches fail to get beyond this stage (see Chapter 7). Products which successfully reach the growth stage are stars, and become cash cows at the mature stage. Products in decline are known as dogs.

So far no different, but the advance comes in the way the marketer places his products into these categories by using the two variables of market growth and market share. Products in the top half of the box are in the early stages of the product life cycle. They are in growth markets, like the coffee market up to 1975. Other things being equal this means they are products with a future, tomorrow's breadwinners, and should be invested in. However, although all these products consume the company's cash, they are not all equal. Those on the left hand side of the box enjoy a high market share. If not market leaders they will not be far behind the market leaders. Nescafé was a star, as was Blend 37 in the 1960's and Gold Blend in the 1970's. Such products, though they may be unprofitable in the short term due to high development and promotional costs should receive continued financial support as breadwinners of the future. Not so problem children. Their sales have never really taken off and they have a very poor market share. Sometimes called 'question marks', the firm must really scrutinise their performance and ask if they are ever likely to be a real commercial success. If not, it may be better to withdraw them straight away rather than waste funds on the marketing of losers, since those funds could be more profitably allocated to supporting stars or the development of new products. Nescoré was never very successful in this country and is no longer found in supermarkets in the U.K.

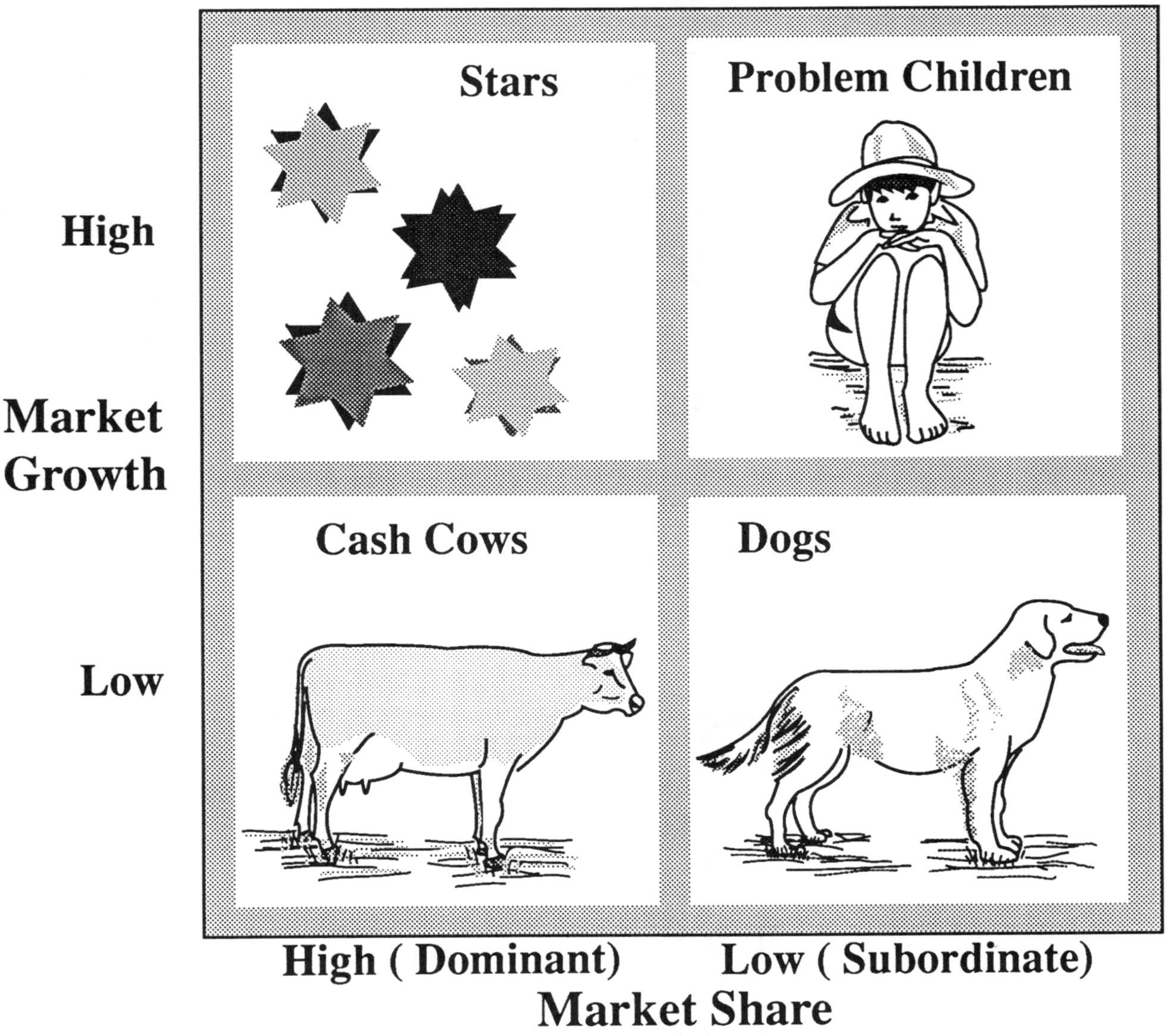

Figure 5.9 The BCG Portfolio Approach.

Products in the lower half of the box are in the later stages of their life cycle. They are in mature markets whose growth has slowed or even stopped. This is not necessarily a bad thing, because a cash cow, a mature product with a high share of its market segment, is usually a very profitable product. Nescafé is an excellent example. Although it advertises heavily, expenditure of 10 million per annum is relatively small when compared with annual sales of 280 million. Its development costs have long since been recovered, and high production volume leads to economies of scale which keep down costs. Allied to the fact that Nescafé is not a cheap product (it costs twice as much as the average own label coffee and more than its main branded competitors) it can be seen that it must be a very profitable one. It is said that cash cows should be 'milked' to provide the funds to support stars, problem children which do appear to have good future prospects and the development of new products. This suggested internal flow of funds is shown in Figure 5.10.

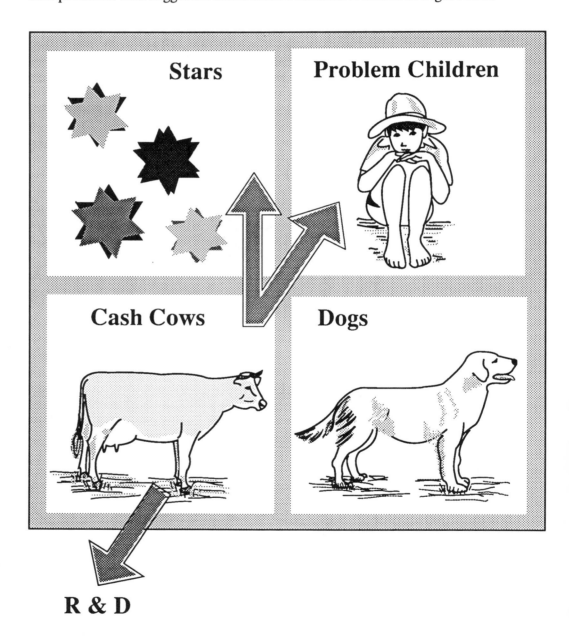

Figure 5.10 BCG Analysis - internal flow of funds.

Dogs have the twin characteristics of low share and low growth. They tend to have low profits, even losses, and poor future prospects. If the dog is relatively close to the market leader and can maintain a positive cash flow in a stable market then it may be a 'cash dog'. By minimising marketing costs such as promotion and product development, cash dogs can sometimes be milked like a cash cow. If, on the other hand the product is a genuine dog, with no prospects for an extension of its life cycle or for its introduction to another segment (e.g. an export market), then liquidation, either immediate or gradual will be the only strategy.

Another American firm of consultants, Marketing Intercontinental suggested the rural analogy 'sow/grow/harvest/plough' to describe the policies that should be applied to the products in the problem children, star, cash cow and dog categories respectively. Application of the BCG or the Marketing Intercontinental approach to product portfolio management should lead to the ideal product development sequence shown in the diagram below.

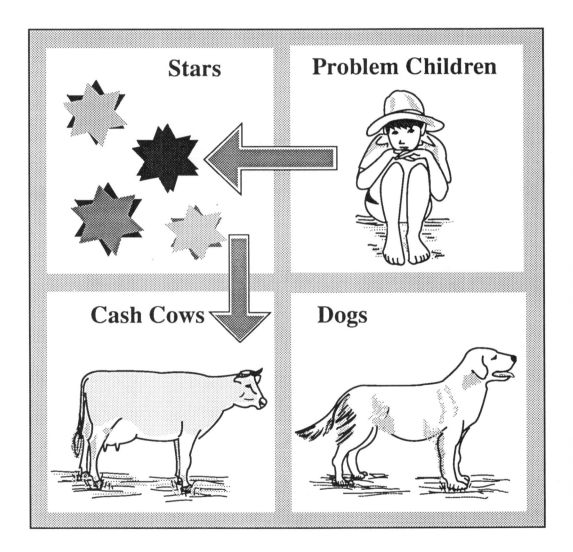

Figure 5.11 The ideal product development sequence.

The BCG approach also provides a very useful framework to help companies forecast the likely outcome of their current marketing policies. The firm's products can be plotted on the BCG framework (often with the aid of a computer these days) so that managers can see at a glance how well each product is performing. The result that might appear is shown in Figure 5.12. The circles represent each of the company's four main products. The size of each circle is used to show the level of sales, so we can see that product C is the firm's best selling product. The shaded circles show the anticipated future performance of the products at a given time in the future, usually twelve months ahead. According to the projections two products are expected to perform in a satisfactory manner. Product C should strengthen its position with sales expected to increase as a result of an increase in market share. This should be a very profitable product. Product A is also showing satisfactory growth, though this appears to be coming entirely from the growth in the market since its own market share is expected to decline slightly, a worrying trend which would need to be carefully watched and corrected. However, on balance, product A seems to be heading in the right direction. The same cannot be said for product D. Although its sales are not expected to fall, they are going to remain static in a buoyant growth market. This represents a very poor performance with market share being lost to competitors who are obviously exploiting the growth market much more successfully. Unless this decline in market share can be arrested it is difficult to see how product D can have a promising future. Product B has no future at all. A genuine dog with sales and market share falling, early withdrawal is likely to be the only sensible strategy for this product.

According to this picture the company's sales are set to rise in the next twelve months. However, looking further ahead prospects may not be quite as good. With the certain demise of product B and the possible decline of product D the company seems to have an urgent need for at least one new product. An early decision will probably need to be made on the futures of both these products so that resources from product C can be channelled into new product development if necessary.

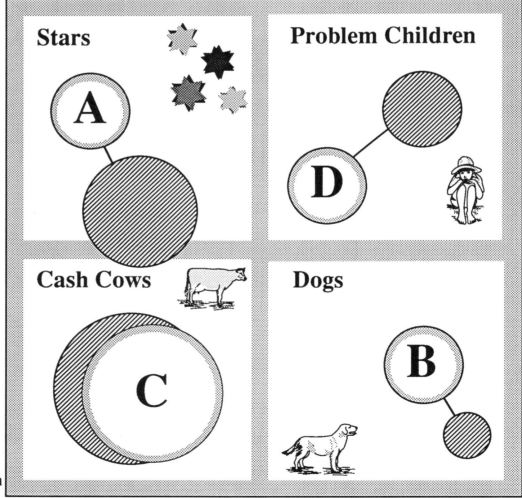

Figure 5. 12 Using BCG analysis to forecast future market position.

5.2.5 The product mix

As we have seen in the previous section it is a good idea for most companies to offer a range of products, each at different stages of their life cycles if future profitability is to be ensured. The total set of products a company sells is called its 'product mix', which may include a number of 'product lines' and a large number of products.

(a) The product line

A product line consists of a group of products that are closely related because they are intended for the same end use (e.g. running shoes), are sold to the same customer group (e.g. Next Accessories, aimed at the 25 - 45 year old woman) or fall within a certain price range (e.g. budget records and cassettes).

(b) Breadth of the product mix

Breadth refers to the number of different product lines in the product mix. The product mix of large firms is tending to become broader, largely as a result of amalgamations. When Cadbury merged with Schweppes the confectionery and hot drinks product lines of the former were added to the soft drinks product lines of the latter, thus increasing the breadth of the product mix. Although this trend towards broader product mixes is also apparent in the larger retailers it is still considered that a company's product mix should be as consistent as possible, in other words, that the product lines should be complementary rather than unrelated.

(c) Depth of the product mix

Depth refers to the number of items within each product line. Some large companies try to crowd smaller companies out of the market by increasing the depth of their product lines. The two detergent giants, Unilever and Proctor and Gamble both have very deep washing powder lines to the extent that they are prepared to risk some of their brands competing with each other. However, the strategy seems to be effective because even the supermarkets' own label products find the market difficult to penetrate.

(d) Evaluation of the product mix

It is the responsibility of top management to review whether the current product mix is suitable for achieving the firm's sales and profits objectives (see Chapter 14 for organisational aspects of marketing). There will be two main aspects of such an evaluation. Firstly the firm's whole product mix will be evaluated in order to allocate marketing budgets according to the needs of various products. This decision is likely to be made as a result of BCG analysis. Whether a product is at the sow, grow, harvest or plough stage will determine the level of marketing resources it is allocated. The second fundamental decision concerns the timing of additions or deletions to the product range. Dogs or problem children may need to be deleted, or there may be an urgent need to introduce new products. Most companies devote resources to new product development programmes (see Chapter 7), but many large companies also see acquisition as a more direct route to broadening or strengthening their product mix, hence Nestlé's 2.5 billion purchase of Rowntrees.

5.3 Branding

As we said in the introduction to this chapter, it was the Rowntree brands which attracted the Nestlé top management and for which they were prepared to pay an extraordinary premium. But what exactly do we mean by a brand? According to Margaret Crimp:

'A brand is a product or service which has been given an identity; it has a brand name and the added value of a brand image.'

We might mention other distinctive aspects of a branded product. It is likely to have recognisable packaging, like the Nescafé jar, it might have a logo or a trademark. Its brand image will enable people to recall identifiable aspects or benefits of the product. These may be directly related to the product such as the quality of the coffee, the strength of the toilet paper, or they may be less tangible such as the Dulux dog or the Andrex puppy. Many people go further than Crimp and say that a brand is a product with a personality, which consumers can see almost as a friend rather than just a purchase. You can see this idea coming through in the advertising of many consumer products, such as 'mild green Fairy Liquid - kind on your hands'.

However, there is more to the concept of branding than giving a personality to a product. In fact, there are four main advantages of branding from the marketer's point of view, and in this section we will examine each in turn.

5.3.1 Differentiation

Differentiation quite simply means making things different, and it will always be one of the main objectives of the marketer to differentiate his product from its competitors. Occasionally you get a new product which is so innovative that it differentiates itself from other similar products. The first Polaroid camera did not need a creative genius to distinguish it from conventional cameras. With some products differentiation is not quite so obvious but is not too difficult for marketers to achieve. Cars, for example look distinctive and have their own unique performance characteristics which can be stressed by the marketer, although as time goes on, cars are becoming more similar.

Some products, however, are known as 'undifferentiated products'. The definition of an undifferentiated product would be: standard products produced to a commonly accepted specification, usually the subject of a routine purchase decision, ordered in response to basic and essential needs.

Examples are soft margarine, sugar, petrol, floppy disks, paper clips, screws, steel and polythene bags and many, many more basic products in consumer and industrial markets. Such products are essentially indistinguishable from other products in their class and one wonders whether there is any role for marketing to play or whether the markets for these undifferentiated products come close to the economists' model of 'pure competition', where prices are governed solely by the laws of supply and demand.

In fact, certain world commodity markets do seem to resemble this model, as seen in the huge price fluctuations in the crude oil, tin, sugar and coffee markets for example. However, there is a fundamental difference between the four commodity markets above and any of the undifferentiated products listed in the previous paragraph. All those products have been through a manufacturing process. Value has been added to them, and whenever value is added it gives the marketer an opportunity to differentiate that product from its competitors. As we said at the beginning of this chapter, the customer is not just buying the generic product, but a package of benefits, a total product. Steel itself may be an undifferentiated product, but as we saw at the beginning of this chapter, individual suppliers can add value to that core product in the eyes of customers. Branding will be one of the key weapons which gives an identity to an undifferentiated product. There are a number of ways in which this might be done.

(a) Brand name

There can be a lot in a brand name. Beanz meanz Heinz to a lot of people. The main reason why a lot of products are perceived as undifferentiated, especially in industrial markets is that their manufacturers don't even try to differentiate them. They do not even take the first step of giving them a name. There can be a lot of promotional mileage in a name, especially if it is distinctive. The Guinness - 'pure genius' advertising is one good example. Look at this list of the top ten selling sugar confectionery counter lines in the U.K.

1. Rowntree's Fruit Pastilles.
2. Opal Fruits.
3. Polo.
4. Trebor Extra Strong Mints.
5. Tunes.
6. Chewits.
7. Wrigley's Spearmint.
8. Basset's Liquorice Allsorts.
9. Locketts.
10. Cadbury's Chocolate Eclairs.

Sweet eaters or not, we all recognise those names. Ideally a name should be short and it should mean something. Both of those things help it to be recognised and remembered. One of the best examples of a recently named product is the Compaq computer. The name is short, and it describes the product itself, a compact portable computer. It is generally agreed that this wise choice of name helped Compaq to establish itself in the fiercely competitive American micro computer market in the 1980's. Surely the most effective name on the list above is Polo, beautifully short, and so complementary to its other distinctive quality - 'Polo, the mint with the hole'.

(b) Trademarks

A trademark can be any word, symbol, picture or device which is associated with a particular product or service brand. Although the brand name is what most people would ask for in a shop the trademark will probably help them to recognise the product they are looking for (e.g. in a self service situation). As well as helping brand identity and recognition, trademarks are also playing an increasingly useful role in the battle against counterfeit products. (See 5.3.4).

(c) Colour

Colour can be used to differentiate almost any product. We mentioned at the beginning of this chapter that radio / cassette players are available in some dazzling colours. Some offices will pay more for coloured paper clips because of the value they place on presentation. The best ever example of the use of colour to differentiate a totally uninteresting product was Pink Paraffin. Adding nothing to the quality or performance of the product it did give it an identity, a recognisable name and the basis of a personality which set it apart from its competitors.

(d) Other recognisable features

As we have seen in some of the examples above it is often better if a name can be linked with some other feature to produce a stronger identity. So for the paraffin, Pink became the name and the colour. The hole in the Polo, the Andrex puppy and the Dulux dog are all universally recognisable, and can all be used by creative marketers to give their brands a likeable personality rather than a simple identity.

(e) U.S.P

A U.S.P. is an advantage much sought after by all marketers. Short for 'unique selling proposition' it is the ultimate differentiating factor. It makes a product unique. Even the most uninteresting of products in consumer and industrial markets can develop a U.S.P. Of course, the more technical the product the easier it is to establish a U.S.P. which is inherent to the product, such as the first Polaroid camera, but any product can develop an intangible U.S.P. such as a mint with a hole, pink coloured paraffin or toilet paper which is associated with a soft cuddly puppy. In such markets being different and recognisable is essential, as we will see in the next example.

(f) Can petrol be differentiated?

In these days of consumerism (see Chapter 16) most people are rather cynical about the kind of differentiating claims that used to be common. People just don't believe that a certain brand of washing powder washes whiter than all the others. People know that there are some parts that even the most famous of lager brands cannot reach. However, despite the logic of all this, clear preferences continue to be shown in the market place for certain brands, even though they may be competing against many other brands which are essentially similar in price, performance and appearance.

Since the introduction of the star grading system, petrol has been a typical example of an undifferentiated product. One brand of four star petrol is generally perceived as the same as another four star brand. (In 1988, in fact it came to light that it literally is the same product. Pressed by a House of Commons Select Committee, several major petrol companies admitted that in order to reduce distribution costs they were actually selling each others' petrol under their own trademark!) Nevertheless, measurable preferences for certain brands exist. Shell's market leadership is not based solely on having more filling stations in superior locations. Research carried out in the 1970's at motorway service stations at a time when consumers had a free choice of all the leading brands of petrol at the same price and with no sales promotions showed motorists having the same clear preferences for the leading brands. Shell was chosen most often, followed by BP and Esso with the rest some way behind. As this story shows, a basic undifferentiated product can develop a brand image which prompts consumers to distinguish it from its rivals and choose it in preference to its rivals. If like Shell, companies are prepared to spend time and money over a long period telling their markets why their brand is special, it will eventually become differentiated from its competitors in the eyes of customers.

5.3.2 Added value

We said in 5.3.1 that the first reason to brand a product is to distinguish it from competitors. This is true, because if products really are seen as totally undifferentiated commodities then they will almost certainly be sold mainly on price, thus making the marketer redundant. So differentiation is important, but it is not everything. It is no use being perceived as different from the competition if this distinction is negative or adverse. It is no good being known for the least reliable cars or the most rusty cars. The marketer must therefore aim to be different from and better than the competition. So branding must differentiate the product in a favourable way. It must add value.

There are two main ways in which marketers seek to add value through branding. The first is to associate the brand with high quality and the second is to associate the brand with excellent customer service. The benefits of quality and service do of course lie at the heart of the marketing philosophy. We will examine each in turn in the context of branding.

(a) Quality

It is generally recognised that quality is an important factor in success in the market place. Research carried out for books like 'In Search of Excellence' and 'The Winning Streak' showed that successful companies like Marks and Spencer, Sainsbury, Clarks Shoes, MacDonalds, IBM and many more all place great emphasis on maintaining quality standards throughout the organisation.

Quality should be seen as 'fitness for purpose'. MacDonalds do not serve the most 'cordon bleu' dishes in town, but that is not the point. For what the consumer expects from a fast food hamburger restaurant, MacDonalds can rarely be faulted. Sainsbury's are so keen on quality that they have an objective that all their own label products should be of higher quality than their branded equivalents even though they usually sell for a lower price.

The importance of quality has also been demonstrated by the PIMS study in the USA. A tracking study which monitored the performance of over a thousand American companies the PIMS research showed that company profitability tends to rise with quality and that inferior quality substantially harms profitability.

Adding value through quality involves both substance and image. The substance of quality has to be there, and the PIMS study showed that no amount of promotional expenditure will make up for poor quality. Equally though, it is no use having a high quality product unless it is widely perceived by consumers to be a high quality product. Companies must therefore tell their target market about the quality of their brand and they must keep reminding people about it.

Looking through the examples of well known brands which have been used in this book, the importance of quality is clear to see. Let's consider some of them:

Beanz meanz Heinz

Although baked beans do have the aura of an undifferentiated product many people do insist that Heinz beans do taste better. The company does put a huge amount of resources into maintaining and developing product quality and it is quite common for directors to have tasting sessions where they compare their own and competitors' brands.

Nescafé

Always at the forefront of quality improvements, Nescafé has run basically the same advertising campaign for over ten years reminding consumers of the brand's quality.

PG Tips

A third market leader which has a large and loyal following of consumers who prefer this product over its rivals. Like Nescafe it has been consistently reinforcing the quality message in its advertising for decades. According to the chimps, 'it's in the taste'.

Kelloggs

Even boring old corn flakes, now with a host of own label competitors still have their loyal followers. Kelloggs are fanatical about quality, and constantly differentiate themselves from the lower quality competition by reminding us that 'if its not Kelloggs on the packet its not Kelloggs in the packet'.

Fairy Liquid

Another very mature product, it has been very successfully advertised in recent years by unfavourably comparing the amount of washing up which can be done by competing brands.

Chum

The use of expert witnesses (top dog breeders) praising the high quality of Chum has been used consistently and very effectively by Britain's top selling dog food for many years.

Whiskas

Perhaps the most audacious approach is adopted by Whiskas. They have been telling us for years that eight out of ten cat owners (who expressed a preference), prefer Whiskas, helping the brand to become perceived as a very high quality product, which may explain why it has retained market leadership in this highly competitive market for many years.

All the above products have used branding to add value. They are all sold at premium prices and are very profitable, even after the expenditure of their very large advertising budgets. But they all have the substance as well as the image of quality.

(b) Customer service

Branding can also add value in customers' eyes by establishing an association with high levels of customer service. IBM have always maintained that not only is their product quality the highest but so is the service they offer to customers. Theodore Levitt has pointed out that the more technologically sophisticated the product, the more customers are dependent upon the service back-up offered by the supplier. The buyer of a new computer system may need installation, he may need help in the choice of software, he may need training for his staff in how to use the computer and he will require maintenance support in the future.

Services can also use branding to great effect in this respect. The American car hire company Avis, number two in the market behind Hertz, ran a very successful advertising campaign with the slogan, 'Because we're second we try harder'. There is no doubt that some companies do build a reputation for offering unusually high levels of customer service. The best example is Marks and Spencer, where the customer knows he is always right.

5.3.3 Self service

Attaining high levels of customer service is not relevant to some products because they are sold in circumstances where the consumer serves himself. Branding however is also very important in this self service situation. There are two main factors here, packaging and merchandising.

(a) Packaging

In the supermarket, products have to speak for themselves, and sometimes customers will certainly select the brand which shouts the loudest, i.e. the one that is most visible on the shelf. Companies devote considerable resources to designing and testing packs which will stand out in the self service situation. There are two factors here which are rigorously tested. Firstly there is the visual impact made by the pack, compared to a selection of similar packs, and secondly there is the 'find time'. The manufacturer may have no control over the shelf space or position allocated to its brands by the supermarkets, so it will want to ensure that loyal customers who do recognise the pack are able to identify it quickly even if it is placed in a very obscure position.

The pack also has to reinforce the brand's image. In other words it has to project those qualities which make the brand different from and better than its competitors. There is evidence that when a consumer comes across a new product in the supermarket the decision about whether or not to try it is influenced by ideas about that product conveyed by the pack. Conveying the right impression is no easy task, but image tests on new packs are carried out by showing respondents two or three different packs (e.g. for toothpaste) and asking them to describe what they think the product inside would be like. They have to do this without having tried the product and if it is for a well known brand the name would have to be changed for the purposes of the test.

The packaging also needs to incorporate the brand name, trademark, any slogans used by the brand and, perhaps, some additional promotional material which is to be carried on the pack.

(b) Merchandising

Merchandising is a part of sales promotion which is covered more extensively in Chapter 12, but here we will consider its link with branding, especially in the self service situation. If products have to speak for themselves in the supermarket then anything which can help them to shout louder must be considered. Money off, flash packs offering some extra product, premium offers and competitions are all promoted on packaging in the hope of giving consumers that extra little incentive to buy. (see Chapter 12).

As far as branding is concerned however, merchandising which reinforces the brand image is ideal. POS (point of sale) display material which can convey more of the product benefits is of great value, but many supermarkets refuse to accepts such items, preferring to be in full control of their own in-store displays. Sampling sessions can also be useful as can anything which reinforces the brand image such as permanent storage jars (e.g. Mr. Homepride flour).

5.3.4 Protection against imitators

Brand piracy has become a serious threat to all well known products. Highlighted by the Olympic Games, which put the spotlight on Seoul, one of the counterfeiting capitals of the world, the problem has been growing for well over a decade. According to articles in Business Week in 1984 and 1985, the following well known names are fighting battles against the copiers: Apple Computers, Raleigh bicycles, Cartier watches, Rolex watches, Gucci shoes, Nike running shoes, Singer sewing machines, Chanel perfumes, Boeing aircraft parts, Ford car parts, Wrangler jeans, Levi jeans and Johnny Walker whisky.

The names above represent no more than the tip of a very large iceberg, and the problem is growing all the time. The registration of trademarks and names is useful in the fight against counterfeit, although it fails to dissuade many in the Far East.

Any kind of shape can be registered with the Patent Office, giving the owner the statutory right to the exclusive use of that registered trademark. Many trademarks are instantly recognisable. The Kellogg's cockerel logo, the Adidas symbol, the Lloyds Bank black horse. a recognised trademark adds a stamp of authenticity, giving reassurance to buyers.

Although marks, symbols and graphic designs can be patented as trademarks, physical objects can not. This was established in 1985 when Coca-Cola, who had thought for over sixty years that they had the sole right to their distinctively shaped bottle, had an appeal against its reproduction by other companies rejected in the Court of Appeal. It was ruled that although a drawing in the shape of the bottle could be registered as a trademark the bottle itself could not.

In general names, logos, trademarks and other visual images which represent brand identity are well respected in western markets and are of key importance in helping the top brands to maintain their image.

Conclusion

In this chapter we have seen how a product is much more than a tangible lump of hardware. It should be seen as an augmented product and even as a potential product. It is likely to include many intangible benefits, such as after sales service, in addition to the core product itself. Even more importantly firms must accept that products do not last for ever. They follow a life cycle, which, sooner or later will move into its decline stage. Marketers should therefore have a range of products, with a regular stream of new products being developed to replace those which reach their decline stage. Branding of products is also important because it helps customers to associate with them and to remember their benefits, which can be particularly important in the self-service situation.

Assignment   S.K. Electricals Ltd.

For the past nineteen years the two Robinson brothers, Steve and Ken, have manufactured low cost portable radios. Although they missed the real portable radio boom of the 1960's they were able to establish their company in the early 1970's in a market which still retained several years of good growth. Working from a modern but small industrial unit in Birmingham, S.K. Electricals built its success mainly on two models. The S.K. Mini exploited the interest, mainly from young people, in a tiny transistor radio which could be carried around with ease in a large pocket or in a bag, allowing the owner to listen to his favourite radio programme at home, in the park, in the classroom or at the football match. The sound quality from the single small speaker was poor, but it was always positioned as a low cost, affordable product. The S.K. Maxi was altogether a higher quality product. With FM (very new when the Maxi was developed) as well as long wave, medium wave and short wave bands, the radio was much larger than the Mini and the sound quality from its single large speaker was excellent.

Throughout the 1970's the Mini and the maxi sold very well. On the whole S.K. used direct marketing to reach potential customers, placing small box adverts (typically 6 column centimetres) in publications such as Exchange and Mart, Dalton's Weekly and local newspapers in the Midlands. They also attracted trade orders in this way, mainly from small electrical shops whose buying power was insufficient to secure good prices from the larger manufacturers. Trade customers were given 20% discount off the list price regardless of the volume ordered. A good base of loyal trade customers was gradually built up in this way, though many of these small retailers were beginning to find the competition of the high street multiples increasingly hard to handle. S.K. had suffered a number of bad debts as a result of trade customers going into liquidation, though fortunately none had ever amounted to a cripplingly large sum.

Although the company's growth had been built on the success of the Mini and the Maxi in the 1970's, neither product had performed as well in the 1980's. The Mini had been particularly hard hit by cheap far eastern imports and by the trend away from small radios. With sales of around 8,500 units per annum at its peak in 1980 sales of the Mini had slumped to 6,990 in 1981, 6,216 in 1982, 5,478 in 1983, 4,871 in 1984, 4,011 in 1985, 3,383 in 1986 2,518 in 1987 and only 1,665 units sold in 1988 of which 45% went to the trade. Foreign competition dictated that prices should be cut to the bone, so the Minis were sold at £8.95 list price, plus 60p, postage and packing (always charged at cost by the company). S.K.'s costings showed that each Mini cost a total of £6.98 to produce.

The Maxi had fared a little better because it was still a very good product for those requiring a basic work top radio producing a clear sound. In this respect it was ideal for small workshops, where the brothers had developed a nice niche market, partly through direct mail and partly through the use of a freelance salesman, Eddie Peters. Although below their 1979 peak of 11,245 units sold, sales had remained reasonable at 10,834 in 1980, 10,472 in 1981, 10,516 in 1982, 9,340 in 1983, 9,616 in 1984, 9,488 in 1985, 8,821 in 1986, 8,473 in 1987 and were still just about satisfactory at 8,216 in 1988 of which only 14% were destined for the trade, though a further 40% were sold through the salesman who received a 15% commission. More importantly at a list price of £29.95 (plus £1.95 p. & p.) and a production cost of £20.72, the margins were much better than those achieved by the Mini.

However, in total the Mini and Maxi sold only half as well as they had done at their peak, ten years earlier, and the profit margins were less. For some years the brothers had turned a blind eye to this trend, since they were reluctant to undertake the hard work and absorb the cost of developing new products. By 1983 they knew they must act, though the results of their 'new product development' programme can be described as too little too late. Noticing the growing sales of radio cassette recorders S.K. introduced the Duo in 1984. Although it appeared to be little more than a Maxi with a single cassette deck, the addition of this extra facility had necessitated considerable redesign to the interior of the product, changing a number of components and circuits to enable the Duo to be housed in the Maxi case. Development costs had therefore been higher than expected and were to be written off at £5 per unit over the first 4,000 sales. So far, to say the least, sales had been disappointing. From 102 in 1984 they had risen to 541 in 1985, 687 in 1986 and 794 in 1987, only to fall back to 638 in 1988. S.K. found it difficult to offer a really competitive price, the list price being £39.95 plus £1.95 p. & p. with production costs of £28.63 excluding development costs. Trade sales had been very disappointing accounting for 52 in 1984, then 326 in 1985 as retailers stocked up, but trailing off to 301 in 1986, 235 in 1987 and 116 in 1988. Eddie had sold 36 in 1985, 54 in 1986, and, encouraged by an increase in commission to 17.5% (only for the Duo) had sold 223 in 1987 and 190 in 1988. He was not, however optimistic about the product, saying that customers complained about the lack of stereo, the inability to copy tapes and the rather boring old fashioned appearance of the product.

Of course, the Duo had been outdated before its introduction. Taking advice from a number of people in the trade, the two brothers decided to develop a much more fashionable range. Called the Englander range, there were three models. All were stereo radio / cassettes and all were available in a choice of black, white, grey, cream or red cases. Moreover, with the help of an industrial design student from the local Polytechnic a much more distinctive, rounded design had been produced. Based on fifties fashions the product was actually very trendy as well as functional and aesthetically pleasing, to the extent that S.K.'s student had won the prize for the best final year industrial design project from any British degree course. Under the fifties exterior however the product had been completely redesigned, with high quality components and all the latest features. The Englander 1 offered stereo sound, a single cassette deck and the same high quality components and sound reproduction to be found in the more expensive models. The Englander 2 came with twin cassette decks and a pre-set push button facility for radio tuning. The England 3 also offered a graphic equaliser, a digital radio frequency display and a self seek station selector.

Despite the use of the Polytechnic design services the development costs of the Englander range had risen beyond the brothers' plans until a total of £80,000 had been invested. They planned to write it off at £8 per unit over their first 10,000 sales. Despite the fact that they had removed unnecessary features such as the existing models' short wave facility, their costs were inevitably higher than the far eastern imports, although the Englander's quality, both in terms of appearance and sound quality was clearly superior to most competitors. Excluding development costs S.K. worked out their total production costs to be as follows:

Englander 1: £42.60 Englander 2: £49.25 Englander 3: £56.70.

The retail list price was to be:

Englander 1: £75.95 Englander 2: £85.95 Englander 3: £99.95

The Englander range first went on sale towards the end of 1986, too late to really take advantage of Christmas sales. The Englander 1 sold 82 units, (52 to the trade), the 2 sold 127 (including 46 to the trade) and the expensive 3 headed the sales league with 182 units sold of which 80 went through the trade. In 1987 the company's sales and marketing policies continued much as before. The adverts in the small trader press and local newspapers were expanded to spread across two columns in order to provide enough space for the expanded range of models, trade discount remained at 20% but the freelance salesman was offered an increased commission of 20% on the new range only, to encourage him to concentrate on the Englanders. Sales of Englander 1 reached a rather disappointing total of 320 units (of which 190 were at the standard Englander discount of 20%). Englander 2 performed better with sales of 982 in 1987 of which approximately 74% were discounted, and the Englander 3 was again the most successful model reaching sales of 1300 units, 78% of which went through Eddie or other traders. A number of trends were becoming apparent during 1987. Firstly, the company's traditional direct marketing methods were not working very well with the new range. The Robinson brothers decided that whilst consumers were happy to buy a very cheap product via mail order from a relatively unknown firm, they were much more inclined to seek the reassurance afforded by a proper retail outlet when buying more expensive products. Ken, who was responsible for direct sales had noticed that for the Englanders a much higher proportion of the direct sales were to local people who collected their product from the factory.

The other noticeable trend in 1987 was the increased interest from a number of retailers. Steve was convinced that this was due to two factors. Firstly the product itself was of a very high quality, both from the technical and design point of view. Secondly it was British designed and built, a very unusual feature in that market. Normally these factors, like most of S.K.'s activities would have gone almost totally unnoticed by the radio buying public, but this time other promotional factors were at work. Due to the success of the student's design, the student himself, the Polytechnic and the Design Council had made efforts to publicise the design, resulting in articles in a large number of magazines and journals and in three national newspapers, the Sunday Times, the Sunday Telegraph and the Daily Mail. This good PR had given S.K. Electricals a higher profile in the trade than it had ever previously enjoyed and enquiries had been received from quite a large number of retailers, mainly small independent businesses but including some very up-market shops. Ken had insisted that the company commission some good quality brochures for these enquiries and that the trade discount be increased to 25% for the Englander range only, in order to encourage more trade business. 1988 Englander sales were as follows: Englander 1: 540 units total, 420 units trade, 32 units Eddie Peters. Englander 2: 1,736 units total, 1,050 units trade, 96 units Eddie Peters. Englander 3: 2,214 units total, 1,738 units trade, 62 units Eddie Peters.

It was also notable that 86% of direct Englander sales were made to buyers in the West Midlands.

By the end of 1987, the two brothers were buoyant, with the new range seemingly on the verge of a break through. In addition they had received an enquiry from one of the leading high street electrical retail chains which had resulted in Ken making several sales calls to the company's headquarters. Negotiations were difficult however, with the retailer demanding a 40% discount, (although Ken felt that retail price could be raised slightly). The retail buyer was also unhappy about S.K.'s direct marketing of the range and wanted to see the outline of a three year new product development programme from S.K. Steve felt that the deal with the retailer would not be 'worth the hassle', but Ken thought that with the increasing domination of the high street retailers the company had to adjust to the times and move to being a trade supplier.

Some very difficult decisions lay ahead.

Task

1. Draw a graph showing sales volumes of all S.K. models from 1980.

2. Compile a sales analysis for 1988 sales for each model covering the following information:

Model: Total sales value: Total production cost: Profit contribution.

3. Using the data at your disposal, plot S.K.'s products on a BCG matrix showing the 1988 position.

4. Advise S.K. Electricals on their product strategy for the next three years.

Chapter 6
Services

Introduction

It has been stressed throughout this book that for marketing purposes, a distinction should not be drawn between goods and services. Since the role of marketing is to identify an unsatisfied need and then to organise the resources of the organisation to meet that need, it should not matter in principle whether the need is for a product or a service. We have said that a company's product should be seen as 'whatever it sells', whether it is a tangible good or an intangible service.

So why should we now have a chapter on services? There are two principal reasons. First is the fact that services are now such an important part of our national economy - indeed of the economies of the whole western world. This will be considered in greater detail in section 6.1. Secondly, there are certain differences which arise in the marketing of services. The principles of marketing remain the same, as do the service marketer's long term planning activities and the marketing research which underpins that planning. In the short term tactical aspects of marketing management however, the service marketer needs to adapt to certain special factors which are inherent in the nature of services. The remainder of this chapter will explore those differences of emphasis.

6.1 The importance of services

In the UK more people are employed in the service sector than in all other sectors of the economy put together. It is the same in the USA and in most western economies. In Britain, income from services contributes more than any other sector to the Gross National Product, and income from selling services overseas, called 'invisible earnings', plays an increasingly important role in our balance of trade.

The standard definition of a service is that provided by the American Marketing Association, which says:

> *'Services are activities, benefits or satisfactions which are offered for sale or are provided in connection with the sale of goods'.*

The problem with this definition is its similarity to the augmented product concept. William Stanton has modified this definition to make it more suited to pure service industries. According to Stanton, services are:

> *'Those separately identifiable, essentially intangible activities which provide want satisfaction and which are not necessarily tied to the sales of a product or another service. To provide a service may or may not require the use of tangible goods. However, when such use is required, there is no transfer of the title to those tangible goods.'*

Though long winded this is a good definition. Firstly it points out that services which are sold as stand alone activities (for example, an independent repair service for domestic appliances) are different from the same service which is part of an augmented product, (for instance, the five year parts and labour guarantee bought with a new automatic washing machine). Secondly the definition makes it clear that services can involve tangible goods, for example, the hire of cars or industrial equipment, as long as the goods themselves are not permanently sold.

6.1.1 Examples of services

With over half the workforce employed in the service sector, you would be right to expect the range of service activities to be vast. In this section we will merely attempt to demonstrate the breadth of the sector by highlighting a few examples.

(a) The financial services industry is probably the most buoyant area of the service sector. It includes high street banks, building societies, merchant banks and stockbrokers. Insurance, (incorporating property insurance, motor insurance, life insurance and pensions) is another growth market.

(b) Professional services include accountants, solicitors, consultants of many kinds, architects and surveyors.

(c) Marketing services are growing as are advertising agencies. There are market research companies, PR companies, hospitality companies and sales agents.

(d) Catering is also buoyant, including hotels, restaurants, fast food takeaways.

(e) Leisure and recreation covers sports centres and clubs, theme parks, zoos, amusement arcades, libraries, cinemas, sports events and music.

(f) There are cleaning services such as contract office cleaning, domestic cleaning and window cleaning. Decorating covers internal and external painting, sand blasting and interior design.

(g) Transport services employ thousands of people, as do health services (both in the public and private sectors), education and training, social services, travel agents, telecommunications, the delivery of letters and hair dressing.

The list could go on, but it does illustrate the point that service industries are many, varied and crucial to our national economy and way of life.

6.1.2 Reasons for the growth of services

As manufacturing industry creates wealth with ever fewer people and ever increasing use of technology, western governments have had to place more emphasis on the development of the service sector. Reduction of employment in manufacturing industry, since productivity has continued to increase, has not meant less wealth. On the contrary, western countries continue to grow richer and as they do so there is an ever increasing demand for all the kinds of services mentioned above.

In the years after the Second World War the introduction of the welfare state led to a huge growth in public sector services. Since 1979 privatisation has begun to reduce the activities of the public sector, although the core services, health, education and social services are still provided mainly by the state. Increasing competition from the private sector however, is being seen throughout these services. Stimulated by government policies and social changes since 1979, there has been tremendous growth in private schooling at all age ranges, private medical care and private social care such as homes for the elderly or nurseries for the children of working mothers.

The buoyancy of the service sector has resulted in increased competition and greater investment in marketing by service companies. One clear sign of this is the growth of service sector advertising. For over twenty years TV advertising was dominated by well known branded goods. In the 1980's the big grocery brands have seen increasing competition for the audience's attention from the banks, building societies, insurance companies, airlines, telecommunications companies and the government advertising its own services such as the Youth Training Scheme.

Service companies therefore are facing exciting growth opportunities and are keen to recruit marketing expertise to help them to exploit their markets. We will now turn our attention to the role of the marketer in the service sector.

6.2 The nature of services

There are a number of factors which make services different from physical goods. They are, **intangibility, inseparability, perishability, heterogeneity** and **ownership**.

6.2.1 Intangibility

Unlike goods, services cannot be seen, touched, smelt, tasted, tried on for size or stored on a shelf. They are intangible. This makes services much harder to buy. If you walk through a shop, physical goods are everywhere. They can be touched, seen and felt. If they look very attractive, they will often tempt people to buy them. Once bought, the shining new television can be taken home and will remain as tangible evidence of the purchase for years. If it is still working well after five years, people will make statements like 'We've had our money's worth out of it', or 'that television doesn't owe us anything'.

It is more difficult to make statements like that about services. If you sell your house you may use an estate agent and a solicitor, and they can cost a lot of money. Although the vast majority of people would not be able to move house without these two services, the fees are often paid rather grudgingly. People can't really see what they've had for their money, and how this intangible concept can be worth so much.

Some services are more intangible than others. A counselling service is totally intangible. The customer has nothing of a tangible nature to show for it. The estate agent produces a leaflet, a big sign in the garden and adverts - small identifiable proof of the service. A hairdresser actually takes something tangible from you, but you can see what you have paid for, and any kind of hire service, for example, a library, offers very tangible evidence of its service, though not permanent evidence.

Some goods have a greater element of intangibility than others. Salt is almost one hundred percent tangible, but cars are often sold with additional intangible benefits such as after sales service and credit. Perfume is a tangible purchase, but the liquid itself is only a small part of the reason for purchase. The service it performs, the hope and confidence it inspires form the larger, less tangible part of this product.

Lynn Shostack has produced a diagram showing this gradual change from a clearly tangible good to a totally intangible service. Her dividing line is fast food, which is very apt, since both product and service are equally essential to customer satisfaction.

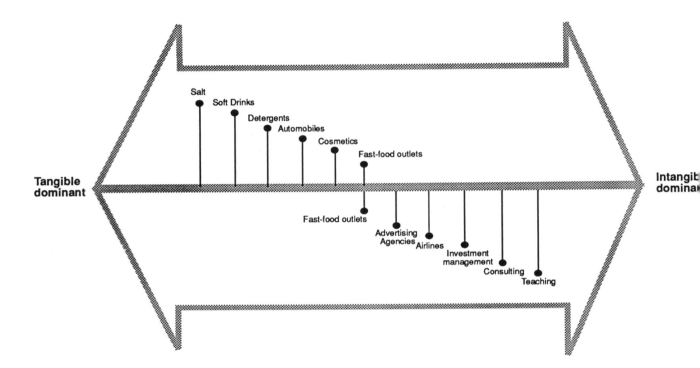

Figure 6.1 Goods and Services - from tangible to intangible. (From G.L.Shostack, *'Breaking Free from Product Marketing'*, Journal of Marketing April 1977.)

6.2.2 Inseparability

The production and consumption of services are inseparable. If you have your hair cut you have to be sitting there at the same time as the hairdresser is working. To take advantage of a bus service, both you and the bus must make the journey at the same time.

Having stated the obvious, let us now examine the implications. Inseparability means that the consumers have direct experience of the production of the service. They are, in effect, in the service factory at the time of production. This has profound implications for the staff in service industries.

When you buy a product, such as a hair dryer, it comes nicely packaged, in a shiny bright colour, with instructions. Your initial impression of that product is formed entirely by the box and its contents, and marketers have plenty of time to plan these aspects of product management to ensure that customers are pleased by what they see. If the first packaging idea they came up with looked hideous, the consumer will never know that. If the first instructions translated from Japanese were virtually incomprehensible it does not matter as long as they are improved. If two per cent of the production of the hair dryers are defective in some way and the faults have to be corrected before they leave the factory or the products rejected, you will never know, nor will you care so long as your hair dryer functions perfectly. What if the workers on the factory floor where the hair dryers are made are badly dressed, have not shaved for two days, pass the time shouting and swearing at each other? What if the method of manufacture is very noisy or pungently smelly? Well, who cares, as long as you never have to go near the place.

But if you do not dry your hair at home, but receive that service from a hairdresser you do have to go right inside the shop and you will start to care a lot about all of those things. If the hairdresser's hair dryer doesn't work and you can't have your blow wave you will feel that the service has not been provided, however expertly your hair has been cut. If the hair dresser has bad breath, body odour, dirty overalls and unkempt hair, you will notice and will not be pleased. If the environment at the hairdresser's is at all unpleasant you will not be happy, because although it is a place of production it is also a place of purchase and consumption and you have to sit there for up to an hour.

As you can see, the task of satisfying customers for the provider of a service is in many ways much more difficult than it is for the manufacturer of a product. In service industries everything has to be right first time, all the time, and any mistake can prove very costly in terms of lost custom. How service personnel conduct themselves in the customer's presence, what they say, what they don't say, how competent they are, how personable they are or how presentable they are, can determine whether the customer buys from the firm again.

The simultaneous occurrence of production, purchase and consumption of some services contrasts starkly with the lengthy time scale which can separate the production, purchase and consumption of a product.

6.2.3 Perishability

You cannot find a 'product' which is much more perishable than a seat on a bus, train or aeroplane or in a theatre, cinema or football ground. Since production and consumption are simultaneous, services are instantly perishable if they have not been sold by the time of production. If you miss the Sunderland versus Leeds United match on October 27th you will never see it, which may come as a great disappointment or a great relief to you. For the supplier of the service however, it is a lost sale that can never be recovered. The empty train seat, the half empty football terraces, the empty hotel bed or dentist's chair all represent a lost opportunity. Unlike the manufacturer of goods, they cannot just keep on producing the service and store it up for a future sale. For service industries, striking the right balance between supply and demand, between capacity and sales is extremely difficult.

Moreover, the problems of perishability can be made even more acute by fluctuating demand. Demand can vary during the day, during the week or from season to season. Many seaside hotels are full for only two months of the year. They are half empty for another four months and completely empty for the rest of the year. Capacity may therefore be insufficient to meet demand at peak times, but way in excess of what is required at slack times. The telephone system suffers from exactly the same problem on a daily basis, as do the railway and bus services, especially in and around cities where people are commuting to work. The problem is illustrated in the diagram below.

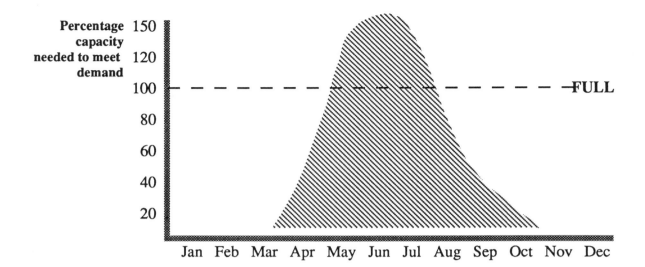

Figure 6.2 The problem of fixed capacity versus seasonal demand for a seaside hotel.

All service companies therefore face difficult decisions about the level of service they will provide and about how they will react in times of above average and below average demand.

6.2.4 Heterogeneity

Products are often made in batches. Some products, manufactured in very long runs, such as ball point pens, pots of 'thick and creamy strawberry yoghurt' or Ford Sierras, may result in thousands of identical items being mass produced. Services are never identical. One cut and blow wave is never quite the same as another, one lecture or training session (even one on the same topic presented by the same tutor) will never be identical to another. The human element ensures that services will be heterogeneous, which simply means varied.

This is understandable, but it does make it very difficult for potential purchasers to evaluate services. A topical subject in the U.K. is the increasing parental choice over their children's education. Many people feel that parents should have more choice over the primary and secondary school attended by their children. It is said that this would result in good schools receiving more applications, which would enable them to expand, whilst the opposite would be true for poor schools, thus causing them to contract, and perhaps eventually to close down. The main problem here is how parents would determine which are the good schools and which are the bad. Certainly the comparison of exam results may not be a truly reliable guide, and there are so many less tangible elements of any assessment such as the happiness of the children, the extent of their social development or the quality of their sports coaching.

Similar difficulties arise if one tries to evaluate medical services. There may be two or three GP practices in a town. But how do customers choose between them? Do they ask to see the doctors' graduation results, do they look at the annual mortality figures for each practice or do they ask people in the town which doctors are the most friendly? It is very difficult to find an objective assessment of competing services. Although extreme cases of poor service may be widely reported, information about less serious variations in the quality of service may not be available to buyers. As a consequence buyers of services are often looking for yardsticks against which they can measure their performance. This buyer uncertainty can be seen as an opportunity for service marketers as we will see in section 6.3.

6.2.5 Ownership

When a customer buys a good, there will often be a document, such as an invoice or a receipt, which transfers ownership from seller to buyer. The buyer then owns that product and is free to do whatever he likes with it.

When a consumer buys a service he does not usually receive ownership of anything tangible. He hires a car, but never owns it. He books a hotel room, but owns nothing in it. Even a credit card actually remains the property of the issuing company. Service buyers are therefore buying only access to or use of something.

These five special attributes of services do tend to change the emphasis of a service marketer's task compared to that of a product marketer. The next section examines these effects.

6.3 Points of emphasis for service marketers

6.3.1 The fifth 'P'

Jerome McCarthy coined the phrase 'the four P's' in the 1960's to simplify the marketing mix concept voiced initially by Neil Borden some years earlier. Since that time many writers have claimed that the four P's are not sufficiently comprehensive, and have suggested other central aspects of marketing such as public relations and packaging. In 1986 Yoram Wind even suggested that it should really be 'the eleven P's'. Well, not many writers would agree with that and in fact most of the more commonly suggested additional P's do already seem to be included within McCarthy's four P's. Public Relations and Packaging for example, are part of 'promotion' and 'product' respectively.

There is however a fifth 'P' which is frequently suggested which is not encompassed within McCarthy's four P's. This fifth P is 'people' and there is now a growing view among marketing academics and practitioners that it should be seen as a valid and important part of the marketing mix. The fifth 'P' is explored in greater detail in Chapter 9 under the heading of customer service, but it has important implications for the marketing of services, which must be explored here.

Peters and Austin, in their book *'A Passion for Excellence'* (a sequel to *In Search of Excellence*) have suggested that the differences between winning companies and those of mediocre performance will often be slight, just like the difference between the gold medal winner in an athletics race and the athlete who finishes almost unnoticed in fifth place. The difference may be only a couple of metres over a 1,500 metres race but it's the winner who receives all the acclaim. To win therefore you only have to be a little better, and this tiny difference may be provided by the fifth 'P', by the way a company's employees behave. If employees go out of their way to give customers immaculate service at all times, those customers will gradually form a favourable impression of the company as a 'caring company' and this will be a significant factor in their decision to buy from that company again. Customers who receive poor service, or simply form the impression that 'this company isn't really interested in me, they're more concerned about themselves', will soon label that company as uncaring, and will begin to search elsewhere for a supplier.

This is seen as important in manufacturing industries. Companies like the car manufacturer Jaguar and Komatsu who make heavy earth moving equipment, both invest money and spend time explaining to all their employees the importance of putting the customer first. Retailers like Next and Tie Rack with high prices and profit margins invest a proportion of that profit in training their staff in the importance of customer care. If customer care is of such importance to a manufacturer and a retailer, how much more important it is to a service company where the customer often has no tangible features to evaluate and spends much of his purchasing and consuming time in direct contact with the staff of the service provider?

In service industries the behaviour of the staff can lead to fundamental rather than marginal differences in customer satisfaction.

British Airways has invested in a major staff training programme called 'Putting People First'. Their marketing research had shown beyond any doubt that staff attitude towards and treatment of customers strongly affected sales. The objective of the training programme was to help staff concentrate on the two most important aspects of company performance - satisfying the customer and beating the competition. Theodore Levitt puts this in a more erudite way when he states:

> 'If marketing is about anything it is about achieving customer-getting distinction by differentiating what you do and how you operate. All else is derivative of that and only that.'

Everybody in the organisation must focus on giving the customers what they want and doing it better than the competition, and in service industries this often boils down to the way staff treat customers. In service industries even the little things like offering the customers a nice cup of freshly ground coffee whilst they are visiting the solicitor or being measured for a new suit can make all the difference.

6.3.2 Managing image

Due to the difficulty of evaluating services, consumers are often more aware of the image making factors which surround the service. These can include the company's premises and the equipment used in the performance of the service. Since both premises and equipment will be seen by customers, service companies should devote attention to keeping both in good condition. Clean vehicles, new equipment, attractive, tidy, welcoming premises are all important because they are factors which the consumer can easily evaluate. The demeanour, politeness and smartness of staff will also be noticed as will things like the company's literature, letter-heading and order forms.

6.3.3 Creating tangible features

In addition to the premises, equipment, staff and literature, the service company may be able to create additional tangible features with which consumers can identify. The credit card companies place great emphasis on the design of their cards. Access take the branding process a stage further by endowing their 'flexible friend' with a brand personality. Lloyd's Bank have the black horse, Swinton Insurance Brokers the big glasses and Caledonia Airlines used to build their advertising around the air hostesses. These features may not offer measurable benefits to customers but if they help people to differentiate the service provider from its rather amorphous competitors they will make a very useful contribution.

6.3.4 Marketing to attract employees

Since the fifth 'P' is so important to service companies it follows that they should place considerable stress on the recruitment of the best staff. It therefore makes sense for them to use marketing techniques to help them to attract, keep and motivate the right kind of employees. By maintaining high morale amongst their staff, service companies will usually improve the quality of service offered to customers.

6.3.5 Price discrimination

Companies should try to set their prices according to the level of demand in the market place. This creates difficulties for many service companies since extreme fluctuations in demand can occur. Their reaction is usually to adopt a policy of price discrimination, charging high prices during periods of peak demand and much lower prices during times of slack business. Hotels offer greatly reduced prices during the spring and autumn in order to encourage people to take their holidays out of season. Any additional business which they can attract at times when they have spare capacity provides useful extra turnover to help cover their overheads.

Price discrimination is practised by many service businesses. British Telecom have three price bands which apply at different times of the day, and much of their advertising is designed to encourage off peak social use of the telephone. British Rail attract a lot of business with their saver tickets. Airlines have standby tickets, which can be sold very cheaply to people who are prepared to wait and take the risk that a seat may not be available.

There is one potential problem which can result from the use of the price discrimination weapon. If full price customers begin to feel that they are being treated unfairly in relation to cut price customers they may decide to switch to the cut price service or to another service provider where their status will be better preserved. Thus, if British Rail allowed unrestricted use to holders of cheap tickets and these low fare payers were taking scarce rush hour seats, the regular commuters may become unwilling to continue paying high prices for their season tickets. Equally, first class air travellers who are paying considerably more for the same core service than a club class passenger will expect to encounter visible benefits in return for their expensive ticket. They will expect a much higher level of service, failing which they may take their business to a competing airline.

6.3.6 Exploitation of the customer base

Existing customers are valuable assets to all businesses. They are the best source of new business, because having received satisfaction once, they feel much less uncertainty about buying from that company on subsequent occasions. If this is true for manufacturers and for retailers, it is even more relevant to service companies simply because the purchase of a service typically holds more uncertainty for the buyer. This can be seen in the fact that customers do not usually change banks, building societies, insurance companies, solicitors or accountants. The tendency is sometimes vividly illustrated by people who move from one part of the country to another but retain their original bank or solicitor despite having moved many miles away. Logically it is not in their best interests to be so far removed from these services. That they choose to accept this inconvenience shows the extent of the uncertainty they feel about changing to a new provider of the same service.

This makes it very difficult to win competitors' customers, so difficult in fact that one study estimated the cost of winning competitors' customers to be seventeen times higher than the cost of retaining an existing customer. This explains the valuable incentives which are often offered to new customers by service companies. For example, the banks offer considerable incentives to students to open new accounts, incentives often worth over £50. Dairies frequently offer free milk to new customers on new housing estates, occasionally up to eight weeks free supply, also worth around £50 to a family. In both cases the incentive seems high, especially since there are no strings attached, but in both cases the outlay will pay off for those companies because their customers are most unlikely to ever change to a competing supplier as long as they continue to receive good service.

Service companies will also adopt strategies to retain and strengthen the loyalty of existing customers. Airlines frequently run promotions offering customers tokens for flights booked which can be used against the purchase of future flights. People undertaking a large number of business trips would be motivated to remain with the existing airline or might use their tokens for a holiday flight which could represent additional business for the airline. Accountancy practices may offer free information to their clients about topical matters such as tax changes following the budget. This free information may be in the form of a seminar or a booklet but it represents an added benefit which helps to keep existing customers loyal.

6.3.7 The customer ladder

It is often said that customers move through a ladder of feelings as they get to know and trust a company. The customer ladder can be expressed as follows:

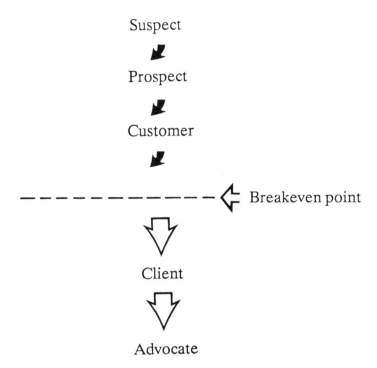

Figure 6.3 The customer ladder.

This explanation of buyer behaviour is particularly appropriate to consumers' reaction when faced with buying many services. Let's use the example of private medical insurance. As with many other services (such as life insurance) consumers will initially be very suspicious of the whole concept, partly because they do not understand the benefits, and are thus prepared to dismiss them. As time moves on however, they may become a little more interested in the concept as their concern about the future grows. Still somewhat suspicious, they may nevertheless clip and return a coupon from a national newspaper advert for one of the leading private health care companies. As far as that company is concerned they have now become a prospect. The company will send them literature, they will be visited by a sales person and may be invited to visit one of the organisation's hospitals to see the facilities and talk to the staff and some satisfied customers. They may organise special events such as wine and cheese evenings with films and an authoritative speaker. They will probably bombard the prospect with further persuasive literature. At the end of all this the prospect may be persuaded about the benefits of becoming a customer. However, he may still not be entirely convinced that the benefits are worth the considerable fees involved, but the company may have a trial period membership scheme for twelve months, and, as an extra incentive might be offering a free weekend at a health farm for new customers taking up the trial membership scheme. This may be enough to make our doubting Thomas become a customer. Our customer, however, is still not a regular buyer. The health care company may have to apply yet more persuasion or offer a further incentive if the customer is to agree to become a full member paying a regular annual subscription. In many cases it is only when the customer becomes a regular client that he becomes profitable to the company. In some businesses, such as life assurance, or time share accommodation, the whole of the first year's income can be insufficient to recover the marketing costs involved to convert that person into a customer. It is through the remaining years of the client's loyalty to the service provider that the profits are made.

Once people are sufficiently convinced to become clients, they often remain loyal for many years, and also tend to become enthusiastic supporters of the cause. Ideally, from the company's point of view they will become advocates, singing the praises of the service and its provider to their friends and acquaintances. This favourable 'word of mouth' promotion can be of much more value to the company in attracting 'suspects' than any amount of advertising. Service companies of this kind often give clients incentives to introduce new prospects to the company.

6.3.8 Promotional emphasis for service marketers

Service marketers often find themselves in the rather strange position of having to concentrate their promotional efforts at either end of the communications spectrum. (See Chapter 10 for more details of marketing communications). On the one hand, due to the intangibility of services and the defensive way in which 'suspects' view new or unknown providers it is very important for service companies to work at the 'soft sell' end of the spectrum to educate people with the objective of 'wearing down' their natural resistance. This public relations work might involve extensive use of press releases to generate favourable publicity in the media, the production of detailed literature and testimonials from satisfied clients which can be perused by 'suspects' without any pressure in their own homes. Open days may be held, quality assurance will be promoted and employees will be trained to create a consistently good image. Budgets permitting, these PR type activities can be supplemented by image building advertising on the TV and in the national press.

However, service companies also have the problem of perishability. The seat in the airline, the room in the hotel, the accountant's time or the hire car have to be sold today, or that revenue is forever lost. Therefore service marketers must also place significant emphasis on the 'hard sell', immediate end of the spectrum. This may involve short term sales, promotion incentives, considerable emphasis on personal selling and perhaps tele-sales. The personnel involved in the selling will need to be highly professional and very well trained. Considerable effort will also be devoted to securing repeat business from existing customers.

This dichotomous promotional effort which is typical of the marketing communications of many service companies is split between the 'soft sell' at one extreme and the 'hard sell' at the other. It is shown in the diagram on the next page.

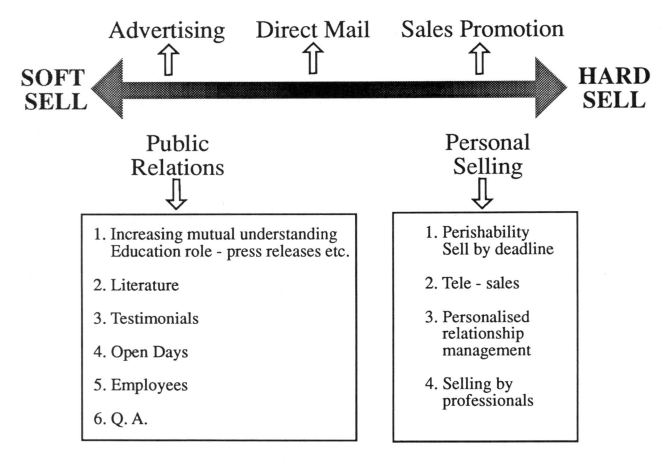

Figure 6.4 Points of emphasis for service promotion.

Conclusion

Our fundamental proposition throughout this book has been that the marketing of any product, whether a physical good or an intangible service follows the same basic marketing principles. Many highly respected academics refuse to accept that there is any difference between goods and services. Theodore Levitt, following the logic of the augmented product and total product concepts maintains:

'...there is no such thing as service industries. There are only industries where service components are greater or less than those of other industries.'

In reality this statement is compatible with the scale of intangibility we displayed in Figure 6.1. We can say that although the principles of marketing apply to both products and services there is no doubt that some products, and some services are more tangible than others. As we have suggested in this chapter, the emphasis placed by the marketer on different aspects of the marketing and promotional mix will vary according to the intangibility of the offering and the level of uncertainty faced by the buyers. The marketing of services is a new and rapidly growing area. Due to the lack of research and published material on the marketing of services, providers of specific services may have to be prepared to experiment a little with the kind of marketing tactics outlined in this chapter.

Assignment State of the Art Ltd.

Three years ago State of the Art Ltd. was formed by three ambitious college lecturers, Liz Carter, Beryl Knowlson and Jenny Riley. Based in Manchester, the company offers a broad range of interior design services from helping with ideas for the redecoration of someone's lounge to designing the interior of a suite of offices. The firm has done very well during its three year existence with Beryl and Liz mainly looking after the administration, the finances and the selling and Jenny providing the main creative inspiration. This year they secured the contract for the interior design of the new office block for the U.K. headquarters of a major American computer manufacturer and they have also been responsible for the refurbishment of two major hotels in Manchester. The extra work resulting from such contracts has enabled the company to appoint two young graduates to assist Jenny with the design work.

State of the Art is able to offer a complete interior design service including the initial design (or redesign) of a room, its furnishings and its decoration. They can also manage the project which includes the selection and purchase of materials, furniture, fittings and equipment and the hire and supervision of contractors to carry out renovation or decoration work or install equipment and furnishings. Such a 'turnkey project' would leave all the responsibility with State of the Art who would simply hand over the keys to the client when the premises were ready for occupation. On the whole the sub-contractors did a good job, but they did require extensive supervision, and any poor workmanship or unacceptable behaviour, which did sometimes arise, invariably reflected badly on State of the Art. Indeed, they had lost one important client the previous year when their regular painter and decorator, Terry Loftus, upset a tin of apple white emulsion paint over a mini computer wiping out five years of customer records and sales analyses. Terry was very apologetic and still carries out much of the contract decorating mainly because he is a friend of many years standing.

Although the company had a good growth record, the three partners were not entirely happy. They still felt they were following a rather hand-to-mouth existence with the level of business fluctuating wildly. Sometimes, when they had a large project to manage everybody was working frantically in order to meet the deadline. At other times business was very slack with work in progress perhaps for only two or three small clients. At times like these the three partners would turn their thoughts seriously towards selling. At various times in the past they had placed adverts in local publications, sent out mailshots and on one occasion even taken exhibition space at a North West Business exhibition at the G-mex centre in Manchester. They had found it very difficult to evaluate the effectiveness of these promotional initiatives. Usually they had not been followed up, as a new large job, often the result of a personal contact, would come in and take their minds away from their promotional work. They were now, however, becoming increasingly unhappy with this 'stop-go' promotional policy and were determined to build a more secure client base for their business.

In the past they had budgeted £6,000 per annum for marketing expenditure, and, apart from the year they attended the exhibition, had usually spent less. They were however prepared to increase this budget if they could be more confident that discernible results would follow. 'What we need', said Beryl, 'is a proper marketing plan'. Strangely enough, the following evening she saw an advert on Channel 4 for the DTI's Enterprise Initiative, part of which is to offer financial help to small companies to improve their marketing. Under the scheme it would be possible to have a marketing strategy and written marketing plan prepared by a professional consultant, half of whose fees would be paid by the Government under the Enterprise Initiative scheme. Beryl sent off for the details and all three partners agreed that they should apply for the grant.

A month later, having approved their grant application, the DTI sent a marketing consultant to visit State of the Art's small but attractive offices. John Varley had worked for many years in marketing in the hotel trade, but for over five years now he had owned his own successful marketing consultancy which specialised in the marketing of services. Full of charm, John got on very well with the three directors, and they were all very impressed with his marketing experience and knowledge. It was agreed that John should take on the three ladies and prepare a marketing plan on their behalf.

It was decided that John should spend the first two days of the assignment talking to the owners and staff of State of the Art. Together they carried out a SWOT analysis for the company with the aim of matching its internal capabilities with appropriate opportunities in the market place. John then visited and interviewed a sample of eight existing or past customers of the company and a further eight potential customers. The analysis and market research confirmed John's feelings that the hotel and catering growth market would offer the best opportunity for State of the Art. Three market segments were highlighted:

1. Medium sized independent hotels in the North of England.

2. Restaurants in Greater Manchester.

3. Up-market pubs in Greater Manchester, particularly those interested in developing the catering side of their business.

John considered that it was vital that State of the Art concentrated its marketing resources on a particular sector of the interior design market rather than continuing with its undifferentiated marketing approach. The problem now was to work out a detailed marketing programme for each of the three segments he had identified.

Task

You work as a trainee in John Varley's consultancy and he has asked you to become involved with the State of the Art assignment. Initially you must work on one of the market segments identified by John and prepare some draft notes which would help John to make a progress presentation to the client in seven days time. John would like to present some ideas to the directors of State of the Art on the following topics.

1. The most important general aspects of service marketing which the three directors should be aware of.

2. A draft promotional plan which would help State of the Art to make itself known to this market segment.

3. Some ideas for a four page brochure to be targeted at this segment.

Chapter 7
Developing New Products

Introduction

The theories that we examined in Chapter 5, including the product life cycle, Peter Drucker's breadwinners and the BCG matrix all demonstrated the fact that products do not continue to satisfy their markets indefinitely. Consequently, all companies must see new product development programmes as the cornerstone of their future profitability. Developing new products is however, a very difficult and risky business. As we will see later, most new products fail. In this chapter we will presenta a framework for new product development. Such a framework cannot guarantee success but can help to minimise the risks of failure. We will consider in turn each of the steps in the new product development process shown in the diagram below.

Step 1

IDEAS

    Step 2

    SCREENING

        Step 3

        MARKETING
        ANALYSIS

            Step 4

        PRODUCT DEVELOPMENT

                Step 5

                TESTING

                    Step 6

                LAUNCH

Figure 7.1 The new product development process.

7.1 Ideas

Ideas are the basis of all new products. Some products are more innovative than others. Some, such as penicillin, nylon, kevlar or the jet engine represent a totally new break through, often the result of many years of slow and expensive research and development. Other new products are 'adaptive', which means that they are improved versions of an existing product. The degree of innovation in an adaptive product can vary enormously, but they are not classified as inventions, just modifications. Some new products do not appear to offer any kind of improvement or modification compared to existing products in the market place. Such products are often referred to as 'me - too' products.

Whether genuine inventions or modifications of existing products, all new products must have started as an idea. The first task therefore of an organisation intent on an effective new product development programme is to create an atmosphere in which the communication of new ideas flourishes. Hewlett - Packard has been one of the most innovative companies in the world since 1945. Its founders, Bill Hewlett and David Packard made it their top priority to create a corporate culture in which individuals would be able to form, express and develop new ideas. (More details of the HP corporate culture will be given in Chapter 14).

In addition to sustaining the kind of corporate culture in which ideas can flourish, a number of specific techniques may be used to stimulate idea generation.

7.1.1 Brainstorming

A brainstorming session would involve a number of people, (usually around eight to twelve), placed in fairly comfortable, relaxed surroundings with a leader to guide the session. The leader will have already prepared certain key words or concepts which he thinks would be appropriate for stimulating the thoughts of the participants. The leader introduces one of these words and the other participants shout out the first word or idea that comes into their head. It does not matter how ridiculous the idea appears, the participant should shout it out because the whole session relies for its effectiveness on group dynamics. One person's banal suggestion might spark off another idea from a second participant which in turn prompts a really good idea from a third member of the group. Most ideas will be voiced spontaneously, so it is often chaotic and might at times degenerate into one big joke. A record would, however, be kept of all points (ideally on tape) and if two or three good ideas emerge from a session it would be deemed time very well spent.

7.1.2 Forced relationships

The process of forced relationships is a simple one. Different products, items or concepts are forced together to see if the germ of a new product results. A simple example would be the radio / cassette player, which could easily have resulted from such an exercise. Taken a stage further the result is a music centre.

7.1.3 The suggestion box

Internal idea generation can be maximised by involving the entire workforce of the company in the process. Many companies have suggestion boxes with financial incentives to contribute. Employees whose suggestions are taken up are paid for their suggestion according to how much money it makes or saves for the company. Suggestions may not be exclusively concerned with new product development. They could include ideas for cost savings on the factory floor, or for a new way of promoting a product, but new product ideas will often be a significant proportion of all suggestions. Many of these are successfully implemented. Smiths, for example successfully introduced square crisps on to the market, an idea originally suggested by a shop floor employee.

7.1.4 Research and development

Many companies, especially larger firms such as ICI employ very large numbers of staff in their research and development (R & D) departments. Being at the forefront of new technological development is important for many companies but in some industries such as pharmaceuticals or computers it is essential.

7.1.5 The sales force

It is often said that the sales force is the company's eyes and ears in the market place. This information gathering role should always be fully exploited by companies, because the close relationships which sales people often have with customers can be a very fruitful source of new product ideas. Sales people should be encouraged to write regular reports about customers' needs and their own ideas for new products or improvements to existing products. Their reports should be circulated to R & D staff as well as the marketing department.

7.1.6 Marketing research

For many companies, especially those in consumer markets, marketing research will be the most fruitful source of ideas for new product development. At its most basic level it need involve little more than developing methodical approach to the use of existing sources of information about the market place as a way of finding out where new market opportunities are occurring. Publications such as Mintel, Euromonitor or Key Note can be very useful in this respect.

However, such general market studies can do little more than suggest attractive areas for the introduction of new products. To generate specific ideas the research must be taken a stage further. This will often involve personal interviews, or various kinds of 'friendly martian' techniques (which were explained in Chapter 4) where people are asked to look at their needs and priorities in a certain product area in a completely different way, perhaps by drawing pictures or acting out plays. These very sophisticated marketing research techniques can often uncover unsatisfied needs which people would have been unable to articulate if asked direct questions, such as the need for a soothing pain killer described in Chapter 4.

7.1.7 Competitors

It is fairly common for firms to use competitors as sources of new product ideas. Most companies gather and file all their competitors' literature, and some take the process a stage further by buying, using and dismantling their competitors' new products. Although it is essential to maintain extensive and up to date knowledge of competitors' activities, to make sure your own company is not slipping behind, using competitors' products as sources of new ideas is of much more dubious value. At best, the copying of a competitor's product results in a 'me-too' product. At worst, the firm may find itself copying a product for which there is no demand, particularly if the competitor has not based the product on a thorough analysis of customers' needs.

7.2 Screening

The purpose of idea generation is to develop as many new ideas as possible. From the start of the screening stage, the new product development process concentrates on reducing the number of ideas down to the tiny number which are worthy of launching on to the market. The first step in this idea reduction process is to screen the ideas for their suitability for the market and their compatibility with the company's strengths.

7.2.1 Compatibility with company strengths

Many ideas can be eliminated quickly and easily on the grounds that they are not really appropriate to the company's strengths and resources. If the firm believes that other organisations would be better at developing a particular idea, they should abandon it, (or possibly sell it to another organisation.) The company must believe that it has staff whose expertise is appropriate to the development of this new product, it must ensure that it has the financial strength to absorb the costs of development and it must be confident that it has the marketing skills to successfully launch the new product on to the market. At the screening stage most ideas can be eliminated if the company makes a ruthless assessment of its own ability to exploit them. Ideas which are allowed to progress at the screening stage despite the fact that they touch on an area of company weakness will inevitably be added, sooner or later, to the long list of new product failures.

7.2.2 Compatibility with existing products

The company must also ask itself how well a prospective new product would fit in with its existing range of products. If the new product is complementary to existing products it will impose less strain on the company's resources because it will build upon existing customer relationships, sales visits, and distribution channels. If the new product is totally different to the company's existing products the costs of introduction to the market will be much higher. A new complementary product might also increase total sales of the existing products if it fills a gap in the range and therefore improves the image of the whole range in customers' eyes.

However, what if the new product is too similar to an existing product in the company's range? The result will be competition between the firm's own products which can only result in sales for the new product being achieved mainly at the expense of sales of the existing one. In marketing jargon, the new product would 'cannibalize' the existing one. This may be acceptable if the existing product is approaching the decline stage of its product life cycle but if it is still performing well there would be no advantage to the company in introducing the new product at this stage.

7.2.3 Value engineering

Having decided that the new idea is compatible with the company's strengths, financial resources and existing product range, it may still need to satisfy itself that the manufacture of the product is feasible. For more complicated products this may involve carrying out a value engineering exercise to assess factors such as manufacturing costs, material and component requirements, or design efficiency with a view to spotting new products which may end up being so difficult or costly to produce that the likelihood of their becoming profitable would be rather low.

7.2.4 Concept testing

The company will obviously want to eliminate new product ideas which are of no interest to customers. The difficulty arises in ascertaining customers' reaction to a product which does not exist. They may not really understand the proposed new product, or they may have a natural tendency to prefer the existing products with which they are familiar. On the other hand, the company wants to avoid the high costs of developing a tangible product before it has consulted customers. The compromise is 'concept testing'. The new product idea is made as tangible and understandable as possible for customers, perhaps with the aid of detailed technical drawings, artist's impressions or scale models. Customers' reactions to the new product concept can be sought, usually at clinics where a full discussion can be held to ensure that the customer understands the product idea and that the company understands the customers' views.

7.2.5 Market demand

Assuming that the product idea is considered to be compatible with the company's strengths and financial resources, that it seems to be feasible to make, and that potential customers appear to be attracted by the concept, the final screening step would involve a quick assessment of the likely demand for the new product. The aim at this stage would be to identify those ideas for which the likely demand would be too small to generate sufficient sales to enable the company to recover the anticipated development costs of the new product.

The whole point of the screening stage is that it should be performed quickly and inexpensively in order to identify early those products which are unlikely to make it through the remainder of the process before too much money has been invested in their development. This need for economy is bound to result in some good ideas being rather hastily screened out of the process at this stage. For example, it is said that Kodak eliminated an idea called Xerography on the grounds that market demand would not be sufficient and that Stanley Tools rejected an idea for a collapsible, portable bench for the DIY man on the grounds that it would never catch on. Xerox and Black and Decker decided differently! However, although it is easy to point to such mistakes, it is normally in the organisation's best interests to be ruthless at the screening stage, because the much more likely mistake is to allow through too many unsuitable ideas which end up failing at some stage, after the organisation has invested a considerable amount of money in their development. After the screening stage, as we will see, the new product development process really does start to become expensive.

7.3 Marketing analysis

As can be seen from Figures 7.2 and 7.3, most of the original ideas have been eliminated by this stage, but the costs incurred in the development of those which remain begin to escalate, especially from the product development stage. The objective is still to eliminate potential losers at the earliest possible stage in order to minimise the potential loss. It is now therefore that a comprehensive marketing analysis and forecast is made since the company wishes to satisfy itself that the new product is a potential winner before the very costly product development stage is entered.

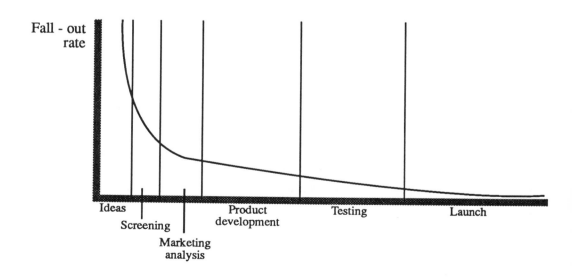

Figure 7.2 The new product fall - out rate

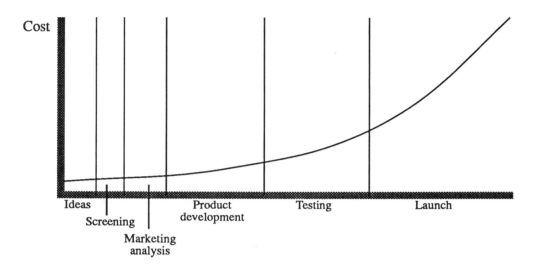

Figure 7.3 The cost of new product development.

The task of the marketing department is to carry out a full appraisal of the commercial feasibility of the project. This will involve desk research and primary marketing research to compile as much information as possible concerning the product's acceptability to potential customers, the kind of detailed features and benefits which will be required by customers, the type of packaging required and the channels through which it will be distributed and promoted to consumers. The costs of developing these features and benefits and promoting the new product will have to be estimated. A price, acceptable to the market and sufficient to meet the company's costs will have to be set and a detailed programme for a launch, with its associated promotional activities, will have to be prepared and costed.

The marketing department will also need to consult all known qualified opinion both inside and outside the company with the aim of assessing the likely sales potential of the new product. By this time the marketing department will have all the projections necessary, prepare budgets and estimate the likely profitability of the new product. We will examine in this section the way in which these forecasts would be prepared.

7.3.1 Volume or value

It is normal for forecasts as well as accounts to be prepared in value rather than volume terms. Volume is the number of units sold whereas value is the amount of income received. Of course, a company is interested in the value of its sales, but reliance on sales value as an indicator can be misleading because factors such as inflation on the one hand, or promotional price cuts on the other hand, may disguise the reality of what is happening in the market place. Forecasts should therefore be prepared and monitored in volume terms. For the purpose of preparing budgets or cash flow forecasts these volumes can be converted into values at a specified price.

7.3.2 Assumptions

As we have already implied, assumptions, such as the prevailing price level, will have to be made if any forecasting activity is to take place. Assumptions will have to be made about any environmental, economic or market factors which could have a significant impact on the performance of the product in question.

The preparation of a cash flow forecast for a petrol station would involve making assumptions about the following:

- inflation,

- changes in the rate of taxes levied on petrol,

- changes in the price of oil,

- the effects of legislation or other political activity on consumption of lead free petrol,

- price changes made by competitors,

- sales promotions (own company or competitors'),

- other changes in the level of competition such as the opening of new petrol stations in the locality,

- opening hours,

- changes in the level of service offered, such as the introduction of a new convenience food store which may generate more forecourt traffic.

There will undoubtedly be still more factors which will affect the volume of petrol sold from a service station over a given period of time. Unless assumptions about these factors are clearly stated, any forecast becomes meaningless. Some companies take this principle a step further. They specify their assumptions and state their view of the likelihood of each assumption applying in reality. They then prepare three forecasts, an optimistic forecast, a pessimistic one and a 'most likely' scenario. The 'most likely' forecast is the one used for planning purposes, but the optimistic and pessimistic forecasts are useful in demonstrating just how good or how bad sales could be if certain external factors prevail.

7.3.3 Market potential

The first step in any sales forecast is to arrive at an estimation of the market potential, the maximum number of products which could be sold by all the suppliers in the market to all the customers, given complete awareness of the product. As shown in the diagram below, actual market size (i.e. the total current sales of all the suppliers) is almost invariably less than market potential. The gap between the existing market and potential market size is a function of the level of marketing effort made by the industry. The more complete consumers' knowledge of a product and its benefits, the closer the existing market will be to its potential maximum size.

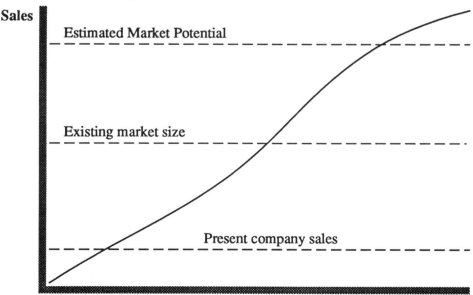

Figure 7.4 Market size and potential.　　**Level of industry marketing effort**

Equally, the share of the potential market achieved by an individual firm will depend partly on the extent of customer knowledge of its product (although other factors will also affect single company performance, such as the relative merits of its product compared to competitors, its relative price, and the extent of its distribution.)

By comparing its estimation of market potential with existing market size, the marketing department can project annual growth figures for the market as a whole and by assessing the market share likely to be achieved by their own product, sales figures can be projected. (N.B. for a totally innovative product for which no comparable market currently exists, projections will inevitably be less certain.)

There are a number of forecasting techniques which marketers may use to arrive at these figures.

(a) Survey

A common method of predicting sales, particularly for new, previously unsold products is to carry out market research. a sample of potential buyers would be questioned about their likely purchase of the product if it were on sale today. In industrial markets the sales force would often be used to ask the questions.

The main problem with this method of forecasting is the difference between peoples' 'intention to purchase' (which is, in reality, what is being asked) and their actual behaviour in the purchase situation. Of course, the researcher would pose additional questions in an attempt to get behind the respondents' real motives and intentions, but the fact remains that for almost all products and services, stated intention to purchase exceeds actual purchase, often by a considerable margin. For an existing product this need not pose a problem since existing data should be available from previous surveys which would enable the researcher to modify his 'intention to purchase' statistics into more realistic sales projections. For a new product, however, there will be no basis on which the researcher can make such a statistical adjustment. It is for this reason that the next forecasting method is often favoured.

(b) The 'delphi' method

This term can be used to describe a number of techniques which involve consulting expert opinion. As far as sales of a new product are concerned a company might seek the opinions of its own senior staff, its distributors such as retailers who may have greater contact with the end user, consultants or industry analysts such as trade journal editors or trade association staff. They will simply be asked to give their opinions of the likely sales of a new product based upon their considerable experience of the industry. Ideally their views will be used in conjunction with data collected from the survey method, with the views of the experts being used to moderate the stated intention to purchase of the potential buyers.

Very often such discussion will take place in committee and discussion will continue until a consensus is reached. Partly because of the difficulty and expense of bringing such a group of people together and partly because of the danger of discussion being dominated by a small number of strong personalities, an alternative (and strictly purer) 'delphi' method can be used. The same group of experts can be used to express the same opinions, but separately, rather than together. A questionnaire may be circulated and responses collated. A summary of these responses may then be sent out with a further set of questions, with the objective of moving the experts closer to a consensus. The procedure may even be repeated again until a consensus is reached. Such a process can be very time consuming, and its accuracy may depend upon the skill and objectivity of the contact person. This use of expert opinion is sometimes called a 'top down' method of forecasting.

(c) Sales staff forecasts

Sometimes referred to as 'bottom up' forecasting, it is often popular with companies operating in business-to-business markets with large sales forces. It involves each sales person in the company making a sales forecast for his own territory. Each sales person then discusses his forecast with his superior (e.g. area manager or sales manager) and an agreed forecast is forwarded to the co-ordinator (e.g. the marketing director) who amalgamates all the territory forecasts into one national forecast. However, sales force forecasts often suffer from lack of objectivity and, as with surveys, can be very difficult to compile where completely new products are concerned.

(d) Mini - test

A full blown test marketing exercise (such as full advertising, promotion and distribution in a TV region) would be too expensive at this stage, but for some new consumer products a more limited and less costly form of test market may be both feasible and informative. Limited but authentic trials afforded by an exercise such as the mini - test labs (see Chapter 4) would fall into this category.

Day	Daily sales	Total weekly sales	Moving average
Mon.	201		
Tue.	272		
Wed.	175		
Thur.	292		
Fri.	348		
Sat.	480	1768	295
Mon.	210	1777	296
Tue.	247	1752	292
Wed.	190	1767	295
Thur.	302	1777	296
Fri.	340	1769	295
Sat.	532	1821	304
Mon.	206	1817	303
Tue.	260	1830	305
Wed.	180	1820	303
Thur	290	1808	301
Fri	358	1826	304
Sat	501	1795	299

Table 7.1 Moving averages - beefburger sales.

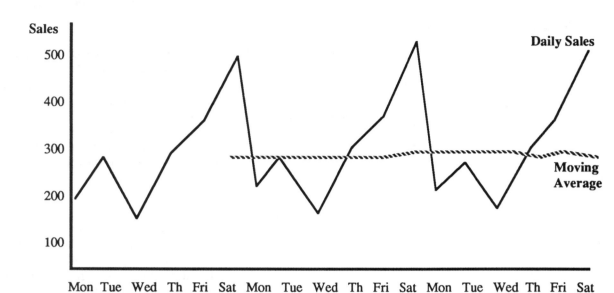

Figure 7.5 Beefburger daily sales and weekly moving averages shown in graph form.

(e) Moving average

If relevant historical data is available, which it often will be for new products which are essentially modifications of existing products, there are a number of statistical techniques which could be employed. The most simple is the moving average, which takes a series of figures and identifies the underlying trend. Let's assume that a company which sells beefburgers in a fast food setting wants to keep a weekly moving average of its sales. This means the average number of beefburgers it has sold in the last week. Therefore, each day they would have to add on the sales of that day and knock off the sales of the corresponding day a week ago before dividing the total number of beefburger sales by the number of days open in order to arrive at the new weekly moving average. As you can see from the graph, the effect of the moving average is to smooth out the rather uneven daily sales figures, thus identifying a more authentic underlying trend.

(f) Exponential smoothing

As you can see from the graph and table above, the moving average does not fully reflect the most recent changes in sales, (e.g. the excellent performance on the second Saturday) since these are counterbalanced by the sales of the previous five days. As far as daily sales trends are concerned this is usually seen as a good thing because exceptionally high or low daily figures are probably not typical and the more consistent moving average is probably more representative. However, if the figures cover much longer time periods such as annual sales the moving average does suffer from its failure to respond sufficiently quickly to recent changes. To overcome this drawback exponential smoothing can be used. This technique gives more weight to more recent data inputs. The skill resides in how the forecaster judges the representativeness of earlier compared to later data and the weightings he correspondingly attaches to each. For example, if an attractive new shop has opened close to the beefburger outlet, increasing the pavement traffic, the forecaster might want to place more emphasis on recent sales figures, since the opening of the new store, rather than the earlier figures which preceded it in order to reflect his company's increased optimism for the future in the light of this new development. The simplified example below, looking at a six week moving average of weekly sales figures attaches a weighting of 1.2 to sales after the new store opening but only 1.0 to sales before that date. As you can see in the graph (figure 7.6), the exponential smoothing technique, in this case, presents a more optimistic view of the future than the moving average.

Week	Weekly sales	Moving average	Weight	Exponential trend
1	1768	1.0		
2	1821		1.0	
3	1795		1.0	
4	1804		1.0	
5	1822		1.0	
6	1960	1828	1.0	1828
7	1952	1859	1.0	1859
8	1871	1867	1.0	1867
9	1834	1873	1.0	1873
.....................new store opens............................				
10	1901	1890	1.2	1953
11	1940	1910	1.2	1974
12	1960	1910	1.2	2040
13	1966	1912	1.2	2108
14	1995	1933	1.2	2195

Table 7.2 Weekly beefburger sales using exponential smoothing to take into account opening of new adjacent store.

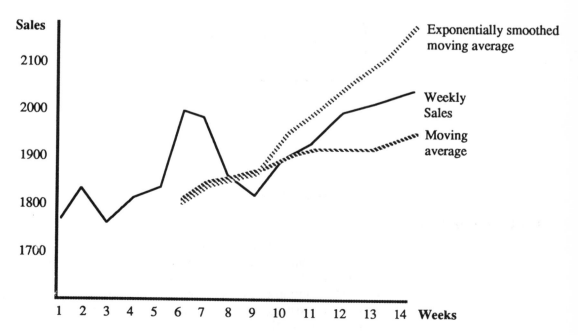

Figure 7.6 Graph showing the effects of exponential smoothing on moving averages of beefburger sales.

The graph also shows the disadvantage of a technique such as exponential smoothing. It is only as good as the person who determines the weightings. The graph above shows the beneficial effect of exponential smoothing around weeks 10 to 12, but beyond that, as the figures from before the new store opening are progressively eliminated from the moving average, the exponentially smoothed average begins to portray an over optimistic picture.

(g) Time series analysis

Both moving averages and exponential smoothing are a type of time series analysis in that they identify a trend over a period of time from a series of figures. When sales fluctuate wildly, e.g. in seasonal businesses, where significant fluctuations in sales tend to be repeated on a fairly predictable basis, the use of time series analysis can identify the underlying trend behind the sharp seasonal variations. The statistical techniques used are too complex to be described in this text, and these days, time series analysis would certainly be carried out by computer. However, suffice it to say, that as shown in the graph below (Figure 7.7), this forecasting technique would average out the peaks and troughs and would produce an underlying trend which would be of much more value for forecasting purposes than the raw sales data.

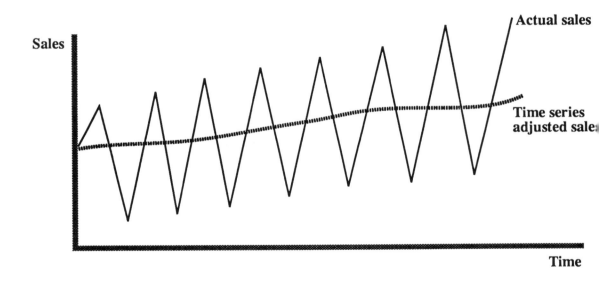

Figure 7.7 Time series analysis.

(h) Lead indicators

As we have stated on a number of occasions in this section, it can be very difficult to use standard forecasting techniques to predict sales of a genuinely new product because of the lack of existing sales data. The use of lead indicators may be a way for some companies to overcome this problem. If a new product will be complementary to an existing product, sales patterns of the existing product can be used to forecast sales of the new product. For the manufacturer of double glazed hardwood window frames sold mainly to the builders of new luxury homes, the building of up market houses will act as a lead indicator. His sales of windows are likely to rise and fall in line with the sales of such houses. Lead indicators do not need to be other products. They can be factors such as demographic trends. a manufacturer or retailer of baby products for example, will use changes in the birth rate as an important lead indicator of its own sales.

(i) Diffusion models

This is another technique which can be very useful in predicting the sales of totally new products with no past sales records. The method is based upon the product life cycle and innovation adoption models discussed in Chapter 5. Briefly, it is suggested that all new products will follow a life cycle, the exact shape of which is unknown but the general trend of which is well established. Moreover, theories such as the innovation adoption concept help us to explain how the product life cycle develops as it does. It is possible therefore to identify factors in the market place which are likely to affect the unfolding life cycle of the new product, and, using sophisticated computer techniques, project sales, at least through the introductory and growth stages. If some hard data, such as sales from a mini test lab are available to underpin the forecast it will probably have a significant degree of statistical validity. Once the product reaches the launch stage, real sales figures can be fed into the computer to update the projections on a regular basis.

7.3.4 Business analysis

As we said right at the beginning of this book, the marketer is not just interested in sales, he is interested in profitability. He will therefore need to convince himself at this analysis stage not only that the market is large enough to yield a satisfactory level of sales for the new product but that this volume of sales will be worthwhile for the company in terms of profit. Since most new products struggle to break into profitability in the short term, it is common practice to compile a cash flow forecast which will show the stage at which a profit contribution will start to be made. The three year projected cash flow below shows the anticipated performance of a new children's bicycle which will have to absorb considerable development costs due to extensive use of high performance plastic components in its construction. All figures shown are in thousands of pounds.

	Year 0	Year 1	Year 2	Year 3
Sales		10000	20000	30000
Direct costs		5000	9000	13500
Gross margin		5000	11000	16500
Development cost	5000	0	0	0
Marketing costs		10000	7000	7000
Overhead		1000	2000	2000
Net contribution	-2000	-6000	2000	7500
Cumulative cash flow	-2000	-8000	-6000	1500

Table 7.3 Cash flow forecast for a new bicycle.

As can be seen from the above forecast, which is fairly typical, even if all goes according to plan, the new product is not expected to make a small profit contribution until it has been on sale for three years. Before that the company will have to absorb heavy losses. However, if the forecasting is accurate, the product should be a good bread winner after its first three years, and on this basis it would probably be given the go-ahead by senior management.

Some projects however will be cut short at this stage, perhaps because projected profitability is too low, or negative, perhaps because the time scale before profits are due to be achieved is too long or perhaps because the assumptions on which the sales forecasts are based are deemed to be too uncertain, thus involving the company in too much risk were the project to go ahead.

7.3.5 Marketing plan development

Having forecasted sales and profits the marketer must now produce a plan explaining the marketing strategies which will be deployed by the company to ensure that those sales are achieved. All aspects of the marketing mix will need to be covered in this plan, including product policies such as branding, packaging and product benefits, pricing and distribution. In some markets distribution will be of critical importance (see section 7.7), but for most new products companies will devote considerable thought at this stage to the promotional strategies they will need to deploy to ensure that sales target are achieved.

7.4 Product development

If the new product idea has successfully negotiated the marketing analysis stage, it is time to translate it from a concept into reality. A physical product will now be developed. It is at this stage that the costs of the project really begin to escalate. There are three main steps involved in this stage of development.

7.4.1 Manufacture

The first step is to involve appropriate technical staff such as R & D staff, design engineers or industrial designers to actually make a physical product. Initially a prototype will be made, which will approximate as closely as possible to the finished product but will probably not be identical because the machinery needed to mass produce the product may not be commissioned until the prototype has successfully come through the test stage. The technical staff will need to ensure not only that the product can be manufactured efficiently but that the benefits desired by the marketing department can in fact be reproduced in the end product.

7.4.2 Packaging

As we said in Chapter 5, for many fast moving consumer goods the packaging can be as important to the success of a new product as its contents, at least in stimulating trial purchase. In the self service situation the pack must assume much of the responsibility for selling the product, so at this stage the company will invest heavily in its design. It may also need to fit in with a house style, where a company uses standard colours, logo, typeface or other trademark to strengthen corporate image. The designers of the pack will also have to bear in mind that packaging also serves a functional purpose, having to protect the product, possibly keep it fresh, make it easy to handle and use and efficient to store and transport.

Since packaging can perform such an important role, marketers must never forget that the packaging itself can be the innovation even though the product inside has not changed. There are many successful product launches which have been based on the repackaging of existing products such as UHT cream in aerosol containers, toothpaste in press top dispensers, beer in ring pull disposable glass bottles or fruit juice in small tetrapaks (the square card containers) complete with straw for immediate drinking.

Innovatory packaging can also be a fruitful source of new product development in industrial as well as consumer markets. In 1988 Bowater Containers (Heavy Duty) Ltd. introduced their 'Square Deal' bulk container made from their own high performance cardboard and with a capacity of 250 litres, twenty percent greater than the standard 200 litre steel drum normally used for the transportation of this volume of liquid. The square container is more economical on space than the round drum, it is more attractive since it can have names, logos and designs printed on it, and when empty it can be stored and transported flat. Such a basic product is an ideal example of the important role that innovation has to play in the marketing of all kinds of products.

7.4.3 Branding

The branding of a product is a vital and integral part of the development of the product and should be handled at this stage so that it can be tested along with the product itself and the packaging before a full scale launch is considered. As suggested in Chapter 5 the brand name is very important here and ideally should help to convey the benefits of the product. Names like Prontaprint are ideal in this respect. Also, names should be easy to say and recall, such as Daz or Kodak or be associated with product quality such as Gold Blend. The marketer also needs to position the product carefully in its target market (see Chapter 4) so that a brand image consistent with the benefits desired by potential buyers can be developed.

7.5 Testing

Once the product is developed it must be tested before it is launched onto the market. Despite having undergone the most thorough development process imaginable there may still be unexpected problems once the product is on sale and in use. By initiating a small scale trial it should be possible to spot these problems and rectify them before the costs of a full scale launch are incurred. Apart from the cost of launching the product nationally, any unexpected teething troubles could adversely affect the image of the product and the company, which must be avoided if at all possible. There are two basic ways of testing the product.

7.5.1 Test market

Once lab tests (either clinical or involving customers) have been satisfactorily completed, some new consumer products will be tested by putting the product on sale in the market place and monitoring its performance very carefully. However, in order to keep down the costs and minimise the adverse publicity generated as a result of any problems, the size of the market place is restricted to a small proportion of its intended market. In the U.K. the test market will often be a town (Portsmouth and Plymouth are popular choices) or a TV region (usually one of the small ones with low advertising rates such as Border or TV South West). A TV region is the most authentic test market for any new product which will use television advertising when launched nationally. For products which will only ever be promoted using the press, local radio, poster or direct mail, a much more limited test area can be perfectly acceptable. If the test market is as authentic as possible, and provided the test is of sufficient duration to assess customer adoption rather than just trial purchase, the performance of the product in the test market should offer a very accurate guide to its likely success nationally. If performance is unsatisfactory, the marketer must find out whether it is the product itself which is unacceptable to customers or whether the fault lies in some other aspect of the marketing mix. The distribution may be wrong, it may be a little expensive or, most likely, the promotion in the test market wasn't good enough, leaving too many potential buyers unaware of the product or its benefits.

Although a test market is the best way of testing most consumer products prior to a national launch, there are some disadvantages. Timing may be a problem for some products, e.g. drinks which need to be ready for a national launch before the pre-Christmas booze bonanza. Secrecy may be a problem for other products, such as the latest microcomputer, with a new wonder function which must not be brought to the attention of competitors until the last possible moment. Whatever the disadvantages of a test market, companies which skip the testing stage may live to regret it. Therefore, if there really are sound reasons for avoiding a regional test market they may consider adopting the kind of testing methods often employed by industrial marketers.

7.5.2 Testing in use

Industrial marketers generally have a much smaller number of customers than consumer marketers, so the notion of a test market will often not be suitable. Secrecy can also be important to them and the ruthless testing of the product in use is often critical. For these reasons industrial marketers will often try to reach a private arrangement with a very small number of potential customers to give their new product a full trial. A new machine, for example may need a three month trial, (or even longer) in use day and night, before the customer and the manufacturer can really be convinced that it is up to the job. Potential customers are often quite willing to be used in this way if the new product appears to offer them genuine benefits. After a few successful trials with customers who are typical of the target market the product will usually be launched straight onto the national market.

7.6 Launch

By now the costs are becoming enormous. A full scale national launch can be extremely expensive, largely due to promotional costs. TV airtime costs for example, have doubled in real terms over the last ten years. The marketing expenditure supporting a typical new fmcg product during its first year will often exceed half its total sales revenue (and be well in excess of its gross profit). As a result, manufacturers are often happy if a new brand is beginning to break even by the end of its third year on the market. Despite these huge costs, it is only a small proportion of the new consumer brands which reach this stage which become very successful - around 10%, a point demonstrated in our case study (see 7.7).

Because of these huge costs many marketers prefer a 'rolling launch', even in the comparatively small British market. This involves launching the product in one region, almost invariably a TV region in the U.K., and often one in the affluent south east. When certain sales targets are met the launch will be rolled out to a neighbouring region, and so on until the whole country is covered. This allows the marketing mix to be fine tuned if necessary as the launch proceeds.

As has already been indicated a significant promotional effort will be made with the launch of a new product. Advertising and public relations will be used to spread awareness of the product and its benefits and sales promotions such as samples, money-off vouchers and premiums will be used to stimulate trial, as will in-store merchandising. Further details of these promotional techniques can be found in Chapters 10 to 12 of this book. To illustrate the difficulty of launching a new consumer product, let's examine the following case study.

7.7 Bar wars

Budweiser is the world's best selling beer. In the autumn of 1984 it was launched on to the British market by its wealthy American parent Anheuser-Busch. There was no shortage of financial strength or marketing expertise behind the launch. Watneys, chosen to brew and distribute the beer in the U.K. predicted that it would become Britain's best selling beer within a decade. Four years after the launch it is way off that optimistic course having so far failed to capture even 1% of the British market. By comparison, a lager called Fosters, launched on the U.K. market by its Australian owners Elders IXL in 1981 has already won a 6% share of the market. The contrasting performance of these two products demonstrates the importance of the whole marketing mix in the successful launch of a new product, especially in fiercely competitive consumer markets.

Firstly the product. Bud was launched as the ice cold, all American beer, determined to disprove the belief of the average British drinker that American beer is tasteless, gassy and weak. Anheuser-Busch have steadfastly refused to modify their product to conform more closely to the growing British taste for a carbonated light coloured lager. Fosters by contrast was soon modified to appeal more strongly to the British taste buds and pub drinking habits. It lost its early beery taste and darker colour and became virtually indistinguishable from most of the other cool yellow lagers. Also very important, its strength was reduced to make it more compatible with the British habit of 'session drinking', involving the consumption of large quantities during an entire evening in the local pub. Ironically therefore, Budweiser is a strong beer that many perceive as weak. Fosters is just the opposite, but it is the Elders' product which most closely meets the needs of British consumers.

Price also has an important effect, especially for a mass market product. Due to its new lower strength Fosters pays less duty which helps it to sell for a significantly lower price than Bud.

In the British beer market, however, distribution is critical. Nearly 75% of sales come from drinkers downing draught pints in pubs, and more than half of Britain's 80,000 pubs have ties with a brewer which obliges them to sell its brands. Realising the importance of the pubs, Elders was determined to own a brewer, and when Hanson put Courage on the market they did not hesitate, especially since 5,000 tied pubs were part of the deal. After the Courage takeover, Fosters retained its licensing agreement with Watney and has since bought stakes in Scottish and Newcastle and Greene King giving it a distribution network of around 20,000 pubs and restaurants. On the other hand, Watneys chose to sell Bud only in up market pubs, and even now, draught Budweiser is on sale in only 3,500 outlets. Although Bud matches Fosters in the relatively small market for take home canned beers, its lack of distribution gives it an enormous handicap in the fight for market share.

Fosters' promotion has also been much more successful. They were rather lucky that the star of the ads, the role model of the tough Australian lager drinker, Paul Hogan, shot to world fame soon afterwards on the back of his starring role in the highly successful film *Crocodile Dundee*. But it was Fosters' skill in communication with their target audience which really made the difference. According to marketing consultant and brewing industry expert Norman Strauss:

> *'Fosters got into the British lager drinking culture with the humour of its ads and an unerring eye for the pub lifestyle. When Budweiser first came they basically were selling America without addressing British pub culture.*

Fosters have spent very heavily on advertising in the U.K. and have followed the same consistent creative theme, resulting in the ads, Paul Hogan and consequently the lager itself reaching virtual cult status among the young lager drinking target audience. By contrast, Bud's promotional activity has been much more cautious. They did sponsor British television coverage of American football, very compatible with the American image they wished to portray, but its advertising has not been memorable and the beer has not caught on, apart from in the 'yuppie' take home market in the south east. In the summer of 1988 Anheuser reorganised its international management team after the sacking of several top executives, Watney was given a greater role in the U.K. promotion of Bud and a determined effort is to be made to establish the beer as a mass market brand. But even the Watneys officials see Bud as 'a beer for the 1990's rather than the 1980's'. We will see.

Conclusion

We have seen in this chapter just how difficult and risky the new product development process is. Involving the six steps of ideas, screening, marketing analysis, product development, testing and launch it is easy to see how the process of getting a product on to the market can be both time consuming and expensive. As the Budweiser case shows, even with the backing of considerable financial and marketing resources, success is by no means guaranteed. Trying to short cut the process however can greatly increase the risks of failure, as demonstrated by some of the more notorious new product failures such as the Sinclair C5 electric vehicle. The whole point of the new product development process is to maximise the product's chances of success in the market place by thoroughly implementing the marketing philosophy. a target segment for the new product must be identified, and the company must ensure that the potential buyers in the segment do appear to want such a product. Once a need is identified the company must satisfy itself that sufficient potential sales exist to cover the costs of developing the product and yielding an adequate profit within a satisfactory time period. It must also decide how it will market the product to ensure that the projected sales are achieved. The company must then develop the actual product, always ensuring that it does offer the benefits required by potential buyers, and before launching the product it must test that it has got the whole product and marketing package right.

As we said at the beginning of this chapter, most new product ideas do fail, especially in consumer markets. The objective of the new product development process is therefore also to spot failures as well as successes. Since the costs of new product development escalate as the process unfolds, the earlier a likely failure can be identified, the lower the loss to the company will be. However, it must be stressed that no matter how far down the development process the new product has gone, once ultimate failure is feared the project should be terminated. Regardless of how much time, money and effort has already been invested in the product, continuation would only increase the losses. The marketer must always be objective, but never is this more important than during the new product development process.

Assignment

Trans World Expedition

John Taylor was 20 years old and a trainee data processing manager with a local authority. He liked his job but he also liked the outdoor life, travel and adventure. He was sometimes accused of living in a dream world. The recent Trans World Expedition had really fired his imagination. He had spent hours monitoring its progress, collecting press cuttings and magazine articles and building up a file of the expedition's activities. He even planned imaginary expeditions of his own, getting carried away with all kinds of adventures. He had a large map of the world, plotted distances, worked out budgets, considered tactics to overcome a vehicle breakdown in the Brazilian jungle or African desert.

As a boy, the same vivid imagination had made John an obsessive games player - Monopoly, Risk, Cluedo - he was an expert at all of them. Suddenly, one evening John realised that with all his 'day dreaming' about the Trans World Expedition he had virtually invented a game of his own! All the ingredients were there. All he had to do was to organise his material and think up some rules.

John set to work, every night and all weekend for several weeks perfecting his game. His parents wondered if he had gone into solitary confinement. One evening he came downstairs and invited them up to his room. There it was, his map of the world, modified with simulated jungles, deserts, mountains, snow, rough seas etc. There were some vehicles, budget cards, little boxes of provisions of various kinds, bundles of bank notes, chance cards and dice. Everything had been worked out for a Trans World Expedition game for up to six players.

John's father was amazed. He thought it was brilliant and could have commercial possibilities. As a successful businessman himself he thought he was a good judge of these things. Mr. John Taylor senior had come from a poor family but had started his own delivery service with a rusty old van in 1961. He now had a thriving transport business with a fleet of heavy lorries and light vans. He owned a large expensive house and could afford a very comfortable lifestyle.

Father and son began to discuss the possibility of starting a business to manufacture and market the game. Both were very keen on the idea, but John's natural enthusiasm was tempered by his father's greater experience and knowledge of potential pitfalls. Although he could easily afford to finance such a business, Mr. Taylor senior did not want his son to rush into any venture without doing his homework properly. He therefore suggested that he would be prepared to finance his son for an initial period of twelve months during which time John was to concentrate on research and development, with the objective of reaching a position from which he could launch the product on to the market, or, alternatively, discovering that it would be more prudent to abandon the whole idea. However, before going ahead even with this preliminary stage, John's father wanted to know how John would spend that time and money.

Task

Assume you are John Taylor and you can't wait to get your business into operation to produce your game. However, your father needs convincing first. You must write a report which will demonstrate to him that your new product idea is worth pursuing for the twelve month development period. You will also need to show that you are fully aware of the risks involved in developing and successfully launching even the best of new product ideas. You will therefore have to convince him that you will follow all the steps in the new product planning process in order to maximise your chances of success and minimise your financial losses should the idea not be quite as good as you think. You have clearly passed the idea generation stage, but you will need to show your awareness and understanding of all the steps from screening to testing, and to explain exactly how you would tackle each stage. In addition to demonstrating your knowledge of the new product development process which you will put your new board game idea through, you must also state and justify the resources, financial and non-financial, which you would need to undertake your twelve month task.

You should submit your work as a formal report.

Chapter 8
Pricing

Introduction.

Having researched the market and developed a product or service offering to meet an identified need, the product must be priced. The price is a value which the seller attaches to his product. If the customers regard this price as offering good value for money the product should sell well.

Price is a very important element of the marketing mix. It is not just an accountancy task but a central part of the marketing package that the company is to offer to its customers. There are four reasons why price is such an important element of the marketing mix. They are **quality, image, a fair price** *and* **price bands.**

8.1 Price

8.1.1 Quality

As stated elsewhere in the book, everything about the product and the company communicates messages to the customer. This is certainly true of price. Above all, the price communicates messages about a product's quality. Customers often have a very incomplete knowledge of the real attributes of competing products. They may have seen a few adverts, heard opinions from friends and tried some but not all of the product choices. In the absence of complete knowledge customers tend to assume that more expensive products are of a higher quality than cheaper competing products. The more complex the product and the less extensive the technical knowledge of the consumer, the more the conclusions will be drawn. Hi-fi equipment is a good example. The enthusiastic but rather bewildered consumer tends to gaze at the shelves of competing products, all with flashing lights, computer assisted controls and an impressive array of functions, often with very little ability to distinguish the real merits of competing products. His fear of demonstrating his abysmal ignorance to the sales assistant may also prevent him from asking as many questions as he should about the differences between the products. He may listen to them, but in the hubbub of the store they all seem to sound rather similar. In the end it is hardly surprising that the perplexed buyer, probably subconsciously, makes assumptions on quality based largely on the price tickets before his eyes.

8.1.2 Image

Some products have pose value. They are the car, the jeans, the pub or the wellies to be seen in. In some pubs the tables are covered by empty lager bottles. They are shapely bottles with attractive labels and gold foil around the neck. The lager inside costs around twice as much as the humble draught variety, although it costs no more to make and its taste may be virtually indistinguishable. The consumers are buying the image of the bottles more than the lager inside, which is why they go to the trouble of bringing the bottle as well as the glass back to the table. Those bottles are like badges. They make a statement about the buyers. They have pose value. A relatively high price is essential if a product is to have this prestige value.

8.1.3 A fair price

There is evidence of a 'plateau effect' in price. People resist a very expensive price which seems to be a 'rip-off' but are also suspicious of a very cheap price, which tends to be associated with poor quality. Most people are price conscious, seeking good value for money, but this does not usually result in their buying the cheapest available product.

8.1.4 Price bands

Although the price plateau principle almost certainly applies it may exist at different levels for different groups of buyers. When buying groceries an affluent middle class family will have a different notion of 'good value for money' than an unemployed family. Therefore marketers will often try to offer a range of products priced within certain bands roughly in line with what the customers expect to pay, e.g. £9.99, £14.99 and £19.99. This price banding is particularly popular in the clothing market.

In setting prices the marketer will aim to arrive at a price which will maximise long term profits. As we will see, this is not necessarily the highest price he can get away with, nor the lowest price at which he can afford to sell. As explained in the next section a number of factors will influence the final pricing decision. It is also important to bear in mind that there are two types of pricing decision, strategic and tactical. Strategic pricing involves the setting of a long term pricing level, the attaching of a value to the product. From time to time however, short term tactical price changes may need to be made, often for promotional reasons (see Chapter 12), which do not aim to change the basic value ascribed to the product. We will look at both strategic and tactical pricing in the next two sections.

8.2 Strategic price setting

If a company is introducing a new product or reviewing the price structure for its existing products it must take seven main underlying factors into account.

8.2.1 Costs

(a) Cost plus

In arriving at a price, most companies will start with their own costs because they will not want to sell at a price which is insufficient to cover those costs. In its simplest form this results in 'mark-up' or 'cost plus' pricing. This involves the addition of a pre-determined percentage to the firm's costs, and is particularly popular with some retailers. For example, a clothing retailer might work on a 50% mark-up. This would involve adding 50% to the purchase price of all products. A pullover bought from the manufacturer for £16 would be sold in the shop for £24. This 50% margin would cover overheads and profits. It would probably be an 'industry norm'. In other words, years of experience would have taught the industry that a 50% mark-up would be a sufficient margin to yield a satisfactory profit. This may work well as long as traditional conditions prevail, but in a changing market environment it can be very dangerous to rely on cost plus methods of pricing.

(b) Target pricing

A more scientific approach would be 'target pricing'. To start with, a breakeven analysis as shown by the diagrams would have to be worked out.

Figure 8.1 shows the firm's fixed costs. These are the costs that the firm must bear whether it manufactures one item per week or one thousand. They include costs such as rent, rates, depreciation, loan repayments, bank charges etc. The line is horizontal, because with the company's existing premises, plant and equipment these costs do not change. They are fixed at £10,000 per week.

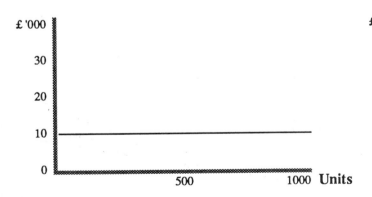

Figure 8. 1 Fixed Costs

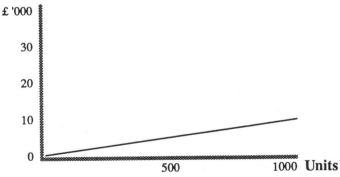

Figure 8. 2 Variable Costs

Figure 8.2 shows the firm's variable costs. If it takes 2.7 kilos of polyethylene granules to produce one plastic moulding it will take 270 kilos to produce one hundred mouldings. Labour charges also rise in proportion to the number of units produced. Thus if the variable cost of one unit is £10, the variable cost of producing 1,000 will be £10,000. Figure 8.3 simply shows the fixed and variable costs added together. The line represents the total cost of production for increasing volumes of output showing that whereas the total cost of producing one unit per week would be £10,000 the total cost of producing 1,000 units is £20,000 or £20 per unit.

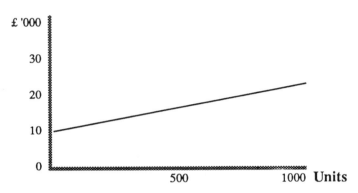

Figure 8. 3 Total Costs

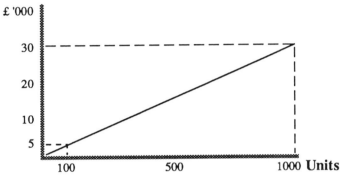

Figure 8. 4 Sales

Figure 8.4 shows the sales projections. At a selling price of £30 per unit, sales of 100 units would generate £3,000, sales of 1,000 units would generate £30,000.

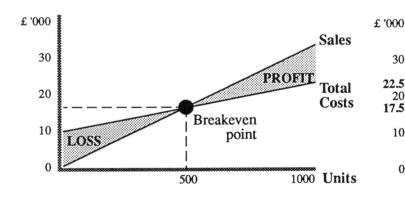

Figure 8. 5 Breakeven point

Figure 8. 6 Target pricing

It is Figure 8.5 which produces the important information. By superimposing the sales and total cost curve the break even point can be found. Where the curves intersect, the minimum level of sales for the firm to break even is shown. In this case the break even point is sales of 500 units at £30 per unit. Lower sales (to the left of the break even point) result in a loss. Higher sales (to the right of the break even point) show a profit. Using this method it is possible to compare the break even points at different pricing levels. It is possible to adopt a target pricing strategy by determining the level of sales and price level which would produce a certain target profit. As Figure 8.6 shows, if the firm wants to make a profit of £500 per week it must sell 750 units at £30 each.

The big drawback with all cost based approaches to pricing is that they are inward looking. They take into account only factors internal to the firm. In reality, factors outside the firm are much more likely to influence the price that the company will be able to charge.

However, break even analysis is very useful for establishing a base line for pricing, a price below which the firm cannot trade without making a loss.

8.2.2 Company objectives

It cannot be taken for granted however that the company will not under any circumstances be prepared to trade at a loss. Company objectives will therefore be a second relevant factor to consider when setting prices. The company's goals may influence pricing in a number of ways.

(a) Marginal costing

If a firm has spare capacity due to a shortage of work, the directors of the company may have the objective at least in the short term, of seeking work at virtually any price in order to keep the factory busy and avoid making employees redundant. They may therefore have a 'marginal costing' policy which seeks to cover the variable cost and only a contribution to overheads. The remainder of the fixed costs, which are not covered would represent a loss to the company.

The concept of marginal costing is particularly appropriate to service industries. As we saw in Chapter 6, if a commercial aircraft takes off with empty seats, the opportunity to sell those seats on that flight has been lost for ever. If the airline had managed to sell tickets for some of those empty seats, even at a greatly reduced price, it would have been better, financially, than leaving them empty. The small additional revenue brought in by the cut price tickets would have helped to offset a small proportion of the very high fixed costs. This is why airlines offer cheap stand-by tickets for passengers who are prepared to travel at very short notice on a flight with spare capacity. The same marginal costing policy leads to tour operators offering bargain holidays, again for buyers who are prepared to book at very short notice.

(b) Buying market share

Pricing at below break even level could result from a very different objective. A strong company seeking to expand may choose to sell at less than a break even price in order to drive competitors from the market place. If it believes it can sustain the losses for longer than the competition, such a pricing strategy, known as 'penetration pricing' may be viable. When it has secured a dominant position in the market, prices can gradually be increased. The Japanese penetration of the British motorcycle market was achieved in this way.

(c) High profit margins

Far from selling at a loss some companies want to achieve very high profit margins. This may be feasible with a new type of product such as the first Polaroid camera, video recorder or compact disc. With such an innovative product in a new market there may be an opportunity to make unusually high profits, with prices set well above costs. This is known as 'price skimming', the high price skimming the cream from the new market. This is often feasible because some customers are willing to pay for exclusivity and the latest developments. As time passes the firm can lower prices to draw in more price sensitive groups of customers. Price skimming enables a firm to recover its development costs quickly. This can be necessary in markets with unusually high R & D costs, e.g. pharmaceuticals, and essential in fast changing markets such as fashion.

8.2.3 Demand

A firm cannot decide on the price for a product without looking outside the company at conditions in the market place. One of the most important factors will be the level of demand. As explained in Chapter 7 products tend to follow a life cycle. During the early stages of that life cycle when demand is strong and growing it is usually possible to charge higher prices than in the later stages when demand is weakening. Products at the decline stage of their life cycle will often have to be priced at a low level. End of season fashion sales would be an example of products reaching the decline stage of a very short life cycle. Cheap black and white televisions are the result of a product having reached the decline stage of a somewhat longer life cycle.

Sometimes demand fluctuates as a result of trade cycles beyond the control of the manufacturer. When industry was depressed in the early 1980's demand for steel fell considerably. The steel producers were forced to lower their prices as a result. By the end of the decade renewed world economic growth coupled with reductions in capacity made by most steel producing countries in the early 1980's had substantially altered the balance of demand and supply and prices had risen considerably.

Demand can also fluctuate on a more regular and predictable basis. Companies can often respond in a planned way to these changes in demand by charging different prices for the same product under different conditions of market demand. This is known as 'price discrimination'.

There are many examples of price discrimination. Seasonal products such as holidays are much cheaper in the low season. The buyer of fourteen days on the Costa del Sol in May receives exactly the same product offering for a much lower price than the sun seeker who departs on August 1st. Telephone calls are cheaper when demand is less in the evening and at weekends, as are rail fares. In this way the seller can try to sell spare capacity at times of low demand by offering attractive prices.

Sometimes essentially the same product can be sold at different prices at the same time. Airline and theatre tickets would be a good example. Relatively minor changes in the product offering can lead to large changes in price, based not on the difference in cost to the seller but on the difference in demand from customers. Airlines therefore divide their market into segments such as business travellers, personal travellers and holidaymakers, and adopt a different pricing policy for each segment.

8.2.4 Perceived quality

As stated earlier consumers tend to associate a high price with high quality. This quality may be perceived in the mind of customers rather than inherent to the product, but if it is there sellers can charge for it. Leading brands of perfume can command a much higher price than less established brands. It is debatable whether the core product is significantly superior, but the augmented product, enhanced by stylish packaging and years of successful advertising has attained a very high value market position, and is priced accordingly. This is known as 'perceived value pricing.'

A variation of this pricing strategy can be adopted for the luxury versions of standard products. Known as 'product line pricing' it involves charging significantly higher prices for 'top of the range' products due to their higher perceived value. Cars would be a good example. The top of the range Cosworth Sierra costs almost three times as much to buy as the cheapest two door 1.3 litre version. It does not cost three times as much to produce. The profit margin is much higher, but the pricing is in accordance with the relative values perceived by customers.

8.2.5 The competition

Some companies base their prices largely on those charged by the competition. This 'competition oriented pricing' is very common in extremely price sensitive markets and is more likely to be practised by the weaker companies. Petrol companies often respond to competitors' price changes within hours. Supermarkets and retailers of electrical goods in the same town will keep a keen eye on prices charged by their competitors. It is now common for retailers to offer to refund customers the difference if they can find the same product sold cheaper elsewhere.

Competition oriented pricing can be very dangerous, leading to rash price cutting and a downward spiral in prices which only leaves the industry as a whole much less profitable. Many of the most successful companies are those which have refused to cut prices, relying instead on their higher quality, better service or some other benefit which offers the customer value for money. Kelloggs do not try to be as cheap as their own label competitors. Rover refused to respond to competitors' heavy discounting when it introduced its new 800 model because of the adverse effect such price cutting could have on perceived quality.

In today's highly competitive markets however, virtually all companies must take some account of the prices charged by competitors. However good the rest of their marketing mix, few companies can afford to be too far out of line with the rest of the industry.

8.2.6 Distributors

In some industries distributors exert a powerful influence over the pricing strategies of manufacturers. Today, the large retail chains in the U.K. often dominate their smaller suppliers (see Chapter 9) and can, if they choose to, more or less dictate prices to them.

Even where the manufacturer is stronger and is in full control of his pricing strategy, if he sells through distributors he must take account of their needs. Retailers and wholesalers need a sufficient margin to make an adequate profit. It would not be sensible for a manufacturer to set a price which was very attractive to consumers but did not allow a sufficient margin to interest the distributors. Without a good network of distributors the manufacturer's market share may fall however competitive his prices.

8.2.7 Legal constraints

In some countries there will be extensive legal constraints on pricing. There are no longer statutory controls on pricing in the U.K. but there are certain rules designed to ensure that consumers are not misled by pricing. Under the Consumer Protection Act 1987 for example, the once common practice of buying in special cheap goods for sales and advertising them at apparently massively reduced prices is no longer permitted. Only genuine price reductions can be marked up or advertised. Goods displaying a price reduction (e.g. Now only £19.95 - was £35) must have been previously stocked and sold at that higher price.

8.3 Tactical pricing

A company's pricing strategy will probably result not in a single fixed price but a price range, a minimum and a maximum price at which the company will sell. Tactical pricing refers to the task of setting specific prices within that range and altering them if necessary as conditions change or to secure a short term tactical advantage over the competition. There are many examples of pricing tactics, some of which are described below.

8.3.1 Promotional discounts

Sales promotions are described in much more detail in Chapter 12. They are a very popular form of price cutting. To be effective they must offer the customer sufficient incentive to buy extra, or to change brands, and they must have a time limit in order to induce action now. It is also believed that price discounts which are clearly of a short term nature do not have a detrimental effect on the product's perceived quality, because consumers see them as a promotion and not as the 'real price'.

8.3.2 Loss leaders

Loss leaders would be a small number of products promoted at an incredibly cheap price (a loss making price). They are designed to attract customers into the store in the hope that, once there, they will also buy many normally priced items. Very popular with retailers, especially supermarkets at one time, this pricing tactic has become less common in recent years.

8.3.3 Psychological pricing

How many prices in the shops end in 99p? Probably the overwhelming majority. £4.99, £9.99, £19.99 etc. There are good psychological reasons for charging £9.99 rather than £10. Research has shown that although many customers will mentally round up the price a significant number will round it down, particularly if, subconsciously, they want to give themselves a reason for buying.

8.3.4 Customary pricing

Sometimes customers become accustomed to seeing a certain price for a product or product type. It becomes difficult to raise the price without having a major adverse effect on demand. Chocolate bars would be a good example. Rather than increase the price a supplier might be tempted to reduce the amount of product, aided perhaps by a creative re-design of the packaging. These tactics led to the phenomenon of shrinking bars of chocolate in the inflationary 1970's, which in turn created the conditions for the success of Yorkie, as Rowntree recognised the demand for a decent sized, chunky, chocolate bar.

8.4 The case of low alcohol beer

In 1988 Allied Breweries spent £3.5 million advertising Swan Light, an Australian lager with an alcohol content of only 0.9%. A market which was virtually non existent as recently as 1985, has suddenly exploded, helped by political and social factors such as increasing pressure against drink driving and longer pub opening hours. Although low alcohol beer still accounts for less than 1% of the market, over a hundred million pints per annum are already being drunk.

Don Swan, the sun tanned Australian star of the Swan Light TV commercial, was designed to appeal to 18 to 30 year old males in professional occupations. His message is that Swan Light is ideal with lunch for those with a busy afternoon ahead. And it tastes good! This is the message reinforced by Lennie Henry and other stars brought in to raise the image of low alcohol beers in an attempt to overcome the memory of the rather plastic, watered down taste of the early low alcohol and alcohol free beers.

And it seems to be working. Low alcohol's current 1% of the market is predicted by many industry experts to grow to around 5% over the next few years. And that is big business because low alcohol drinks are very profitable since they escape excise duty.

The threshold for duty is 1.2% alcohol. Below that level no duty is paid. The normal pint, containing 3-4% alcohol contributes 20p in duty to the Exchequer. Does this mean that low alcohol beers cost 20p per pint less than ordinary beer? Certainly not! Why should they? The customer does not perceive them as being worth any less. In fact they tend to cost more, most being priced towards the top end of the beer price range. After all they do offer benefits, being able to drive the car, being able to work efficiently in the afternoon, being seen as 'smart', which are not offered by conventional beers.

This perceived value pricing is making low alcohol beers a very profitable business to be in, which explains why the big brewers are happily spending so much money advertising their low alcohol products.

(Source: 'Sober approach to heady profit', *Sunday Times* 19/6/88.)

Assignment — Apricot Dance and Fitness Studio

The Apricot Dance and Fitness studio is a women's health and fitness centre run by fitness fanatic Rachel Davis, only 26 years old but already a very successful business woman. Husband Andrew, the other director, is a PE teacher and is heavily involved in the business. One full time secretary is employed together with a part time cleaner and several part time instructors.

The studio has been open in Crewe for two years and is located in the town centre. Facilities include a large gym, a small gym, a weight training room, changing facilities with sauna and sun bed and a pleasant coffee lounge / bar.

The studio is open from 10am to 9pm on weekdays and from 9am to 6pm on Saturdays, but is closed on Sundays, despite a number of requests from members, largely because Rachel does not think she can forego her one remaining weekly lie-in.

The core activity is a thirty minute dance session which takes place hourly. Rachel, unwilling to tear herself away from the practical side of the business still leads many of the sessions, but three very reliable part time assistants lead some of the sessions and would be keen to take on more. The small gym is used for specific activities such as yoga, self defence, judo and aerobics etc which tend to take place around two or three times per week and are all supervised by specialist instructors. Despite some growth in these activities the small gym is heavily under utilised. Use of the weight training facility is free to members but after an initial burst of enthusiasm, most members now largely ignore the facility. Andrew runs a supervised weight training programme three evenings per week which is better attended. There appears to be a strong demand from men for such a facility but Apricot is currently unable to respond to this demand due to the lack of a male changing area.

All clients have to be members, apart from the well advertised, monthly taster sessions which are open to anybody, and are still the studio's main source of new members. Membership costs £40 per annum, a figure which has not risen since Apricot's opening. Members also pay £1 for each organised session they attend. This charge does not vary regardless of the type of activity or the time of day. There are charges for the sunbed and sauna which are quite well used and income is also generated by the bar. However, although the lounge is well used by women for coffee and soft drinks during the day, custom at the bar during the evening is disappointingly low despite the fact that prices are held slightly below pub prices in the hope of attracting more trade.

The clientele of the studio varies during the day. The morning sessions are very popular with mothers of young children who have not yet returned to work and whose children are probably attending a morning nursery. The lunch time sessions are well attended by working women. There is a lull most afternoons, with retired women forming the majority of the small number of customers followed by a popular early evening period as people call after work, starting with teachers from 4pm and ending with the ambitious career minded women at 7pm. The evenings are mainly quiet apart from some popular yoga and aerobics classes. Saturday mornings are busy but the afternoons very quiet.

Although Apricot grew very rapidly during its first year and Rachel still makes a good living from the business, sales seem to have reached a plateau. This is disappointing because Rachel hoped to make sufficient profit to open a second centre after two years, a target which is not now going to be met. If Apricot is going to expand changes will have to be made to improve profitability.

One of Rachel's neighbours, and members, Lesley James, worked in marketing before leaving to start a family. Arising from casual conversations about improving Apricot's marketing, Lesley has agreed, for a small fee to help Rachel, and has started by carrying out a market research survey of studio members. Three focus groups were held, one with non-working mothers, one with retired members and one with working women to gather general views about the studio and its facilities. This information was used to compile a questionnaire which was sent to all members. A year's free membership was promised to the first completed questionnaire drawn from a sack, and a response rate of over 90% was achieved.

The main points arising from the survey were as follows.

1. Virtually everybody considers Apricot's charges to be very reasonable with only a handful considering them to be expensive.

2. Most regard the choice of physical activities as excellent. In fact the majority of members would not object to dance sessions being less frequent at off peak times.

3. Weight training is not very popular and not considered by most members to be very feminine, but a significant number stated that their husbands would be interested in such a facility.

4. Although some women, mainly from the retired group, place a high value on the female-only nature of the studio, the majority expressed a preference for a mixed club. This view is strongly held by unmarried members, and young married women also stated that they would be more likely to visit the studio and the bar in the evenings if their husbands could accompany them.

5. There is little demand for the studio's facilities on Saturday afternoons but a good demand for Sunday morning and evening opening especially if membership were mixed and the social aspect of the club were improved.

6. On the social side a number of members during the focus groups had compared Apricot unfavourably with other sports clubs such as the local squash club. Here activities such as discos are organised and the bar is much more of a social meeting place. The survey showed most members to be in favour of such developments.

7. Other new services are also in demand. In particular many members would like Apricot to become more of an all round health centre. Sessions on diet, make-up, skin care etc would be popular as would more individual counselling, with a tailored individual health and fitness programme much in demand, as much for its motivational as for its educational benefits.

8. Many members considered Apricot's promotion to be poor, and felt that more people would join if the studio's facilities were more widely understood. Some members felt that the monthly free group sessions may be rather intimidating for some people who may prefer a more low key, personal introduction to the studio.

9. Retired women felt that a more limited and cheaper way of using the facility, preferably with a tailor made programme for older people could produce a lot more interest from people of their own age group.

TASK

Both Rachel and Lesley felt that the survey had produced some very worthwhile information. Rachel was still determined to expand Apricot by opening new studios, but felt that she ought to get the formula right in Crewe before proceeding. With this in mind she asked Lesley to write a full report outlining ways in which Apricot's profitability could be improved. In particular Rachel felt that the report should concentrate on two areas:

(a) how Apricot's mix of services could be changed for the better,

(b) a review of Apricot's current pricing policy.

If, however Lesley felt there were important recommendations to make in other areas, or any additional information requirements, Rachel was happy that they should be mentioned in the report.

Write Lesley James' report.

Chapter 9
Distribution

Introduction

Having developed a product or a service and determined a price, the company needs to decide how to distribute it to customers. This is the third 'P' in the marketing mix and is all about place. In fact distribution is about places - places where the product will be made, stored, bought and used. Two words accurately describe the concept of distribution, 'availability' and 'accessibility'. A company needs to ensure that its products are available, that it is in fact possible for customers to buy them. This sounds obvious, but in the 1960's and 1970's lack of availability was one of the big failings of British industry. As competition increases however, being widely available may still not be enough to ensure success in the market place. Consumers can be notoriously fickle and very lazy. They will often opt for the product which is easiest to buy rather than the ideal product. It must always be an important objective of any marketer to make his product or service more accessible (easier to buy) than those of his competitors (although, as we will see later in the chapter, the exclusivity associated with some 'difficult to buy' products can be highly valued by some customers).

9.1 Basic definitions

Place - As an element of the marketing mix, place or distribution involves those management tasks concerned with making the product available and accessible to buyers and potential buyers.

Availability - Availability describes the fact that a product or service is capable of being acquired and used by buyers and potential buyers.

Accessibility - A product is accessible if buyers and potential buyers find it easy and convenient to acquire and use.

Physical distribution - The management tasks concerned with efficient movement of goods and services both into the company and outwards to the customer.

Channels of Distribution - The system of organisations through which goods or services are transferred from the original producer to end users.

Middlemen - Middlemen, or distributors, are those organisations which handle goods or services in the channel of distribution between the producer and the end users.

9.2 The economics of middlemen

There is a cost attached to using middlemen. They have to be given their cut of the profits. So why do manufacturers use middlemen, and so keep all the profits for themselves? There are two reasons why many manufacturers feel it is beneficial to use middlemen. They are lower costs and higher sales.

9.2.1 Lower costs

(a) Fewer lines of contact

The basic economic reason for the use of middlemen is that they reduce the lines of contact between producers and end users as shown in the diagram below.

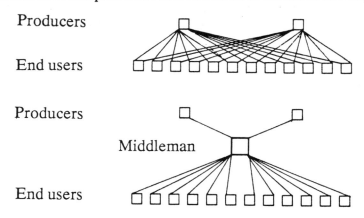

Figure 9.1 The economics of middlemen.

Without the middleman there are 24 line of contact. With the middleman there are 14 lines of contact. The cost of delivering goods to one middleman rather than twelve end users will be much lower. Clearly it is more efficient to use middlemen. Imagine how much more efficient it becomes when there are millions of customers rather than twelve.

(b) Lower stockholding costs

Using middlemen saves the producer money because he does not need to hold as much stock. The middlemen assume the responsibility of holding sufficient stocks to meet end user demand.

(c) Lower sales administration costs

If the manufacturer is dealing with thousands of customers his sales administration costs will be enormous. He will need to employ a small army in tele-sales for incoming orders and the associated paperwork with confirmation of order slips, delivery notes, invoices and statements will be very costly. Dealing with a relatively small number of distributors only relieves the manufacturer of a large proportion of these costs.

(d) Lower sales force costs

With distributors a much smaller sales force can be employed. The distributors' sales people perform that task in their local area leaving the manufacturer's sales force to sell to the distributors themselves and possibly to a small number of very important customers.

9.2.2 Higher sales

The second broad reason for using distributors is that it should enable a manufacturer to increase his sales. There are three main reasons for this.

(a) Accessibility

Being placed in the area, hopefully in a good location, distributors make it much easier for customers to buy.

(b) Knowledge of the local market

The locally based distributor is also much closer to his customers in other ways. He understands their needs and priorities much better than a remote manufacturer. This would be especially true when referring to export sales.

(c) Specialisation

Manufacturers specialise in manufacturing. That's what they are good at. Retailers specialise in displaying large numbers of goods and making it easy for customers to buy them. That's what they are good at. Time after time research into successful companies has shown that an important factor in their success is that they concentrate on what they're good at, but do not try to be good at everything.

9.2.3 The functions of middlemen

The basic role of middlemen therefore is to make the product more available and accessible to customers and potential customers in a more cost effective way than could be achieved by the manufacturer alone. They do this by performing some or all of the following functions:

(a) Breaking bulk

They take goods in the large quantities which the manufacturers want to sell but are prepared to sell them in the much smaller quantities that end users usually wish to buy.

(b) Storage

This relieves manufacturers' storage problems and costs and increases availability to customers.

(c) Stockholding

The buffer stocks held by distributors reduce delivery times to end users and reduce the risk of stock - outs.

(d) Delivery

Whereas manufacturers typically deliver to distributors with 38 ton articulated lorries, the distributor probably delivers to many small customers with a small van, thus increasing accessibility.

(e) After sales service

Dealers often provide a valuable local point for after sales service, as in the case of cars or electrical goods.

(f) Price setting

Distributors may have the authority to decide their own pricing or may be required to sell at prices laid down by the manufacturer.

(g) Promotion

Local distributors often perform a valuable role promoting manufacturers' products on a local basis. Sometimes manufacturers will recognise this and reach co-operative advertising agreements with their middlemen with both parties sharing the cost.

(h) Personal selling

This can take two forms. A local retail outlet provides an obvious sales advantage to a manufacturer. For industrial products a similar cash and carry type sales desk may exist but the distributor may also have its own sales force calling on local companies. This is a valuable extension to the manufacturer's selling capabilities.

(i) Extending credit

Industrial distributors often sell on credit to their customers thus removing a significant cash flow burden from the manufacturer.

9.3 Physical distribution

Physical distribution management (sometimes called 'PDM') is of great importance to all companies. It is an important factor in ensuring the availability of products to customers but it is very difficult to carry out efficiently and can become very costly. Many companies therefore have specialist managers in charge of PDM. They are responsible for designing and operating all the systems concerned with controlling the movement of goods into through and out of the factory. It is the job of the distribution manager to ensure that the company delivers the right goods to the right place at the right time and in the right condition.

The aim of PDM is quite simply to achieve the highest possible level of customer service at the lowest possible cost, an objective which is simple to state but extremely difficult to implement. Let's look at the two different aspects of this objective.

9.3.1 Maintaining a high level of customer service

Many factors contribute to giving customers the impression that they have received a high level of service, but we can highlight a number of factors that do come within the distribution manager's control.

(a) Short delivery time

Nobody wants long waiting lists. Consumers certainly don't want to wait at all. They want the item to be on the shelf. Retailers therefore want quick delivery to ensure that they never do run out of stock. In an ideal world deliveries would be made on a daily basis, but in practice that would be extremely expensive for the manufacturer, so weekly or twice weekly deliveries are more likely to be the norm for many products.

(b) Reliable delivery times

In reality, provided delivery times are not ridiculously long, most customers are less worried about the speed of deliveries than the reliability of the delivery promises. Broken delivery promises are extremely irritating and will be enough to make many buyers change suppliers in future. A manufacturer therefore must not fall into the trap of promising short delivery times which will be difficult to meet. It is far better to offer a slightly less attractive delivery time and to guarantee its reliability.

(c) Condition of goods

It is no use ensuring that the right goods arrive in the right place at the right time if they have been damaged in transit. If goods arrive in the wrong condition they are not 'available' in the full sense of the term. Strict control over packaging, handling and transportation are critical if goods are to arrive in the right condition.

(d) Prompt replacement of defective goods

If goods do not arrive in perfect condition prompt replacement will at least make the customer feel a little better about the supplier.

(e) After sales service

For many products, e.g. machinery, vehicles or computers, the customer is equally concerned that the product remains in the right condition. Failing that, the customer wants the manufacturer to get it back into the right condition. The manufacturer therefore has to manage the distribution of spare parts and servicing. This may be through dealers or it may be direct from the factory. One of the claims of Xerox is that every Xerox photocopier in the USA would be no more than three hours away from a maintenance engineer. Very good customer service, but a very expensive guarantee to honour.

(f) Minimum order size

In general, buyers like the minimum order size to be the smallest quantity they ever want to buy. Manufacturers prefer to supply in economic quantities. PDM must try to strike a balance between the costly implications of having no minimum order size and the possible loss of goodwill if an unreasonably large minimum order size is imposed.

9.3.2 Minimising distribution costs

Distribution costs are a significant proportion of the total costs of many companies. Certain industries tend to have very high distribution costs. Some examples are shown in the table below.

Machinery 9%

Paper 15%

Wood 17%

Chemicals 21%

Metals 22%

Food 25%

Table 9.1 Distribution costs by industry as a proportion of total costs.

It is easy to see how a food processing company would regard the control of distribution costs as a key management activity. However, to manage distribution costs effectively they must be broken down further. The table below shows how distribution costs are typically made up across manufacturing industry in general.

Administration 17%

Transport 29%

Handling 8%

Packaging 12%

Warehousing 17%

Inventory 17%

Table 9.2 Breakdown of distribution costs.

In recent years technological developments have enabled companies to make efficiency improvements in some of these areas of distribution cost. Computers have certainly helped to reduce the cost of order processing and are also beginning to have an effect on the control of warehousing and materials handling with specialised computer software now available to control those activities. Multi-tier racking and even materials handling robots are contributing to greater efficiency. The widespread adoption of bar coding in consumer goods industries is leading to significant cost savings. Packaging improvements are continuously being made. Automatic packaging machinery and the use of cheaper raw materials are also having a beneficial effect on costs. Glass bottles are being replaced by much cheaper PET (plastic) and by tetra-bricks (the card containers, in which fruit juice is usually packed) which are so much more efficient to store, handle and transport. Some distribution costs are much more difficult to reduce. Although lorries have become bigger and more efficient, the only way to make meaningful cuts in transport costs is to reduce customer service by delivering less often. Inventory (or stock holding) costs are also very difficult to tackle without reducing customer service. In effect inventory costs rise in direct proportion to the level of stocks held. Reducing these costs therefore means holding less stock which inevitably means reduced customer service as stock - outs become more common and delivery times longer. In fact some aspects of distribution costs have risen. Storage costs are growing with the cost of premises, especially in the southern half of the country. Insurance costs have also increased as have shrinkage (pilfering) problems, especially at the retail end of the distribution channel.

PDM must therefore be constantly striving to reduce the costs of physical distribution but must avoid doing so at the expense of customer service. Those distribution costs which can be reduced by improving internal efficiency must be tackled first. The distribution manager is always trying to reconcile two incompatible objectives. Maximising customer service and minimising distribution costs are contradictory. The one normally improves only at the expense of the other. The distribution manager must therefore try to strike the right balance between the two. He must strive to reduce distribution costs to the lowest level compatible with the maintenance of good customer service. Costs must be kept as low as possible, but as a marketer we must always put the needs of customers first even if this results in slightly higher costs and prices.

9.4 Channels of distribution

The marketer has a number of decisions to make as far as channels of distribution are concerned. He must decide how many middlemen (if any) are required between the manufacturer and the consumer, what kind of distribution network would be most suitable for his product, how to select individual distributors and how to manage the system once it is in place.

9.4.1 Channel levels

The number and type of middlemen in a channel of distribution can vary as shown in Figure 9.2.

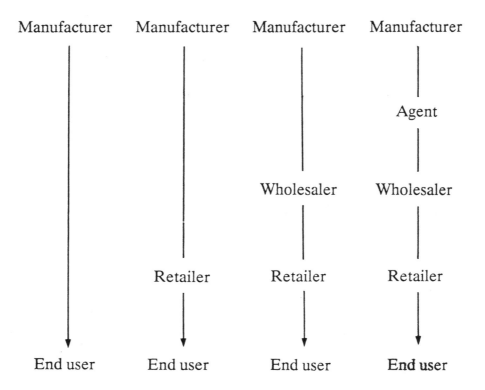

Figure 9.2 Channels of distribution.

As shown in the diagram, the number of levels or tiers between a manufacturer and end user could be as few as none (a zero level channel) or could be as many as three (a three level channel). It could even be more but that would be fairly unusual. One level or two level channels are by far the most common.

A zero level channel is more correctly termed direct marketing and is growing in popularity. Mill shops attached to large textile factories are becoming more common and many small companies concentrate on selling their products direct to the end user.

In consumer markets the one level channel is becoming the most common because of the growth of the large retail chains who buy direct from the manufacturer rather than from wholesalers. In business to business markets, many transactions are made without middlemen, but where channels are used one agent or wholesaler between manufacturer and end user will be the most normal arrangement.

Two level channels are still common in consumer markets since many small retailers do not have the buying power to purchase directly from the manufacturer and therefore have to buy their stock through wholesalers. Sometimes small retailers band together into a buying syndicate (e.g. Spar, or Mace) to increase their buying power. An organisation like Spar in reality acts as a wholesaler, but since it is owned by its customers (the retailers) its margins are lower than those of an independent wholesaler.

Agents differ from distributors in that they do not normally hold stock or own it. They concentrate on promoting and selling manufacturers' products and receive a commission on all sales from the manufacturer, who delivers the product straight to the customer. Such practices are common with items such as machinery which is often purpose built or would be very expensive to hold in stock for long periods of time.

Most manufacturers will not choose between these different channel levels. They will adopt some combination of all four. A computer manufacturer for example will deal directly with its largest customers who are spending very large sums of money. Medium sized computer systems typically bought by smaller businesses will be sold through professional local dealers, fully qualified and competent to provide advice, training, installation, servicing etc. Their cheapest products, perhaps a small home computer, may be available from many high street shops and small computer dealers. If the manufacturer has a minimum order size, the small dealers will have to buy through wholesalers. The manufacturer may also use agents, especially abroad, where the company may not be well known, which makes distributors reluctant to carry stocks.

9.4.2 Channel networks

Not all one level or two level channels are the same. Distribution networks can vary and a manufacturer needs to decide on the type of network which best suits his product. There are three broad choices.

(a) Intensive distribution

The aim of an intensive distribution strategy is to secure as many outlets as possible in order to maximise availability and accessibility to potential buyers. This type of distribution is most suited to products where convenience of purchase and impulse buying are important factors influencing sales. Examples of products requiring intensive distribution would be petrol, cigarettes, ice cream and crisps. The manufacturer of such products wants his brands on sale in every conceivable outlet. A regional manufacturer of soft drinks for example will want his products on sale in supermarkets, small grocery shops, fish and chip shops, newsagents, confectioners, pubs, cafes, fast food outlets, vending machines, and any other outlet which will stock the product.

(b) Exclusive distribution

At the other end of the spectrum, availability and accessibility are deliberately restricted. Prestige products which need to protect their image of up-market exclusivity will grant sole dealerships to distributors in each area. The dealers will be chosen very carefully because their image and competence must match up to the high standards demanded by the manufacturer. You would not expect to find Porsche cars sold by any old back street garage. A dealer for IBM business computers has to meet a number of very stringent requirements.

(c) Selective distribution

Selective distribution involves the use of more than one but less than all of the distributors who are willing to stock the product in a particular area. The manufacturer may want the distribution of the product to be as intensive as possible but may also want to protect the image of the company and its brands by exercising some control over the type of retailers selling it. A good example would be white goods (e.g. washing machines), brown goods (e.g. televisions) and other domestic appliances. Competition is fierce and a manufacturer will want his brand on show in as many retail outlets as possible, but there will still be some criteria that retailers are required to meet, such as minimum stock holding levels and standard of premises.

9.4.3 Vertical integration

In addition to the three broad classes of channel network described above, other variations are possible. Vertical integration describes a co-ordinated channel of distribution where all the members work together for the common good with the aim of achieving greater efficiency and therefore a competitive advantage. Vertically integrated channels may or may not be under common ownership.

In the past Burtons was the ideal example of a vertically integrated channel. Their motto used to be 'from sheep to shop' and they did indeed control all activities involved in transforming the wool from the sheep's back into a made to measure suit bought at a Burton's high street store. Nowadays Burtons is a retailer, sourcing much of its merchandise from other manufacturers.

Thorntons is a good example of 'forward integration'. The Derbyshire manufacturer of quality confectionery has gradually developed a network of its own high street shops.

C & J Clark the shoe manufacturers, practise both forward and backward integration, acquiring retail outlets at one end of the chain of demand and building up a substantial shoe machinery business at the other.

Channel members in vertically integrated channels do not have to be under common ownership. Many large retail chains practise backward integration by exercising very tight control over their suppliers. Franchising is a very popular method of forward integration. Benetton shops for example are all franchises. A Benetton shop is an independent business which was started by its owner under a franchise arrangement with Benetton. Under a franchising agreement the franchisor (Benetton) agrees to supply the shop with merchandise, and to provide management and promotional help. In return the franchisee (the individual store) agrees to buy exclusively from Benetton and to pay the franchisor a royalty on all sales. Franchising is an increasingly popular form of business ownership.

9.4.4 Selecting channel members

For all but the most intensive of distribution networks the manufacturer will need to exercise some control over the recruitment of channel members. A number of criteria may be used.

(a) Image of the product

The more exclusive and expensive the product, the more up-market the image of the distributor will have to be.

(b) The standing of the company

Distributors buy a large volume of goods on credit from manufacturers. The manufacturer will therefore want to satisfy himself that all his distributors are of sound financial standing and able to meet their debts.

(c) Complexity of the product

Technical products such as business computers demand a high level of knowledge on the part of dealers. The ability to train buyers' staff and to service products may also be required.

(d) Perishability of the product

Products requiring special equipment such as freezers can obviously be sold only through outlets with the correct equipment. Manufacturers requiring intensive distribution (e.g. ice cream companies) will often supply the middleman with suitable equipment.

(e) Location of customers

Manufacturers will obviously want more middlemen in areas where they have the greatest concentration of customers.

(f) Competitors' strategy

It is normal for manufacturers to strive to match the distribution strategy of their competitors. It is however possible to take the opposite view. Avon cosmetics developed a significant niche in the market by following an alternative distribution strategy and meeting the needs of those customers who prefer to choose their cosmetics at home.

9.4.5 Managing the distribution network

The aim of the manufacturer is to maximise co-operation and minimise conflict in the channel. This is an important management task because conflict is inherent to the channel system, simply because everyone in the channel wants to maximise his profits and there is a great temptation to try to do so at the expense of other channel members.

Distributers in competition with each other will also inevitably come into conflict. A certain amount of conflict is healthy as competing retailers for example, seek to maximise their market share by improving customer service. However, a tactic they often turn to is price cutting and this can have detrimental effects on the manufacturer's brand image and, in the longer term, on the industry as a whole.

Manufacturers must therefore attempt to manage their distributors. Ideally, they should be firm on pricing policies and the amount of discounting allowed by individual channel members, particularly if discounting is used to poach customers from other channel members. Of course it is only if the manufacturer is IBM and the distributors are all much smaller companies, that this kind of strict channel management becomes perfectly feasible. If, however, the manufacturer is a small food processing company and the distributor is a major supermarket chain, the manufacturer will have little control over the behaviour of the distributor, (see 9.5).

Manufacturers may also need to motivate distributors to sell their brands. If a retailer stocks four similarly priced washing machines from four rival manufacturers why should he try to sell brand X rather than brand Y? The manufacturer of brand Y will always want to motivate distributors to sell his brand. He will try to do this by offering the distributor healthy margins, by offering support in the form of display material, quality brochures, and help with advertising. He will try to build dealer loyalty by organising conferences (perhaps in attractive locations such as the Canary Isles in the autumn), by running competitions for dealers and their staff with worthwhile prizes for dealers who meet certain sales targets, and they will devise a regular stream of promotional offers.

9.5 Channel Power

It has been implied so far in this chapter that the manufacturer is in control of the channel, selecting, controlling and motivating channel members. Traditionally this would have been the case, but increasingly in the U.K., channels of distribution are becoming retailer dominated due to the phenomenal growth in retailer power since the Second World War.

Very often now retailers control manufacturers. They specify the kind of products they want to stock, the quantities, the delivery dates, the packaging and often the price. The custom of the large retailers is so valuable to the manufacturer that they have to go along with all the retailer's wishes. A result of these developments has been the growth of own label products, especially in groceries, but also in clothing, electrical goods and even furnishings. As a supplier of an own label product the manufacturer is reduced virtually to the status of a sub-contractor. Some of the larger manufacturers have resisted this trend. Kelloggs proudly proclaim that 'if it's not Kelloggs on the packet it's not Kelloggs in the packet'. Kelloggs can be sure of their shelf space in the supermarkets because their brands are demanded by the public. Smaller companies with lesser known brands cannot afford to be so strong willed. They have seen their own market share eroded by own label goods and eventually have had to become an own label producer to keep their plant fully occupied.

Channel power can therefore rest with the manufacturer or the distributor. In practice the larger companies will almost always wield power over the smaller ones, but whereas the balance of power used to rest with the manufacturers it is currently swinging steadily in the retailers' direction.

Assignment Detectagas Ltd

Inspired by reports in newspapers about explosions and fires caused by a build up of gas, often from tiny gas leaks which had gone unnoticed for some time, Bill Owens has invented a very accurate and compact method of detecting escaping gas. The gas detector is so small that together with an alarm system it can be incorporated in a box no larger than an eight centimetre cube. Bill's real stroke of genius was to realise that if the alarm were to use mains power rather than batteries it could be incorporated into an ordinary looking domestic plug. This would be very convenient since the electrical socket would form a permanent anchorage point. Sockets are usually situated in close enough proximity to gas appliances and plugged into the wall the detector would not look out of place.

Bill has produced ten prototype units and had them strenuously tested. They work very well. They can detect very small traces of gas which makes them emit a loud high pitched intermittent sound which can be heard outside the house if the owners are not at home.

People are becoming ever more safety conscious. Burglar alarms have penetrated a significant proportion of households. The market for small smoke detectors has grown rapidly in recent years and Bill's gas detector meets a very similar need. Potentially the market is every household which uses gas, and many houses would require two or three since one needs to be located close to each gas appliance. Many houses have a gas boiler, gas fire and a gas cooker. Bill realises of course that penetration of the market would be slow and that some segments would be more likely buyers than others. However, he is convinced that there is a potentially huge market awaiting his invention and has formed a company, Detectagas Ltd. to exploit it. He has also taken the precaution of patenting his product. There are other methods of detecting gas which cannot be covered by his patent but they are all less compact and would require housing in a unit roughly twice the size of Bill's.

The components for the gas detector cost a total of £4.80 if bought in sufficiently large quantities. Using a sub-contract assembler, Bill has been quoted £8.70 per unit, ex works and excluding VAT, provided he orders in batches of at least 1,000. Bill would of course have to add on his own profit margin to cover promotional costs, general overheads and postage and packing costs which would amount to around 85p if units were sent individually to customers.

Bill has done some costings and has worked out that if he leased a small factory unit and employed his own assembly staff he could produce the units for around £8.00 provided he could sell at least 10,000 a year. If he used a sub-contractor from the Far East, costs would come down further, possibly to as little as £7 provided at least 50,000 units could be ordered.

Bill's research suggests that a price tag to the end user of no more than £19.95 is essential if it is to prove sufficiently attractive to the mass market. He feels that his big problem is distribution.

Task

You have been called in as a marketing consultant by Bill Owens. Write a report which outlines the distribution options for Detectagas, explaining the advantages and disadvantages of each option. You should also explore the implications for pricing and marketing communications of each option before making recommendations and summarise the reasons for your choice of distribution channel.

Chapter 10
Marketing Communications

Introduction

In this chapter we will examine the nature of communications in general and marketing communications in particular. We will look at the kind of tasks that marketing communications have to achieve and at the methods which can be used to carry out these tasks successfully. We will also consider the methods used by organisations to measure the success of their communications.

10.1 Communicating

All organisations need to communicate with their customers. They need to communicate with their past customers, their present customers and their potential future customers. They also need to communicate with other groups such as their own employees, shareholders, trade unions, government bodies, the local community and possibly the population at large. Although an organisation's communication task, as outlined above, can be an extremely complex process, we must start by looking, in very simple terms at what we understand by the concept of 'communicating'.

10.1.1 Stimuli

A stimulus is something that provokes an action or a response. We are constantly absorbing and reacting to stimuli. Some responses will be premeditated, some measured, some habitual and some reactive. And others so instinctive that we are often not consciously aware of either the stimulus or of our response.

(a) Simple response

If it is very warm, the pores of our skin will gradually open, but it may be only when we are sweating profusely that we become aware of our instinctive reaction. Sometimes we are painfully aware of the stimulus but our reaction is virtually automatic. If we walk from a dark room into bright sunlight we react by screwing up our eyes and looking down. Simple instinctive or reactive responses can be displayed as follows:

Figure 10.1 Simple response model.

(b) Operant response

Other responses are habitual as proved by Pavlov's famous dogs who began to salivate from habit when they heard a bell because they associated the sound with the arrival of food. Pavlov showed that our instincts can be modified through environmental and social experience. This psychological model of 'operant conditioning' suggests that people may be conditioned to respond in certain ways.

Figure 10.2 Operant response model.

It is on the basis of this kind of theory that advertisers have sometimes been accused of manipulating consumers by stimulating demand for products which are not needed or which may even be harmful. It is for this reason that the Advertising Standards Authority has prohibited the direct linking of cigarettes and alcohol in adverts with benefits like social, sexual or sporting success.

(c) Cognitive response

Sometimes however we think about our response carefully before we react. The simple question 'what would you like to drink?' provokes long thought processes in some people before they finally deliver a carefully considered response. This is based on the 'cognitive' model of human behaviour which suggests that our actions are based more on our own thoughts and decisions than on external conditioning. This can be represented by the following model where 'O' represents some evaluation process internal to the human mind.

Figure 10.3 Cognitive response model.

(d) Complex response

Most behavioural scientists would agree that reality usually falls somewhere between these two schools of thought. Let's illustrate this with the sequence of events that may follow the launch of a new product.

New high energy yogurt drink is introduced and heavily promoted with adverts showing fantastic benefits for trendy, enthusiastic consumers.

Many people who want to be trendy and energetic are stimulated to make a trial purchase of the new product. They buy and consume it.

After consuming, they decide whether or not they are satisfied with their purchase. Did they like the taste, did it make them feel good, did it make them look good in front of friends to be a buyer of this latest new product? A very complex thought process (as described in Chapter 2) results in the development of an 'attitude' towards the new product. Regular purchase will result if the attitude is very favourable, no future purchase if it is very unfavourable.

The debate occurs over whether the third stage of attitude development is really an internal and independent evaluation process or whether it is strongly influenced by other stimuli such as the second campaign of even more persuasive adverts. As described in Chapter 2 it is probably a compromise with external factors such as advertising and the opinions of friends affecting but not determining the formation of the individual's attitude. This process is represented below.

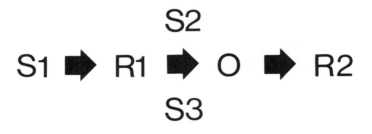

Figure 10.4 Complex response model.

(e) Planned response

Occasionally we anticipate a stimulus and prepare and perhaps even rehearse a response. Such stimuli might include the next challenge from the playground bully, a request from the teacher for the homework which has not been done, or perhaps the next encounter with the girl you are dying to ask out. This increases the probability of a certain response occurring.

Figure 10.5 Planned response model.

The more frequently the response is rehearsed or carried out, as in the salesperson's presentation, the greater the probability that the actual response will be the same as the planned response.

10.1.2 Messages

Messages lie at the heart of the communications process. All forms of animal life communicate with each other through sending messages.

(a) Oral messages

Birds and animals in the jungle shriek and scream to warn others of impending danger. The human baby cries to inform its mother of its hunger. Orally, a wide range of messages can be sent without using words. The cat purrs and we understand. The more simple and clear the message, the more completely it is understood.

(b) Visual messages

Sound does not accompany all messages. Many animals have elaborate courtship rituals involving colour, size perception, and manoeuvres all designed to communicate a message to the opposite sex. Many humans exhibit similar behaviour. Words like make-up, high heels and body language would all be applicable to this primitive and instinctive behaviour.

(c) Verbal messages

At a certain stage in human evolution, primitive man began to develop consistent noises to denote certain common activities or commodities. Sounds like 'eat' and 'meat' became understood by both the sender and receiver of a message and led to great economies in grunts and gesticulations.

(d) Written messages

Many years later man developed the ability to express these verbal messages in the form of written symbols. People could thus communicate without being face to face or within earshot. They could be miles apart and communicate with the written word. Coded messages became more complicated with technological developments leading to Morse Code and wartime demands leading to the development of fiendishly clever codes to confuse the enemy. All languages of course are a form of coded message. The more complicated or alien the code, the less likely is the message to be understood. A British person finds it easier to learn French or German than Russian or Chinese.

(e) Electronic messages

The way of the future may be electronic messages. Computers can already communicate with each other, from one side of the world to the other. Some countries, such as France are very advanced in this field, with activities like electronic shopping already quite common in that country.

Marketing managers are extremely interested in messages, and in the way they are transmitted and understood.

10.1.3 The communications process

Two way communication is not easy. Even face to face there is much scope for misunderstanding. As the exercise at the end of this chapter demonstrates, it is not easy to convey an accurate understanding of even simple, factual messages. If face to face communication is difficult, one way non-personal communication, such as advertising must be even more challenging. How do you send a convincing message via a thirty second television advert that Guinness is a sophisticated drink? Before we can begin to answer this question we must examine some of the theory upon which marketing communications are based. The most commonly quoted model of the communications process is the one developed by Wilbur Schramm in 1965 in 'How communication works'.

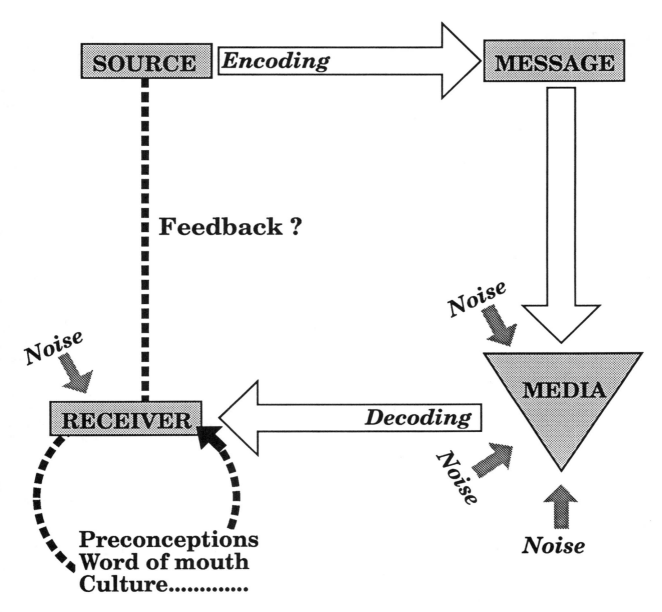

Figure 10.6 Schramm's Communications Model of the Marketing Communications Process.

Let's examine Schramm's model.

(a) The source

The source of the communication is the person or organisation sending it. Normally, the source knows exactly what message it wants to send. In other words, the sender knows exactly what he wants to happen as a result of sending this message. If he doesn't, the communications process has already broken down.

(b) Encoding

Even if your communication is delivered directly to one individual or to an audience it still has to be encoded. It will be put into words, and for an audience may be livened up by the use of visual aids. A letter will take longer to encode, a thirty second TV advert longer still, and a twenty minute company video probably yet more time. For all but the simplest of everyday verbal messages the encoding process involves translating the message contained in the mind of the sender into a form that is suitable for the way in which it must be communicated.

(c) The message

In its newly encoded form we now have a message. It might be in the form of a full colour print advertisement with no words whatsoever on the page. It might be in the form of a four page personalised direct mailshot with two hundred words on each page and three 'p.s.'s' at the end. Is this message exactly the same as the one which was initially formed in the mind of the sender?

(d) Media

Unless communication is face to face it must go through some form of medium. But to what extent does the medium affect the message? If an identical advert is placed in both the *Guardian* and the *Sun* newspapers does exactly the same message come across or do the media distort the message? It is said that up market media such as *Vogue* magazine can enhance the image of the product being advertised whereas a down market publication might be bad for the image of a sophisticated product.

(e) Noise

The whole process is liberally sprinkled with noise. Noise is usually the main factor contributing to the downfall of the message. Noise can be anything which interferes with the reception or understanding of the message. Noise is anything which competes for the attention of the intended receiver or audience. In face to face communication, noise may come in the form of the persistent interruption of a small child who ultimately succeeds in sabotaging all attempts at sensible conversation. Adverts face competition from other adverts, or, in magazines from pages containing information or articles which are of more interest to the reader. Noise occurs during the commercial breaks on TV when the chocolates are passed round, someone goes to put the kettle on, and sometimes when members of the family actually speak to each other. The volume of direct mail received by the average householder continues to increase, the supermarkets are full of special offers and we can even watch adverts whilst waiting in a post office. The sheer volume of competing messages makes it inevitable that many will go unnoticed and very few will be taken in.

(f) Decoding

It is therefore only a small proportion of the intended audience who are giving any real attention to a typical non-personal marketing communication. Those who are paying attention will have to decode the communication. They must interpret it in their own mind and form their own understanding of the intended message. The more complex and subtle the message the more difficult this process of comprehension will be and the more varied will be the results. In other words, apart from the most simple of communications the message changes yet again.

(g) The receiver

During this perilous reception stage the integrity of the message is under further threat from the receiver's preconceptions. Arguably the biggest danger to the understanding and acceptance of any persuasive message comes in the form of the preconceived views of the receiver. The man who has owned an unreliable car will be unreceptive to the messages of its manufacturer for many years to come. And so might his next door neighbour or best friend due to the powerful influence of word of mouth communications. Cultural beliefs make it difficult for some messages to be accepted in certain countries. For example, whereas black is the colour of death and mourning in Britain, it is white in Hong Kong, purple in Brazil and yellow in Mexico. The use of those three colours in the respective countries could have a considerable effect on the interpretation of the message.

(h) Feedback

If you are involved in a two way conversation such as sales negotiations you get constant feedback which enables you to monitor your performance and satisfy yourself that your messages are having their desired effect. Where one way marketing communications are concerned you often have no immediate response to let you know if your message was received and understood.

All communications therefore are difficult. Non-personal marketing communications are particularly difficult because they have to compete for attention with so many other attractions and distractions, they are usually seeking to persuade, or at least to influence peoples' attitudes and as one way messages it is difficult for the sender to judge their success.

10.1.4 Shared meaning

To achieve genuine communications the communicators must understand each other. If we imagine an Italian and a Frenchman who did not speak each other's language but both spoke a little English trying to hold a conversation, the extent of their communication would be determined by their knowledge of English, as this would be their only common ground, or shared frame of reference.

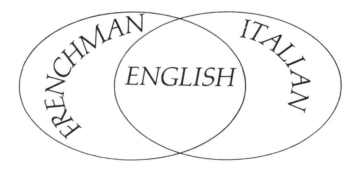

Figure 10.7 Shared frame of reference.

This concept applies even to people who speak the same language. Factors such as different experiences, beliefs, levels of education and ages often make it difficult for people to communicate properly with each other because their shared frame of reference is so small. If the marketer is to succeed with his promotional messages he must always try to understand the receivers' frame of reference. Everything about the message must be designed to fit in with the receivers' language, beliefs and aspirations.

10.2 The communicating job

An organisation must define its communicating task very clearly. It must always have a clear definition of its intended message, and the target audience to which it must be sent. It must also know the anticipated result of sending that message to that audience. It needs to know the best time to send the message, and the best way of making sure that the message actually gets to the audience. In short, the organisation needs to plan a communications campaign.

10.2.1 Planning the campaign

A well planned marketing communications campaign will follow the same basic principles of planning that guide many other areas of the business. These are briefly summarised in the table below.

Stage 1

Where are we now? = **ANALYSIS**

Stage 2

Where do we want to be in ...... years (or months)? = **OBJECTIVES**

Stage 3

How can we get there? = **STRATEGY and TACTICS**

Stage 4

How will we know when we have arrived? = **EVALUATION**

(a) Analysis

The basic principles of planning outlined above apply to planning anything. Their origins lie in the planning of military campaigns. You can imagine the generals studying military maps or poring over models of the battlefield. Before they can plan anything they need to have a very detailed and accurate knowledge of the current position and strength of their own armed forces. They also need as much knowledge as possible about the enemy's position and strength. Thirdly, they need to know all about the wider environment in which the battle is being fought. Good planning can result only from a thorough and accurate analysis of the current situation.

(b) Objectives

This detailed analysis will help the generals to set realistic objectives. Their ultimate objective of course will be to win the war. However, this may not be achievable in the next three months or even the next year, so interim objectives will need to be set. In 1943, for example, the allies took the decision that a key objective for 1944 would be the opening of a new front against Hitler in Western Europe.

(c) Strategy and tactics

Both strategy and tactics are concerned with how you achieve your objectives. Strategy is concerned with broad actions designed to achieve overall objectives. Thus, if the Allies' key objective for 1944 is to invade France they could choose between a number of broad strategies, such as:

to march up through Italy and invade southern France by land,

to invade northern France by sea,

to mount a seaborne invasion from the Atlantic or from the Mediterranean or

to rely on an airborne invasion.

Once the broad strategy is determined, the detailed tactics must be worked out. Having chosen the seaborne invasion of northern France it was necessary to identify the beaches in Normandy which could be used, to plan departure points and times from England, to assign men, ships, weapons, provisions etc. to each element of the plan and to work out many, many more details. Tactics have short term goals and become detailed action plans for everyone in the armed forces who will be involved in that operation.

(d) Evaluation

An army needs to be able to continuously monitor and evaluate its progress. It must therefore have yardsticks which will indicate clearly whether or not it is on course. If one division of the army is on schedule but another division has been held up by heavy fighting, problems will lie ahead if those two divisions have to join up to take a key bridge across a major river on a specific date in the near future. If goals are not being attained, remedial action will have to be taken to regain control of the situation. The army would no doubt have prepared some contingency plans covering how they would react if certain things went wrong. As the unfolding of any battle demonstrates it is possible to stay on course only if you know exactly what the course is and have clearly defined mileposts which enable you to make a regular check on your progress.

We can illustrate this communications task in the campaign planning diagram below:

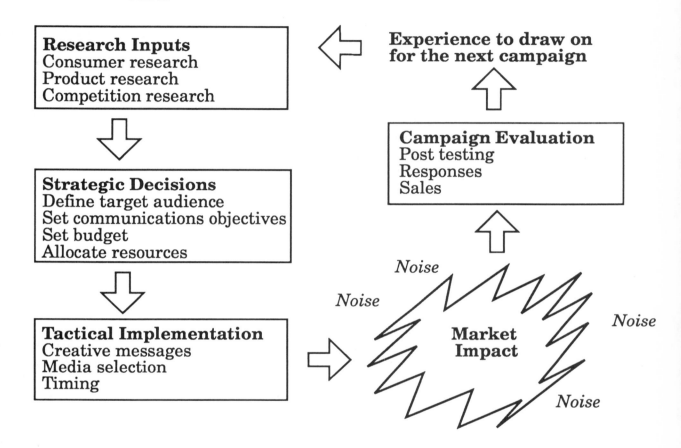

Figure 10.8 The campaign planning process.

10.2.2 Research

As we explained in Chapters 2 to 4, research is a vital part of any marketing job. Without accurate information we can never know where we are now, which is essential if the right decisions are to be made. If we are to establish the right rapport with our customers we need to know all about them. We also need to know exactly what they think of our product and competitors' products.

There is no point in a car manufacturer running an expensive advertising campaign saying that model X is the most reliable car on the market if the public believes it to be the least reliable. The message would not be believed and the campaign would probably do more harm than good.

10.2.3 The target audience

As discussed in Chapters 2 to 4, successful marketing is based on a very detailed knowledge of customers and markets. Any of the methods of segmentation described in Chapter 3 might be used to help marketing managers define and understand their target audience. Accurate segmentation of the market helps the marketing manager to achieve two very important tasks.

It helps him to understand the target audience which is vital if he is to send the right kind of messages that the audience will relate to and it enables him to define the audience which is vital if he is to select the right media to reach the audience.

The car buyer typologies outlined in Chapter 3 would form the basis for Volkswagen's understanding of its target audience. It is on the basis of this understanding that Volkswagen's advertising campaign would be created. However, the typologies themselves are not enough. To develop an effective advert for a car, Volkswagen's advertising agency needs to have an identikit picture of a typical buyer of each individual Volkswagen model. This is the kind of information that Volkswagen's market research consultants produced to guide the advertising agency.

As an example the Polo is both the smallest and the most female oriented car in Volkswagen's range. These two characteristics both point to 'Small is Beautiful' as the primary target market. The secondary target should be 'Frightened' as this also comprises the most 'flight' based male group.

As far as characters are concerned the 'Small is Beautiful' buyers are likely to be women, married with children, in their late twenties or early thirties and upper middle class. Key factors to attract them will be ease of handling and parking, safety and reliability. The more socially conscious in the 'Small is Beautiful' segment will be attracted by low fuel consumption and all ecological matters. Their lifestyle is family based with visiting friends and relatives, holidays and watching sport highly valued. They are unlikely to visit pubs or clubs.

Research has uncovered the fact that the Polo is poorly rated in the 'Small is Beautiful' segment – therefore promotional messages will need to stress Volkswagen's traditional strengths of quality, reliability and safety.

'Frightened' consumers are older and less upper class. They are likely to shop at Marks and Spencer and to enjoy classical music concerts and the theatre. They like car outings in general and visiting friends and family in particular. Their image of Volkswagen is good in terms of safety and average on most other dimensions. Any strengthening in terms of reliability and ease of driving will appeal to this segment. Analysis by social value group suggests that 'self explorers' will comprise a prime target group for the Polo. Key factors to attract them will be all ecology related issues.

On the other hand the Golf GTI/Cabriolet has a different image. Given the characteristics of the car it is not surprising that 'Boy Racer' is an important target group for both sexes. They will be primarily attracted to the car because of its sports performance and unusual exterior appearance. Image and style are everything to this group so it is vital for the GTI to be promoted as the car to be seen in.

The 'Pro-Am' group is also highly attracted to the GTI, but for quite different reasons connected with its performance and engineering from a technical viewpoint. It will be very difficult to appeal emotionally to both these typologies since they are almost opposites in demographic and attitudinal characteristics.

Our feeling is that the best compromise is to concentrate male strategies towards the 'Pro-Am' group which fits in more closely with the car's actual character (well engineered and powerful, but not flashy) and to target female strategies at 'Girl Racers'. It is likely that with correct characterisation (Yuppies), the featuring of 'Girl Racers' will also indirectly appeal to 'Boy Racers'.

'Pro-Am' people can stand an appeal based on technical considerations and press advertising may be appropriate to convey the necessary detail. By contrast, the fast moving audio-visual media will be necessary to attract 'Boy/Girl Racers'. Their image of Volkswagen in terms of performance and excitement is good but less good for stylishness. This latter attribute will be important to attract this group and should be strengthened.

The predominant social value groups are 'Conspicuous Consumers' and 'Experimentalists'. 'Conspicuous Consumers' are acquisitive and concerned about their position in society whilst 'Experimentalists' are materialistic and pro- technology.

'Boy and Girl Racers' have frantic and varied lifestyles. They enjoy eating out, going to clubs, pubs and discos, listening to records/tapes, playing sport, and going on holiday. Men are lager drinkers, girls tend to be wine drinkers. They are fashion conscious and tend to shop at specialist shops such as Next, Principles, Benetton etc.

The above information will help to develop creative messages which should appeal to potential buyers of Polos and Golf GTIs. However, these messages will have little effect unless they reach large numbers of these potential new customers. Volkswagen and its advertising agency therefore need to know about the media habits of each target audience. Below is a summary of the Golf GTI owners' media survey. This information was acquired from a postal questionnaire sent to everybody who had bought a Golf GTI in August 1986. Over 50% of buyers completed and returned the questionnaire.

The affluent 'yuppie' image of the GTI owner is substantiated in the reading habits of the owner body with the *Telegraph* (32%) and the *Times* (30%), the two most popular daily newspapers. The *Financial Times* is also prominent at 24% and is probably read in conjunction with either *The Times* or the *Telegraph*.

Local morning and evening papers are also widely read as is the free local press, with over 40% of owners stating that they received such a paper on a regular basis.

The *Sunday Times,* cited by 52% of owners was by far the most popular Sunday newspaper, although often it appears to be taken in conjunction with another, less serious one, with the *Mail on Sunday* (25%) and the *Sunday Express* the most popular in this respect.

The Radio and TV Times are again popular in leisure reading at 25% and 22% respectively, with the more 'high brow' publications such as *Country Life, Economist* and *Punch* also in evidence to a lesser extent.

The level of readership of specialist car magazines is much higher among GTI owners than for other Volkswagen owners. *Motor, Car, What Car* and *Autocar* are all highly read by these car enthusiasts, with the net effect that these publications bear greater importance as a source of pre - purchase information than is the case for other models.

The TV viewing and Radio listening habits of the target audience also need to be investigated as do the possibilities of reaching it through other media such as the cinema, direct mail or outdoor posters. The result will be a target audience definition which enables the advertiser to reach it with an appropriate message.

10.2.4 Objectives

As discussed earlier in this chapter, setting objectives is vital. Early in this century, Lord Leverhulme, founder of detergent giant Lever Brothers, is said to have coined the phrase: *'I know that half my advertising is wasted but I don't know which half!'*

These days most advertisers devote significant amounts of time and resources to making sure that their advertising expenditure is not wasted.

As Russell Colley emphasised in 1961, the setting of clear communications objectives is vital if a company is ever to know if its promotional money was well spent. Colley's DAGMAR concept has become a fundamental part of good advertising practice. DAGMAR stands for:

Defining Advertising Goals for Measured Advertising Results.

However, in order to define meaningful objectives it is essential to distinguish between marketing and communications objectives. Whereas the key marketing objective may be to sell 10,000 cars this year, communications objectives will usually be expressed in terms of communicating goals rather than sales targets. Only very rarely (e.g. in certain types of direct response advertising) do marketing communications have a direct and measurable effect on sales. More usually they are seen to move the customer towards the act of purchase by gradually convincing him that it is a good idea. As we said in Chapter 2, products are bought on impulse or by habit only in the most routine, low involvement purchase decisions. Normally the buyer goes through a number of stages in his decision making process and it is the task of marketing communications to speed the buyer through this sequence. It is said that marketing communications should have a 'hierarchy of effects', each moving the customer closer to the act of purchase. This hierarchy of effects can be seen as the communication spectrum, illustrated below:

Figure 10.9 The communications spectrum.

If objectives are clearly set in terms of the communications spectrum, their achievement can be measured after the campaign. Examples of good communications objectives would be:

to increase awareness of our company name and its basic product offering from 65% of the target audience to 90%, to increase comprehension of the effective cleaning ability of dish washers to 80% of the target audience and

to raise preference that model X is a 'more reliable car' than model Y from 35% to 55% of the target audience.

It may be that none of those objectives will, in themselves achieve sales, but if successful, they will make sales more likely by moving customers closer to the decision to purchase.

10.2.5 Setting budgets

(a) Percentage of sales

This is the most common method of setting communications budgets and involves allocating a fixed percentage of sales revenue to promotion. There are often industry norms in this respect. Many frequently advertised consumer products such as cosmetics, washing powder or pet food will have as much as 10% of their sales revenue devoted to advertising and promotion. Many more such as breakfast cereals, coffee and chocolate will have an advertising to sales ratio of 5%. More expensive items such as cars or personal computers will usually have a ratio of 1 - 2% and many industrial products will devote only a small fraction of 1% of their sales revenue to advertising.

(b) Competitive parity

Many companies will react to any significant increase in their competitors' promotional expenditure. If one brand of coffee is very heavily advertised, the sales of directly competing brands may suffer unless they retaliate. Some companies regard it as essential to maintain their brand's 'share of voice' for this reason.

(c) Objective and task

In theory, the ideal way to set a communications budget is by the objective and task method. This involves firstly setting the communications objectives that must be attained if the overall marketing objectives are to be achieved. One can then estimate the extent of advertising and other promotion that would be necessary to achieve the communications goals. Working out the cost of this level of advertising would produce the budget figure that it would be necessary to spend. Although an ideal budgeting method in theory, it is little used in practice partly because of the difficulty of working out the level of advertising necessary to achieve certain objectives and partly because companies fear that it would lead to a dramatic increase in promotional expenditure.

(d) Affordable

The affordable method is virtually the opposite of the objective and task method. Rather than asking what we need to spend, it simply asks what the company can afford to spend. The affordable method is commonly favoured by small companies but can have the danger that insufficient funds are allocated to stand a reasonable chance of achieving much impact.

10.3 Ways of communicating

There are many ways of sending promotional messages to the market. The marketing communications mix could involve any combination of the following methods:

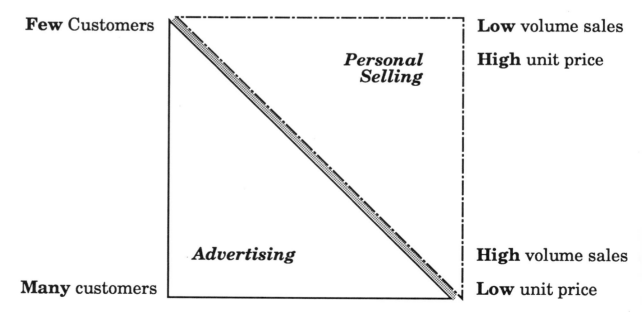

Figure 10.10 The marketing communications mix.

10.3.1 Allocation of resources

Once the marketing communications budget has been set it must be allocated to specific methods of communication. The campaign planner must therefore have a good idea of what each method of communication is good at. He will allocate the most resources to those methods of communication which are best at achieving the kind of objectives he has set.

The list of communication methods shown in Figure 10.10 becomes gradually more personal as you move higher up the list. Personal selling for example involves face to face conversation, usually on a one to one basis. Telephone selling is also one to one, but not face to face. At the other extreme, advertising involves sending the same fixed message to many people, often millions.

As a generalisation one can rate the effectiveness of the different elements of the communications mix in the ways shown in the next two diagrams.

Few Customers   **Low** volume sales

Personal Selling   **High** unit price

Advertising   **High** volume sales

Many customers   **Low** unit price

Figure 10.11 The cost effectiveness of personal versus non-personal marketing communications.(1)

As the diagram suggests, advertising is best at mass marketing, sending messages to large audiences. These will be associated with consumer products, sold in large volumes often at a low price, such as groceries. A new chocolate bar will often be picked off a shelf in a self service supermarket by many new buyers without any persuasion from a sales assistant if it has been advertised and promoted well.

Personal selling is very cost effective if the total number of customers for a product is small as it is in many industrial markets. Also, if products are high cost and sell in low volumes the purchasing process is likely to be longer and involve more negotiation. The two way communication afforded by personal selling is ideal for this high involvement buying decision. For selling cars, houses, complex hi-fi systems or computers it is usually essential for a salesman to speak at length, usually on more than one occasion with the customer before the sale is completed. Personal selling however is very expensive if large numbers of customers or low price products are involved, which is why it has been almost eliminated for many fast moving consumer goods. Telephone selling is a more economical alternative to personal selling, and exhibitions offer the opportunity to speak to larger numbers of customers. Direct mail can be used to send personalised messages to relatively large numbers of buyers, but the communication is only one way.

However, before one can decide on the relative value of personal versus non-personal communications one must also take into account the complexity of the communications task, as shown in the diagram below.

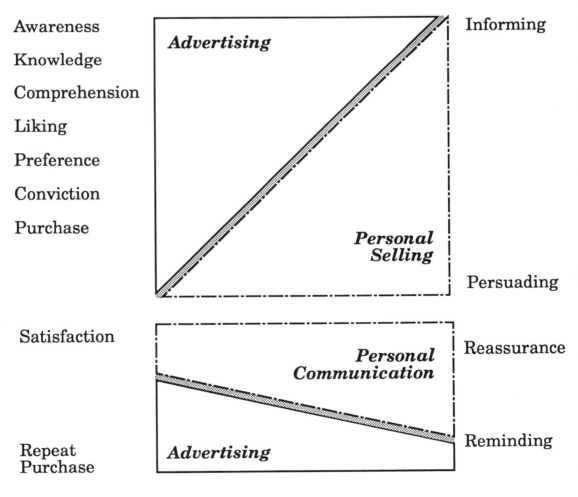

Figure 10.12 The cost effectiveness of personal versus non-personal marketing communications.(2)

Non-personal marketing communications are best at sending simple messages of the kind usually required at the beginning of the communications spectrum. These are typically 'informing' type messages. Simple messages may also be required right at the other end of the spectrum if repeat purchase is to be encouraged. These would typically be 'reminding' type messages. Advertising and sales promotions are very cost effective at conveying simple informing and reminding type messages.

Brochures can effectively convey more complex, technical messages as can direct mail, public relations and exhibitions. These last three can also be more persuasive, and can certainly be useful for sending the kind of 'reassurance' messages that are often required just before and just after purchase. Persuasion however is always best achieved through two way communication, preferably face to face but the telephone can also be very persuasive, as can addressing groups of customers, at exhibitions or public relations events for example.

To arrive at an initial decision for the allocation of resources to the various elements of the communications mix it is necessary to take into account all the variables mentioned in Figures 10.12 and 10.13. This can be a difficult task and experience will often play a large part in the manager's decision making. His experience basically tells him what kind of tasks each element of the marketing communications mix is best able to perform. A summary of the main strengths of each marketing communications tool is given below.

THE MARKETING TOOLS – MAIN STRENGTHS

Personal selling

1. Achieving conviction and purchase – 'closing the sale' to use selling jargon.

2. Negotiating terms such as price, delivery times, credit terms.

3. Explaining complex issues, which is usually an important task with highly technical products.

4. Maintaining good relationships with regular customers.

5. Enhancing the credibility of the 'product' – particularly important for service industries.

Tele-sales

1. Order taking.

2. Qualifying leads and arranging sales calls.

3. Reminding regular customers to place their order.

4. Closing very straight forward sales or sales which have been virtually concluded by previous personal visits.

Exhibitions

1. Demonstrating the benefits of products, especially if they are expensive, complex or technical.

2. Reaching large numbers of potential customers in a face to face situation.

3. Enhancing the company's image through a good display.

4. Selling. (N.B. at some exhibitions no selling can take place, only display and demonstration.)

Direct mail

1. Targeting precise segments of the market.

2. Sending long or complicated messages.

3. Making impact, by doing something special with the mailer contents.

4. Improving awareness and knowledge on a wide scale.

5. Achieving action, e.g. attending a shop opening or applying to test drive a car.

6. Selling simple items, e.g. typical catalogue items.

Public relations

1. Increasing understanding.

2. Sending complex or highly technical messages, e.g. through an article in a specialist magazine or through a conference.

3. Generating awareness or building image, e.g. through sponsorship or open days.

Literature

1. Informing briefly or in great detail.

2. Explaining product benefits.

3. Stimulating interest.

4. Building image.

Sales promotion

1. Stimulating trial or impulse purchase.

2. Provoking attention in stores.

3. Encouraging repeat purchase.

Advertising

1. Reaching mass audiences.

2. Sending simple messages.

3. Generating awareness.

4. Stimulating interest and excitement.

5. Building image.

10.3.2 Implementation

Detailed tactical plans and budgets would then need to be drawn up for each element of the communications mix to be used. This detailed implementation of the communications plan will be examined in the following chapters of this book.

10.4 Measuring results

Following the campaign its results should always be evaluated. Marketers need to know if their message has reached the target audience. If they have used the wrong media a campaign could go virtually unnoticed. Worse still could be a campaign that was noticed but which failed to convey the intended message. If large numbers of people perceive the message incorrectly the product could be harmed. Advertisers will therefore want to satisfy themselves that the campaign did reach its target audience, that the audience did understand the message and that people retained a favourable impression of the advert. There are a number of ways of evaluating marketing communications.

10.4.1 Pre-testing and post-testing

The most common method employed by large advertisers is to test the views of a representative sample of the target audience both before and after the campaign. One possible technique would be to ask a series of questions designed to test the target audience's position on the communications spectrum both before and after the campaign.

Lets examine a possible example with a new chocolate bar.

Customers' Perceptions of BIG-CHOC.

1. Can you tell me the brand names of any three chocolate bars?

2. Can you tell me the name of this chocolate bar? (Here, a photo of BIG-CHOC with its name blanked out may be shown.)

3. If the name BIG-CHOC still has not been mentioned another photo, including the brand name may be shown and the respondent asked, 'Have you ever heard of BIG-CHOC?'

4. Have you ever tried BIG-CHOC?

5. If not why not?

6. If so did you like it?

7. If yes, how often do you buy BIG-CHOC?

In reality questions would probably go into greater detail about exactly what it is about BIG-CHOC that consumers either like or dislike, and how they rate BIG-CHOC compared to competing products on a number of criteria.

However, the questions above should make it possible to place the target audience somewhere on the communications spectrum. Let's assume that the following answers were given.

The market position of BIG-CHOC

1. This question was designed to test customers' unaided recall which tells us how well known BIG-CHOC is compared to other chocolate brands. The answers were as follows: The brands most commonly mentioned in response to this question were:

Kat-Kut 91%

Venus Bar 85%

Milky 32%

Dairy Block 23%

BIG-CHOC 14%

Several other brands were mentioned by a small number of respondents.

2. When shown the photo of BIG-CHOC 80% of respondents were able to correctly identify it.

3. Of those who could not identify it from the photo, half claimed to have heard of BIG-CHOC which means that only 10% of the target audience was unaware of BIG-CHOC.

4. Despite this high awareness, not many people had ever tasted a BIG-CHOC. In fact only 28% of the target audience had done so.

5. The basic reason given by those who had never tried BIG-CHOC was lack of interest in the bar. Although aware of it they had never really considered buying one. Most had little idea how BIG-CHOC differed from other brands.

6. Of the 28% who had tried BIG-CHOC reactions were generally very favourable. 75% of them liked it and 25% claimed to buy at least one BIG-CHOC per week.

In summary we could say that BIG-CHOC does not have a major problem on awareness. Most people have heard of it. They are much more aware of the best selling chocolate brands but that is to be expected. 90% of people have heard of BIG-CHOC, which is satisfactory. The problem comes at the next stage. Most people have not even tried one. They don't seem to be interested in it. Their knowledge of the exact nature of BIG-CHOC is generally poor, and their understanding of its benefits even worse. We can see that there is no problem with the product itself because those people who do taste it tend to like it and a good proportion become regular buyers.

From this research the marketing communications objectives for BIG-CHOC would be clear. The brand manager has got to generate interest in his product. Specifically the main objective would probably be something like this:

'To increase trial of BIG-CHOC amongst the target audience from the current level of 28% to 40% within 6 months.'

This is a good objective since it is specific, it does not try to achieve too much (it concentrates on a precise area of the communications spectrum), it is measurable and it has a time limit.

An objective like this will require an exciting advertising campaign to generate interest in the product. It will involve sales promotion to stimulate trial purchase and may also involve the free distribution of small sample bars in shopping centres, supermarkets or at sporting events.

If the campaign is successful, trial purchase will rise to 40% of the target market. As long as consumers' reaction to the taste of the bar remains the same, those who like the BIG-CHOC (and presumably buy occasionally) will increase from 21% to 30% and regular buyers will increase from 7% to 10%.

At the end of the 6 month campaign it would be a simple task to evaluate the success of the campaign by 'post-testing'. Exactly the same questions as used in the pre-test would be asked to a representative sample of the target audience.

If the campaign has been successful, knowledge and understanding should be much improved. The target audience will be more excited about BIG-CHOC and trial will have increased. Evidence from the previous research suggests that if trial increases, liking, conviction, purchase, satisfaction and repeat purchase will not be problems, but no doubt all of these aspects of consumer behaviour will be the subject of detailed marketing research after the campaign.

10.4.2 Direct response

Pre- and post-testing is based on the assumption that the main effects of marketing communications will be on people's minds rather than on their actions. As we explained in Chapter 2 it is generally the case that actions such as purchase are only indirectly related to marketing communications. A person gradually makes up his mind to buy as a result of many factors. Therefore most companies do not measure the success of advertising and most other non-personal communications on the basis of whether their sales have gone up or down. There are just too many other factors involved.

However, some marketing communications are designed to produce a direct response rather than an invisible effect inside people's heads. A direct response may be the placing of an order or it may be some other kind of measurable action taken by customers. Below are some examples of responses that can be achieved by certain kinds of marketing communications.

(a) The success of a sales person will almost always be evaluated on the basis of the level of sales achieved.

(b) A tele-sales campaign might have the objective of arranging sales calls for representatives. It is quite common for businesses selling new kitchens or double glazing to use tele-sales to persuade potential buyers to agree to a call by a sales person.

(c) Some exhibitions which are open to the public such as the Boat Show and the Ideal Homes Exhibition are mainly designed to achieve sales and orders for exhibitors.

(d) Much direct mail is intended to produce an order. The fantastic prize draws are usually to gain the receiver's attention. The real objective will be a subscription for the magazine, an order for the new gadget, a membership fee for the club etc.

(e) Most sales promotions are meant to stimulate some kind of action, usually purchase of the 'special offer' product.

(f) Some advertising is designed to achieve a direct response. On the one hand the desired response may simply be to fill in a coupon asking for more details of a certain product or, at the other extreme it may be to place an order, perhaps for a dress advertised in a Sunday colour supplement. Many retailers advertise in the local press with the clear objective of attracting customers to their premises, and will know if a specific advert has worked well if they have a 'busy Saturday' as a result.

It is therefore a mistake to assume that marketing communications work only on people's minds. Many companies have a clear intended response when they spend money on marketing communications and therefore expect to have very tangible results to measure.

Conclusion

Communicating is very difficult at the best of times with much scope for misunderstanding. Marketing communications, especially those which are not face to face are confronted by many hazards which can interfere with the correct message being received and understood. In the light of these communications difficulties, meticulous planning is essential if a company is to get the most from its marketing budget. Good campaign planning will begin with thorough analysis based on market research which leads to the setting of specific objectives. A broad message and media strategy is then developed followed by detailed tactical plans which will involve all aspects of designing and sending the right messages.

There are many possible ways of sending marketing messages. One of the key factors in the success of a promotional campaign is the optimal allocation of resources to different elements of the marketing communications mix. The marketing manager must be careful to choose the communications technique (or combination of techniques) which will be best at achieving the specific objective he has set.

After the campaign, evaluation is vital to ensure firstly that a sufficiently large proportion of the target audience was reached, secondly that the intended message was received and understood and thirdly that the campaign achieved the desired effect. Checking on marketing communications' effectiveness is usually done by pre- and post-testing, but various forms of direct response can also be used to measure success.

Assignment

'Dynamo'

Fizoggs Ltd. have introduced a new breakfast cereal called 'Dynamo' aimed mainly at children. An advertising campaign has been run featuring a complete family breakfasting enjoyably on Dynamo before rushing off enthusiastically to school and work, but sales have been rather disappointing. National sales targets had been under achieved by 25% despite the product being sold at a very attractive price. Fizoggs are desperate to know where the problem lies so that they can take remedial action to rescue the brand. Dynamo brand manager is Glen Ainsworth, 27 years old and very ambitious. Failure of Dynamo would be a severe setback to his career so he is determined to do all the right things to identify the causes of the problem and take the best corrective action possible.

If he had had any doubts at all on this score, a one hour meeting with Fizogg's marketing manager Janice Murphy made it crystal clear where he stood. Miss Murphy was a highly successful and very confident career woman in her mid thirties. Glen found it difficult to put his side of the case to her at the best of times and on this occasion the traffic was totally one way. Miss Murphy said that she didn't think that Glen had a sufficiently accurate definition of his target audience. he didn't even know whether he was aiming it primarily at children or adults. She thought the advertising and promotion had been boring and predictable, that, as a result, the public were indifferent to Dynamo and that the supermarkets therefore didn't want to give it much, if any shelf space. Glen preferred to forget some of the comments she made about his determination! Suffice it to say that if he didn't get this one sorted out it would be his job rather than his career that was at stake. Glen was given a month to come up with a plan to rescue Dynamo.

He knew that his first step was to undertake a thorough analysis of the current situation. He therefore commissioned some market research including personal interviews with children, women and men and some focus group sessions which would include tasting of the product and its rivals as well as discussion.

A summary of the results is given below.

Personal interviews

Awareness

Unaided recall amongst all groups was very low with only 12% of respondents being able to correctly identify Dynamo from three clues. (The clues given were a still from the TV advert, a copy of the press advert which included a description of the cereal and a close up photo of the pack. In all cases the name was of course obscured on the photos.) It is true that awareness amongst children was higher because they tend to take a greater interest in breakfast cereals than adults and watch and remember more TV adverts.

Aided recall was slightly better with 39% claiming to have heard of Dynamo when shown a real pack.

Knowledge

Both knowledge of Dynamo and understanding of its benefits were very low. Only 9% could accurately describe the kind of cereal it was. Very few knew anything about the added vitamins and the product's positioning as a high energy cereal.

Liking

When asked to list their favourite three cereals virtually nobody mentioned Dynamo, which is hardly surprising since most were unaware of its existence and of those who had heard of it less than half had actually tasted it. In fact 6% of the target audience had tasted it. This fell as low as 3% for adult women and 5% for girls. 8 to 16 year old boys were most likely to have tried with 11% of this segment having tasted Dynamo. The boys and men also tended to like Dynamo with over 80% of those who had tried it saying that they would choose it again. Women tended to be less enthusiastic with 68% saying they were unlikely to choose it again. About 50% of girls under 16 liked Dynamo.

Focus groups

Sixty four focus groups were carried out in the evening in different regions and in different types of neighbourhood. There were four types of group, all boys, all girls, all men and all mothers. All groups met in a neutral location (e.g a hotel), and contained 12 people. The results were as follows:

Boys' groups

The large majority of the boys loved the cereal. No packets were returned from boys' groups. A very high 45% said they considered it to be better than any other cereal.

They were less enthusiastic about the advertising however which they considered totally boring. They preferred action packed adverts, preferably funny, but definitely interesting. Something had to happen. Some liked adverts with a famous personality such as a pop star or sports personality. The younger boys tended to like in-pack gifts, the older ones competitions. They had no interest at all in the price.

Girls' groups

Girls were less enthusiastic. The response was better than it had been in the personal interviews with 62% claiming to like Dynamo, but only 25% being prepared to list it amongst their favourite three cereals.

Girls quite liked the current advertising campaign, preferring family situations to sports oriented or action packed adverts. They were very keen on any kind of sales promotion which involved collecting something.

Men's groups

Men tended to like the cereal. They said it was easy and quick to eat, which was important since they were often in a rush in the morning and they like the sweet flavour. Some men however suggested that although they like eating sweet breakfast cereals it would be better if the healthy benefits of the product were stressed, especially as far as their wives were concerned. 74% of men said they would choose Dynamo again though many of these stated that their choice of breakfast cereal was determined more by their children. In a nutshell, if the kids demanded that Dynamo be stocked by the household, Dad would probably eat it for his breakfast.

Most men had not seen the TV advertising, and were the least likely of all four segments to watch any TV. They tended to watch a lot of sport and to remember adverts with well known personalities or very attractive women in them. They had no interest whatsoever in any kind of sales promotion.

They thought that the product should be 'reasonably priced'. Their idea of a reasonable price varied from 49p to £1.25 for a 500gm pack! Apart from the 18% of men who did their own shopping or helped with the family shopping, men's idea of the price of cereals in general was very hazy.

Mothers' group

A lot of women did not like Dynamo. 76% said that they would not choose it again. They seemed to think it was too sweet and too fattening. Many stated a preference for more healthy cereals such as muesli.

However, when asked what determined their choice of cereals for the family, 92% of mothers with children over 7 said that their choice was influenced by their children's preferences, although 18% of this group said that however much their children liked it they would not buy Dynamo because it was too sweet. These mothers tended to come from the more educated, higher social class groups.

Not surprisingly mothers were the most price sensitive and the most knowledgeable about price. They thought that Dynamo's current price was very reasonable.

Women were inclined to notice sales promotions. They like flashpacks (e.g. 15% extra in this pack) and they like money-off promotions. Money off the next purchase seemed to be almost as acceptable as money off the current purchase, particularly if the sum was significant. They didn't particularly like collecting tokens, but often allowed themselves to be talked into it by their children.

Task

Assume you are Glen Ainsworth. Your meeting with Janice Murphy is now only four days away. You have decided to enter the meeting positively by calling your report 'Recharging our Dynamos'.

Write Glen's report under the following headings.

1. Summary of the current situation.

2. Six month objectives.

3. The target market.

4. General message strategy.

5. Marketing communications mix.

6. Price.

7. Some initial thoughts on advertising.

8. Some initial thoughts on sales promotion.

Chapter 11
Advertising

Introduction

Advertising is big business. In 1986 £7,620,000,000 was spent on advertising in the U.K. Over £7.5 billion seems like a lot of money to spend on advertising but it's little more than one tenth of American advertising expenditure which totalled £67,374,000,000 in the same period. In fact Britain is only the fourth largest advertiser in the world, with Japan coming second and West Germany third. However, before we look at how and why all this money is spent, some basic concepts need to be defined.

11.1 Advertising definitions and concepts

11.1.1 What is Advertising?

We can define advertising as follows:

'Advertising includes all forms of non-personal communication conducted through paid media under clear sponsorship.'

This includes adverts on the television, radio and cinema as well as print adverts in newspapers, magazines and directories. It also includes roadside posters, usually referred to as 'outdoor advertising'. It does not include any promotional material on a product's packaging, any sponsorship, any articles in the press or news features on TV or radio. Nor does it include special events, company brochures, competitions or merchandising. At one time direct mail was commonly seen as just another form of advertising but as it becomes increasingly prevalent many people are coming to see it as a discipline in itself. All these non advertising forms of promotion will be the subject of subsequent chapters of this book. This chapter will concentrate on traditional forms of advertising.

11.1.2 The advertising process

The basic communications planning concepts examined in Chapter 10 all apply specifically to advertising as well as to marketing communications in general. Analysis, often in the form of marketing research is vital if a good advertising campaign is to be planned. Measurable objectives are essential, and will usually be set according to the DAGMAR model referred to in Chapter 10. A budget will also need to be finalised. A broad message and media strategy will then be developed followed by the hard detailed work which goes into producing an advert and buying the media time or space which is needed to broadcast that advert. Following the campaign a careful evaluation will be carried out to make sure that the objectives were achieved.

As you can see the advertising process as an entity is very similar to the marketing communications planning process described in the last chapter. We will therefore not repeat the material explained in Chapter 10 but will concentrate on more detailed information about the advertising industry, starting with the agencies themselves.

11.2 Advertising agencies

Advertising agencies are big business, and many of the most successful ones are British. The largest advertising agencies in the U.K. are:

Saatchi and Saatchi	£242 million
J.Walter Thompson	£175 m
BSB Dorlands	£156 m
D'Arcy, Masius, Benton & Bowles	£120 m
Ogilvy and Mather	£112 m
McCann Erickson	£108 m
Lowe Howard Spink	£89 m
Young and Rubicam	£82 m
Boase Massimi Pollitt	£74 m
TMD Advertising	£73 m

The figures represent the agency's billings, i.e. the value of the advertising they place on behalf of their clients.   (Source: MEAL June 1988).

Most large advertisers will employ an agency to handle their advertising. We will therefore assume in this chapter that an advertising agency is involved.

However, it must be borne in mind that the use of an advertising agency is not compulsory. Many companies, usually smaller companies, create and run advertising campaigns without the help of an agency. It is likely that most of the advertising you see in your local newspaper has been developed without the use of an advertising agency. Even TV and radio adverts are often produced without an agency since the TV or radio company will often help the small advertiser with basic creative work and copywriting.

Virtually all well known advertising campaigns are produced by agencies so we will begin this chapter by examining the way an advertising agency works. The diagram below shows the basic structure of an agency.

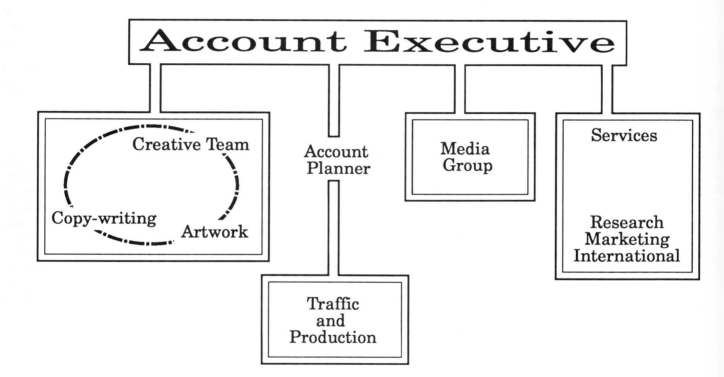

Figure 11.1 Advertising agency structure.

11.2.1 Account management

Advertising agencies refer to their clients as 'accounts'. Accounts have to be carefully nurtured and meticulously managed if the relationship is going to result in an advertising campaign which pleases everyone. The agency therefore appoints a member of its staff to be in charge of each account. An important client will be assigned a very senior account executive. It is the responsibility of the account executive to make sure that the internal departments of the agency work together to meet the objective of the client. He must ensure that the creative people produce a message that fits the client's brief and one which the client is happy with. He must ensure that the media department get the best possible value for money from the client's budget. He needs to ensure that everything is co-ordinated and that the advertising appears according to the schedule agreed with the client. When handling a large account the account executive will almost certainly be assisted by an account planner who will take over much of the responsibility for monitoring the internal performance of the agency. This will involve keeping tight control over 'traffic and production'. Production is the term used to describe all the activities involved in turning the ideas produced by the creative department into something tangible such as a thirty second film which can be transmitted during the commercial break on TV. Traffic involves all the activities which ensure that the agency keeps to the timetable agreed with the client in order to guarantee that adverts appear in the right place at the right time.

The account executive may also need to call on additional services such as marketing research to uncover customers' attitudes and behaviour, marketing consultancy to advise on general matters concerning the brand's position in the market, particularly in relation to its competitors. The campaign may be international, in which case the agency's international department will be called upon to advise on all the implications of running the adverts in other countries.

Smaller agencies are unlikely to have all these services available within the agency. They will tend to buy in research and consultancy from independent specialists, and may have co-operative arrangements with foreign agencies to assist with advertising which needs to be placed abroad. However, any company wishing to run a genuinely international campaign (often called global advertising) will almost certainly appoint a very large multi-national agency which is capable of handling all aspects of the campaign.

11.2.2 The creative department

Once the account executive has agreed a brief with the client he needs to involve his creative department. It is their job to turn the basic message which has to be communicated into exciting and interesting advertising material which is also clear and understandable. Although there are many types of specialists within the creative department, they broadly fall into two camps. Copywriters deal with words and stories such as scripts for TV ads or text for magazine ads. Designers or artists deal with all the visual aspects of the advertising. Between them, the copywriters and designers come up with a creative concept for the client. This is usually produced in the form of a storyboard, a series of hand drawn visual images and key words, slogans or dialogue. For important accounts the presentation to the client will often be an elaborate affair, full of drama with quite a number of agency staff involved.

11.2.3 The media department

There are two aspects to the work done by the media department. Firstly there is media planning which essentially means choosing the best medium, or combination of media to reach the target audience. This relies heavily on the kind of research which tells us about the reading or viewing habits of the target audience. Having determined a broad media strategy the department will then need to work out a timetable of insertions (called a media schedule) which should enable members of the target audience to see the advert the desired number of times. (See 11.4.1)

Secondly there is media buying. Once the client has accepted the agency's proposed media strategy, schedule television time or newspaper space has to be bought. This involves a lot of haggling with the media owners to buy at the best possible price for the client.. If millions of pounds are to be spent on a TV advertising campaign, even a small discount on the rate card price can be worth a significant sum of money. The media buyers also need to book suitable times on TV or radio and the correct positions in newspapers or magazines.

11.2.4 Traffic and production

There are many other jobs to be done inside an advertising agency. Sooner or later ideas and schedules have to be turned into actual advertising. There can also be a huge logistical problem in ensuring that everything happens when it is supposed to happen. Included in this planning must be time for the client to see, consider and approve proposed material at all stages in its development. The client may want to make changes, and time must be allowed for this possibility. Models, actors, photographers, camera crews, musicians and a whole host of other possible players may have to be organised. Equipment may have to be moved to filming locations, risky or difficult film sequences may have to be shot many times before they are perfected. All these logistical problems are called 'traffic' by the agencies.

Traffic is controlled by the production department which is also responsible for making sure that tangible adverts are actually produced. Production staff usually have to liaise with a number of external suppliers such as printers, photographers, film producers etc. to ensure that technically good advertising is produced. This work may not be the glamorous side of advertising but it is essential. The production department has been called 'the nerve centre' of the agency.

11.2.5 Choosing an advertising agency

Some companies stick with the same advertising agency for years and years, but the majority seem to change agencies quite often. It is not difficult for companies to find an advertising agency, though it is arguably more difficult to select the best one.

Advertising is a newsworthy business to be in. Saatchi and Saatchi, for example, became very well known largely as a result of their handling of the Conservative Party's advertising campaign for the 1979 general election. In the business and marketing world many more large agencies receive a lot of publicity as a result of campaigns they have developed for clients.

Advertising agencies are also listed in a number of reference sources. The Advertisers Annual for example lists all agencies together with their clients so a company wishing to choose an agency can check on its credentials. The Advertising Agencies Register goes further and provides videos prepared by the agencies to explain and promote their own services. These videos will usually contain examples of the agency's work.

Companies will use these sources or simply word of mouth, to draw up a short list of up to six agencies. They will then meet with each one, explain what they are trying to achieve, and leave each agency to come up with some ideas. The agency will develop an outline for a campaign, especially its creative elements, and will present its ideas to the client. This presentation is known as a 'pitch'. If a lucrative account is at stake agencies will spend thousands of pounds developing their pitch, but only one can be successful. The client will usually choose the agency which has presented it with the best potential campaign.

11.2.6 Paying the advertising agency

Agencies are traditionally paid by commission. The agency books space or time in the media on the advertiser's behalf. The media charge the advertiser for this space or time and give a commission, usually 15% to the agency. The agency therefore is actually paid by the media rather than the client.

The term 'above the line' (which simply means media advertising) grew up as a result of this practice. It was normal practice for advertising agencies to invoice their clients by first listing all advertising booked on their behalf in the media. These activities would be paid for through the commission which the agency drew from the media. However, the agency may have incurred other costs, not covered by this commission. The agency therefore drew a line across the invoice below which it recorded and charged for these other activities. These 'below the line' activities might include the development of sales promotions such as point of sale material or competitions, the production of brochures or the sending out of mailshots. For these activities the agency does not receive a commission from any third party and therefore has to bill the client for its time. These non media promotional tools are therefore often referred to as 'below the line' activities.

In recent years 'below the line' activities have been growing at a much faster rate than 'above the line' advertising. Many agencies therefore now charge a straight fee for all their services, including 'above the line' work and reimburse to the client any commissions received from the media.

11.3 Creative work

The message to be sent to the target audience will be a major factor in the success of that advertising. The message is a combination of words (spoken or written), symbols, illustrations, stories, colour, movement and sound. The scope for creativity is virtually infinite. However, before we examine how the creative team goes about developing an advertising message, let's step back and analyse what they are trying to achieve.

11.3.1 The communications dilemma

Cast your mind back to Schramm's model of the communications process which we analysed in Chapter 10. If Schramm's model is correct, the inescapable conclusion is that it is a virtually impossible task for a company to get its marketing communications messages across in their intended form to the desired target audience. Inherent in the advertising process are two major creative problems.

1. Getting the message noticed at all.

2. Getting the right message noticed.

In fact these two problems can be mutually exclusive, and form the heart of 'the communications dilemma'.

The Communications Dilemma

IMPACT ⟱ ⟱ UNDERSTANDING

The fundamental problem is that measures taken to get the message noticed in the first place, which often call for a high level of creativity, can often interfere with the communication of the basic message which the advertiser wants the audience to receive. The danger is that the audience remembers the creative gimmick but forgets the less interesting advertising message.

Back in 1960 Alfred Politz drew a very famous analogy when giving his answer to this communications dilemma. This is what he wrote.

"Imagine a room with a large window that looks out upon beautiful countryside. On the wall opposite the window are three mirrors. The first mirror is uneven, spotted and dirty looking. The second mirror is clean, neat and, in addition, is framed by a beautiful ornamental engraving. The third mirror has no frames or ornament, and is nothing but a plain but perfectly flawless mirror. Now, an observer is taken into the room and his guide points in turn to the three mirrors and asks: 'What do you see?' The observer replies firstly, 'I see a bad mirror', secondly, 'I see a beautiful mirror' and thirdly, 'I see a beautiful scene out of the open window'."

(A. Politz, Journal of Marketing, 1960)

Politz's conclusion is that it is the function of a good advert, like a good mirror, to reflect with perfect clarity and perfect accuracy the subject (i.e. product) in question without attracting any attention to itself. He continues.

'Intellectual gimmicks, cleverness, wittiness or ingenious and tricky word combinations do not add to but rather subtract from the effectiveness of advertising. In fact, many of these so-called attention getting devices actually operate as distractions.'

Politz also maintains that

'if a product has features worth paying money for, it must have features worth paying attention to'.

Is Politz right?

One can cite advertising examples both for and against his argument. The use of famous personalities is a very common attention gaining device in TV advertising. When Compaq Computers were trying to penetrate the U.K. market in the mid-eighties they ran a series of TV ads featuring John Cleese. They were very funny and made a lot of impact but the market researchers discovered a significant number of viewers who remembered the John Cleese advert but could not remember the name of the product he was advertising. A follow-up campaign, still starring John Cleese but this time featuring the Compaq product much more prominently was more successful in conveying the intended message.

On the other hand the very famous Campari ads in which Joan Collins drenched Leonard Rossiter in the liquid not only made a great impact but also succeeded very well in achieving the intended objective of increasing the target audience's awareness of the product.

There is of course no definitive answer to this question. We can however make a number of points which will help us to decide what it is that gets an advertising message noticed and remembered.

(a) Exposure

Simon Broadbent, in his book 'Spending Advertising Money' puts forward the 'threshold concept' which simply states that 'unless advertising for a brand reaches a certain level it will be wasted.' A TV ad shown only a small number of times will go virtually unnoticed. If, on the other hand, it is shown over and over again it will inevitably be noticed and remembered. I'm sure that very many people will still be able to remember the 'Tell Sid' campaign to promote the sale of shares in British Gas. At the time of writing it still holds the record for the largest sum of money spent on a single advertising campaign on British television. Sheer exposure therefore is a critical factor in overcoming the communications dilemma, but most advertisers cannot afford a 'Tell Sid' campaign. They can't rely solely on exposure to get their message across and must therefore find other ways. See section 11.4.1 and Figure 11.4 for further details.

(b) Consistency

Companies may not be able to afford the cost of saturation exposure in the space of one single advertising campaign, but if they consistently send the same message over a number of years the exposure effects become cumulative. Over time more and more people notice and remember the advertising. How many people do not know of the PG Tips chimps? Very few. PG Tips consistency also extends to the key message which the chimps utter to distinguish PG Tips from other tea. Can you remember the message? Of course, 'it's in the taste!' Boredom is avoided by regularly changing the little scene acted out by the chimps.

(c) Rapport

It must always be a vital advertising objective to seek rapport with the target audience. People take notice of things which interest them. Therefore the advertiser should find out what his target audience is interested in and ensure that his advertising reflects those interests. It's back to the basic marketing philosophy of being outward looking and putting yourself in the customers' shoes. If you want to sell tennis rackets to young male tennis players, have a picture of Boris Becker in the advert, because being like Boris Becker is what they're interested in. When Levi introduced their '501' jeans their research showed that there was a revival of interest in early rock and roll music amongst their target audience and thus used Eddie Cochran's song 'C'mon Everybody' as a way of successfully winning the attention of their audience.

In ideal circumstances the advertiser's message will be virtually synonymous with the interests of the target audience (e.g. the tennis racket). More often, however, the two will not coincide. The advertiser therefore has to use the interests of the target audience to achieve impact so that their attention has been won for the delivery of the advertising message (e.g. Levi 501's).

(d) Creative brilliance

There is no doubt that creative brilliance can also be responsible for advertising success. However, it is equally certain that it is the most difficult way of achieving that success because we arrive back at the communications dilemma - the problem of successfully marrying that creative brilliance with the clear and simple message that must be sent. In 1988 two car adverts (out of a long list of many forgettable car ads) were commonly cited by advertising practitioners as examples of creative brilliance. Both were ads for new models and therefore needed to make a big impact and both faced an image problem which they had to overcome.

The first ad featured the new Peugeot 405. People had an image of the larger Peugeot cars as rather dull, slow and old fashioned. Therefore, as well as getting the car noticed, the agency had to convey the impression that this new model was an exciting car, not at all in the mould of its predecessors. The creative team came up with an image of the new car speeding through fields of blazing sugar cane. It was dramatic, different and attention grabbing and despite being criticised by some environmental groups, it also contributed to rather than detracted from the fundamental message to be conveyed.

The second ad was all about the new Volkswagen Passat. The one where the car crashes through the floor and lands down on the floor below. Developed for Volkswagen by advertising agency DDB Needham this ad won the Grand Prix prize at the 1988 Cannes International Advertising Awards Festival. This means it was voted the best advert in the world in 1988. It came into being because market research had shown that people associated Volkswagen with small cars. They were not thought to make big, luxurious or expensive cars. That job it was believed, was performed by sister company Audi. The advertising brief was therefore simple, get the car noticed and convey the message first and foremost that it is BIG, and, if possible that it is luxurious. Hence the big, heavy car crashing through the floor; the gimmick once again adding to rather than subtracting from the message.

The Volkswagen ad was exceptional. It was also expensive, costing half a million pounds to make! The vast majority of advertisers don't have that kind of money and cannot reach those creative heights. Although there is a growing tendency for advertisers to try to entertain, especially on TV, they would be well advised before spending huge sums of money on a campaign to pre-test the ad to make sure that the intended message is coming across.

It is suggested that it is not possible to give a firm answer to the communications dilemma. It is possible, however, to draw some conclusions.

If we accept the validity of Schramm's model of the communications process, we can see that it is very difficult for advertisers to be effective because there are so many obstacles which can prevent the intended message reaching the audience.

Of the factors contributing to advertising effectiveness, exposure is the most certain way to success.

Most advertisers cannot afford sufficient exposure to be certain of getting their message noticed and remembered though long term consistency helps in this respect.

Within their limited budgets advertisers can maximise the level of attention they generate by using the interests of the target audience to establish rapport with them, since people are much more likely to take notice of things which interest them.

To make a huge impact, especially as far as TV advertising is concerned, creativity is becoming more important as the competition for the audience's attention intensifies. However, creative brilliance is very difficult to attain, and for every VW Passat advert there are probably many more which fall into the Politz trap of allowing the creativity to obscure or distort the message.

11.3.2 Developing the message

There are three stages in the development of an advertising message.

a. Message generation.

b. Message selection.

c. Message execution.

a. Message Generation

This is where the creative talents of the agency can run riot. There are no rules at this stage. Virtually anything goes. The main thing is to come up with a creative idea which is interesting enough and different enough to be noticed, and hopefully remembered. Many advertisers try to project a unique selling proposition (USP), in other words a clear main benefit not possessed by any competing products. Good examples would be toilet paper which is 'soft, strong and very long' or washing up liquid which is 'mild on your hands'.

b. Message Selection

The creative team will usually develop several messages for an important campaign. They will then test them out on samples drawn from the target audience. People may be shown videos of the alternative ads interspersed with current ads of competing and random products. They will then be interviewed to see which they remember most and which was best at conveying the intended message. Discussion groups may be used to explore the perception of the advertising message in some depth. The more expensive the campaign, the more thorough will be the pre-testing. The result should be the selection of the agency's best creative idea.

c. Message Execution

Most commentators agree that the final advert should concentrate on projecting one simple clear message, stressing the main benefit of the product or service. Print adverts should not use more words than necessary and should not be cluttered. As suggested in section 11.2.4 a lot of work goes into ensuring that adverts are produced to a very high technical standard. Poor photography, filming, sound or colour can ruin the effectiveness of an advert.

11.4 Media

However good the creative concept behind the advert, its effectiveness will still depend very much upon intelligent media selection. There is a vast choice of media through which the message can be communicated to the target market. There are a dozen national daily newspapers and hundreds of regional and local ones. There are over five hundred consumer magazines and even more trade journals. Television offers the advertiser fourteen ITV regions, Channel 4, TV AM, and the growth in cable and satellite stations. There are around fifty ILR (Independent Local Radio) stations, a thousand cinemas and a vast number of outdoor advertising opportunities. Before examining each of these potential media in more detail we must look at the decisions that need to be taken by the media planner.

11.4.1 Media planning

The chief objective of the media planner is to ensure that an acceptable proportion of the target audience (= COVERAGE) sees the advert a sufficient number of times (= FREQUENCY). The media planner must decide what coverage and frequency he should aim for, how much he can afford, and how he can achieve these objectives. The media planner will need to take account of the following factors.

(a) Budget constraints

A small advertising budget will automatically cut out the more expensive media such as television. The media planner will therefore need to be conscious from the outset of his budgetary constraints and choose only between those media which he can afford.

(b) The target audience

The media planner needs a very accurate profile of the members of his target audience. He needs to know their sex, age, social class, income, level of education geographical location and lifestyle.

(c) Coverage

All media publish detailed profiles of their typical readers (viewers, listeners etc.). You can find out the difference between a typical Guardian reader and a typical Sun reader. You can find out the profile of ITV viewers at 9p.m. on a Wednesday evening. Unbiassed breakdowns can be found in directories such as Benn's Media Directory or BRAD (British Rate and Data). The media planner must therefore match his target audience profile to the closest profile of users of different media. It will almost certainly be necessary to send the message via several different media to maximise coverage of the target audience.

It is interesting to note how much difference there can be between the potential maximum coverage offered by each medium, as shown by the diagram.

This graph is based on what the advertising world calls OTS, which means 'opportunity to see'. At some stage during the week, 92% of adults watch commercial television and therefore have an opportunity to see advertisements, whereas only 38% listen to ILR and a mere 2.5% go to the cinema.

(d) Cost effectiveness

If there is a choice of media through which the target audience could be reached the planner will not simply want to use the most effective media, he will want to use the most cost effective media. £1,000 spent on advertising will not reach exactly the same number of people whatever the medium that is used. When you include costs in the calculations, the most effective media e.g. television, may not turn out to be the most cost effective media because of their very high price.

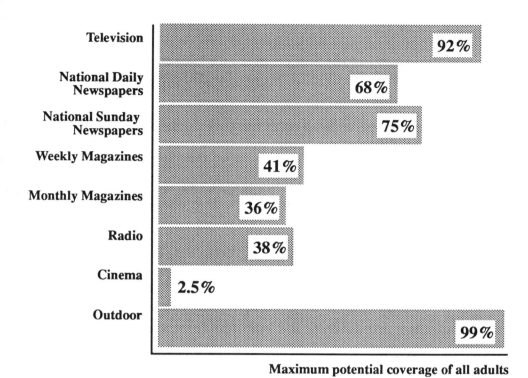

Figure 11.2 Adult weekly coverage potential by medium.
(Source: *Marketing Magazine,* 1987).

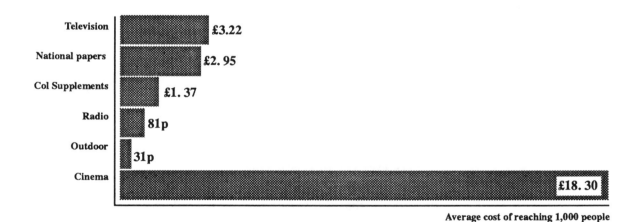

Figure 11.3 Adult cost per thousand by medium. (Source, Marketing, **1987**).

The CPT (the estimated cost of reaching one thousand people in the target audience) is the standard method used by media planners to compare the cost effectiveness of different media. On television the most widely used measure of CPT is the thirty second slot. The audience of a TV commercial consists of the number of people claiming to be in the room with the television set on and tuned to the relevant channel. They do not have to be actually watching the commercial to have one 'opportunity to see' (OTS). For newspapers a full page black and white ad is used and for colour supplements a full page colour ad. Outdoor is the most difficult medium to put a CPT figure on because of the wide variation in prices for outdoor advertising in different locations and the difficulty in measuring audiences. However, all experts agree that outdoor advertising offers the cheapest way of giving large numbers of adults an opportunity to see your message. The cinema comes out very badly on this chart, but arguably it is not a very fair comparison since it is a well known fact that adults in general are infrequent cinema goers. If the target audience were young adults (16 to 24 year olds), the CPT for cinema turns out to be lower than it is for television.

(e) Frequency

It may not be enough simply to cover the target audience, however cost-effective that coverage if the members of that audience do not see the message a sufficient number of times. Simon Broadbent developed the 'threshold concept' (see Figure 11.4) which suggests that unless people are exposed to a message a certain number of times they will remember little if any of it. To be effective advertising must therefore go beyond that threshold level.

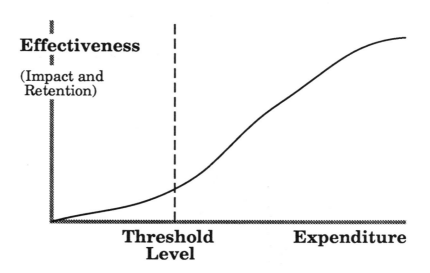

The Threshold Concept.......
'unless advertising for a brand reaches
a certain level it will be wasted' (Simon Broadbent)

Figure 11.4 The threshold concept.

'Frequency' is the word used by advertisers to describe the number of opportunities to see that the target audience should have. For an average budget TV campaign the media planner would probably try to achieve six opportunities to see spread over a period of four weeks. To achieve six OTS, the advert would have to be run many more times than that. Frequency can conflict with coverage, because the more times an advertiser has to run his advert in one medium to achieve the desired frequency, the less money will remain in his budget to use a selection of media to cover the audience more fully.

Most media planners have to end up compromising here. Six OTS for a TV campaign is probably less exposure than most advertisers would desire, but it is probably all they can afford if they are going to use a spread of media to reach those parts of the audience who are not heavy TV viewers. Advertisers with very large budgets will be able to achieve much higher frequency without sacrificing coverage.

(f) Impact

However, knowing the CPT for each of the alternative media still isn't enough, because we are still not comparing like with like. How can you compare the impact made on an individual member of the audience by the following commercials.

A cinema commercial on a large screen in a darkened room commanding the full attention of its audience,

An independent radio commercial in an office, factory or house where the radio is on for a large proportion of the day as background noise,

A newspaper

A poster next to a busy road on the edge of a provincial town.

Of course, there is no single objective yardstick which could accurately judge the impact of these four commercials. We can only make assumptions, based on experience, that the cinema will have the most impact, the roadside poster the least with the radio and newspaper coming somewhere between. It is also true that different products will make more impact in some media than others. TV (or cinema) was the only medium that could do justice to the exciting new concept offered by the first Polaroid cameras, whereas fashions make most impact in glossy magazines. The advertiser often decides that it is worth paying more for a medium which offers greater impact for his message.

In developing his media schedule the planner will have to take into account all these five factors. He must work within his budget, he must choose the right media to reach the target audience, he must cover the whole of the target audience and he must ensure that the target audience has an opportunity to see the message a sufficient number of times. Moreover, not only must he achieve all this in the most cost effective way possible, he must also use media which will enhance the impact of his message.

The media planner therefore usually has to make a compromise decision. Basically he is being pulled in four different directions, as shown in the diagram below.

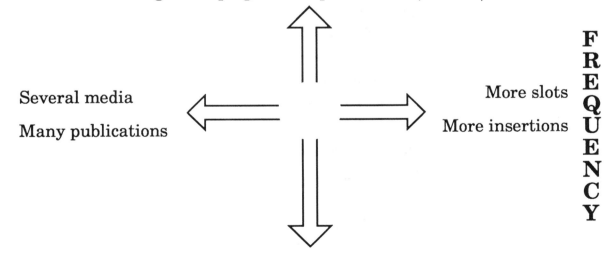

CONTINUITY
Longer campaigns or drip schedules (see 11.4.3)

C O V E R A G E — Several media / Many publications

F R E Q U E N C Y — More slots / More insertions

Longer commercials, colour ads, bigger spaces

IMPACT

Figure 11.5 The media planner's problem.

The forces influencing the media planner's decisions are pulling him in four directions. He can't satisfy them all but must reach the best compromise decision which does not ignore any of the four factors.

11.4.2 Media selection

The success of the media planner in achieving his objectives will depend very much on his ability to select the right media. Each have their own distinguishing characteristics, which we will examine in this section.

In 1986 the £7.6 billion spent on advertising in the U.K. was distributed across the media in the following way:

Newspapers 41.5%

Television 32.5%

Magazines 19.6%

Outdoor 4.0%

Radio 2.0%

Cinema 0.4%

We will now consider the characteristics of each of these different media.

(a) Newspapers

There is a wide range of national newspapers and magazines. New national newspapers have appeared in recent years (e.g. the *Independent* and *Today*) and many new free local newspapers have been launched.

Newspapers vary widely in their circulation as shown by the following table for national newspapers.

Daily Newspapers.

The Sun 4,146,644

Daily Mirror 3,082,215

Daily Mail 1,792,701

Daily Express 1,679,438

Daily Telegraph 1,138,673

The Star 1,013,688

The Guardian 470,023

The Times 450,626

Today 408,078

The Independent 375,317

The Financial Times 286,774

Sunday Newspapers.

News of the World 5,213,901

Sunday Mirror 2,778,935

The People 2,749,246

Sunday Express 2,143,374

Mail on Sunday 1,932,799

The Sunday Times 1,362,743

Observer 749,644

Sunday Telegraph 716,044

Sunday Sport 430,000

Figure 11.6 National newspaper circulation January - June 1988. Source: Audit Bureau of Circulation. Figures show average sales for that period.

It is interesting to note that British people feel they have more time for newspaper reading on Sundays than on weekdays with three million extra copies being sold - 17,646,686 compared to 14,844,086. There is evidence that Sunday newspapers are read more carefully and in a more leisurely fashion than daily newspapers.

Advantages of newspaper advertising

1. **High national coverage.** Over 85% of the population can be reached through national and local newspapers, although in practice, advertisements would have to be placed in a very large number of newspapers to achieve this level of coverage.

2. **Audience segmentation.** National newspapers attract different types of readers which allows advertisers to target specific audiences. The regional and local press allow very accurate geographical segmentation.

3. **Credibility.** It is often felt that people believe the printed word more than certain other forms of advertising, though, of course, some national newspapers will enhance the credibility of the message more than others.

4. **Messages.** Long or complex ones can be sent if a large space is booked and long copy is written.

5. **Frequency of publication.** Some advertising messages have great urgency. The ability to send a message at very short notice can therefore be important. Daily newspapers offer this possibility.

6. **Split runs.** A big advantage offered to the advertiser by most national newspapers is the facility of split runs, where half the print run can carry one form of copy and the other half can carry different copy. This enables the advertiser to test two different adverts.

7. **Economical.** For many advertisers newspapers will prove to be the cheapest way of reaching large numbers of people with an advertising message.

8. **Specialisation.** Certain days become known for special features. A good example would be job advertisements which appear in the quality nationals on certain days for certain careers. This improves targeting as people in the relevant target audience are likely to make a point of buying on that day.

9. **Colour supplements.** An increasing number of colour supplements are now being included with newspapers. Originally offered with certain Sunday newspapers, they have now spread to some of newspapers, such as the *Daily Telegraph,* which offers a colour supplement with its Saturday edition. Supplements help to overcome some of the disadvantages of newspaper advertising. They are appropriate for products which require high quality, colour advertising and they are often read by several people and kept for several days, or even weeks, thus helping to overcome the first two disadvantages of newspaper advertising given below.

Disadvantages of newspaper advertising

1. **Poor impact.** This is due to the volume of competing advertising messages and the fact that newspapers result in rather 'flat', uninteresting adverts, though the use of colour in newspapers is reducing this to a certain extent.

2. **Short life.** Daily newspapers have a short life and are often only partially read.

3. **Quantity.** There is a proliferation of local newspapers making it difficult for national advertisers to make accurate judgements on their value, particularly since there is often a dearth of readership information too. This problem has been exacerbated by the growing number of free newspapers. Usually local or regional, there is often a higher proportion of advertising matter to editorial matter than in a typical paid for newspaper. Often delivered on a door to door basis, the 'opportunity to see', in the area of distribution, is very high in theory, but in practice there is a great deal of uncertainty over the actual level of readership of free newspapers. The net effect of the spread of free newspapers, as far as most advertisers are concerned, is to increase the fragmentation of media and make the media selection process more difficult.

Buying newspaper space

Space is bought either as a double page spread, a full page, half page, one third or one quarter page. Smaller spaces are bought in terms of 'SCC' (single column centimetres). For example, a 30 x 4 space would form an advert 4 columns wide by 30 centimetres deep. Details of costs appear in BRAD or Benn's Media Directory or in the rate cards supplied by the newspapers. The CPT of competing newspapers is roughly equivalent. In other words, a newspaper with a high circulation can charge more for the same space than a newspaper with a lower circulation. The cost of space will also vary according to other factors such as its position in the newspaper. Prime spots such as the front page, TV page etc. will command a premium price. Lack of competition from other adverts also increases the price, so a 'solus' spot (no other advertising on that page), or a 'next matter' position (next to editorial rather than next to another advert) will be more expensive than a 'run of paper' spot which the editor can place anywhere he wishes.

Costs

Costs can vary dramatically between the national and local press. In 1988 the published rates for the Daily Mail for black and white display advertising were as follows:

Full page £24,500

SCC £82

The Holme Valley Express, a paid for weekly covering the Holmfirth area of West Yorkshire would charge somewhat less:

Full page £400

SCC £1.60

In conclusion, many newspapers enjoy reader loyalty which may enhance the credibility of the advertiser's message, which makes them very useful for prestige and reminder advertising. They can also be useful for product launches such as new cars because of editorial support and the newsy, urgent nature of the medium. However, as they are read hurriedly, adverts will often go unnoticed and lengthy copy may be wasted, although the Sunday papers are read in a much more leisurely fashion.

(b) Television

Television viewing is nearly equally divided between BBC and the IBA (Independent Broadcasting Authority) which includes ITV, Channel 4, and TV AM. ITV is split into fourteen regions, each of which is run by an independent company under a franchise arrangement. The list below shows the companies running each region and the share of the national audience which each reaches.

Region	Company	Share of audience
London	London Weekend & Thames (weekdays)	22%
Midlands	Central	16%
North West	Granada	13%
Yorkshire, N.Midlands	Yorkshire	11%
Wales and West	Harlech	7%
South	TV South	7%
North East	Tyne Tees	6%
Central Scotland	Scottish	5%
East	Anglia	5%
South West	TV South West	3%
N.Ireland	Ulster	2%
N.Scotland	Grampian	2%
S.Scotland,N.England	Border	1%
Channel Islands	Channel	tiny

The Advantages of television

1. Mass communication of simple messages. Since it reaches virtually all homes almost everyone has an opportunity to see TV advertising.

2. Impact is very good, helped by colour, sound and often a very high standard of creativity.

3. The message is received in a relaxed atmosphere at home.

4. Regional segmentation is good, provided the regional boundaries are appropriate.

5. Extensive viewing data helps to target specific audiences.

6. Attractive discounts and other assistance will often be available to new advertisers.

Disadvantages of television

1. Airtime is very expensive at peak viewing times.

2. Production costs for highly creative advertising are very high.

3. Coverage is poor with higher income/education groups tending to be light TV viewers and therefore difficult to reach through this medium.

4. Viewers' attention often wanders during the commercial breaks.

5. Remote control has aggravated this problem, with viewers often 'channel flicking' during commercial breaks.

6. The growing use of videos also causes problems as many viewers fast forward the adverts when watching recorded programmes.

Buying Time

Each TV company sells airtime in commercial breaks between and during programmes. There are three or four breaks per hour with a maximum limit of 7 minutes per hour for advertising allowed. Different advertising rates are charged at different times of day, roughly corresponding with audience size, with the highest rate occurring during the peak early evening viewing time. Prices also vary considerably between the large ITV companies and the smaller ones. The prices shown below are taken from the July 1988 issue of BRAD and refer to the cost of 30 second slots.

Peak time ITV:

Thames: £38,500

Anglia: 10,000

Border: 1,600

Off peak 4:

Thames: £250

Anglia: 200

Border: 35

A peak time thirty second slot on national ITV (all regions) could cost around £100,000 but in practice, discounting is prevalent and media buyers often achieve reductions of around 30% in rate card costs. On the other hand, at times of peak demand, such as the run in to the Christmas retailing bonanza, premiums can be paid. ITV companies operate a kind of auction system known as pre-emption. Unless an advertiser pays an extra fee to secure a certain slot, another advertiser can pre-empt up to 24 hours before transmission time.

The buying of TV airtime is highly complex and requires the use of specialist media buyers, but broadly speaking advertisers try to achieve coverage of the whole TV audience or a certain segment of it, such as ABC1 adult women. This is measured in terms of TVR's (television ratings), where 10 TVR's means that a certain slot will have been seen by 10% of the audience in question. Since 100% of the audience would be equivalent to 1 OTS (opportunity to see), the media buyers use the term 'Gross OTS' to express the total number of opportunities to see achieved by a particular campaign. However, since this figure is no more than the sum of the TVR's achieved by each individual slot, a Gross OTS of 4 does not mean that everyone in the target audience with a TV set has seen the advert four times. Some individuals may have seen it twenty times and others not at all. There is no way of ensuring genuine coverage of the target audience through TV advertising.

(c) Magazines

Magazines vary from quarterlies to weeklies and from very general magazines with a wide readership such as the *Radio Times* to highly specialist journals with much smaller circulations. There are well over a thousand magazines of one kind or another published in the U.K. though the numbers are constantly changing. The main difference between newspapers and magazines is that magazines pre-select their audience by their content, and are therefore much better for targeting purposes. We can divide magazines into seven broad categories:

Special interest

Interests of all kinds are covered by specialist magazines from photography to skateboarding, from dog breeding to chess.

General interest

Women's magazines form the bulk of this category but there are also children's magazines, broadcasting magazines and current affairs type magazines.

Trade journals

Aimed typically at the distribution trade they cover items of topical interest and are a major vehicle for supplier information to the trade, either in the form of editorial (written largely from manufacturers' press releases), or advertising. A typical example would be *The Grocer.*

Technical journals

Aimed at companies in manufacturing or service industries, these journals do often contain long technical articles as well as shorter more topical items. Again a large volume of advertising will be found. Typical examples would be *Plastics and Rubber Weekly* and *Woodworking Industry.*

Professional journals

These are aimed across industry divisions at members of specific professions such as accountants, personnel managers, solicitors or engineers. Many professional bodies have their own magazine. Job advertising is prominent in these journals.

Regional magazines

Traditionally these were rather up-market social publications such as *Cheshire Life,* but with the ever decreasing costs of publishing a large number of locally based free magazines are appearing aimed both at the domestic market and at local businesses.

In-house magazines

Most large companies and some smaller one publish in house magazines as a PR exercise. Aimed at their own staff and sometimes also distributed to customers and suppliers, some of these magazines do carry advertising.

Advantages of Magazine Advertising

1. They have a longer life than newspapers and one copy may be read by several people - even by hundreds if it ends up in a doctor's waiting room.

2. Segmentation and targeting can be very precise.

3. Special interest magazines will often be read avidly by enthusiasts who will be prepared to devote considerable time and attention to all of its contents, including the advertisements as well as the editorial. In addition to improving the chances of an advert being noticed, it enables advertisers to use long and complicated copy if necessary.

4. High quality paper and print is suitable for up-market advertising, e.g. fashion, perfume, quality furniture.

5. Some magazines are kept by subscribers as sources of reference.

6. Some respected journals may add credibility to advertising messages.

Disadvantages of magazine advertising

1. High quality production means high cost since very high quality originals are necessary to take full advantage of the glossy medium.

2. Infrequent publication causes long lead and cancellation times and makes really topical advertising impossible.

3. Advertisers face considerable competition for their message from editorial and other adverts.

4. The long life of some magazines makes monitoring and evaluation difficult.

5. Readership details are much less comprehensive for most magazines than they are for newspapers. The smaller journals may not even have independently audited circulation figures.

6. Cost per thousand is typically high but is arguably offset by the greater intrinsic value of the advert to the reader, particularly in the specialist magazines.

Buying Space

The basis of magazine space selling and buying is very similar to the newspaper system. as it has similar categories of space size, special positions, premiums and discounts. However, since magazines usually face greater media competition than newspapers, their sales departments have to be particularly active and frequently offer advertisers special inducements such as special introductory rates for new advertisers, special editorial features to accompany adverts, reader reply services, and advertising space in very flexible shapes such as L shapes, T shapes and even diagonal advertisements.

The one big difference in buying space in magazines rather than newspapers is lead time. Copy dates (deadline for receipt of finished artwork) for colour ads in monthly magazines may be as much as three months before publication, so the space will often need to be booked around six months ahead, with the creative planning having to precede that. This explains why topical advertising in the glossies is so difficult.

Cost of Advertising Space

Costs vary widely according to the circulation and prestige of the magazine. It is best to illustrate this point with some examples. All are taken from the July 1988 edition of BRAD, which is by far the most comprehensive source of advertising media and their costs in the U.K.

Colour page

Woman's Own £19,600

Cosmopolitan £6,400

Just 17 £5,100

Black & white page

Woman's Own £14,000

Radio Times £14,000

TV Times £12,130

Prima £7,500

M & S Magazine £5,950

Smash Hits £5,350

Cosmopolitan £4,230

Weekend £3,700

Elle £3,200

Just 17 £2,800

Motor Cycle News £2,507

Company £2,260

The Economist £1,750

Titbits £1,680

Men Only £1,600

Melody Maker £1,540

Girl About Town £1,400

Autocar £1,150

Running £1,080

Annabel £1,000

Rowing Monthly £375

Black & white 1/8 page

Woman's Own £1,750

Cosmopolitan £535

Just 17 £470

Melody Maker £300

Running £155

Rowing Monthly £65

(d) Outdoor

As well as poster sites, outdoor advertising includes transport advertising opportunities (such as buses, taxis, underground trains and stations, railway stations and airports), sports stadia perimeter boards and even milk bottles, parking meters and balloons. Outdoor posters are usually sited on the sides of buildings, by the roadside, around car parks, in shopping centres and precincts and even on litter bins.

Outdoor advertising does lack many of the attributes of the press and television but is useful for reminding people, building frequency and perhaps reaching some of the less accessible parts of the audience. The concept of visual transfer is often used for outdoor advertising. Research has shown that images from TV commercials remind people of the whole advert, thus increasing the impact made by the poster.

Advantages of Outdoor Advertising

1. By far the lowest CPT of all media.

2. High coverage and OTS - theoretically 94% of the population has the opportunity to see a poster advertisement in a week and almost everyone over a long period.

3. Large poster sites can be very dramatic.

4. Adverts are in full colour.

5. There is a very wide choice of locations and sites.

6. Little direct competition from advertising matter.

7. Some poster sites may achieve 'sole attraction' status, where people have little else to do but read the advert when standing on the underground platform, riding up the escalator or waiting for the bus.

8. Many poster sites are booked for 13 weeks and it is said that poster advertising may come close to achieving the 'subliminal effect' (where people sub-consciously absorb a message without realising it) as people pass the poster site maybe twice a day for 13 weeks.

Disadvantages of outdoor advertising

1. Wallpaper effect. Since they are always there and have very little opportunity to make impact, the main criticism of the outdoor media is that messages go totally unnoticed by many people. The big exception to this rule was the outdoor advertising which accompanied the introduction of Araldite, when a real Ford Cortina, (albeit minus the heavy bits such as engine and transmission) was stuck to a billboard. Needless to say, as well as being noticed on the spot, this creative coup also generated much additional publicity in the media, and was arguably one of the most brilliant pieces of advertising of all time.

2. Printing costs for the large sheets ordered in relatively small quantities are expensive.

3. Booking and cancellation lead times are long.

4. Audience research is very scanty.

5. Grafitti is a problem on some sites.

6. Most sites suffer from plenty of extraneous matter to distract the attention of passers-by, especially drivers.

7. Suitable only for very simple messages due to the often short exposure time (maybe less than 5 seconds) of the audience.

8. Due to the complexities of buying outdoor space, advertisers usually opt for the contractors' packages (explained below). The problem with such packages is that the advertisers never really know what they have bought, in terms of exact location, numbers and type of people to be covered.

9. Production problems make topicality very difficult except at high cost. Sometimes advertisers feel the cost is worth paying as when Shell suffered the embarrassment of having to withdraw their new 'Formula Shell' petrol early in 1988 due to reports that it could harm certain types of engine. Within days Esso had implemented a national poster campaign announcing that their petrol would not harm your engine!

10. Due to TC booking procedures (see below) prime sites can be monopolised by regular advertisers for long periods to the exclusion of others.

Buying Poster Space

The size of poster sites is measured in 'sheets'. Nominally a sheet is 30 inches by 20 inches (the industry staunchly resists metrication) but sites are usually 4 sheet (5ft x 3ft 4in), 16 sheet (10ft x 6ft 8in), or 48 sheet (10ft x 20ft). In addition there are the 'supersites', 10 feet high and sold in multiples of 3 feet widths with 27 and 36 feet being the most common.

Outdoor space is sold by contractors who each own thousands of sites around the country. Well known contractors include Independent Poster Sales, Adshel and Moore O'Farrell. They tend to sell pre-selected packages through the Association of Poster Marketing (a joint sales organisation). These packages include a mixture of sites which supposedly deliver a specified audience. Until recently this was deemed highly suspect due to the transient nature of poster audiences. In 1985, in a bid to improve the status of their medium the poster industry introduced OSCAR (Outdoor Site Classification and Audience Research) which is improving the availability of data to help media planners to make informed decisions.

Poster sites are usually booked for a month or three months but it is possible to book sites 'TC' (till countermanded). This is popular for some prime sites, e.g. outside a busy supermarket, or with continuous poster advertisers such as cigarette manufacturers. It does however cause frustration with some advertisers who complain of the unavailability of the best sites. To help media planners, packages can often be booked nationally or by TV region.

Outdoor Advertising Costs

A single small poster site could be booked for a few pounds, but this virtually never happens. Sites are bought in packages. The Association of Poster Marketing sells a package including 400 sites in a variety of sizes and locations for £68,000 per month. Production costs are also steep, tending to add around 30% on to the cost of a typical package.

Transport advertising is not cheap either. A package of 450 bus backs for one month in the Granada and Border TV regions would cost £19,800. Alternatively a region with less people and even fewer buses, TVSW, would offer 40 bus backs for £1,760.

For the yet more economy minded, parking meters can be booked monthly at an average cost of £2 each and advertising on the back of match boxes costs a mere 5p per box! (All figures from BRAD, July 1988).

(e) Radio

The IBA runs Independent Local Radio (ILR) comprising 47 stations at present. Programming is generally middle of the road in contrast to BBC's four highly segmented national services. Although ILR is currently receivable by around 85% of the population, only about 45% listen in a typical week. This figure rises to over 60% for the 15-24 year olds but gradually declines to below 30% for over 60's. Radio Luxembourg is an important addition to radio advertising, playing pop music during the evenings and reaching large audiences of teenagers. The visual transfer concept can be adapted on an audio level with songs or jingles associated with well known TV adverts helping to increase the impact of radio advertising. A recent ILR development has been networking, starting with the Network Chart show on Sundays, which offers advertisers the possibility of genuinely national advertising on ILR.

Advantages of radio advertising

1. Precise local coverage.

2. Commercials are transmitted serially, so they do not have to compete at that point in time for listeners' attention with other adverts or with programme matter. (Unlike newspapers, for example, where a large amount of competing material faces the reader).

3. Radio is an excellent medium for conveying urgency, e.g. 'hurry to Joe's store on Main Road NOW, while stocks last'.

4. Campaigns can be booked or cancelled at short notice which facilitates topical and urgent advertising.

5. Sound quality is much better than TV which does offer the possibility of making impact through the use of creative sound effects.

6. Production costs can be very low due to very simple production technology. Radio stations will help advertisers with production of their ads.

7. Discounts will be available for first time advertisers.

Disadvantages of radio advertising

1. Planning is difficult because apart from the excellent local targeting, radio research is still not sufficiently comprehensive to enable media planners to plan national campaigns in the way they would like.

2. Radio is generally assumed to be very poor on impact. It is seen as 'verbal wallpaper', always there in the background, but rarely paid full attention.

3. Booked nationally, ILR is an expensive medium.

Buying Radio Time

The ILR radio stations sell airtime in two ways. Firstly there are specialist radio sales organisations selling time on behalf of all ILR stations and mainly aimed at servicing London advertising agencies. Secondly each station sells its own air time on a local basis. Radio Luxembourg sell its own time through a London sales office.

Radio time is not usually bought spot by spot, but by packages of spots which are guaranteed (loosely) by the station to reach a certain audience. The most popular package is the TAP (Total Audience Package) which includes a collection of spots in various segments reaching a cross section of listeners.

Most commercials are 30 seconds in length, although 15, 45, 60 second or even two minute commercials are available. Commercials are vetted locally by the station for their conformance to advertising standards which helps to keep the lead time to a minimum.

Cost of Radio Advertising

Costs vary widely. The samples given below are all official rate card costs from the July 1988 issue of BRAD. Discounts will be widely available, especially for quantity bookings.

The most expensive 30 second spot on a local station would be Capital Radio's price of £1,300 for a commercial on Sunday morning between 10am and 1pm. At the other extreme a 30 second spot on a weekday evening could cost as little as £6 on Devonair or £4 on West Sound (based in Ayr). More typically, most 30 second spots would cost in the region of £50 - £200. Advertising on the Network Chart show would cost £2,500 for a 30 second spot, £1,250 for a 10 second spot. A TAP covering all ILR stations and including 3 thirty second spots per day for a week would cost around £60,000.

(f) Cinema

The number of cinemas has been declining for over thirty years, although it has slowed down considerably over the last ten years. Hit initially by the spread of television the medium has also had to contend with the threat of video rental in more recent years. As a result it has become increasingly dependent upon the latest 'Big Films' with star names and much publicity. There are now less than 700 cinemas in the U.K. and around 1,230 screens in total. The cinema is a very young medium, with 30% of 15 to 24 year olds claiming to attend once a week and 76% attending at least once a month. The attendance figures drop rapidly amongst older age groups, although the audience at cinemas in the West End of London shows an older profile. The cinema is therefore used mainly as a way of targeting this young audience with products like jeans, cosmetics, motorcycles, new bank accounts and local entertainment likely to feature prominently amongst adverts.

Advantages of cinema advertising

1. Reproduction quality of both sound and picture is superb.

2. Local advertising is feasible.

3. Excellent targeting of young adults.

4. Ideal conditions for holding the attention of the audience, with the impact of the big screen and the absence of distractions.

5. Research shows that people recall cinema commercials better than TV commercials.

Disadvantages of cinema advertising

1. Low audiences.

2. Very slow build up of coverage and frequency since commercials are shown only once during a programme and most individuals even in the young adult group will not attend the cinema more than once a month.

3. Production costs are extremely high. Initial filming is no more expensive than for television, but then the costs start to escalate. The cinema contractors demand two very high quality 70mm colour prints per screen, which is a lot of films if a

national cinema campaign is contemplated especially since they cost several hundred pounds each. Thus many advertisers use alternate weeks advertising at each cinema (or screen) to halve the print costs.

4. Many cinema adverts, especially the local ones, are of poor quality, and this image may rub off on the whole commercial break.

5. Buying is arguably more difficult than for any other medium, though attempts have recently been made to ameliorate this.

Buying cinema space

Yes, for some odd reason it is referred to as space. Most cinemas have their advertising 'space' sold through two selling organisations, Pearl and Dean or Rank Screen Advertising. Until recently lack of audience data made it very difficult for media planners to know exactly what they were buying, but the recent formation of CAVIAR aims to overcome this problem. Standing for Cinema and Video Industry Audience Research the body will provide detailed information about cinema attendance in different regions, for different films by different segments of the audience.

Cinema advertising is usually bought in the form of packages which attempt to segment the audience. You can buy a package of cinemas in seaside towns, cities, university towns, the west end of London etc. More specific packages allow advertising to be bought around certain 'big films', or solely for 'X' rated films. Apart from the obvious public cinemas, it is also possible to buy into holiday camp cinemas, cinemas on boats and army camp cinemas. In general, however, media buyers find cinema space very difficult to buy, which may be an important factor in the medium's very low share of advertising revenue.

Cost of cinema advertising

Spots can be booked with individual cinemas at a cost of around £30 for a thirty second spot for one week. Of course, with the production costs taken into account it would make sense only to book a number of weeks (or several different cinemas). To book a thirty second slot nationally on all 1,233 screens for one week would cost £41,070.

11.4.3 Scheduling

Having developed the creative message and chosen the media for its transmission to the target audience the media planner must work out the best timing for his campaign (macro - scheduling) and a detailed timetable of events to make sure that everything appears when it is supposed to (micro - scheduling). Macro - scheduling is concerned with when to spend the advertising budget throughout the year, micro - scheduling is about deciding how to time adverts in various media throughout a campaign.

(a) Macro - scheduling

The basic decision facing the media planner is whether to adopt a 'drip approach', which involves spreading the budget fairly evenly over the year, or whether some kind of 'burst approach' which would concentrate advertising at certain times, would be more appropriate. Many advertisers opt for a burst approach simply because regular advertising of a type to make sufficient impact, would be prohibitively expensive. Also the seasonality of some products makes a burst campaign prior to peak expenditure the most logical strategy to follow. We therefore see heavy advertising for holidays in the new year and for drinks and toys in the weeks preceding Christmas and new bank accounts during the summer months when many young people will be starting university or their first job. If, on the other hand, a product is not particularly seasonal there may be a good case for exploiting 'soft' sectors such as June - August when demand for advertising time / space, and therefore its cost, are lower.

(b) Micro - scheduling

As the choice of media is finalised a detailed timetable known as a media schedule will need to be produced. The media schedule below (Figure 11.7) gives micro - scheduling details for a campaign using print media. It must show the publications to be used, the space size booked in each, the number and dates of each insertion, the individual cost of each advert and the total cost for the campaign. Ideally it should also show the media planners' estimated coverage of the target audience and average number of opportunities to see. Schedules will also need to be produced to show the timing and nature of advertising in other media, although if packages have been bought, details will be limited to the general information on that package supplied by the media owners.

The schedule shown in Figure 11.7 is for the advertising of an industrial product to manufacturers of electrical equipment. Two trade journals have been used, the first one monthly and the second one weekly. The space column gives details of the type of space that has been booked. In all cases it is a 4 colour (which simply means full colour), full page. One insertion in Electrical review will be a front cover, for which a premium has been paid, and all other insertions in both journals will be inside, but FM (facing matter) so they won't be faced with direct competition from any other advertisements. The gross rate card cost shows the premium that has been paid both for the front page and for the FM positions, but the third cost column shows that some discount has been negotiated. This figure multiplied by the total number of insertions shows the total cost due. The final columns show when the adverts will appear. The letters across the top represent the months, starting in August, so this campaign will run from September to January. Electronics and Power is monthly, so a cross is placed in each month when the advert will appear. For the weekly publication, the dates of the issues in which advertising will appear are shown.

Conclusion

Somewhat in contrast to its carefree glamourous image, advertising is a very skilled and highly technical discipline. Creative departments come closest to the common 'way-out' view of the advertising profession. In the intensely competitive world of advertising genuinely creative ideas are worth gold, so good creative people are often allowed to work (and behave) virtually as they like.

In general, however, advertising is about very careful planning, particularly on the media side, where the choice of channels of communication is huge, each offering a different route to the target audience. Buying media time and space is a highly skilled occupation in itself.

Last but not least, campaigns have to be put together. Commercials have to run on TV at the right time on the right day. Films have to be made, photography and artwork organised, posters produced. The account executive who must control all of these activities and keep the client happy may have a glamorous job, but certainly not a carefree one.

STARCHI & STARCHI LIMITED
Incorporated Practitioners in Advertising

Media Schedule

Client	Campaign Period	Job No.	Schedule Type	Date	Page
	Aug 85 - May 86	825	Booked	8. 08. 1985	**1

1986

Publication Data	Space	Rate Card Cost	Gross RateCard Cost	Negotiated Gross Cost	No Ins	Total Cost	A	S	O	N	D	J	F	M	A	M	J	J
ELECTRONICS & POWER (M) 43581	Page 4 Colour F M	1165.00	1233.53	1233.53	3	3700.59		X		X	X							
ELECTRICAL REVIEW (W) 20047	Whole Page 4 Colour Front Cover	1450.00	1535.29	1535.29	1	1535.29							3					
	Page 4 Colour F M	1330.00	1408.24	1260.03	5	6300.15			6	18	15	6						
									27									
Total for this Schedule						11536.03												

Figure 11. 7 A media schedule

Assignment Wentworth Publications

Wentworth Publications has produced a new magazine aimed at full time students in Colleges of Further Education and in Sixth Forms. As well as features of general interest such as music, films, sport etc., the magazine will include serious articles on issues of interest to students. Changes in examination systems, student facilities in colleges, career and higher education opportunities would all feature prominently.

With production planning well underway, the first issue is due out in six months time to coincide with the beginning of the new academic year. Advertising agents Ace Communications have been awarded the account and the creative team is busy working on a brilliantly creative idea which will be suitable for all main media. Media planner Geoff Crowther will therefore be constrained only by his budget in deciding on the best media to reach his target audience. He has a total budget of £190,000 including media and production costs for a burst campaign in September and October. But time is already running short to plan the campaign properly and book the media, and Geoff is still worried about the lack of published research data on this very precise audience. There is plenty of information about teenagers and young adults but this population doesn't quite fit in to either. There is also the problem that students of this age may not have exactly the same media habits as people of a similar age who have already started work. He can therefore see no alternative but to do some market research and has formed a team of four young assistant media planners from his department in order to speed up progress.

Task

In the role of Geoff Crowther and with a team of four assistants, carry out a college student audience research project. The team brief is to:

1. Draw up an audience profile of the target market in terms of

      1.1 Age range

      1.2 Age breakdown as follows: 16 - 18 19 - 21 22+

      1.3 Sex breakdown

      1.4 Living with parents / living independently

      1.5 Main leisure interests.

2. Media Habits 2.1 TV viewing in terms of heavy: over 20 hours per week medium: 11 - 20 hours per week light: up to 10 hours per week 2.2 Radio listening according to the same criteria 2.3 Cinema going as follows heavy: at least once per week on average medium: at least once per month on average light: less than once per month 2.4 Readership of national newspapers, daily and Sunday. 2.5 Readership of local or regional newspapers. 2.6 Readership of magazines.

In each case for 2.4 to 2.6 list the most popular titles with their percentage coverage of the target audience.

It will be essential to carry out a primary research survey to ascertain the information required for points 1 and 2. Use a sample of no less than 100 young people, with a personally administered questionnaire completed by the interviewer.

3. Present your findings in report format.

4. Outline your recommendations for a broad media strategy to reach this target audience, together with your estimation of the costs of production and media and the sort of coverage of the target audience that we could expect from your strategy. Check your figures with BRAD where possible. Comment also on lead time requirements.

5. Complete a media schedule on the normal form (attached) for all print advertising to be used. As far as costs are concerned, consult BRAD as far as possible and simply fill in the rate card cost at present.

6. Provide details of market research questionnaire and tables of results as appendices.

7. Be prepared to make a 15 minute presentation of your work to the whole account team in three weeks time.

ACE COMMUNICATIONS LIMITED

Media Schedule

Client	Product	Campaign Period	Job No.	Schedule Type	Date	Page

Publication Data	Space	Rate Card Cost	Gross RateCard Cost	Negotiated Gross Cost	No Ins	Total Cost	A	S	O	N	D	J	F	M	A	M	J	J

Chapter 12

Other Promotional Techniques

Introduction

In addition to advertising there are many techniques that a marketer can use to stimulate demand for a product or service. This chapter will look at the remainder of the non-personal methods of communication and Chapter 13 will cover personal communications.

12.1 Direct mail

The popular impression of direct mail is a vision of millions of consumers and businesses being submerged each day beneath a mountain of direct mail. This is a misconception. Although the irritation factor caused by individual mailshots which are inappropriately targeted may be very high, the volume of direct mail received – even by businesses – is not particularly large. In fact, British households and organisations receive, on average, only a small proportion of the direct mail that would be received by a typical American consumer or business buyer.

An even greater misconception is that all mailshots take the most direct route to the waste bin, and must therefore be a waste of money. In fact, many transactions are completed as a result of mailshots. Even a seemingly tiny response rate, below 1% for example, can make many mailshots a highly cost effective form of promotion.

12.1.1 Reasons for the growth of direct mail

In reality direct mail is currently the most rapidly increasing form of promotion. In 1986 the banks alone sent out no less than 109 million items by direct mail. Many organisations are beginning to use direct mail because of the considerable advantages it can offer, including:

(a) Selectivity

Targeting can be very precise, and there are many readily available methods, e.g. ACORN, (see Chapter 2) to help users of direct mail to aim their message at the correct audience.

(b) Cost effectiveness

The ability to target precise segments makes it possible to eliminate a large proportion of unlikely buyers. This eliminates the waste factor which is such a problem when advertising through the main media such as TV and national newspapers.

(c) Impact

Mailshots do make impact. A 1986 survey (by Survey Research Associates) showed that 80% of recipients read some of the leaflets included with regular bills, while 40% read most of them. Companies which are prepared to spend money on making an impact (e.g. offering a free draw with a valuable prize) get a very high rate of attention from the audience.

(d) Complex messages

Unlike most forms of media advertising, direct mail can cope with detailed copy, allowing long and complicated messages to be sent. If impact has been made, and the receivers are interested in the general message they will be prepared to read quite lengthy copy. This is ideal for complex offerings such as financial services.

(e) Measurability

Direct mail is the most measurable form of promotion. The marketer knows exactly how many mailshots have been sent and exactly how much the whole campaign has cost. By recording the responses the effectiveness of the campaign can be measured, and since it is usually a simple task to trace the proportion of responses which resulted in sales, it is possible to work out whether the campaign paid for itself.

(f) Testability

More than any other medium, direct mail is testable. A small number of mailshots can be sent out and the response monitored. Individual features of the mailshot can be changed and different versions compared for response rate. Different copy, photographs, mailing lists, envelopes, incentives – almost any variable – can be tested. For a valid test, however, it is important to change only one variable at a time otherwise it would be impossible to isolate the effects of each change.

12.1.2 The elements of a mailshot

There are a wide variety of methods that can be adopted when sending a mailshot, but there are five elements which will usually be regarded as standard practice for any mailshot.

(a) The envelope

This is the first thing the receiver sees. It has tended, therefore, to be standard practice to put a message on the outside of the envelope to stimulate the interest of the recipient. If, for example, you are trying to sell a gardening encyclopaedia to a target audience comprised of people with a known interest in gardening, it is considered to be a good idea to draw attention on the envelope to the fact that its contents are about gardening. However, this philosophy is no longer going unchallenged. For less interesting mailshots, such as financial services or for most business - to - business mailshots, it is feared that an envelope which broadcasts the fact that a mailshot is inside might be counter productive and lead to the letter being consigned to the waste bin unopened. Plain envelopes are therefore often preferred, giving much more creative scope for an attention-grabbing message to appear when the letter is opened.

(b) The letter

Again, the traditional direct mail method of message sending has been a letter. It tends to be very long, with the benefits stated, explained and emphasised. It is usually personalised as much as possible, often printed in hand written style, always includes at least one PS, and traditionally ends each page with an absolute cliff-hanger in mid sentence which will compel the reader to carry on to the next page. The Readers Digest mailshots, much maligned by satirists and comedians, were a typical example of this traditional form of direct mail letter, and have been an extremely effective form of promotion.

Times are changing however, and with the increasing volume of direct mail marketers have had to become ever more original to gain the attention of their readers. Instead of the letter, printed leaflets are becoming much more common. Photographs – perhaps of the high performance convertible car that might be won by anybody who places an order (provided they act within ten days) – can be included. Leaflets can have large print which conveys a simple message to interest readers in the moment when the contents are withdrawn from the envelope. Unless their interest and attention can be won very quickly the communication will almost certainly be discarded.

(c) The booster

The booster is designed to tackle this problem of stimulating readers. Methods used to boost their interest and attention have been many and varied, free prize draws offering large sums of money or fast cars to the winner being the most common. They almost always have a short time limit to prompt quick action, because it is generally felt that unless respondents respond quickly they will not respond at all. In practice this is not entirely true. Although the majority (over 50% but less than 75%) will respond in the first week, the replies will continue for some weeks, albeit at a steadily declining rate.

Increasingly, the booster is being seen as a method of gaining attention rather than as a way of increasing response. Companies will, for example, include a small gift such as a torch with the mailshot simply to gain the interest and attention of the reader. If the mailshot arrives in a lumpy Jiffy bag it will certainly be opened, and provided the gift has some novelty or some perceived value it will almost certainly generate sufficient interest for the message to be read. True to the marketing philosophy, if the product or service being promoted is of interest to the readers they will respond. It can be argued, then, that boosters should be used to gain the attention of the readers rather than to persuade them to respond.

(d) The reply

It is still universally accepted that it must be made as easy as possible for the reader to respond. This is usually done by including a reply paid envelope and a simple to complete card or order form. Use of credit cards will be encouraged and an increasing trend is to promote a telephone reply facility with a toll free 0800 number which is, arguably, easiest of all for the customer.

(e) The list

Mailshots have to be distributed or sent to an audience which, in its simplest form, is lots of names and addresses. The usual way of obtaining these names and addresses (because it is easy and quick) is to buy or rent a mailing list. A special industry has grown up to provide this service. Sources of mailing lists include magazines will provide their circulation list. This can be a very well targeted list for a specialist message. Directories will provide mailing lists of their entries, broken down into various categories. Even if these names and addresses are already available in the directory, renting a list (which comes in the form of adhesive labels ready to stick straight onto the envelopes) saves a lot of time consuming work. Some companies specialise solely in list brokerage. They have huge databases of companies and individuals broken down into various segments – industries, interest groups or past buyers of certain products. Lists can be bought, which means that the buyer owns that list and can mail the names on the list as many times as is wished; or they can be rented, which means that the list can be mailed only once. Some list providers have on-line facilities which enables them to download lists onto the customer's computer and some provide a complete direct mail service handling all the stuffing of envelopes, the posting and the responses. Renting lists can cost up to £100 per 1000 names. Buying can be at least double.

As a result of these high costs, many organisations prefer to develop their own mailing lists. Usually starting with a list of their existing customers, they will add names and addresses carefully selected from specialist directories, exhibition attendance registers, society membership registers, magazine readerships, or any other suitable source. Although this method avoids the cash outlay of renting or buying off-the-peg lists, it is very expensive in management time. Companies have to decide on the most cost-effective method of compiling a list which is suitable for their communications task.

12.1.3 The cost of direct mail

Costs can vary enormously depending on how frugal or how extravagant the marketer wants to be. These examples will give some idea of typical options.

The cheapest form of direct mail is door to door leaflet distribution. There is no reason why the post has to be used. Provided some kind of geo-demographic segmentation such as ACORN is used so that every house in a certain neighbourhood is part of the audience, door to door distribution can be extremely cost effective. Assuming a modest black and white leaflet (or a colour leaflet if large print numbers should bring down the unit cost) the cost per thousand would be:

Distribution £20

Leaflet   £25

Total   £45

£45 per thousand, or 4.5p per household reached, is very low cost promotion. Leaflets will alternatively be delivered door to door by the Post Office at a cost of £35 per thousand.

A conventionally posted mailshot would have the extra costs of postage, envelopes, the stuffing of the envelopes and, for most companies without their own comprehensive database, the renting of a mailing list. The printing would almost certainly be more costly, although very long print runs would help to reduce the unit cost. A booster may also be used. Assuming a target audience of 100,000 households the cost per thousand of a typical mailshot might be:

Postage   £140

Envelopes   £5

Printing   £20

Stuffing   £5

Booster   £200

List rental £40

Total   £410

This is 41p per household reached. Money has been saved by obtaining a postage discount from the Post Office and using a telephone rather than postal reply facility, in the promotion of – for example – time share holiday flats. The objective of the mailshots is simply to attract respondents to a promotional evening in a U.K. hotel to hear more about the accommodation and the location. Assuming a 2% response rate it will have cost £20.50 for each positive response, not an excessive sum in this market. The cost of converting some of those respondents into buyers will be much higher. Note the high cost of the booster, since a good incentive is considered vital to increase response. The booster would probably take the form of a small gift to each respondent who turned up at the hotel, plus a prize draw with a valuable first prize (a £10,000 car would cost £100 per thousand with a mailing list of 100,000).

12.1.4 Response rates

There is, of course an enormous variation in response rates, depending on the type of product or service being promoted, the standard of the mailshot and the suitability of the list. A 'warm' list would include known buyers of that kind of product or service (but not existing customers); a 'cold' list would be much less well targeted, perhaps covering all addresses in a certain area. The rule of thumb response rates given below do, however, act as some guide.

Door to door leaflets 0.2% - 0.5%

GPO door to door leaflets 0.7% - 1.5%

Postal direct mail:

'Cold' consumer up to 2%

'Cold' business-to-business up to 4%

'Warm' consumer up to 7%

'Warm' business-to-business up to 15%

Of course the nature of the response also makes a significant difference. Getting people to part with their money is much harder than getting people to go to a wine and buffet reception in a hotel for the evening. One reason for the generally higher response rate for business-to-business mailshots is that their desired response often involves no more than respondents expressing interest, e.g. returning a reply card requesting additional information.

12.2 Sales promotion

Sales promotions include money off coupons, scratch card competitions, small plastic soldiers inside boxes of breakfast cereals, free samples, buy one and get one free, and they come in many more varieties besides. But what exactly are sales promotions?

The definition of sales promotions is simple. They are: 'short term incentives to buy'.

The objectives of advertising are usually more long term, such as generating awareness and building brand image. The objectives of sales promotions are almost always short term, induce people to act immediately. James Adams writing in ADMAP in January 1987 summed up concisely the difference between advertising and sales promotion. Advertising is 'to increase preference for the brand in the mind of the potential customer through paid for media space or time'. A sales promotion is 'any device for triggering purchase of the brand where it would not otherwise have been chosen.' Adams adds that a sales promotion will usually seek to achieve this objective by 'increasing perceived value for money'.

Other general terms used to describe sales promotions are 'below the line' expenditure (see Chapter 11 for explanation) and merchandising, which usually refers just to in-store sales promotions.

Sales promotion is a significant activity in consumer markets. In 1986 expenditure on sales promotions by the top five hundred advertisers was equivalent to 10% of their advertising expenditure. For smaller advertisers the amount spent on sales promotion tends to become proportionately higher. There are around fifteen thousand promotions in the grocery trade alone every year.

12.2.1 Broad classifications of sales promotions

There are two broad classifications of sales promotions as shown in Figure 12.1. 'Selling into the pipeline' describes those promotions aimed at moving the product from the manufacturer into the channels of distribution; 'Selling out of the pipeline' describes those promotions which aim to move products from the shelf to the end user. It should also be pointed out that there can sometimes be a third audience for a sales promotion, which is the company's own sales force, who may need to be motivated to help move products through the pipeline.

Into the Pipeline

Out of the Pipeline

Marketing Channels
eg. Retailers

(Consumer Sales Promotion)

Main Techniques:
Cash Discounts
Dealer incentives and premiums
Exhibitions and demonstrations
Direct mail shots
Industrial sales promotion

Main Techniques
Sampling
Couponing
Sponsorship
Competitions
Price reduction
Personality promotions
Self liquidating premiums
Merchandising/point of sale
Premiums - in/on/off pack offers

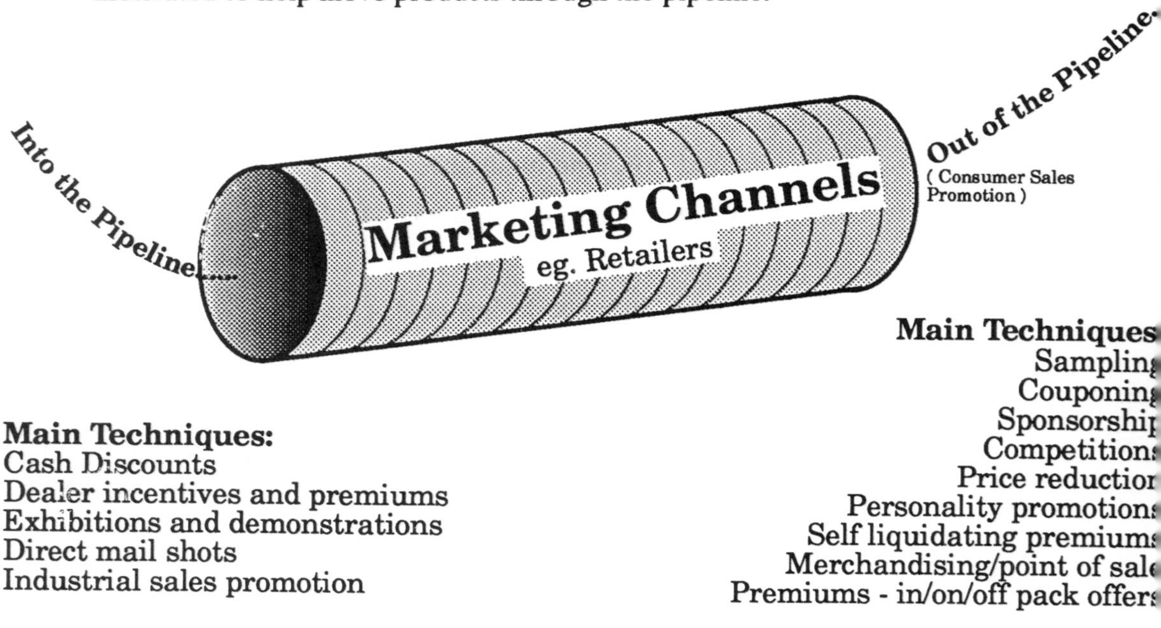

Figure 12.1 Sales promotion - moving products through the pipeline.

12.2.2 Promotions into the pipeline

'Into the pipeline' promotions are aimed broadly at getting more products into retailers. More specific objectives could include securing retailers' agreements to take a new product or to give more or better shelf space to an existing brand. The manufacturer may want a special position in the store, and may want the retailer to become involved in a joint venture to promote the brand. Promotional methods used may include the following

(a) Dealer competitions

These would usually be linked to sales, with a prize for the best performing dealer. The trend is towards motivating the dealer's entire staff, so the prize may be a weekend in a luxury hotel for the whole team of the best performing distributor (e.g. the dealer who sells the most cars in a certain month).

(b) Dealer loaders

These are aimed at getting dealers to stock more: the 'baker's dozen' – one free case with every twelve ordered – for example. More common these days would be a simple discount for large orders placed within a certain time period. This usually has a good effect on sales because, having accumulated the large stocks of a certain brand, the dealer then tries hard to pass them on to consumers.

(c) Deferred terms

Extended credit is a good motivator for dealers, who can thus expect to have sold and received payment for the goods before they have to pay their supplier.

(d) Sale or return

This is sometimes essential in persuading a dealer to stock a new untried product, in order to remove the risk from the retailer's point of view.

(e) POS display material

Point of sales display stands, posters, racks, exterior signs etc. used to be very popular, especially amongst smaller shops. Increasingly, however, they are being seen as an inconvenient intrusion, particularly by the larger retail chains.

(f) Co-operative advertising schemes

This can be much more attractive, especially to smaller dealers, since it enables them to increase their advertising presence in the local press.

(g) Promotional gifts

Usually given at Christmas and typically bottles of spirits, the practice is coming under increasing pressure because of its overtones of bribery. Many large companies have now forbidden their staff to accept gifts from suppliers and have asked suppliers to discontinue the practice.

12.2.3 Promotions out of the pipeline

Moving products off the shelves is big business. The manufacturers are still responsible for the bulk of 'out of the pipeline' promotional expenditure but the retailers are becoming increasingly involved. Typical promotions include the following.

(a) Free samples

The most effective method of getting people to try a new product, and also the most expensive. It can be done on a door to door distribution basis, or, as is more popular nowadays, as part of a joint promotion of non-competing products, such as the bounty packs of baby products given to mothers who have recently given birth.

(b) Coupon offers

Usually in the form of 'money off', they can be distributed door to door, be part of a press advertisement, or be on-pack and offering money off the next purchase. Sometimes coupon offers are distributed as part of an 'FSI' (a free standing insert). An FSI would typically be found in a magazine such as *Prima* or *Woman's Own*, and would contain nothing but adverts and coupons for non-competing products. Coupons do, of course, involve the buyer in some effort and therefore have a redemption rate of only around 20%.

(c) Reduced price

Usually in the form of 'money off', these promotions are very popular with consumers but are the most expensive of all for the manufacturer or retailer concerned. It is far cheaper to give away free products or other merchandise which can be purchased in bulk quite cheaply. Also some of the money given away in reduced price offers will be wasted since regular purchasers of the product would have bought anyway.

(d) Banded offers

This type of promotion takes two forms: 'two for the price of one' (is very common with soap and shampoo) or a well known brand carrying a sample of another non-competing product.

(e) Premium offers

There are three main types of premium offer:
The free gift
This may be contained in the pack (plastic animals in breakfast cereals or cards in tea). It may be the pack itself (instant coffee in storage jars), or it may be given at the checkout (for example a free mug with every gallon can of oil purchased). A common objective with such promotions is to build brand loyalty through encouraging a collecting habit.
Free sendaway gift
This type of promotion offers a free gift in exchange for the proof of purchase of a certain product, usually demonstrated by a collection of tokens or packet tops. The consumer has to claim the free gift by sending away the tops. An example would be a free guide to the Tour of Britain cycling race in exchange for eight Kellogg's Bran Flakes tokens. This can be a cost effective form of promotion for the manufacturer since many of the people who buy the product and start collecting the tokens in fact never send off for the free item.
Self-liquidating premiums
Here the consumer has to send both money and proof of purchase to obtain the premium offer. Through buying in bulk and maybe striking an agreement with the manufacturer of the offered item (who gains valuable publicity) the self-liquidating offer can appear to be very good value to the consumer but actually pays for itself.

(f) Competitions

Interest in competitions can be considerable, particularly if there is an attraction of a very large prize coupled with a sufficient number of small consolation prizes to encourage people to try their luck. It is popular with petrol companies: the Shell 'make money' promotion (packets containing half a bank note which had to be matched with its corresponding half) was both very original and very popular with motorists.

(g) Personality promotions

This type of promotion is limited to big brands with large advertising budgets. The promotion involves the offer of a prize to customers who can prove that they have purchased the product, if the personality stops them in the street or calls at their home. They were very popular in the 1960s with personalities like Miss Camay and the White Tide Man. More recently they have been popular with national newspapers, particularly in the summer when the personality will roam the holiday resorts giving prizes to buyers. This can be very effective because although newspaper buyers are normally highly brand loyal, they may be tempted to change their normal habits whilst on holiday.

(h) Demonstrations

Giving away samples of the product or demonstrating a durable product at the point of sale can be useful for generating interest. It tends to be very expensive and is now generally considered to be less cost effective than advertising for achieving the same objective.

(i) Trading stamps

The use of trading stamps developed rapidly in the 1960s. Trading stamps were an updated version of the Co-op 'divi' (possibly the longest running British promotion). The Co-op 'divi' was a simple dividend based on purchases, which enabled each Co-operative store customer to accumulate a cash sum which could be spent on items in the store or deducted from the shopper's bill. Each customer had a personal number and a 'divi' book, and expenditure was laboriously recorded in the book with every purchase. Periodically, the 'divi' total was worked out and the shopper could cash in the 'windfall'. Co-op stores still use the same basic system, but the 'divi' is now accumulated in the form of trading stamps, such as Green Shield stamps. Financed by the retailer the stamps lost popularity in the mid 1970s due to hyper trading stamp inflation (for example, petrol stations offering 10 and 20 fold Green Shield stamps). They have actually made a reappearance in the late 1980's but it remains to be seen whether they will re-establish themselves. The Co-op 'divi', now in the form of stamps, has continued to thrive throughout this period.

(j) Bonus packs

Sometimes called 'flashpacks' they come usually in the form of a brightly coloured extra portion on the pack containing extra product such as '20% extra free'. These promotions can be very popular with consumers since the extra value is obvious, and they are popular with manufacturers because giving away free product is less costly than knocking money off, while the packs have considerable impact in the store and the promotion can sometimes be part of a campaign to trade customers up to larger sizes. The disadvantages are the considerable extra packaging costs incurred and the logistical problems of fitting the larger packs onto supermarket shelves, pallets and lorries.

(k) Charity promotions

Customers collect box tops or wrappers and send into the manufacturer who makes a donation to charity for each wrapper sent in. The Ski yoghourt Stoke Mandeville appeal is typical. Sporting appeals, e.g. donations to help athletes train for the Olympic Games, are also popular. Probably the best example is the Andrex appeal for guide dogs for the blind. In addition to focussing on a very popular cause, the labrador connection was a strong reinforcer of brand image. Such promotions can have major publicity spin-offs and can result in the involvement of fund raising organisations like schools, scouts and even children's television programmes, all of which is good public relations and might stimulate purchase.

12.2.4 Promotions to the sales force

Ideally the manufacturer should also involve its own sales force in any sales promotion, to help push the product into the pipeline. The sales team can be used to raise retailers' awareness of the promotion, persuade them to participate and can subsequently walk round the stores to ensure that the necessary shelf space, POS material etc. is in fact in place.

Promotions to the sales force will often take the form of competitions, with a special bonus or a prize – such as an exotic holiday – for the salesman with the largest increase in retailer orders for the product in question.

There is evidence that such promotions do motivate the sales force, less because of the financial incentive than the element of competition and the urge to win, especially if the prize is high profile, such as two weeks in Barbados.

12.2.5 The effects of sales promotions

The effectiveness of individual promotions can vary enormously for a host of reasons, but in general most people are agreed on the following effects of sales promotions:

a good sales promotion will lead to a short term increase in sales,

a good sales promotion with complementary support into the pipeline and sales force incentives will have a favourable effect on shelf space and positioning,

most sales promotions will have little or no effect on brand loyalty and long term sales,

although the promotion might have a positive effect on short term sales, 'next period' sales (i.e. in the few weeks after the end of the promotion) may fall to a lower level than normal as consumers use up the higher stocks they have purchased while the offer was on.

Finally, it follows that manufacturers of staple products, such as toilet paper or toothpaste, should not see sales promotion as a way of stimulating extra purchase because consumption cannot increase. They should see sales promotions only as a way of tempting buyers of competing brands to switch. However, manufacturers of luxury products such as aperitifs should see sales promotion as a way of increasing purchase and attracting new users.

12.3 Public relations

The most generally accepted definition of public relations is:

activities to increase the mutual understanding between an organisation and its publics.

There are two very important points in this definition. Firstly, PR is not about selling product or about persuading people to do something. While sales promotion is about short term objectives, PR is about long term objectives such as brand awareness, interest and image. Secondly, PR underlines the fact that a company's communications programme should not only be about communicating with customers. In the long run there are many publics whose goodwill is important to any organisation and PR activities can be an important way of sending messages to those publics.

Relevant publics for a company can include any or all of the following:

customers   industry

the local community   its own staff

shareholders   suppliers

distributors   local and national government

the city   the media

opinion leaders   public opinion

special interest groups   educational bodies

trade unions.

The philosophy of PR was perfectly summed up by Frank Jefkins when he said that PR is all about transforming negative feelings into positive ones. He amplifies this concept in his PR transfer process.

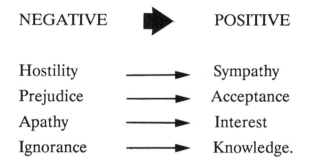

12.3.1 PR activities

As with sales promotion there are many different manifestations of PR activity. Some of the more common examples are listed below.

(a) Press releases

Much of the editorial content of local newspapers and trade journals has its origin in press releases received by those publications. Even publications employing many journalists will still use material from press releases if it is sufficiently interesting, as will TV and radio. Companies therefore have nothing to lose by sending out press releases if they think the subject will be of interest to any of the publics previously mentioned. Common subjects include large orders won, new staff employed, new technical developments made and export achievement. Anything which shows the company in a favourable light can be a useful basis for a press release. It must always be remembered that editors are very busy people who receive a very large number of press releases, so the story must be relevant and of interest to the editor's readers, and the press release must convey that information very quickly. The tone should be strictly informative with superlatives and silly claims avoided, since its objective is to increase mutual understanding rather than to sell. Press releases are also written to a standard format, which should be followed, because this also helps to make the editor's life easier. This format is shown in Figure 12.2.

(b) Press conferences

When companies have something particularly newsworthy to say they organise a press conference. When Amstrad took over Sinclair in 1987 the deal was kept secret until Monday April 7th, when a midday press conference – which had been publicised early that morning – took place in a central London hotel, with Alan Sugar

How to Write a News Release

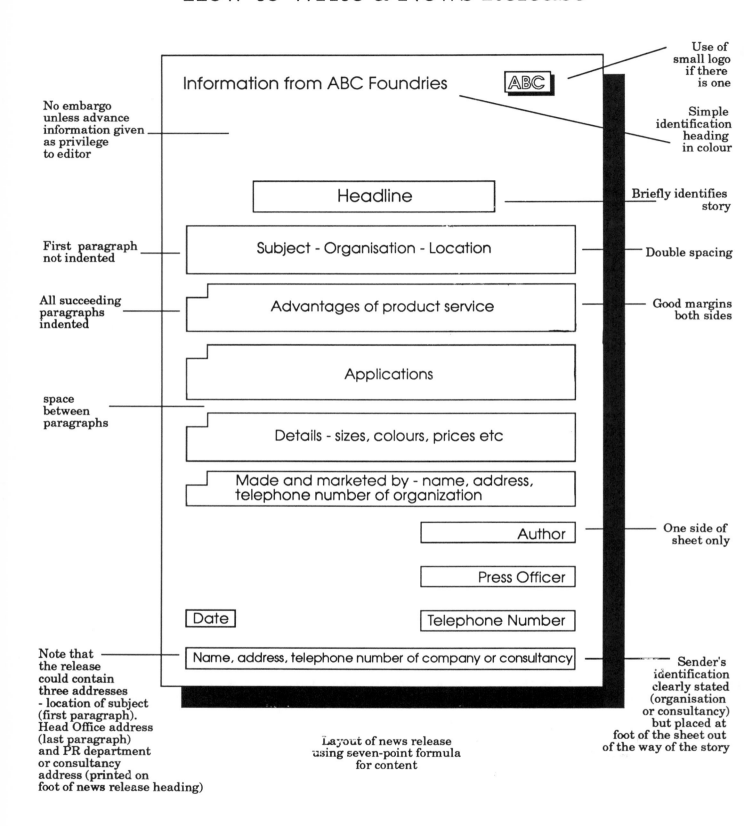

No embargo unless advance information given as privilege to editor

First paragraph not indented

All succeeding paragraphs indented

space between paragraphs

Note that the release could contain three addresses - location of subject (first paragraph). Head Office address (last paragraph) and PR department or consultancy address (printed on foot of news release heading)

Information from ABC Foundries

ABC

Use of small logo if there is one

Simple identification heading in colour

Headline

Briefly identifies story

Subject - Organisation - Location

Double spacing

Advantages of product service

Good margins both sides

Applications

Details - sizes, colours, prices etc

Made and marketed by - name, address, telephone number of organization

Author

One side of sheet only

Press Officer

Date

Telephone Number

Name, address, telephone number of company or consultancy

Sender's identification clearly stated (organisation or consultancy) but placed at foot of the sheet out of the way of the story

Layout of news release using seven-point formula for content

Figure 12. 4 Standard press release format

and Sir Clive Sinclair making a joint appearance on the stage. With rumours having built up over the weekend, everybody was keen to find out the real story and one hundred and fifty journalists attended. There were interviews for the lunchtime

World at One on Radio 4, for BBC and ITN news, all of which covered the story extensively that day. On Tuesday all the four quality national newspapers led with the story, and the *Money Programme* spent four days filming at Amstrad to feature the company in its Sunday evening programme on BBC 2. Amstrad enjoyed a week of exceptionally high visibility, and the free media time and space which they achieved was worth a vast sum of money at advertising.

(c) Event sponsorship

Sporting and cultural events are increasingly seen as offering good PR value, both for the promotional opportunities they afford and for the image enhancement that a well chosen event can bring to a brand or a company. Cigarette manufacturers particularly favour sponsorship as a result of the partial ban on cigarette advertising. The audiences attracted by the Embassy World Snooker Championships, screened on BBC, must be worth millions of pounds in advertising terms to the sponsors. Sometimes events can be selected for image building purposes. The Milk Marketing Board chose to sponsor events like the Milk Race (cycling) and, earlier, the Milk Cup (football) partly to counter the boring and effeminate image of milk.

(d) Event staging

Sometimes a company can be even more ambitious and stage an event. Richard Branson did it twice to generate publicity for his new Virgin Atlantic airline. Crossing the Atlantic by speedboat, and breaking the record for the fastest crossing, followed by the first attempt to cross the Atlantic by balloon, cost Branson's company huge sums of money. However, the investment paid off many times over in the value of the publicity received by Virgin, in terms of both its volume and its very positive effect on Virgin's image.

(e) Visits

Open days are a very popular PR activity. Organisations can invite members of any of the publics previously mentioned with the aim of furthering mutual understanding. The best known current example of this activity would be the public visits to Sellafield organised by British Nuclear Fuels to assuage fears about the plant.

(f) Hospitality

Some companies choose to entertain people at top sporting events. This is a favourite method used by businesses to get to know their customers. Football matches, golf tournaments, racing, motor racing and power boat racing can all be important hospitality venues. Perhaps the most prized hospitality venue of all is Wimbledon. The All England Club allowed its first hospitality marquee at the tennis in 1975. In 1988 there were forty four marquees booked by a total of one hundred and seven companies during the fortnight. Most of the marquees are run by hospitality companies who hire out the use of the lavish marquees to companies wishing to entertain guests. Without exclusive use of a marquee it could cost a company £10,000 to entertain ten guests for a day, but with a ticket for No. 1 or Centre court, prawn and avocado cocktail, plenty of champagne and – of course – strawberries and cream, they all seem to think it's a good investment.

(g) Charitable donations

Very good for company image and sometimes linked to sales promotions (as in the Andrex example), support for charity is often seen as excellent PR. Many smaller companies support local 'good causes' (e.g. the restoration of the village hall) for the good local publicity.

(h) Awards and competitions

These activities can be another good way of generating favourable publicity. It is important to support an activity which is appropriate for the target audience the company would like to reach. The National Westminster Bank's sponsorship of the annual Engineering Marketing Awards affords it valuable publicity amongst the industrial community.

(i) Company videos and magazines

Both very popular and capable of reaching large and diverse audiences, these tools normally portray very general company information.

(j) Customer magazines and technical guides

Officially a way of providing useful information (often of a technical nature) to customers, these publications can be an effective way of increasing customer loyalty.

(k) Clubs

Similar in purpose to customer magazines, the club atmosphere further boosts loyalty. Home computer user clubs are an example.

(l) Seminars

Often of a technical or educational nature seminars, can be a useful way for companies to meet potential new customers as well as rewarding existing clients. A highly polished, professional seminar is good for a company's image with both existing and potential customers. Hewlett-Packard run informative seminars on subjects like Computer Aided Design to attract companies who may be future buyers of CAD systems.

(m) Signed articles

Learned articles on scientific, technical or business subjects published in respected journals are also a way for companies to enhance their credibility.

12.3.2 The effects of PR

PR can be used for a number of purposes. It is very good at building image over a long period of time, e.g. portraying a company as being at the forefront of technology. It is good at delivering information about the company or its products, whether a relatively simple statement that a new transatlantic airline service is operating, or very complex information about a new computer breakthrough. Public companies make use of PR to build financial confidence in the city. A second category of effects would revolve around the ability of PR to reach certain audiences that might otherwise be difficult to reach or get to know. Hospitality is much used for this purpose. Seminars and signed articles perform the function in a different way. Finally, PR is another way of motivating people, whether it is customers through clubs and events, distributors through conferences or employees through high profile events or a simple company newsletter.

PR works much more effectively at the top end of the communications spectrum.. It is good for increasing awareness, knowledge, comprehension and liking. Further down the spectrum its strengths diminish. PR is not good at persuading. It should be used for increasing mutual understanding and not for selling.

12.4 Literature

Company and product literature is usually in a similar category to PR. Its purpose is to improve customers' knowledge, understanding and liking, but with a few exceptions (such as mail order catalogues) brochures are usually designed to inform rather than to sell.

Brochures have a much larger role in business-to-business marketing than in consumer marketing for several reasons. Firstly, companies are often less well known than typical suppliers (retailers) in consumer markets. Customers therefore like to have a brochure simply in order to find out a little more about the company.

Secondly, products and services are often much more complex, with a large amount of detailed information to be conveyed to potential customers. Brochures are ideal for this purpose and are used in consumer markets for high involvement purchases like cars, dish washers or fitted kitchens. Thirdly, a high quality brochure can enhance a company's image and increase its credibility. Conversely, a tatty brochure or the absence of literature will almost certainly be harmful to a company's image in most markets.

12.5 Exhibitions

Exhibitions offer the opportunity to combine the strengths of personal selling with non-personal communications activities. They bring together many elements of the communications mix including PR, sales promotion and personal selling. Some exhibitions, mainly business-to-business ones, are much more geared to the PR end of the spectrum. Transactions do not take place at these exhibitions but there is an opportunity for potential customers to see, feel and hear the company's products in operation. There is an opportunity to meet the staff and discuss problems. There is an opportunity for both sides to commence the process of building a relationship which can be further developed after the exhibition.

On the other hand, some exhibitions are more like traditional markets, cluttered with little stalls all clamouring for the customers' attentions and eager to peddle their wares. Many consumer oriented exhibitions are like this. The Ideal Homes Exhibition and the Boat Show are good examples. True, both have their larger exhibitors attending very much as a PR exercise. The full sized fully equipped show homes built in days by the major builders, or the top of the range fifty foot yachts and motor cruisers, are examples of image building exhibitors. However, most stands at both exhibitions are small and are booked by small companies eager to take advantage of a highly targeted market of thousands of people who have travelled to the exhibition, usually with money to spend. For many of these companies 'a good show' is fundamental to the success of their whole financial year.

At both types of exhibition, attendance for exhibitors is very expensive. The total cost of a medium sized stand at a week long trade exhibition would almost certainly exceed £50,000, and the larger companies in the industry could spend five or even ten times that sum. A small company with a small stand at the Boat Show will not be able to undertake the exercise at a total cost of much less than £10,000.

The high cost of exhibiting makes it essential for companies to have clearly defined objectives for any exhibition and to evaluate after the event whether these goals were met. For some companies it will simply not be cost effective to attend exhibitions.

Conclusion

It has been seen that there is a huge range of promotional techniques available to the marketer. This makes planning and, especially, allocation of resources between those techniques (see Chapter 10) of critical importance. Having determined the promotional objectives it must be ensured that resources are allocated to those techniques most able to achieve the communications goals which have been set.

Assignment   Ripley College

Don Rippon is the marketing officer for Ripley College of Further and Higher Education. The college management has recognised that there will be increased competition between Ripley College, the nearby polytechnic and other colleges offering similar courses for students in the near future. Don has been given the task of enhancing the image of the college by giving it a higher profile in the community, in particular in relation to targeted audiences.

Task

In the role of Don Rippon, write a report for senior management in which you outline the use that the college could make of the five marketing communication tools covered in this chapter.

Chapter 13
Personal Selling

Introduction

The standard definition of personal selling is:

'Oral presentation in a conversation with one or more prospective purchasers for the purpose of making sales.' (**Philip Kotler**).

This is a good definition of the traditional view of personal selling which is seen to involve a sales presentation, the objective of which is to persuade someone to buy something. Increasingly, however, the role of personal selling is being seen as something much wider than the very narrow view of the hard sell door-to-door salesman. In the vast majority of cases the final act of the marketing process involves personal contact between buyer and seller. The act of personal selling is usually the culmination of the marketing mix. A product which meets customers' needs has been developed and produced, it has been priced, it has been made available and accessible to buyers, promotion has raised their awareness and stimulated their interest and finally a deal has been struck between buyer and seller.

13.1 The importance of personal selling

In arriving at an acceptable deal the importance of personal selling will vary between different types of business, but in general it is important in three ways:

(a) Making sales

Whenever a sale is made the role of the sales person can be critical. Even for the most mundane of items well trained sales people will always sell more than untrained sales people.

(b) Relationships

Sometimes sales are the result of a much longer dialogue between suppliers and customers. In this situation personal interaction between buyers and sellers is very important because the final sale may be the culmination of long negotiations, possibly over many years.

(c) Service

Making the sale and fostering the relationship which precedes it are very important, but together they still do not fully encompass the personal role in successful marketing because if the marketing process is all about the delivery of satisfaction to customers there is a much more central role for people to play. People are fundamental to the winning and keeping of satisfied customers, so much so that it is now suggested that the marketing mix should have a fifth 'P' - People.

In fact, 'personal communications' would be a more accurate term to fully describe the role and importance of personal selling in the marketing process.

13.2 Personal communications and making sales

A sales person has five broad tasks which must be performed well if selling success is to be maximised.

Prospecting, preparation, active selling and delivering maintenance skills.

A sixth area which is increasingly being seen as fundamental to successful selling is the ability of the sales person to cope with the particular stresses and strains of the job. We will call this Coping Skills, and will look in turn at each of these six important aspects of the sales person's job.

13.2.1 Prospecting

Any sales person needs to identify 'prospects' (people or companies that can perhaps be sold to) before any selling can be done. Increasingly companies are using other methods to provide prospects for the sales force but many companies still leave the individual sales person with the responsibility for identifying potential customers. In that case there are a number of methods which can be used.

(a) Cold calling

This often means knocking on doors and asking if it is possible to speak to someone about the product or service you are trying to sell. Someone selling burglar alarms might knock on the door of every house without an alarm. Someone selling office supplies might go into every factory on an industrial estate. At the best of times this method can be inefficient and demoralising, so most experienced sales people try to adopt methods which are a little less random.

(b) Research

For the majority of sales people random cold calling would be ridiculously inefficient because their product or service can realistically be sold to only a small minority of businesses or individuals. If, for example, you are offering a tool making service to companies with plastic injection moulding machines, you do not knock on the door of every company on the industrial estate because the vast majority will not have such a machine. It is much more efficient to first spend time identifying prospects, i.e. companies which possess injection moulders. There are many trade directories, both national and local which sales people can use to identify potential customers in the right kind of business. It is also a good idea to look in trade journals and local newspapers to look for news items which could mean that a firm has a need for your product or service. A firm announcing redundancies, for example, might have a need for a redundancy counselling service. An expanding firm might have a need for a recruitment agency. In other words, as in all areas of marketing, research should help people to target their efforts more effectively.

(c) Word of mouth

An experienced sales person will already have a lot of customers and contacts and will constantly ask them about developments in the industry. Most industries have a thriving grapevine and a sales person who asks questions will identify a lot of leads in this way.

(d) Enquiries

Many companies will use advertising or direct mail as a way of stimulating enquiries for sales people to follow up. It works on the principle that if people are sufficiently interested to telephone or write off for additional information in response to an advert they must be potential buyers, and therefore worth a sales call. However, in reality this is not the case. Often over half the responses to an advert will not be from potential customers. A good proportion may be from students seeking information for their projects! Experienced sales people will therefore have a method for 'qualifying' enquiries, perhaps by telephoning them and having a short conversation to identify likely purchasers. The sales person will then visit only these 'qualified leads'.

13.2.2 Preparation

Some people say that good sales people are born and not made. In other words, selling is a matter of personality and not training. Most companies no longer subscribe to this belief and devote significant resources to training their sales people to help them become better at selling. The sales person can be better prepared in a number of ways.

(a) Sales training

Training courses can improve a sales person's active selling skills. The sales person's presentation of certain product benefits can be prepared and rehearsed, and as a result of experience can be evaluated and refined. Prospects may have certain common objections or questions. With good preparation a sales person's skill at handling them and identification of the best ways of closing the sale can be improved.

(b) Product knowledge

Good sales people are experts on their product; how it is made, what its benefits are, how it works etc. All this has to be learned. Nothing lets a sales person down more than the inability to answer a prospect's questions about a product or service.

(c) Customer knowledge

It is very difficult selling to customers about whom you know nothing. Customer knowledge and good relationships are a great help to the sales person who should therefore invest time in developing them. A good sales person will keep comprehensive records on customers which will be updated after each visit and read through before making a call. Notes should be made of the individual buyer's name, needs, interests, family, previous purchases and any other matters of relevance to making a sale or building a relationship with that individual.

(d) Competitor knowledge

A sales person also needs to be an expert on the competitors' products; how they differ, their advantages and disadvantages. Again, any questions on these subjects must be well handled.

13.2.3 Active Selling Skills

There are a number of stages in making a sale and the good sales person will be well prepared for each one.

(a) Making appointments

Getting an appointment to see a prospect is not always a foregone conclusion. It is sometimes necessary to sell the appointment by offering a benefit or a reason over the telephone. The sales person might, for example, mention a special offer which could save the prospect money.

(b) Opening

Having succeeded in making an appointment, the sales person will visit the prospect. At the outset it must be decided whether to launch straight into a sales presentation or whether it would be better to spend a few minutes chatting to the prospect to build a relationship. Most sales people will prefer the latter approach, but some customers may regard this as time wasting and prefer to get the appointment over and done with as quickly and efficiently as possible. The sales person's tactics will, therefore, be based on knowing his customer.

(c) Probing

Probing is all about getting to know the prospect better. An experienced sales person will ask a lot of questions at this stage, designed to find out about the prospect's, needs and priorities. The sales person will be just the opposite of the stereotype of the loud mouth salesman who never shuts up, and will be trying to decide at this stage what kind of things will make the prospect act, what kind of things will make the prospect decide to purchase the product or service in question.

(d) Matching

Once the sales person has found out what the prospect wants, it can be attempted to match the offered product or service to the prospect's needs. The information gleaned from the probing in stage three enables the message to be targeted in stage four. The successful salesperson does not make a long speech covering every conceivable benefit of his product. Those benefits of interest to the prospect are selected and highlighted. A good analogy is the difference between a Second World War anti-aircraft gun and a modern surface-to-air heat seeking missile. The anti-aircraft gun works on the machine gun principle of continuously spraying the air with shells in the hope that one or two might hit the target. The heat seeking missile constantly adjusts its trajectory in order to keep on target and is a much more efficient use of resources.

The sales person, like the heat seeking missile, must continuously ask whether s/he is on target. The product or service is tailored to the needs of the prospect and presented as a solution to the prospect's problems.

This raises an important ethical question which will be explored more fully in Chapter 16. In short, it is not the salesperson's objective to sell people things they don't want. Apart from being unethical it is not in the seller's long term interests, because there will be no further success with the same customer. If the salesperson's objective is to sell, this can be done most effectively by matching the benefits of the product or service to the needs of the customer. A salesperson who believes in the product will always find it easy to do this with a clear conscience, and when he or she comes across prospects for whom his product is not suitable, he or she must say so. That is the way to win the goodwill for a potential future sale.

(e) Handling objections

Even when a salesperson does have a product or service which genuinely meets the prospect's needs, the latter may still be reluctant to be committed to the purchase. The prospect may have various reasons for this. These reasons are known as 'objections' and it is the duty of the sales person to try to 'handle' or overcome these objections because failure to 'close the sale' on this occasion may end up with the prospect buying from a competitor with a more persuasive salesperson.

Research into this subject has led to three main conclusions.

Firstly, many objections are not inherent to the buyer but are caused by the sales person. Experiments have shown that inept sales people have to handle up to five times as many objections as expert sales people.

Secondly, if it is true that poor selling creates objections, the solution is not to become better at handling objections but to become better at selling. Many sales people create objections by attempting to rush into their selling without spending enough time probing and matching beforehand.

Thirdly, objections come in three varieties; genuine objections, misunderstandings and excuses. Most people have a natural fear of making the wrong decision and are therefore likely to try and defer difficult decisions. Many objections arise from this understandable reluctance on the part of the prospect to be committed. Experience and good training can help a sales person to overcome these objections either through logical argument or perhaps through some incentive (e.g. a discount or promotional gift) to encourage the prospect to act now. If on the other hand the prospect isn't just making an excuse not to go ahead, the sales person must find out if the objection is valid or based on a misunderstanding. By going over the main points again it may be possible to clear up a misunderstanding in the prospect's mind. However, some objections may be genuine areas of mismatch. The benefits offered by the sales person's product do not match the needs and priorities of the buyer. If the sales person wishes to retain the goodwill of the prospect they will withdraw gracefully with the aim of renewing their efforts when benefits can be offered which more closely match the prospect's needs.

(f) Negotiating

Even when a buyer and seller have agreed a sale in principle there may still be some details (such as exact price, delivery dates installation arrangements, credit terms etc.) left to negotiate. There is always a danger that the sales person is so pleased to have made a sale that they relax and give too much away at this point.

Let's look at price negotiations as a typical example. As shown in Figure 13.1 there are three fields in any area of negotiations. Firstly, there is a range that the buyer is happy with but not the seller. Secondly, there is another range which is acceptable to the seller but not to the buyer. Thirdly, there should be an area of overlap which they can both agree to.

£500------------------------ Seller's ideal price

£480------------------------ Buyer's upper limit

£470------------------------ Seller's lower limit

£450------------------------ Buyer's ideal price.

Figure 13.1 Price negotiations.

In this example, the area of overlap is quite small. Neither the buyer nor the seller can achieve their ideal price but there is a range which will be acceptable to both. The sales person's objective must always be to reach an agreement at the top end of the range of overlap. This is done by not giving away too much at once, and by trading concessions. In other words, if the buyer insists on a lower price, the sales person agrees, but only in return for quicker payment.

(g) Closing the sale

The next step for the sales person is to 'close the sale'. This means getting a signature on an order form, or completing the transaction in a shop. In some major sales it may mean securing agreement on a particular point of difference so that the parties can proceed to the next stage of negotiations at their next meeting. At this stage the experienced sales person will always know how to lead the prospect to the point where business can be requested without appearing to adopt high pressure sales techniques.

13.2.4 Delivering

Having closed the sale, the sales person's job is not necessarily complete. To ensure that a very satisfied customer is retained there may be a number of details to be monitored to make sure that the customer gets what is expected. One of these details may be prompt delivery, others may be installation, providing technical information or training the customer to use the product. They are all aspects of good service and will be covered more fully in section 13.4.

13.2.5 Maintenance skills

In addition to being good at selling, sales people must be efficient at organising their own time. Sales people have to work independently for long stretches of time. An export sales person might be away from the office for up to three months and a domestic sales person may visit the office only once per fortnight or once a week. How effectively they organise their time during those long periods when they are effectively their own boss will be a critical factor in their level of achievement.

Research has shown that the average sales person spends only around one sixth of his time actually selling, (see Figure 13.2). Through better planning it may be possible to increase selling time by reducing travelling time or perhaps chat time, particularly since research has also shown that the most successful sales people spend relatively little time on chit- chat.

13.2.6 Coping skills

It may well be however that being more efficient is not the only key to increasing selling time. Some sales people, perhaps suffering from job related anxiety, may be using the non-selling times as excuses to avoid selling.

Face to face selling can be a very stressful job. In addition to spending long periods alone, away from contact with colleagues in the office and perhaps away from the family, sales people experience a higher degree of rejection than the average worker. Clearly a sales person cannot expect to make a sale with every prospect, but every time failure can be taken as personal. Circumstances can easily combine to make a sales person feel rejected and depressed. It is therefore vital that management encourage the sales force, help them to cope with the loneliness and anxiety of the job (perhaps by arranging periodic meetings where sales people can exchange experiences and ideas of how to cope), and train them as professionally as possible because competence and success are the best motivators for anybody in any line of work.

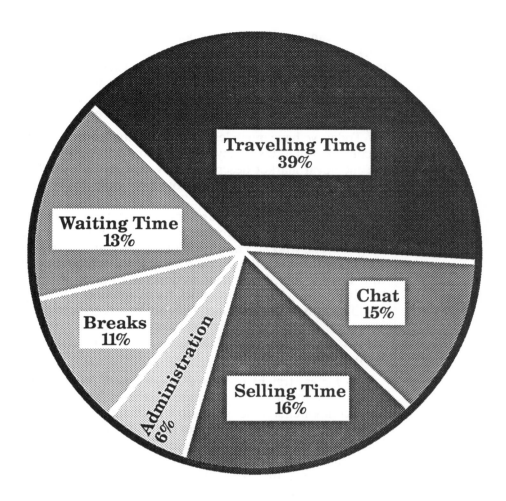

Figure 13.2 Selling time expenditure (industrial products).

13.3 Personal communications and relationships

In 1982 two American management consultants, Thomas Peters and Robert Waterman published a book called 'In Search of Excellence'. It has been a world best seller and will be responsible for re-shaping management theory and practice for some years to come. Peters and Waterman spent some years studying America's most successful companies (such as IBM, Hewlett-Packard, McDonalds, Proctor and Gamble) and the result is their analysis of what makes those companies successful. Peters and Waterman have distilled their findings into eight key success factors. The marketing philosophy pervades several of these factors but it is synonymous with one of them - 'closeness to the customer'.

You cannot provide customer satisfaction unless you know exactly what customers want, in its broadest (augmented product) sense. The best way to keep in tune with customer needs is to be genuinely close to them. This means spending time with customers, talking to customers, listening to customers and understanding them. In short it means building a relationship with them. You don't need to carry out a research survey to discover the wishes of your own family. You have a close relationship with them. Successful companies tend to have close relationships with their customers, so that they understand them almost instinctively. They have empathy with their customers.

You can appreciate the importance of relationships if you think of a medieval market. Everybody in the small town would know everybody else. The traders and the customers would all know each other. These relationships would enable traders to understand with a high degree of certainty what customers wanted to buy. And they would have to supply it because the buyers would know all the traders and would avoid a trader who did not meet customers' needs.

Today we have much less complete knowledge of our market places, especially in consumer markets. Many industrial markets, however, are much more similar to the medieval market described above. Many industrial purchases, e.g. specialist production machinery, are available from only a very small number of suppliers. Buyers probably know them all. They have received visits from the suppliers' sales people and maybe from more senior managers too. They may have direct experience of buying from a given supplier before, and even if they haven't, they can talk to other buyers, who all know each other through the trade association. The buyers also know that after the purchase of a new machine they will have a lot of dealings with the supplier. They may be dependent on that supplier for installation, for training on the use of the product, for maintenance and repairs and perhaps future modifications of the machine. They are not, therefore going to buy from a supplier in whom they do not have complete confidence. So even for many new task purchases in organisational markets (see Chapter 2) relationships are a significant factor leading to the sale.

As far as straight re-buys are concerned, relationships will often be of even greater importance. The purchases in themselves may seem much less significant, small components to be built into a machine or a car for example, plastic granules to make into polythene sacks, but in reality the smooth running of this relationship is of critical importance to the buyer. Imagine the Ford assembly line, with finished cars running off the end every few seconds. What if they ran out of just one component, e.g. the switch that operates the windscreen wipers? The line would stop, and it could cost Ford millions of pounds. What if a batch of those switches were of poor quality, and failed after a few months in use. That would lead to high warranty costs and worse still would damage Ford's reputation. All manufacturers like to be able to have complete confidence in the suppliers of even the most trivial components. It therefore pays suppliers to keep close to their customers and to maintain relationships at many levels, as shown in the diagram below.

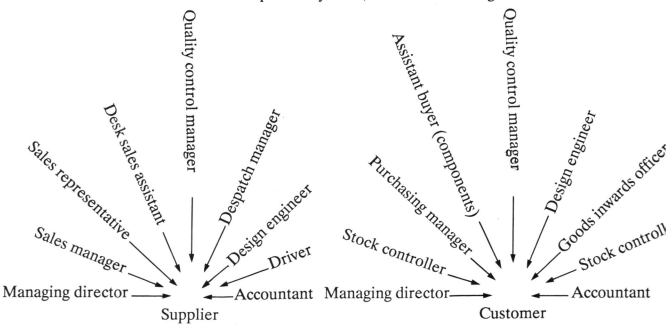

Figure 13.3 Buyer - Seller Relationships.

In a situation where a manufacturer and a component supplier are both large companies the pattern of relationships shown above could easily develop. All those people in the buying company are affected by the performance of the supplier, so all their counterparts in the supplying company should regard it as a key priority to maintain good relations with the customer. If they are close to the customer they will know immediately a slight problem arises, because good relationships will lead to good communications. The supplier should then be able to solve the problem before it becomes serious. In most straight re-buy markets, the maintenance of strong relationships with customers is probably the most important factor in a company's success.

Even in consumer markets this factor is present. Many villages and small towns will have more than one newsagent, more than one greengrocer, more than one pub. Why do people buy from a particular corner shop, fish and chip shop or butcher? Sometimes it's convenience, but often they'll buy from one a little further away. Very often it's down to relationships, some of which go back decades not just years.

So the fifth 'P' is very important to the marketing success of many companies. Yes, you do need a good product at the right price, well promoted and efficiently distributed, but all of those things may not be enough if relationships with customers are neglected.

13.4 Communicating as providing service

As stated earlier, successful companies are close to their customers. As a result they are particularly sensitive to changes in the environment and can adapt quickly to them. Moreover they see it as the responsibility of everyone in the company (not just the sales and marketing staff) to be responsive to customers' needs. This is what the fifth 'P' in the marketing mix is all about.

Research carried out by British Airways showed that for every one customer who makes a complaint there are a further seven dissatisfied customers who vote with their feet and that on average each unhappy customer tells another six people about his dissatisfaction. Therefore even if the complainants are dealt with to their total satisfaction, a total of forty two people could be gaining a bad impression of the supplier for each complaint that the company is aware of.

To understand the key role to be played by all the company's staff in keeping customers satisfied we have only to think of our own experiences as customers. What is it that gives us a bad impression of a supplier? It might be something very serious such a faulty product which the supplier is reluctant to replace but it might be something much more trivial such as the rudeness or lack of concern of a shop assistant. Very often it is these small things which make consumers choose a certain shop or a certain supplier. That is why successful companies like Marks and Spencer, Next and McDonalds invest so much money in staff training to ensure that polite and efficient service is always given to the customer.

There is also no doubt that companies as well as individual consumers also buy service. They do not just choose the cheapest supplier but will be prepared to pay a slightly higher price for the confidence of a reliable and helpful supplier whom they know to have the customer's interests at heart.

Work by Dr. John Nicholson of London University suggests that internal communications and motivation are inherent to a firm's ability to consistently provide good customer service. According to Dr. Nicholson: *'You can't treat the customer better if you're not treating the staff better too.'* These kind of views are gaining in popularity and have resulted in many leading companies to holding regular seminars to emphasise to all staff the importance of putting the customer first and to discuss ways of improving customer service.

In short, communicating with customers is not something which can be left to the sales people and the advertising agency. Everybody in the company communicates with customers. The telephonist communicates by her manner, the technical person by his eagerness to find a solution, the accountant by the way in which he asks for a bill to be paid, the delivery driver by his politeness and promptness. Things as well as people can also communicate. A dirty delivery van, a badly packaged parcel, a maintenance engineer with dirty overalls, a badly laid out letter with spelling mistakes can each give an impression that the company does not really care.

13.5 Telephone selling

Because of the high total cost of maintaining a sales force (estimated at over £30,000, including overheads, to keep one sales person on the road for a year) and the relatively small proportion of sales force time spent selling, companies are always looking for ways to increase the efficiency of their sales effort. In recent years this has led to a rapid growth in tele-sales, a method of selling now employed by many companies.

It is not usual for telephone selling to replace all the tasks of the sales person described in section 13.2. It can be feasible for the sales of fairly simple, low value products bought on a repetitive basis. A good example would be supplies of tea, coffee, milk, sugar etc. to replenish drinks machines. Lots of companies have these machines and need to re-order supplies weekly or monthly. To employ a sales person to drive round to take orders in person would be very expensive, but a tele-sales operation can be used to ring customers on a regular basis to take their orders.

More usually tele-sales will be used to take over part of a sales person's job with the aim of increasing his selling time. Prospecting and making appointments are tasks that can be performed on behalf of the sales person by tele-sales. Typical examples would be suppliers of fitted kitchens and insurance services. Virtually all households are potential customers for both organisations. It is therefore possible for them to cold call over the telephone or to send a mail shot followed up by a telephone call with the objective of identifying those consumers who have an interest in the product or service. Having identified someone who is interested, the tele-sales person makes an appointment for the sales representative who therefore only has to visit 'warm' prospects. Since he also does not have to spend time prospecting or making appointments his active selling time should be greatly increased.

Conclusion

Personal selling is a very important part of the marketing mix of most companies. Most sales still require personal contact between buyer and seller at some stage. Moreover, the good relationships which must be maintained between suppliers and their customers if trade between them is to continue, are often based, at least partly, on personal relations between individuals. Although it is mainly through the sales force that most organisations maintain good personal relations with their customers, many other employees within the organisation have an important role to play in this respect. Finally, it is important to note that due to the increasing cost of personal selling, the telephone is being increasingly used as an alternative to face-to-face contact. It is possible to use the telephone to fulfil all aspects of the personal selling process, including the maintenance of relationships, but is most commonly employed to carry out the more straight forward tasks such as prospecting, qualifying leads or taking routine orders.

Assignment   Roberts Supermarkets

'Roberts Supermarkets' is a small local supermarket chain with seven stores in mid-Lancashire. It is a family firm, currently run by three brothers, Alan, Cliff and Steve who are in their late thirties and early forties. The three brothers are increasingly conscious of the fact that their company has an image problem, being neither a large chain on the one hand nor a small intimate corner shop. Most of their stores are in small towns, close to the town centre. At the time they were opened (between 1966 and 1975) they were in excellent locations but recent out of town shopping developments have seriously weakened this advantage. Their stores vary in size but average around 5,000 square feet of sales space. When first opened they were considered to be large supermarkets but in the late seventies and eighties they have been overtaken by developments in the trade which have seen the average size of stores increase considerably. After 1975 Roberts' growth virtually ceased as Mr. Roberts senior decided that the company was 'quite big enough'. It is now two and a half years since Mr. Roberts' retirement and the three brothers realise it is of vital importance to do something about the stores' market positioning. For many years the company has essentially sold on price, which was fine in the early days when they were competing mainly against corner shops but has become increasingly untenable as the main supermarket chains have become larger and more dominant. These developments have posed a number of problems.

1. The size of the main supermarket chains gives them immense buying power which makes it impossible for Roberts to match their prices.

2. The range and quality of the large chains' own label products far exceeds anything that Roberts can achieve.

3. Many individual stores are now as much as three or four times the size of Roberts' stores and therefore carry a much wider range of goods.

4. The larger stores tend to be located out of town, with large car parks and with the spread of car ownership and increasing traffic congestion in town centres, these out of town stores are becoming more and more popular with people for their weekly family shopping.

As the first step towards a new market positioning strategy the Roberts brothers commissioned some market research, an action that would have been unheard of in their father's time. Briefly, the main findings were as follows:

1. Most people use the Sainsbury, Asda or Tesco superstores for the bulk of their family provisions which they buy either weekly or monthly.

2. This is supported by the fact that Roberts average basket size (average amount bought by each customer) is £6.21 whereas the average basket size of the local superstores would be over £30.

3. Families with cars would quite happily drive fifteen to twenty miles to shop at one of the superstores, even if their own local town had a Roberts store. Some people without cars even used the special buses that provided a service to some of the superstores.

There were however things that shoppers disliked about the superstores including:

1.Lack of staff availability to offer assistance or advice. Fresh produce (meat, fruit, vegetables, bread) was often criticised and was often bought at local greengrocers, butchers or bakers.

2. The trend towards eliminating price stickers from individual items and relying instead on the bar code and a computerised print-out from the till was generally disliked.

3. Long queues at check-outs at busy times were also widely condemned.

Roberts however did not have a good image. A number of problems were mentioned and also several interesting pointers to future developments.

1. The shops were seen as suffering from poor displays, a lack of space, and a general image of tattiness bordering on uncleanliness.

2. The staff were considered to be scruffy and rather unhelpful.

3. The 'Hi-Value' own label goods (commissioned by Roberts as part of a consortium of small chains) were considered in fact to be 'Low-Value' and poor quality, but Roberts stocks and prices on well known branded goods were considered acceptable.

4. Roberts was considered very poor on fresh produce.

5. A significant number of people expressed a desire for a local delivery service.

6. Mothers with young children complained about the difficulty of manoeuvring prams or buggies inside the congested store. Some respondents expressed a preference for small shops e.g. the greengrocer's and butcher's because of the good personal contact they afforded with the owner and staff.

7. A large number of people expressed a demand for more convenience items such as pre-packed sandwiches for lunch, pre-packed salads and quality cook-chill meals for the evening. These items were currently being purchased at small sandwich bars or at Marks and Spencer.

8. There was considerable demand for longer opening times especially in the evenings.

The report was very interesting and convinced the three brothers about two things.

A major repositioning of their business was long overdue and a huge effort had to be made to improve all aspects of the personal service provided to customers.

The brothers were sure that these two priorities were related but felt that they needed professional help to clarify their thinking and to suggest some fresh practical ideas for implementing any changes.

Task

You have been called in as a consultant by the three directors of Roberts Supermarkets Ltd. to tackle the two points outlined above.

Write a report to the directors which:

1. Summarises the company's main strengths, weaknesses, opportunities and threats.

2. Outlines a medium term (three years) strategy for repositioning the company.

3. Explains in detail the measures which could be taken to improve service to customers.

4. Makes specific recommendations concerning any staff training considered essential to the successful implementation of these changes.

PART THREE SPECIAL ASPECTS OF MARKETING

So far in this book we have covered the analytical aspects of the marketer's task, which, if carried out successfully, will enable him to correctly identify a gap in the market, which his company would be in a good position to exploit.

Part Two of the book then went on to examine the implementation of a marketing strategy which would arise out of such an analysis. We looked at the development of a product or service, its pricing, its distribution and its promotion to the relevant target market.

In this final part of the book we will look at some of the special aspects of the marketer's job. These special aspects will not change the marketing principles stated in Chapter 1, but they may influence the way a marketing manager applies those principles to his particular job.

Chapter 14 looks at the organisation itself and explains how factors such as the structure and the culture of the organisation can have a significant effect on its marketing. Chapter 15 explores the fact that by no means all organisations are typical profit seeking companies, and examines the application of marketing principles in non-profit making sectors. The final chapter of the book looks to the future and examines some of the social, political and environmental trends which are having an ever increasing influence on the work of the marketing manager.

Chapter 14
Marketing Organisation

Introduction

We have talked in great detail in the previous chapters of this book about the kind of programmes that marketing people have to develop with the aim of meeting the needs of their customers. To win and keep satisfied customers, the firm must translate these plans into action, and to do that a sound organisation will be necessary. Many well prepared plans and good intentions fail to materialise due to poor organisation. There are two broad aspects of a firm's organisation. Firstly there is its structure, the kind of tangible organisational features which can be shown on a chart. It is this organisational structure which underpins most firms and ensures that they function efficiently. There is also a second, less tangible aspect to the way in which a firm organises itself. Usually referred to as organisational culture it concerns the way a firm motivates its staff. In the marketing context the right kind of organisational culture is particularly important for ensuring that staff are constantly motivated to deliver satisfaction to customers. This chapter will examine both the structural and cultural aspects of marketing organisation.

14.1 Organisational structure

In any organisation, people must work with colleagues in their own department and in other parts of the organisation. For example, it would be silly for sales and marketing staff to devote a large proportion of their time and resources to selling and promoting a product the company was finding it difficult to produce, perhaps due to a shortage of an essential material or a temporary staffing problem. Equally it would be foolish for the production department to keep manufacturing for stock a product which the marketing department was finding hard to sell. People in production and in marketing must communicate with each other if such problems are to be avoided, as must staff from other functional areas of the company.

According to Peter Spillard,

'An organisation is a more or less permanent grouping of people established to undertake specific tasks in order to achieve a given set of objectives.'

It is for this reason that companies are run by a board of directors which includes the heads of the major functions within the organisation. Good communications begin at the top and it is the responsibility of the directors to ensure that all departments and individual employees work together to implement the firm's objectives. The company's organisational structure should facilitate this co-operation, as shown by the chart on the next page.

The chart is of course incomplete. In a large company, each functional area would include many more managers and some areas, such as purchasing or research and development might be formed into departments in their own right. However, the purpose of the 'family tree' is to clarify areas of responsibility so that everyone in the organisation knows whom to approach when they have to deal with matters which affect other functional areas of the company. Thus, in the example illustrated above, the sales manager may have an important customer who requires a few slight modifications to a standard product. If so, he will need to consult the chief production engineer about the feasibility of incorporating such changes before making any promises to the customer. The market research manager may wish to buy a powerful new statistical analysis programme to improve the efficiency of his operation. If the price of the software is higher than the sum his department is authorised to spend, he will have to seek the approval of the finance director. Perhaps the advertising manager would like to take on a bright young assistant. If so, he would need to ask for the assistance of the graduate recruitment manager. The purchasing manager may have found a new, less costly source of supply for an important component in one of the company's products. Before placing an order with the supplier however, he must check with the marketing director or sales manager that there is likely to be no adverse customer reaction to the change and he will also need to liaise with the quality control manager to ensure that the new supplier is capable of meeting his firm's quality standards.

We can therefore define organisational structure as:

'a framework which defines areas of responsibility for carrying out all activities which contribute to the success of the organisation.'

Due to the wide ranging nature of its responsibilities, marketing tends to interact with other departments more frequently than do most other functions. Since it is the duty of marketing to identify the needs of customers and to ensure that the firm organises its resources to meet those needs, the extent to which the organisational structure facilitates or hampers this process is often considered to be a vital factor in the firm's success. For example, the demise of the British motor cycle industry is often attributed to the fact that marketing was given a very low level of seniority in the organisational structure of most British manufacturers compared to the high

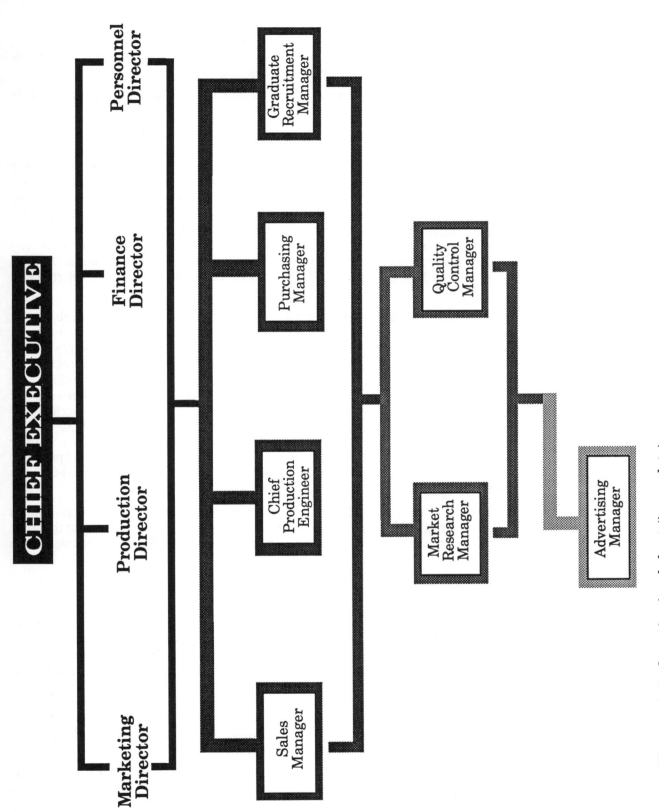

Figure 14. 1 Organisational chart (incomplete)

status of the traditional engineering and accounting functions. This led to a misreading of needs in the market place and the consequent dismissal of the Japanese threat until it was too late.

In this first section of this chapter we will examine four different ways of organising the marketing function within the company.

These are traditional structure, product structure, market structure and matrix structure.

14.1.1 Traditional structure

The diagram above shows a typical marketing department organised along traditional lines. It is most commonly found in single product, single market companies where all the firm's efforts need to be organised in this one clear direction. The structure is very simple. It is clear to everybody where responsibility lies for different activities. Since the structure is hierarchical (the layers of management are organised in tiers or levels, from top to bottom) it is also clear where the authority lies if a disagreement arises between two members of the department. A sales representative, for example, would not ignore the wishes of the market research manager.

Such a hierarchical structure also helps to demonstrate how corporate objectives and strategies, determined by top management are translated into action by ordinary employees. For example, the board of directors will determine the company's overall sales and profit objectives. These will be translated by the marketing director and sales manager into detailed sales objectives broken down into specific products and markets. The sales manager will then divide these detailed objectives between the three regional sales managers who will, in turn, divide their regional objectives into detailed sales targets for their sales representatives. They will fix these targets according to their perception of the potential offered by each territory and their view of each sales person's ability to maximise that potential. Incentives will probably be offered to individual sales representatives to motivate them to achieve their sales targets.

The example shown in Figure 14.2 is illustrative of a typical department. It does not mean that all marketing departments contain each of those positions or that they always have the same titles. Each one of the managers just below director level (often called middle management) will probably have a small department below him, though in most companies the sales department will be larger than the others. The advertising and promotions manager might have junior managers responsible for advertising, public relations and other promotional activities and each of those junior managers may have one or more assistants. The advertising and promotions department may handle all marketing communications activities without the assistance of outside agencies, as might the market research department. In many companies however, these tasks will be delegated to outside agencies, and consequently the size of internal departments will be much smaller. The task of the appropriate manager becomes one of setting objectives, liaising with agencies and monitoring their performance. In fact, in this situation the advertising, market research and customer service functions will often be merged in one department with one manager, usually called the marketing services manager.

If there is a customer services department, it is usually responsible for all aspects of giving customers a good service. This will include matters such as responding swiftly and correctly to enquiries, ensuring that products are delivered on time and in the right condition, providing support such as installation, training, maintenance or perhaps helping the customer to arrange finance to pay for the product.

The sales manager will often have junior managers below him responsible for different regions of the country, or Europe or the world, if the company is an

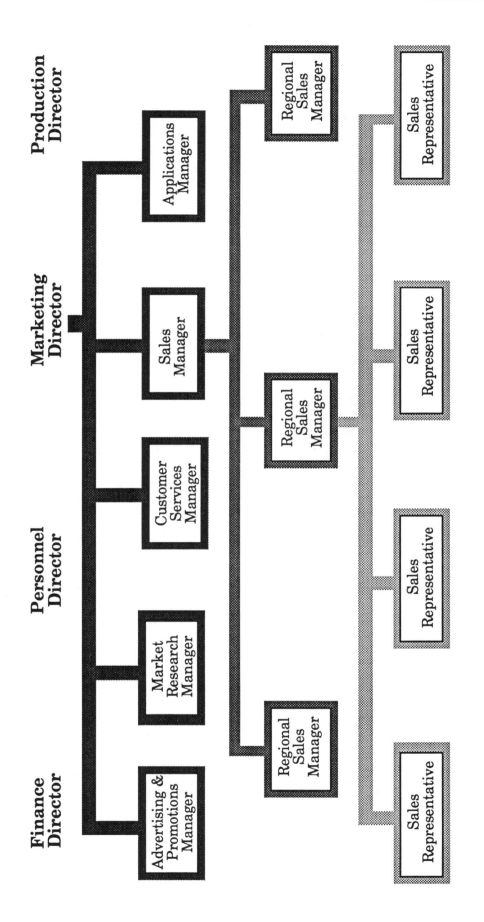

Figure 14. 2 A traditional marketing department structure

exporter. Sales departments can be very large, particularly in companies involved in business to business markets. It is not uncommon for more than fifty sales representatives to be employed, with a regional manager in charge of about ten salesmen.

The applications manager is in charge of new products or new applications (uses) for existing products. This title is very common in the engineering sector, but new product development would be more likely in the FMCG (fast moving consumer goods) sector. Whatever the title, this department performs a vital role, building a bridge between market research, customers and R & D (research and development) to ensure that the firm always has a steady stream of 'tomorrow's breadwinners' progressing through the new product development process.

The traditional structure is therefore very simple, clearly defining everyone's role, responsibilities and authority. However, its advantages in straight forward single product, single market situations can cause difficulties in more complex multi-product, multi-market situations. In a company with a diverse range of products it is difficult for individuals to decide how much of their time and resources to devote to individual products. The danger is that some products will be neglected, or at best receive much less attention than others. To overcome this threat, multi-product companies will often base their organisation on a product oriented structure.

14.1.2 Product structure

A typical product structure is shown in Figure 14.3. It is very common in consumer goods companies, particularly the larger ones which have a wide range of products. Product managers are often called brand managers and are seen as the champions of their brand, fighting to defend or improve its position internally within the company as well as externally in the market place. Some companies, such as the detergent giants Proctor & Gamble and Unilever are quite happy to see their brand managers competing with their own colleagues in the market place if their products are relatively similar.

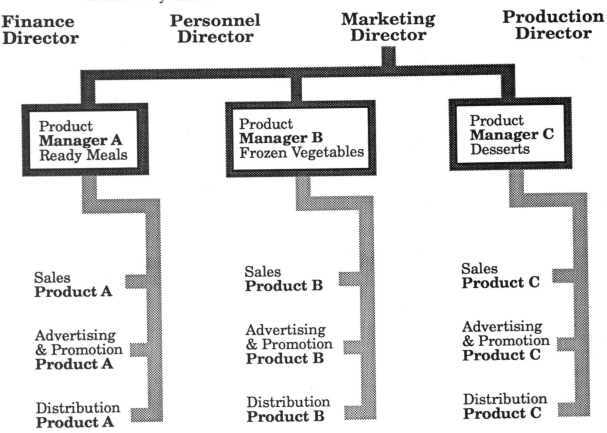

Figure 14. 3 A product oriented structure

The great advantage of this structure to a multi-product company is that each important product or product range gets its fair share of time and attention from each of the important marketing activities. Thus, the ready meals product manager has his own advertising and promotion manager who will probably carry out consumer research, and work with the advertising agency to develop highly tuned advertising to support his brand(s). Product specific sales promotions will be developed, probably with the aid of a specialist promotions agency. A PR consultant may be used to help with activities such as press releases, news features, sponsorship, hospitality and product literature. The advertising and promotions manager will probably also be responsible for packaging, and, if used, for direct mail and exhibitions.

The distribution manager for ready meals will devote his efforts entirely to improving distribution for that product range and ensuring that outlets are fully stocked and receive the right kind of service. Likewise, ready meals will have its own sales staff, perhaps including tele-sales and office sales staff as well as outside sales representatives whose task is to keep in very close touch with all major outlets to ensure that the product is being given adequate shelf space, that it is never out of stock, to encourage retailers to participate in promotions and to keep them informed of any new developments. (If the company were small, several product lines may be handled together at the salesforce level). In this product specific role, individual sales representatives can develop a very high level of product and product application knowledge, which can be very important if complex technical products are being sold. Even for washing powder and ready meals there is evidence that staff who are part of a relatively small team, all united in support of a single brand, will be more highly motivated than staff in a traditionally organised department because the small product specific team can see the results of its actions much more clearly and directly.

Although this type of structure does have some strong advantages for the multi-product company it also has some weaknesses. The main weakness is that the company risks creating a confusing image in the minds of customers. This is particularly evident where two or more products are being sold into the same market by different product managers and sales staff. In general customers do not like to deal with more than one person or department when buying similar things from the same company. This problem can be magnified if the competitive spirit between the brand managers is taken too far and they end up promoting the benefits of their own product to a customer to the detriment of one of the company's other products.

Office systems company Kalamazoo experienced exactly this problem. Traditionally well known as a supplier of manual administrative systems it had also developed a computerised arm. Sales and marketing were organised along product lines. Apart from the confusion as to whether Kalamazoo was a supplier of manual or computerised systems, the real damage was done when the same customer was demonstrated all the benefits of a computerised system by a Kalamazoo salesman, followed later by another representative from the same company (but different department) who explained how he would benefit from a manual system. Such a lack of co-ordination can easily happen in a marketing department organised along product lines. Apart from the waste of resources if two teams are selling to the same customers, it can also damage the company's reputation. It is for these reasons that some companies, including Kalamazoo, have decided to reorganise along market lines.

14.1.3 Market structure

This kind of structure, in its purest form would be identical to that shown in Figure 14.3, except that markets A, B and C would replace products A, B and C. It is particularly appropriate when a range of products of relatively low technical complexity is sold to a number of diverse end users who are less interested in the product itself than in its application to their particular industry or manufacturing process. In business to business oriented markets the market will often by defined by industry type or SIC code. (The Standard Industrial Classification Code was explained in Chapter 2). A market orientated organisational structure enables sales and marketing staff to develop a deeper understanding of the end user markets they serve and helps them to monitor changes and trends in that industry which might affect future demand for the company's products. In other words it helps them to follow Peters and Waterman's advice to stay 'close to their customers'.

A similar structure results from the concept of 'key account management', where some large customers are so important (key accounts) that a unique marketing programme is tailored to their needs. Large companies may have different buying practices than smaller customers. They may demand more sophisticated sales skills, a higher level of technical information, extensive customer service and perhaps special 'just in time' deliveries. Key accounts may therefore be served by·a special team drawn mainly from the ranks of more senior sales and marketing staff.

A market based structure also enables the firm to allocate resources and effort specifically to winning new business or entering new markets. This structure can recognise that gaining new customers is a specialised activity requiring different skills than the maintenance of market share in current markets achieved mainly by keeping existing customers happy. To enter new markets the team needs to place emphasis on marketing research, on promotional activities which disseminate information and generate leads and on 'missionary selling' where the sales person will need the strength of character to accept higher rejection rates than normal and the patience to cultivate relationships before attempting to close sales.

It is clear that both product and market structures have their own advantages. However, they both share some fundamental weaknesses. Firstly they are very heavy on resources, with each product or market team having its own manager, and its own functional specialists for advertising, sales, customer service etc. This almost inevitably increases the overheads of the company. Secondly the responsibility for marketing planning falls on the shoulders of the product (or market) manager who is naturally concerned only with his own product or market. As we stressed in the first chapter of this book, marketing planning should concern the whole company and is about matching the resources of the company to the most profitable needs in the marketplace. Thirdly, such a structure can make co-operation with other company functions (such as production and R & D) more difficult because there is no single point of responsibility within the marketing department for such relationships. It is for these reasons that many multi-product, multi-market companies prefer to adopt a matrix structure.

14.1.4 Matrix structure

The simple matrix structure outlined in Figure 14.4 shows how this method of organisation leads to greater flexibility and increased communication within the department. Each product range still has its champion, who may be called a product sales manager as in the diagram or a product or brand manager. Companies organised as a group with several operating units may have 'Operating unit A General Manager', 'Operating unit B' etc. down the vertical axis. General marketing services such as advertising and marketing research are not duplicated but are provided on a company or group basis to be used by individual product managers or operating units. Hence the matrix structure, allowing the product managers to relate to all the group marketing services and vice-versa.

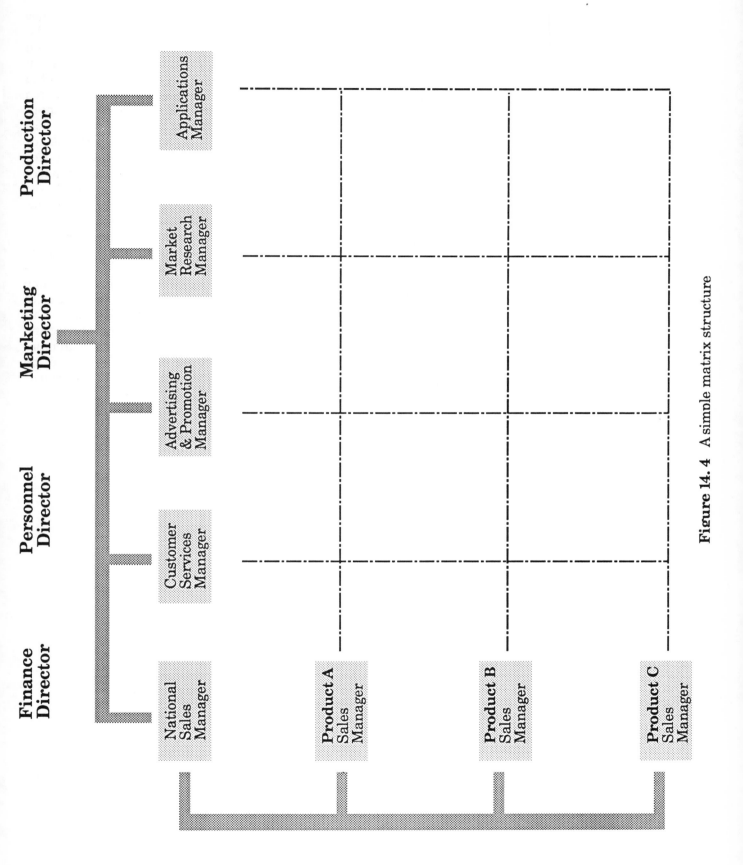

Figure 14. 4 A simple matrix structure

As companies grow and their activities proliferate, matrix structures may become more complex. The structure shown in Figure 14.5 seeks to exploit all the advantages of both the product structure and the market structure. As you can see from the diagram, the product managers report to a group product manager who in turn reports to the head of the marketing organisation. They are responsible for the longer term planning activities and will therefore tend to liaise with market research and new product development teams. Product managers will also usually be responsible, in conjunction with the advertising and promotions manager for the non-personal communications concerning their product. The sales staff are responsible for shorter term selling activities. They may be organised along straightforward geographic lines, e.g. Sales Manager North, Sales Manager Midlands and Sales Manager South. However, if the multiple market problems mentioned in section 14.1.3 exist it may be more beneficial to organise the sales function along end user market lines as shown in Figure 14.5. Sales staff thus become experts in the applications requirements of their own customers. This means that they can help customers with technical problems such as the application of a component or a material to the customer's particular manufacturing process. The firm can also avoid costly duplication and embarrassing contradictions when different sales staff serve the same markets. If a customer requires high level technical support or information the sales staff can always call on the assistance of the relevant product specialist. Sales staff will also use appropriate group marketing services, particularly customer service and distribution. As you can see, the matrix has become more complicated, with more lines of contact, but as long as areas of responsibility are clearly defined and the structure is working within the right kind of corporate culture this kind of matrix organisation can be very effective.

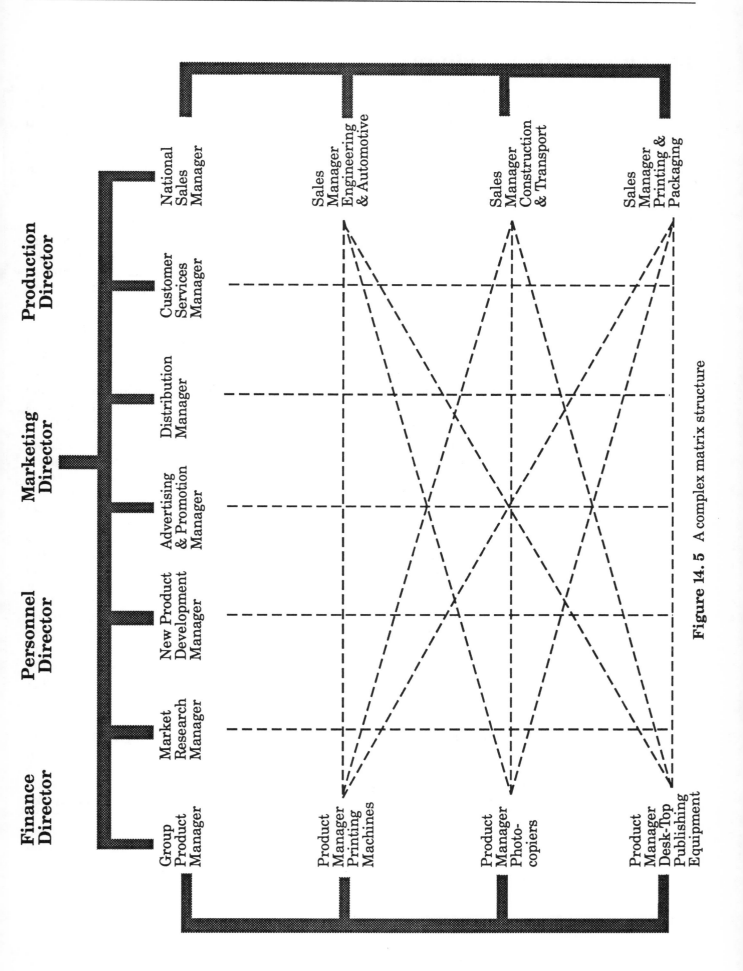

Figure 14. 5   A complex matrix structure

14.2 Organisational culture

The point was made at the end of the preceding section that even the most complex organisational structures can work if supported by the right kind of organisational culture. By itself even the most carefully designed organisational structure is no more than lines and boxes on a chart showing where responsibility for different activities resides. It takes people to translate that chart into effective action and the determination, enthusiasm and effort which people put into that action will often depend largely on the organisational culture.

14.2.1 Relationships

The lines on the organisational chart represent the many formal working relationships that enable the company to function correctly. Some people to people relationships will be formal, occurring in committees, management meetings or through written memos or reports. Other relationships will be much less formal, having their roots in casual conversations and social activities, often resulting from the natural tendency of human beings to develop mutually beneficial relationships.

Let's examine the concept of internal relationships through the eyes of a product manager in a company with a complex matrix structure. If he is to be successful in achieving his own work objectives he will need the willing, rather than grudging, cooperation of many other staff. He will be dealing mainly with other middle managers who are his equals or with more junior staff who are not directly under his authority. Figure 14.6 illustrates some of his likely relationships with other staff.

The product manager's ability to achieve his own work related objectives will often depend on the willing cooperation of people towards the outer edge of the diagram with whom his relationships will be relatively informal. A formal approach to the distribution manager to squeeze in an urgent delivery to an important customer may receive approval, but 'only on condition that Mary (the van driver) and Joe (the fork lift operator) can fit it in.' Joe and Mary's willingness to co-operate will depend partly on their social relationship with the product manager and partly on the prevailing culture (positive or negative) within the organisation. Equally the manager will often depend upon favours, or at least goodwill from other people in the organisation for example, the credit controller to avoid pressing too hard for settlement of an overdue invoice from a valued customer; the recruitment officer to speed up the appointment of a new secretary; the design engineers to examine the possibility of a slight product modification; the PR or hospitality officers to help him squeeze a little extra value out of his limited promotional budget; the researchers to carry out a small piece of 'ad hoc' research on his behalf or from the sales representatives to bring feedback from customers on a new product offering.

14.2.2 What is organisational culture?

It was stated above that Mary and Joe would be more likely to give their willing cooperation to the product manager if the organisational culture were positive, but what exactly do we mean by organisational culture? In sociology, culture refers to the whole of the knowledge, values, ideas and habits of a society, which are passed from one generation to another. Thus, ethnic groups in a multi-racial country like the USA often retain their own distinctive culture for many generations. There can also be 'subcultures' which are distinctive sets of values which exist within the mainstream culture. Subcultures will be different, but not in opposition to the main culture. 'Contracultures', distinctive sets of values which challenge the main culture, can also develop.

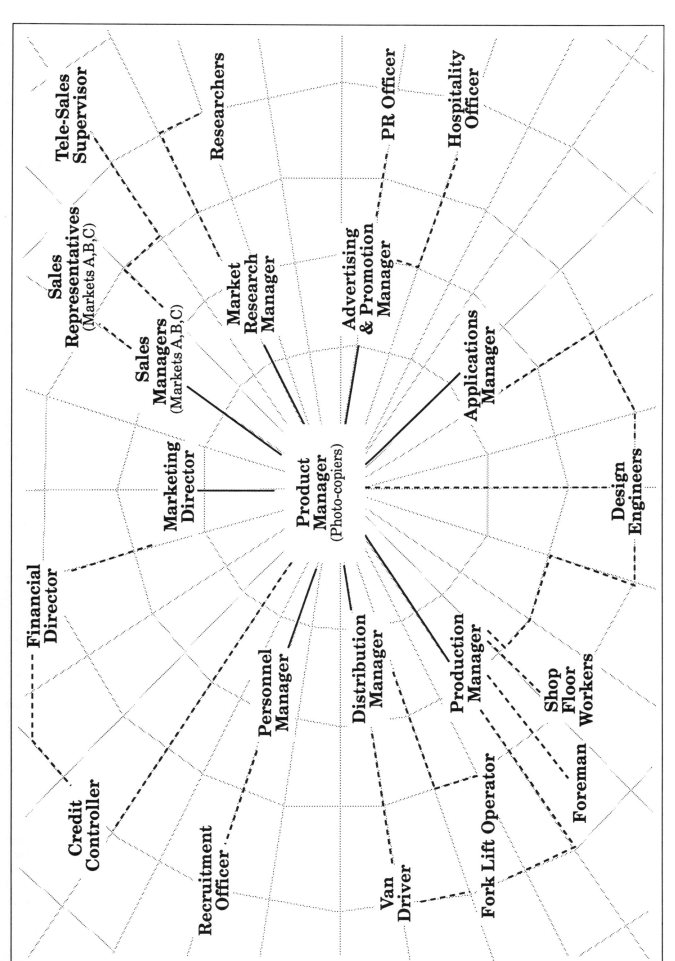

Figure 14.6 The web of relationships

Any culture will be made up of a number of elements.

(a) Beliefs

These are general, sometimes vague opinions about the world and the nature of society. Some cultures believe in a spiritual life after death, others in reincarnation.

(b) Values

Values are strongly held beliefs about what is right and wrong. They lead people to take certain forms of action. In the U.K. it is still a core cultural value that people marry before they have children.

(c) Norms

Certain ways of behaving are expected. They are norms. In most cultures there are unwritten guidelines on how people ought to behave in different situations. For example, people usually form an orderly queue when waiting in the post office or at the bus stop.

(d) Roles

Particular positions in society often have clear patterns of behaviour associated with them. A salesman is often expected to be outgoing and confident whereas a researcher is considered to be more thoughtful and introverted.

(e) Role conflict

Sometimes people have to play a number of different roles. In family terms a person may be simultaneously a father, a husband and a son. Other roles for the same person may include being a teacher, a local councillor and a friend. These various roles may come into conflict, sometimes because incompatible actions are required from two different roles and often because there is not enough time to do justice to all roles.

(f) Status

Some people are held in higher regard than others. Some roles or positions have more prestige than others.

Organisational culture simply refers to work related values, beliefs and behavioural norms common to all members of the organisation. Even the smallest firms develop their own culture. Japanese companies in the U.K. are often said to have an organisational culture which is different from that of the traditional British company. It is said that the Japanese company (with British employees) will be harder working, less prone to industrial disputes and more egalitarian than its British owned counterpart. One of the key aspects of organisational culture is the extent to which all staff work willingly and enthusiastically in pursuit of common organisational goals. Some companies go to great lengths to foster a positive culture within the firm. They run training seminars for staff, they offer incentives, they provide social facilities and they ensure that senior management are seen to conform to key corporate beliefs, values and norms. The establishment of a common cultural base for interactions between staff will almost always be beneficial to company performance. Like a football team, a company is more than the sum of individual performances. The team effort is very important.

14.2.3 Positive corporate culture at Hewlett-Packard

Hewlett-Packard was started in a garage in Paulo Alto, California by William Hewlett and David Packard in 1939. Gradually it grew into the world's leading manufacturer of electronic test and measuring instruments for engineers and scientists. In the 1960's the company moved into analytical equipment for medicine and chemistry and into computers. Today it manufactures over 10,000 products, has a turnover of around $8 billion per annum and employs 82,000 people in countries around the world, including Great Britain.

Based on the assumption that the company will prosper only if those 82,000 employees are committed to doing a good job, HP has always given a high priority to developing the right kind of corporate culture. This corporate culture became known as 'The HP Way'. One of the cornerstones of this positive culture is good internal communications which are upheld by two well known HP philosophies, 'Management by Wandering Around' (MBWA) and the 'Open Door Policy'. MBWA involves maximum contact between managers and all the staff who work under them. Managers are responsible for training their staff, monitoring their performance and looking after their well being. The Open Door Policy is a logical extension of MBWA. No middle or senior management doors are closed to HP employees. They all have the right to walk into any office to discuss any matters or to air any grievances.

The HP Way is particularly concerned that people should be allowed and encouraged to perform to the best of their ability. They generally promote from within, give high priority to post-experience training and have a highly developed system of 'management by objectives'. Objectives start at the corporate level and are interpreted and handed down to each successive tier of management. Each manager of an operating group is responsible for ensuring that the objectives for the team are understood and accepted by each individual team member. The objectives help managers to guide their team and give employees goals to aim for.

According to HP:

'People want to work for a successful company in a friendly atmosphere and to have their potential recognised. Through the HP Way, the company sets an example of balanced management philosophy where personal aspirations and corporate objectives are as close together as any business organisation can achieve.'

There is little doubt that people do seem to like working for Hewlett-Packard. As a result they are quite happy to work harder and to work longer hours if necessary to help the company succeed. The teamwork aspect of the organisational culture is very strong. This is very important, and will give HP a huge advantage over any competitor with a negative, authoritarian or confrontational culture. However, as marketer we have to go one step further and say that a positive hard working culture is still not enough, unless it is also a customer oriented culture.

14.2.4 Customer oriented culture

At the beginning of this book it was stressed that companies must be outward looking. They must regard their primary objective as meeting the needs of customers. They must therefore base their organisational structure and culture on this goal of winning and keeping satisfied customers. For many years Hewlett-Packard has been seen as a product oriented company. They put a huge amount of resources (never less than 10% of net revenues) into R & D, and produce innovative and high quality products, but they have tended to place less emphasis on researching the needs of the marketplace. They have excellent communications with their own employees, but have communicated less well with customers and especially with potential customers. HP has now mounted a campaign to become more market oriented. If successful it should make the company an even stronger force in the computer field.

Comet is a company which is already customer oriented. The following statements are taken from the company's advert which appeared in a number of magazines towards the end of 1988.

'If we're not as good as we say we are, this pledge could put us out of business'

A short paragraph then explains how much Comet values its customers and states: 'To us, customer satisfaction is a matter of principle'. The second page of the ad then outlines the 'Comet Customer Policy', as shown below in Figure 14.7.

It is an obvious truism to state that only if the customer buys and keeps buying will the company continue to have a business. Whilst this makes common sense, not all companies put this principle into practice. Several British car manufacturers were accused of ignoring it during the 1970's, turning out poor quality, unreliable cars losing a lot of customer loyalty in the process. Even a manufacturer of prestige cars such as Jaguar was criticised in this respect. It was only with the arrival of John Egan that this was rectified. In the 1980's Jaguar has been organised around customers' needs. Reliable products that do not go rusty or have niggling little faults have been produced. Customers have been followed up a few months after purchase to ensure that they are happy with their vehicle and this customer oriented culture rescued Jaguar from the brink of bankruptcy and has enabled it to flourish as an independent company.

Research carried out in April and May 1988 by Chapter One Direct (a direct marketing consultancy) showed that many companies ignore the most fundamental of factors when it comes to meeting the needs of customers. Chapter One Direct spent two months filling in every coupon attached to advertisements in national newspapers. In response, 10% of advertisers sent absolutely nothing to the prospective buyer and many more sent something entirely inappropriate, some taking as long as six or seven weeks to do so. Quick and thoroughly appropriate responses were actually few and far between which goes to show that companies can be putting a huge amount of resources and effort into activities they see as marketing (in this case expensive advertising) whilst ignoring the basic marketing principle of putting the customer's needs at the heart of the company's activities. Included in Chapter One Direct's list of poor responders were such famous names as BMW, Barclays Bank, Pilkington Glass, IBM, and Eagle Star.

Whether it is responding thoroughly to customer enquiries, dealing quickly and honestly with customer complaints, giving customers an absolute guarantee of quality and replacing the product without question if the customer is not satisfied or whether it is just being polite, friendly and helpful, the goal of serving customers' needs should be at the heart of an organisation's culture. To appreciate the value of a customer oriented philosophy one has only to consider successful companies such as Marks and Spencer, Sainsbury's, MacDonalds and Jaguar.

COMET CUSTOMER POLICY

Our aim is to help you make the right choice and to ensure you remain satisfied with your purchase.

1. To help you make the right choice, product buying guidelines are displayed and we'll demonstrate any product wherever practicable.

2. Delivery can be arranged anywhere in the UK, in the morning, afternoon or evening - 9am to 8pm Monday to Friday, 9am to 5pm Saturdays. When we deliver, we'll also remove your old (disconnected) appliance if you wish.

3. When you buy a Comet extended warranty, parts and labour are included and you do not have the inconvenience of paying the engineer for repairs and then claiming it back.

4. If you buy any product from Comet, then find the same offer on sale elsewhere at a lower price within 14 days, we'll willingly refund the difference, plus 10% of that difference.

5. If the product doesn't suit, simply return it within 14 days - as new and with original packaging - and we'll exchange it for another product of equivalent value or, if you prefer, give you your money back.

6. We want you to enjoy continuous use of any product you purchase from us, and as we have one of the biggest, dedicated service operations in the country, you can be confident of our specialist attention should the need arise. If the product can't be repaired in the first twelve months, we will of course, replace it.

7. When you make a purchase, you will automatically be given the names of both your sales assistant and the store manager, together with the store telephone number, in case you have any subsequent queries.

8. Comet's aim is total customer satisfaction. If you think we fail to achieve this, please let us know by writing to: Peter McTague, Customer Services Director, Comet Group PLC, George Street, Hull HU1 3AU.

Figure 14. 7 An example of a customer policy agreement.

Conclusion

Perhaps we can leave this chapter almost where we began the book. We said that marketing should be seen as a philosophy, an outward looking philosophy about meeting customers' needs and that the role of the marketing department was to get close to customers, to build a bridge between the company and its customers. In this chapter we have expanded on these principles and we can therefore display this 'bridge building' role of marketing in the diagram below.

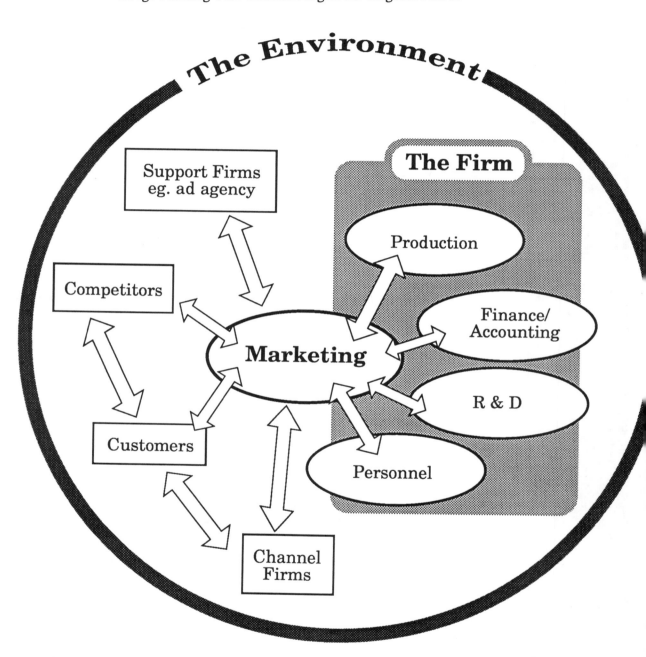

Figure 14.8 **The bridge building role of marketing.**

As we can see from the diagram, marketing's role is to build bridges not just to customers but towards all the external organisations which can affect the company's success. More importantly, the role of marketing is to persuade and encourage all the other functions of the company to be outward looking and to regard meeting the needs of customers as their most important objective. It is vital that both the organisational structure and the organisational culture are designed to help the marketing department make all staff outward looking. The company must be organised not for its own convenience and efficiency but for the convenience and benefit of customers.

Assignment Premier Pumps

Premier Pumps Ltd. is a manufacturer of small and medium sized pumps employing around 350 people. Over the last couple of decades they have seen the gradual intensification of competition which has been further aggravated by the steadily increasing share of the market held by importers, especially in the small pump sector. As a result of these changes in the marketplace the company has found itself competing increasingly on price, although Premier does take pride in offering what it considers to be the best level of service in the market. Pumps can be supplied to the customer's exact requirements, often from existing drawings and tooling, but the company's design engineers will be pleased to come up with a new pump to meet the customer's needs if the company does not have, or cannot locate a suitable specification. Despite this ability the salesforce often has to compromise on price to secure orders.

This commitment to a very extensive product range has enabled premier to compete for virtually any potential business in the market. The twelve sales representatives, under two area managers, are able to cover the whole country, actively seeking out new prospects, servicing regular customers and trying to win business from the competition. However, despite their ability to offer a pump to suit the specific needs of any buyer, the salesforce is increasingly finding that it has to compromise on price to secure orders. This can be very disconcerting, particularly when some of the foreign competitors seem to be selling pumps for no more than it costs Premier to make them. Many orders have been taken at rock bottom prices simply to keep men employed and plant occupied but the company's profits have nevertheless been steadily declining. Lack of profitability is having an adverse effect on the company's ability to keep up with new technology, develop new products and invest in new production machinery.

Measures have been taken to address these problems. Bob Jones, the Works Director, has achieved marked improvements in labour productivity and considerable cost savings through efficient energy management, clamping down on wasted materials and other sloppy practices, and, with the help of the company accountant and buyer, reducing inventories through tighter stock control and purchasing procedures. With the help of the data processing manager, Bob is now in the process of developing a computerised database to describe and classify the company's range of pumps (currently estimated to stand at over three thousand, although nobody is really sure of the exact number). When complete, it should enable the production department to avoid unnecessary design and tooling work and a computer print-out manual should help the sales force to identify whether a list model exists which corresponds to the customer's specification, This should help the salesforce to be more competitive on price and should considerably improve the efficiency of sales order processing.

The sales manager, Jim Browning, has also been making improvements of his own. Convinced that the sales force could improve its efficiency he has recently introduced one of the proprietary sales management systems which records the activities and whereabouts of each salesman, details of each sales call, statistics on orders taken and general information on customers and developments in the marketplace. Currently a manual system, it could be computerised if required, which would enable it to produce revealing cumulative data which should help sales management decision making.

However, Jim Browning can't help feeling a little uneasy about the whole thing. It's quite clear that some of the sales staff (a large proportion of whom have been with the company for many years) resent the new system. Apart from a natural aversion to paperwork, they seem to view it as a 'big brother' exercise. Jim knows they don't make any effort with the optional information sections and even doubts the accuracy of some of the factual details. He is sure that the current sales force could achieve more, as seems to be proved by the performance of the most recent recruit. A graduate in his mid-twenties, Peter Walton's more determined approach seems to be winning some useful new customers in a difficult territory.

Despite his concern, Jim has tended to abide by the advice of his two area sales managers who are strongly opposed to 'rocking the boat' because of the adverse effect it might have on the morale of the salesmen. As a result, the salesmen still receive a basic salary with no commission element, and rather than reduce their perks, (type of car and expenses) Jim has sought economies in other areas. He has virtually eliminated advertising, in which he has little confidence anyway, is taking a hard look at exhibition expenses (even questioning attendance at two of the three annual exhibitions) and has managed to reduce printing costs by only producing leaflets for new products. He doesn't waste any money on gimmicks like direct mail or tele-sales, but does still maintain a small promotional budget spent mainly on small Christmas gifts for customers.

Exports have been disappointing over the last few years. Premier's management team tends to feel that if it can't match the cheap imports on price in the home market it stands virtually no chance overseas. Little effort has therefore been put into exporting with the result that many traditional export lines have declined, although a small number of special pumps have shown a steady increase in overseas sales.

There was no doubt that Premier's senior management team was committed to improving the situation, and that the company was much more efficient than it had been ten years previously. However, although sales volume had been showing steady increases (apart from the worst recession years of 1980 - 1983), profits had continued to decline during the eighties, and there was a growing awareness that the company's products were not technologically advanced. In order to try and overcome this problem Bob and Jim had put their heads together and had created the post of applications manager to bridge the gap between sales and production. They had appointed Jeremy Sadler, a bright young design engineer to the post. In his late twenties, Jeremy had been sponsored through university by Premier and had plenty of enthusiasm for improving and updating the company's products. However, he had no training in sales or marketing and was never too sure whether he reported to Bob Jones or Jim Browning, which perhaps helps to explain why his achievements had been fairly limited, despite a lot of hard work.

Finally, under strong pressure from the parent company, Richard Lambert, Premier's MD, had agreed to the creation of a marketing department. It was decided that the following year should be declared 'The Year of the Customer', and, with the aid of a leading recruitment company a new, well paid marketing manager was appointed. To stress the importance of the new role it was emphasised that the marketing manager's post was expected to be raised to director level within two years.

The new marketing manager was John Gregory. Aged 34, John graduated from a well known university with a good degree in economics in the mid-1970's. He spent six years with a well known confectionery company, successfully completing their graduate training programme and rising to be brand manager of 'Choc- Shapes' before moving on to a well known market research company to broaden his experience. From 1985 he had been assistant marketing manager, with responsibility for research, advertising and other promotional activities, at the UK head office of a successful, foreign owned manufacturer of white goods. In 1986 John had gained his MBA following three years of dedicated part-time study, the final year of which had been devoted to his dissertation on the marketing of dish washers. John was new to industrial marketing but was looking forward to the challenge and was keen to show how a strong marketing effort could pay off.

His enthusiasm received a sharp jolt within days of joining the company. In a series of short, informal meetings designed to introduce John to key members of staff, a deep scepticism about the value of marketing was revealed. Bob and Jim were particularly suspicious of the new department and the effect it might have on their own areas of responsibility. Jim was particularly blunt, pointing out that he and Bob had a very good working relationship, had achieved some important successes in recent years, and he found it difficult to see how John was going to improve things.

Towards the end of his first month John was due to make a short presentation to the Premier Pumps board. He was to concentrate on two areas:

(a) why marketing was so important to the future of the company,

(b) his own role within the company.

In view of the somewhat less than rapturous welcome he had received from other senior staff, John was acutely aware of the importance of this presentation. He was determined to make the right impression.

Task

Assume your role is advisor to John Gregory. Produce a briefing document for John in which you:

(a) identify the main points that John should get across to the board in his presentation.

(b) advise John as to the manner in which he should make his presentation in an attempt to engender the best possible working relationship with the other key managers of the company.

Chapter 15

Marketing for Non-profit Making Organisations

Introduction.

So far it has been an implicit assumption of this book that the type of oganisation implementing the marketing principles it advocates would be a commercial firm, ultimately concerned with making a profit. However, there are thousands of non-profit making organisations in the U.K. and in most other western developed countries. They include charities such as Oxfam, local authorities such as Cheshire County Council, cultural organisations like art galleries, religious organisations such as the Methodist Church, government organisations such as the Department of Health or one of its hospitals, educational organisations such as Oxford University, pressure groups such as Friends of the Earth, political parties and many more types of organisation. None are commercial, profit making bodies. Although their purpose and behaviour will often differ from that of a typical profit oriented company, it is now generally accepted that the marketing philosophy and marketing techniques are of value to non - profit making organisations. This chapter will examine the application of marketing principles to these organisations.

15.1 What is a non-profit making organisation?

According to Keith Blois a non-profit making organisation is:

> *'an organisation whose prime goal is non-economic. However, in pursuit of that goal it may undertake profit making activities.'*

Blois suggests that it is misleading to refer to the kind of organisations listed in the introduction to this chapter as non- profit organisations because it implies that they try to avoid making profits and are thus, in some way, not business like. In fact, many of these organisations employ sores of accountants and financial planners because the ratio of their income to their expenditure is just as important to them as it is to the private company. If their expenditure exceeds their income for long they will certainly run into severe difficulties. Thus, over a prolonged period of time, they must not make a loss. From that point of view it might be more accurate to describe them as 'non- loss' organisations. However, this is not really accurate either because many such organisations do engage very forcefully and effectively in profit making activities. Oxfam has hundreds of high street shops, which it runs along commercial lines and whose objective is to make a profit. However, the distinction between Oxfam and its next door neighbour on the high street is that for the Oxfam shop, making a profit is not its prime motive. Its main purpose is feeding the hungry, and running profit making shops is just one of the ways in which it generates income to be used for its main purpose. Therefore, in contrast to a company, the income generating activities of a non-profit organisation are not an end in themselves but only a means to an end.

There is no single form of ownership for non-profit organisations. Many are in the public sector, part of central government, local government or a nationalised industry (coal) or utility (railways). Since 1979 government policy has been to return many such organisations to the private sector and the process will continue in the 1990's, probably affecting the two bodies mentioned above. Many non-profit making organisations are in the private sector, and for these the most popular status is that of a registered charity, due to the tax benefits they enjoy. A charity has to be non-profit making, but non-profit making organisations do not have to be registered as charities. They could be public or private companies, partnerships or sole traders.

15.2 Why are non-profit making organisations different from commercial firms ?

There are a number of reasons why the management of a typical non-profit making organisation differs from that of a typical profit oriented company.

15.2.1 Less precise objectives.

Making a profit is clear, unambiguous and measurable. The company can easily evaluate its performance by this yardstick. However, if your objective is helping the needy, or providing a good education to students of business studies, both the nature of the objective and the organisation's success in attaining it are much less clear. Moreover, organisations may have multiple objectives which can make them difficult to manage because it is often difficult to determine the relative importance of the objectives; an essential prerequisite if resources are to be allocated efficiently. For example, how does a college compare the importance of engineering courses and history courses. Some might argue that engineering is more important because qualified engineers are needed in industry, but others might argue that there should be more places for history students because more young people want to study history. Non-profit organisations are often afflicted by this kind of philosophical debate, which can make them difficult to manage.

15.2.2 Multiple publics.

Non-profit organisations, particularly those in the public sector often have the difficult task of attempting to satisfy many diverse client groups, all with differing aspirations and priorities. As we said in Chapter 12 when we looked at public relations, all companies are faced with quite a number of different publics, such as customers, employees, shareholders, unions, the local community, public bodies etc., any of which could have some effect upon its activities, and all of which therefore should be seen as relevant target audiences for public relations messages. However, there is little doubt that for a commercial firm, customers are unarguably the most important public, and their needs must be met above all others. The issue is often not so clear cut for non-profit organisations. The publics of a college will include students, past, present and future, parents, lecturers, other staff, educational accreditation bodies (such as BTEC), local businesses, local government bodies, the Department of Education and possible private funders. The managers of the college somehow have to keep all these publics happy. The students come closest to being customers, but they are not necessarily more important than some of the other publics.

15.2.3 Attracting resources.

Many non-profit organisations find it difficult to make their resources cover their expenses. They may be publicly funded, but not to a sufficient level. They are therefore constantly having to seek additional sources of funding. Once again, colleges are a good example. They try to run additional profit making courses, they apply for additional pockets of public funds such as certain Training Agency schemes and, though they are not charities they try to attract charitable donations. There is often a lot of competition for these resources, and, in the case of charitable donations, funders are often being asked to part with money or other gifts in return for no clear tangible benefit.

15.2.4 Unmeasurable outputs.

Even if the organisation's objectives are clear, ways of measuring its level of attainment of those goals may be far from obvious. Assessing the achievement of a general practitioner for example is very difficult. Statistical monitoring of the death rate amongst his patients, though objective and clear would hardly be fair. The danger lies in the trap that in looking for performance indicators one begins to measure inputs rather than outputs. One could, for example judge a doctor by how many patients he sees each day, and pay him accordingly. This does not in any way assess how well he deals with those patients. It measures activity but not results or effectiveness.

15.2.5 Political pressures

Public sector organisations are frequently subjected to extreme political pressures, which can have a tremendous effect on their resources, their objectives, even in some case their existence. A change of government may lead to radical changes in management and operational style which can be very difficult for staff and clients to adjust to. In other words, management very often do not have full control over the destiny of the organisation.

15.3 The role of marketing

As we have seen, non-profit organisations do display many differences from typical commercial firms but they also face many problems and tasks which are very similar to those faced in the profit sector, and which are commonly tackled in that sector with the aid of marketing techniques. The Oxfam shops referred to earlier are just one example of this. Let's have a look at some of the problems or tasks, faced by non-profit organisations, which commercial firms would tackle with the aid of marketing techniques.

15.3.1 Changing environments.

Non-profit organisations operate in the same dynamic, fast- changing environments faced by commercial firms. Both opportunities and threats lie ahead of them. All the factors mentioned in Chapter two (political, economic, social and legal) are applicable to an analysis of the environment facing a non- profit organisation.

15.3.2 Segmentation

Non-profit organisations must analyse their present and potential customers - even if they do not call them customers. Clients, patients, students, members, recipients, passengers, visitors, taxpayers or citizens, whatever they are called they are the target group whose needs the non-profit organisation is concerned to meet. Therefore the techniques mentioned in Chapters 3 and 4 of this book are highly relevant. The non-profit organisation should research its target 'market' to find out about the needs of its 'customers'. It should also segment them, because if it is true that people do not all have the same needs or behave in the same way when buying groceries it must be equally true that they are not all the same when satisfying their need for education or health care. The National Health Service does have to offer health care to the whole population, but it does not have to regard the British population as one mass market. It should and does segment that market, tailoring certain services towards particular segments.

15.3.3 The product

If non-profit organisations exist to meet the needs of their customers they must satisfy those needs with some kind of product offering. Whether it's a visible product or service, or something very intangible like meeting people's need to help those less fortunate than themselves (by making charitable donations), non- profit organisations, like commercial firms, are offering customers a way of meeting a particular need. Therefore, as we described in Chapters 5 - 7 they must take steps to ensure that their 'product offering' meets customers' needs as closely as possible. Moreover, since non-profit organisations are operating in the same dynamic world as profit oriented companies (15.3.1), they must accept that their product offering and the basic need they meet is also likely to display a life cycle. Non-profit organisations must therefore develop strategies to change with the times, modifying existing product offerings as necessary and maybe developing new ones. If they are contemplating new product offerings they will have to do their market research and their forecasting very carefully indeed.

15.3.4 Pricing

Non-profit organisations will not always use the word price. They may say fares, fees, fines, levies, donations, charges, tolls, rates, taxes etc, but, like price, they are talking about a mechanism to ration a scarce resource. Many non-profit organisations such as public leisure centres, museums, private schools and hospitals and the public dental service do use the price mechanism as a way of regulating demand (either totally or partially). If they do not use price they have to ration their product offering in some other way. Health authorities do not charge patients for operations, but where demand exceeds the ability to supply, the scarce resource has to be rationed in some other way-and the usual device in this case is the waiting list which can stretch from months to years in some areas for non-urgent operations. Public libraries do not charge a fee for their books, but ration them by time. On the other hand the same library lending records or cassettes may impose a fee to ration that scarce resource.

15.3.5 Availability and accessibility

Non-profit organisations often need a distribution strategy. In fact, the contribution that can be made by marketing management to increasing the availability and accessibility of the organisation's product or service will often be one of the most critical factors in increasing customer satisfaction. A typical example designed to improve the availability of a public service can be seen in the health service. The supply of GPs to a certain area is controlled by the local Family Practitioner Committee (a branch of the Local Health Authority). Any doctor who would like to start practising as a GP must firstly receive the consent of the Family Practitioner Committee for that area. FPCs have four categories of location, ranging from the kind of area most in need of more GP's to an area already very well served by GPs. The categories are based on the ratio of patients to GPs in each area. In a needy area, new GPs will often be given incentives to start a practice. They are often inner city areas, not attractive places to live, but with a shortage of doctors. The most desirable places, rural, wealthy and with few social problems are usually very well served by GPs. In such areas it will be virtually impossible for a new GP to be authorised unless he is replacing a retiring doctor in an existing practice.

Increasing the accessibility of a service can also be a very important part of the marketing of a non-profit organisation. This can be defined as 'making the service easier to use', or more user-friendly. (See Chapter 9 for more information on the concept of accessibility.) Efforts are constantly being made to improve the accessibility of the social security system for example. A fundamental factor here is overcoming the problem of ignorance. If people are not made aware of the benefits to which they are entitled or cannot understand how to claim them they will not take advantage of the service. One of the objectives of the Social Security Department is to reduce its remoteness from its 'customers' by making its literature more simple and by rationalising the benefits system. They can also make it less remote by improving its physical accessibility through the convenient location of offices, ensuring that the opening hours are acceptable to clients, minimising waiting and providing adequate accommodation for those who do need to wait.

15.3.6 Promotion

Marketing communications may be used to increase demand or they may be used to regulate demand or even to reduce it (see Chapter 16 for 'demarketing'). Very often marketing communications are not used to persuade the target audience to buy, but simply to make them better informed.

The Department of Trade and Industry therefore 'promotes' its grant aid schemes for industry. They are advertised in newspapers and magazines and on the television The objective of this advertising is not to maximise demand. Since there is a limited fund available to support the grant initiatives maximising demand would be counter productive. There would not be enough money in the fund to satisfy all the claimants. The objective of the promotional activity is simply to make all the potential applicants fully aware of the range of grants which are available so that they can make a knowledgeable decision on whether one or more of those grants is suited to the needs of their company.

However, some non-profit organisations may wish to use marketing communication techniques in their more conventional role of stimulating demand. The NHS may wish to increase the demand amongst the people of the U.K. to become blood donors. The health service wants as many donors and as much blood as it can get so the advertising is aimed at those people who have a need to help other people. One way they can satisfy their need is by becoming a blood donor.

Sometimes non-profit organisations will use promotional techniques to improve or change the image of their product or service. The Department of Employment did not need to increase demand from 16 - 18 year olds for places on the Youth

Training Scheme. Since the government decided that unemployment should not be an option for young people, that they should either remain in full time education, find a permanent job or join the YTS, opting out of the scheme would not be possible. However, the research carried out by the Department of Employment showed that young people had a very poor image of the YTS, seeing it as little more than cheap labour with little or no useful training element. The DoE therefore felt the need to improve the image of the YTS, which it did, partly by modifying the product itself (increasing the training content) and partly by spending several millions of pounds on an advertising campaign promoting the success stories of the YTS using the young people who spoke of their enjoyable experience on the YTS, the valuable training they had received and the good job to which it had led them.

Non-profit organisations may even use a technique like sales promotion, designed to be a short term incentive to buy. A very long running and successful sales promotion has been Blackpool's illuminations. Their promotional purpose is to give people an extra incentive to visit Blackpool after the end of the main holiday season, and they have been very effective in achieving this objective.

15.3.7 Evaluating performance.

One of the central principles of marketing management is the control and evaluation of performance. The marketer will constantly monitor and assess his activities and their results to ensure that his objectives are being met. It is often the desire to improve profitability which drives on these evaluative activities. Since non-profit organisations are not profit oriented it is often assumed that techniques designed to monitor, control and evaluate their activities or the performance of their staff are not necessary. In fact, evaluation procedures are a vital element in the effective functioning of any organisation.

Non-profit organisations may not be motivated by profit, but, as we said at the beginning of this chapter, they certainly do not want to be 'loss-making organisations'. Simply to avoid making a loss organisations, (particularly large ones), need a tight budget control system which is capable of comparing budgeted revenues and costs with actual revenues and costs and can take corrective action if costs begin to exceed revenue by an unacceptable margin. To balance the books, revenues can be increased or costs cut. If the organisation chooses to increase revenues it can usefully call on many of the marketing techniques described in this book, such as marketing research, segmentation, new product development or promotional activities.

However, their are other types of evaluation besides budgetary control. These revolve around the question of how well an organisation is meeting its non-financial objectives. A hospital does need to balance its books, but its core objective is to provide people with good health care. A hospital might therefore evaluate its performance by sending questionnaires to patients after their discharge asking them about the quality of nursing, physician care and even the quality of the food and the adequacy of other services such as entertainment. Such evaluative procedures tackle the fundamental question of the organisation's success in achieving its core objective through meeting the needs of its 'customers'.

15.4 Marketing the 'unmarketable'

How do you market income tax? Is this such a clear example of attempting to market the unmarketable that the Inland Revenue would be best advised to dismiss any notion of employing marketing techniques? The answer is clearly no, because although tax itself probably cannot be marketed, the system for dealing with it certainly can. The service can improve its accessibility and certain negative feelings towards the organisation can be overturned.

The Inland Revenue's first objective was to promote a fair and helpful image, on the grounds that if taxpayers are confident that the system is fair they will co-operate with it much more fully, and tax will therefore become easier to collect. The organisation's strategy for achieving this objective is to promote the people behind the service. If taxpayers can see tax inspectors as ordinary, fair, reasonable people they will be less afraid of them and more inclined to co-operate, and even to approach them for help. Staff from the Inland Revenue have therefore appeared on local radio stations to project this friendly image and in some areas they even have set phone-in times when listeners can telephone to ask the advice of tax officials who are not only independent of the local tax office but are also specially trained in broadcasting skills. A further initiative has been the introduction of a number of mobile advice centres which move from town to town acting as an advice bureau and are specifically designed to make the wary customer feel at ease. They also, of course, greatly improve the accessibility of the service.

As with many other public service organisations one of the main marketing tasks of the Inland Revenue is the simple communication of basic information about the service. A common problem with many public sector services is that 'customers' do not fully understand their rights or their obligations. The Inland Revenue has therefore produced a wide range of free explanatory leaflets. They are available from libraries and Citizens Advice Bureaux as well as from tax offices.

There are little customer care touches too. A survey conducted by the London Evening Standard showed that the Inland Revenue is one of the quickest national institutions to answer the telephone! The organisation is determined to make the system more acceptable by promoting the human face of the Inland Revenue.

(Source: 'Making a virtue out of necessity', Marketing Business, October 1988.)

Assignment　　Ingledale School

Although it was situated in the centre of a very wealthy village which was part of an increasingly desirable semi-rural residential area around forty minutes drive from a large city, Ingledale School was not sharing in the prosperity of the neighbourhood. It was a relatively small primary school with less than three hundred pupils, and, like all state schools, had been badly affected by cuts in central and local government funding. The school's resources had inevitably suffered. Books, sports and craft equipment and computers were in short supply. The building was beginning to look rather shabby, both inside and out, and the annual school trip had recently been abandoned.

All of these developments would represent severe setbacks for any school but for Ingledale they were potentially disastrous. The school faced two severe threats. Private education was growing, and as the prosperity of Ingledale had grown, so had the ability of its families to pay for such an education. Secondly, the Government had been promoting the principle of freedom of choice within the state education system. People no longer had to send their children to their local school. They were free to apply for entry to other local schools. Even amongst those Ingledale families who had no desire to remove their children from the state education system there were many two-car families who could easily transport their children to neighbouring schools. If the facilities of Ingledale School continued to decline it was quite possible that many parents would take up one of these alternative options. Withdrawals from the school, though by no means alarming, were increasing. To counter these threats, the school would have to raise the standard of its facilities and equipment, but its revenue was clearly insufficient to cover the cost of doing so.

The school did, however, have a number of strengths. The Victorian building was very attractive architecturally, and, for a school of its size, stood in enormous grounds (which were far from being fully utilised by the school). The pupils came mainly from middle class families who were very genuinely concerned about the standard of their children's education and were therefore keen to help the school. They also had the financial resources to help.

In practice, fund raising from parents had been very disappointing. The annual sponsored walk and sponsored spell seemed to be losing their appeal. Even worse, the school fete, once one of the highlights of summer entertainment had also been in decline for several years, with the previous year's attendance showing a catastrophic fall, making the fete hardly worth running as a fund raising event.

It was the approach of the time for the planning of this year's fete that seemed to have focused the minds of the school's staff on its growing problems. The issues had been extensively discussed in the staff room and it was decided that the forthcoming meeting of the Parent Teachers' Association should be used to initiate a full debate about the school's financial problems with the objective of galvanising the parents into action on the fund raising front.

Headmaster John Brightwell sent a letter to all parents outlining the purpose of the meeting and urging them to attend. The response was encouraging. The school hall was full, and more chairs had to be brought in. John Brightwell stood up and addressed the meeting, outlining very honestly the problems facing the school but also stressing its benefits especially the dedication of its staff, their extensive teaching experience and, despite the shortage of resources, the very good education which the pupils received. However, he ended his speech by pointing out that good teaching may not be enough to ensure the survival of the school in the long run unless resources could be found to improve its facilities.

Parent after parent then stood up to thank John for calling the meeting, for being so frank and to offer their support. They were all optimistic, each pointing to successful ventures that other schools or similar organisations had mounted. Somebody mentioned a series of village barn dances that had been run through the winter which had raised £1,050 towards redecoration of the village hall. Someone else mentioned a trivial pursuits knockout competition, someone a sponsored vegetable garden which the children could run, someone else suggested a series of wine tasting evenings and so it went on. It was mentioned that in many fund-raising situations a committee is appointed and each of its members is responsible for mounting a fund raising initiative designed to bring in a certain amount of money.

People were also full of ideas for the forthcoming fete. The school could get a famous personality to open it, perhaps a footballer who could then take part in a penalty shooting game. They could have other modern attractions such as children's motor cycles instead of offering only the traditional coconuts and tombolas, and they could combine it with the school sports day.

In addition to enthusiasm there also seemed to be plenty of managerial and entrepreneurial talent in the school hall. Surely these people who had such successful careers could deploy some of their abilities to the benefit of the school. There was the chief executive of a well known electric lighting company, the manager of a very large department store, the group financial controller for a public company, the personnel manager of a building society plus several people from professions like medicine, law and accountancy.

There were also two marketing professionals. One, Fiona Robinson was a consultant specialising in the marketing of services who had been involved in several assignments with non-profit making organisations. She made the point that if the school were to be really successful in the long run it should not just be examining fund raising activities but all the aspects of being a good school which meets the needs of all relevant 'customer groups'. She said that there is no point raising money unless it were to be deployed to best effect in achieving the school's objectives. The other marketer was Alan Gilbert, an account executive in one of the leading provincial advertising agencies. He stressed the importance of promoting the summer fete much more effectively than in previous years in order to increase its appeal. If much higher costs were to be incurred attendance would have to be increased dramatically over last year's poor turn-out if a surplus were to be produced.

Everybody agreed with Fiona Robinson and Alan Gilbert. It was decided to appoint two committees and Fiona was nominated as chair of the Marketing Committee with Alan heading the Fete Committee. Both faced urgent tasks if they were to mobilise their committees into early and effective action.

Fiona knew that she had to explain the basics of marketing to the committee and succeed in making them understand that their tasks would range much wider than the organisation of a few fund raising events. She decided that at the first meeting she would have to outline all the marketing activities that Ingledale School would have to consider adopting and appoint small groups to investigate each one. To get her message across she would also have to underline the benefits that marketing could bring to a non-profit organisation by giving some examples of its use in other similar organisations.

Alan was afraid that many people underestimated the task of mounting a successful fete. He knew that the fete itself would have to be meticulously *planned to offer families the kind of weekend entertainment they wanted, and that it would then have to be promoted very effectively to the right target audiences. He knew that money would be limited for promotion but that labour would be plentiful and free. However, he knew that at his first meeting he would have to outline a suggested action plan for the forthcoming fete which the committee could then discuss.*

Task.

Working in two groups, one of which will represent the Marketing Committee and one the Fete Committee, role play the opening meetings which will begin with opening addresses from the respective chairs.

Chapter 16
Marketing and Society

Introduction

It now seems appropriate to look briefly at the wider impact which marketing is having on society. Is marketing good for society? Some people think not, others are convinced of the opposite. Some people think that marketing has become such a central and valuable part of contemporary society that its role should be enlarged and its principles related to much wider social issues. Other people still see marketing as a narrow discipline, of dubious morality designed solely to help companies sell more products. What do you think after reading the first fifteen chapters of this book? Hopefully, this final chapter will clarify your thoughts on the matter.

16.1 Consumerism

Over the last three decades a concern about the power and activities of big business has developed in western countries. Certainly it is difficult to explain exactly what consumerism is but the general feeling is that it is concerned with consumers' desire to obtain greater value for money from their purchases and often encompasses the fear that powerful businesses can exploit and manipulate individual consumers. It is probably also underpinned by an unwelcome feeling that human values are gradually giving way to material values in society at large.

Kotler suggests that consumerism is

> *'a social movement seeking to augment the rights and power of buyers in relation to sellers.'*

This refers to the basic notion that consumers may need to be protected against powerful businesses. Consumerism however, is more than just buyers' rights. Aaker and Day widen the definition to encompass the protection of the individual in dealings with organisations of all kinds including government, public services and businesses large and small. The following definition can therefore be suggested:

> *'Consumerism is a loose movement which believes that individuals need protecting in their relationships with more powerful companies and organisations.'*

16.2 The rights of buyers and sellers

For many centuries exchange relationships were conducted with little interference or regulation. Buyers and sellers were considered to be more or less equal in their ability to judge criteria such as product quality, price, performance features etc. Kotler lists traditional buyers' and sellers' rights as follows.

16.2.1 Traditional sellers' rights

(a) Sellers have the right to sell any product as long as it is not dangerous. Even hazardous products can be sold with the right warnings, storage facilities and controls (e.g. guns in the U.K. can be sold by licensed dealers to buyers with a gun license).
(b) Sellers can set their own prices.
(c) Sellers have the right to promote their product in any manner of their choosing, unless specific regulations eliminate some options, such as the advertising of cigarettes on television. They can spend as much money as they choose on promotional tools such as advertising and can send any promotional messages provided they are not untrue or misleading.
(d) Sellers can encourage purchase by offering any buying incentive scheme of their choice.

16.2.2 Traditional buyers' rights

(a) Buyers have the right to buy or not to buy any product.
(b) Buyers can expect a product on sale to be safe.
(c) Buyers can expect a product to be exactly what the seller claims it to be.

16.2.3 Additional rights for buyers

As suggested at the beginning of the chapter, as sellers have grown larger and more powerful, and products have become more sophisticated and complex, consumers feel that they have lost equality in the marketplace. They have turned to organised movements and to governments for protection. Advocates of consumerism would claim the following additional rights for buyers:

(a) The right to be fully informed about all important aspects of the product such as all the ingredients (and their quantities) in processed food.

(b) The right to be protected against questionable products or marketing practices.

(c) The right to influence products and marketing practices in socially desirable directions, such as not using CFC chemicals in aerosols which will damage the ozone layer.

As we will see in the remainder of this chapter consumerist groups in Britain have made great strides towards the achievement of these three objectives, although they would argue that much still remains to be done.

16.3 Reasons for the growth of consumerism

Consumerism has gathered momentum steadily in most western countries since the 1950's. Its growth can be loosely connected with a number of factors:

16.3.1 Greater democracy

With greater equality, democracy, freedom of speech and educational attainment in the Western world people have become more inclined to voice their protests. The huge growth in the number of people being educated to degree level has fed this movement, with students themselves frequently taking the lead.

16.3.2 Inflation

Inflation always produces winners and losers. It generates uncertainty, and usually makes people feel poorer. Analysis has shown that the growth of consumerism tends to be more prominent after a period of rapidly rising prices which cause a fall in purchasing power, giving them the impression that the buyer/seller balance of power has tilted further away from buyers.

16.3.3 Improvements in communications

Mainly due to television people are becoming increasingly knowledgeable about the world around them. Programmes such as Esther Rantzen's 'That's Life' and Roger Cook's 'Checkpoint' have exposed many fraudulent or unethical commercial practices. This kind of programme is very beneficial to the consumer but the publicity generated from a small minority of firms who exploit customers often casts a shadow of suspicion over the large majority who do see the serving of customer needs as one of their main goals.

Bad news seems to travel particularly fast. Witness this headline in a Sunday newspaper in October 1988, complete with a photograph of Trading Standards Officers inspecting merchandise in the store concerned:

'B & Q hits more trouble over prices.'

The article went on to explain how the Birmingham branch of the DIY chain had been found overcharging for the second time in a week, by as much as 24%, on a range of items. The same trading standards office had also discovered pricing discrepancies at branches of Boots and Texas Homecare. The problem has arisen due to the change over to EPOS (electronic point of sale) tills which read the bar code on the product item and automatically print out the price and the product name on the till receipt. This has enabled the stores to dispense with the labour intensive practice of pricing each individual item. EPOS stores simply show the price on the shelving or the display unit for each brand, so unless the consumer writes down each price as he goes round the store he does not know whether the till has printed out the correct price or not.

The stores are not in the habit of deliberately showing one price on the shelf and charging a higher one at the till but a problem can arise when prices are changed. Normally price changes are fed through the telephone lines from the head office computer to the branch computer over the weekend, or in exceptional circumstances overnight during the week. On Monday morning therefore, before the opening of the store the staff have the task of going round and manually changing the shelf display price of all the items whose price has been changed. Whether or not the staff have changed those prices by the time the store open on the Monday morning the EPOS till will read the bar code and automatically charge and print out the new price. Hence the possibility, especially on Monday mornings of the store displaying one price and charging another, higher price. This was the cause of the problem at B & Q which received such publicity. The company blamed the problem on human error and assured the press that it was not a widespread practice. However it is easy to see how, in our well educated, well informed and vociferous society, such episodes feed the growth of consumerism. People again feel potentially vulnerable as customers and all stores with EPOS tills will fall under suspicion.

Consumer protection organisations then press for safeguards. In this case, Mr. Harry Holding, head of consumer protection on Birmingham City Council, immediately called for tighter controls on EPOS systems. He demanded that all items should be individually priced so that customers could compare the label against their till receipt. (Of course, this would remove one of the main benefits of EPOS from the retailer's point of view). He also called for powers to demand from stores computer lists of bar code prices so that inspectors could compare all displayed prices with prices actually charged by the tills. It will be interesting to see how the use of EPOS systems is regulated over the next few years.

16.3.4 Health and safety

In recent years society has become much more conscious of health and safety and much more aware of products that can have an adverse effect on health and safety. Cigarettes have been the target of many pressure groups such as the BMA and ASH and for many years their advertisement has been banned on TV and health warning messages have appeared on packaging. Healthy diets have also become an important area of concern for many people. Artificial ingredients in processed food have fallen under particular suspicion following the publication in 1984 of Maurice Hanssen's book *'E for Additives'* (billed by the publishers as 'the best seller that started a food revolution').

16.3.5 Social problems

Alcohol has fallen under particular attack in recent years. Many people believe that Britain has a drink problem and that it is getting worse. In particular increasing crime amongst the 18-24 year old age group has been linked with growth in alcohol consumption. The problem is not restricted to petty vandalism and unsocial behaviour of the so-called 'lager louts' but has been connected with much more serious offences. The graph below shows the percentage of incidents in which alcohol was considered to be a contributory factor.

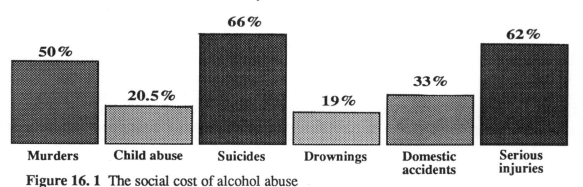

Figure 16. 1 The social cost of alcohol abuse

Britain is listed as only twentieth in the world league table of alcohol consumption per head of the population. Superficially its per capita annual consumption of 7.1 litres of pure alcohol compares favourably with most other western countries – being only half that of league leaders France for example. Britain however, seems to suffer disproportionately from drink related problems because drinking is concentrated among a minority who drink to excess, especially in the 18 - 24 age group. In this age group, Derek Rutherford, director of the Institute of Alcohol Studies, believes that 25% of males and 8% of females drink above the level where they significantly increase the risk of social and medical problems (though in the case of the latter it might be years before they surface).

Derek Rutherford is one of many people who blames the dramatic growth in alcohol consumption amongst young people on the marketing campaigns of the brewers. He points out that forty years ago this age group had the lowest alcohol consumption of any age range (over 18), suggests that the brewers became concerned at 'missing out' on the youth market and began to target advertising at them. This, he says, caused massive growth in drinking amongst young people such that the peak age for alcohol consumption is now 20.

Excess drinking is just one example of a social problem which has been blamed on the marketing profession. Of course there are other possible causes such as films and television and social changes which have led to young people 'growing up' earlier. However such charges are very serious and later in this chapter we will see how consumerist pressure has affected the alcohol market and how marketers can respond to such pressure.

16.3.6 Selling false dreams

One of the main complaints of the consumerist movement is the misrepresentation that a small proportion of marketers are guilty of. This could involve misleading advertising, misleading labelling or the failure of products to live up to promotional promises. Products from time share apartments to slimming aids have come under fire, and the bad publicity has often been magnified by consumer programmes such as those mentioned in 16.3.3. Mail order has often been criticised in this respect, with people sending their money and either receiving nothing for a lengthy period or receiving unsuitable products. Sinclair Research was condemned in this respect, particularly with its QL model which was advertised by mail order before its product development process was really complete. Its introduction was accompanied with much hype and many mail orders were received but some of the early customers had to wait for months before they were in possession of a fully operational machine.

Much of the concern in this respect has focused on criticism of advertising, fuelled in particular by the publication of Vance Packard's book, 'The Hidden Persuaders' in the early 1960's. Consumerists argue that advertising is sometimes deceptive, leaving consumers with an impression or belief which is different from the one they would form if they had perfect knowledge. If advertising were factually untrue then deception could be said to exist, but as we will see in section 16.4, considerable efforts have been made in recent years to uphold ethical standards in advertising.

16.3.7 Pollution

Pollution has been a source of great social concern for several decades. Some of the earlier evils such as smoke from domestic and factory chimneys have been virtually eliminated but they have been replaced by new worries. Nuclear contamination has probably been the greatest source of concern to environmentalists since the Chernobyl disaster in 1987 but lead in petrol, pollution of rivers by industrial waste, pollution of beaches and acid rain are all examples of the same problem. Consumerists argue that society has got its priorities wrong, putting the pursuit of wealth before the preservation of the planet. In some countries the 'Greens' have become a significant political force (e.g. West Germany), and though not yet represented in the House of Commons, the Green Party now has considerable support from some sections of the community.

16.4 The results of consumerism

16.4.1 Pressure groups

Consumerism itself may be an informal social phenomenon rather than a specific organised group but it has led to the formation of a large number of strong pressure groups each with its own particular area of interest. The closest any British organisation comes to being a general manifestation of consumerism would be the Consumers' Association. Almost according to the true Kotler blueprint the Consumers' Association is designed to increase the power of buyers in relation to sellers by providing buyers with information to help them in their purchasing decisions (through the Association's *'Which?'* magazine) and by helping to expose faulty products, misleading product claims and examples of commercial bad practice.

Pressure groups can exert very strong pressure on businesses and government organisations over a period of time. We have already mentioned the growth in ecological pressure groups, known collectively as 'Greens', and although they have not made any formal political progress themselves they have had a remarkable effect on political life in the U.K., with all the main political parties competing in their claims to be the best guardians of the natural environment. The granting of tax concessions to lead free petrol is an example of government support for 'Green' values, but it must be said that there are still many issues on which Government and ecologists part company, e.g. nuclear power.

Many commercial organisations have so far done much more than the Government to meet the demands of the 'Greens'. A recent survey of food retailers, 'The Green Check-Out: Merlin's Supermarket Survey' showed that some stores have made considerable progress on a number of ecologically desirable criteria, while others still lag far behind.

Safeway has the best environmental record. It was the first supermarket chain to stock organically grown produce and set a precedent (now followed by some other stores) of purchasing its organic foods only from Soil Association approved producers. (The Soil Association carries out research and sets standards for organic agriculture). Safeway also has a good 'Green' record in other ways too. It has contributed to Friends of the Earth, UK 2000, The Soil Association and The National Trust. It has bottle banks outside quite a number of its stores and its own label aerosols contain no ozone damaging CFC's.

Other stores are responding to 'Green' pressure in other directions. Tesco, for example has introduced lead free petrol at all its service stations and is only buying company cars which run on unleaded fuel.

A book called 'The Green Consumer Guide' by John Elkington and Julia Hailes says that no supermarket chain has yet moved anything like far enough to satisfy all ecological requirements. The book, which has sold thousands of copies and was near the top of the non-fiction best sellers for several weeks (showing the popularity of the 'Green' movement) actually compiled a 'Green league' table showing that Safeway followed by Sainsburys are the most ecologically minded chains with Asda and Tesco in joint third place. Gateway and Waitrose come next, with Marks and Spencer right at the bottom of the pile. M & S does not yet stock organic produce and their high standards for unblemished and perfectly shaped fruit and vegetables can usually be achieved only through the use of agrochemicals and intensive farming methods.

16.4.2 Government action

Over the years the government has responded to consumerism by creating a number of official bodies to represent consumer groups. The Office of Fair Trading, the Advertising Standards Authority and the British Standards Institute would be examples. The Monopolies and Mergers Commission can be called upon to investigate mergers or takeovers which appear to be creating such a powerful force within a particular industry so that customers or the public in general may be threatened.

If matters become serious, the Government can pass legislation. Recent laws passed to increase the power of buyers in relation to sellers include the Consumer Protection Act 1987, the Sale of Goods Act 1979, the Unfair Contract Terms Act 1977 and the Consumer Credit Act 1974. Cigarette advertising is no longer permitted on television and in response to pressure group activity and general social concern guidelines concerning alcohol advertising have been tightened.

In 1987 the Government formed a ministerial group to look into alcohol abuse under the chairmanship of John Wakeham, Leader of the House of Commons. Rather than pass legislation on standards of alcohol advertising the Government prefers to put informal pressure on the industry's own self-regulating body, the Independent Broadcasting Authority to exercise more rigidly its authority to approve or censor all TV advertisements. This pressure has already resulted in a voluntary agreement to keep spirits advertising off the TV screens. There is, however a view that beer advertising is too good, too effective in encouraging people to drink. In response to Government pressure to tone down beer advertising the IBA insists that nobody featured in beer commercials should look under 25 years of age, and that adverts should not link alcohol consumption with sexual, sporting or social success. One can see the effect of such measures in the evolution of certain campaigns. For example, George the Bear, the cocky hero of the Hofmeister lager campaign is less macho and less cool that in his original commercials. No longer the tough king of the disco and football field, his 1988 commercials depicted him as a more vulnerable, cuddly teddy, with a tree falling on top of him!

Many pressure groups are calling for a complete ban on TV advertising of alcohol. Led by the BMA, which proposed a ban back in 1985, its supporters now even include the Campaign for Real Ale, which shares the medical profession's concern for over excessive consumption. However, there are strong interests opposing a ban. The ITV companies still derive almost 7% of their revenue from drinks advertising and the industry spent over £200 million advertising its products in 1986 (of which £125 million was on TV advertising).

16.4.3 Management responses to consumerism

Management responses to consumerism are summed up very well by the last example. Companies want to promote their products and will therefore oppose any measures which prevent them from doing so. However, as pressure against the promotion of a product grows, management will usually make concessions to their opponents, as the drinks industry has done, rather than run the risk of a total ban.

As a result of the growth of consumerism and pressure groups of all kinds, management has responded in a number of ways. It is not an exaggeration to say that in general companies have a much greater 'social conscience' than they did in times past and this shows through in some of the 'consumerist' initiatives that companies are now taking.

(a) Customer care

Many companies are now making strenuous efforts not only to give customers good service but also to demonstrate their genuine concern for customers. The rectifying of customer grievance is given a much higher priority than it used to be twenty or even ten years ago. They are keen to get improved feedback about the level of customer satisfaction and are quick to point to new consumer benefits such as improved safety features on cars.

(b) Self regulatory bodies

Many industries are keen to demonstrate their awareness of the social implications of their activities by forming self regulatory bodies designed to stamp out examples of bad practices in the industry. A good example would be the Association of British Travel Agents (ABTA) whose purpose it to set standards to ensure that unscrupulous operators do not exploit consumers and to demonstrate to the public that the industry is concerned about ethical behaviour.

(c) Public relations

Companies are becoming more aware of the total social costs and benefits of their activities. They are becoming more concerned about matters such as the environment, and helping society in general. This desire to be seen as a 'good corporate citizen' is often particularly marked among companies likely to have a poor public image such as those working with dangerous processes or materials and foreign companies trying to build a strong position in an overseas market. PR, in its purest sense, increasing mutual understanding between an organisation and its publics (see Chapter 12), can be of great value for companies in this position. In this respect PR should be seen not as 'glossing over the truth'. Most companies now realise that total honesty is the best policy in the long term. Therefore when Shell discovered in 1988 that its 'new formula' petrol was not suitable for all cars and in fact could cause serious engine damage in a tiny minority of cases it made an announcement about the problems, withdrew the product from the market and suffered only very short term damage to its image.

(d) Striving to become a good corporate citizen

British Nuclear Fuels plc (BNFL) provides the fuel requirements for all Britain's nuclear power stations. It has orders which will keep it busy for the next ten years and in 1987-88 made a profit of £196 million on a turnover of £792 million. It spends millions of pounds per annum on advertising and PR, not to improve its order book but to improve its image with the general public because although BNFL has a highly satisfied customer base its problem is with the public at large.

BNFL feels that a large proportion of the public's concern about its activities is based on misinformation and the bulk of its PR budget is consequently devoted to improving the publics understanding of its operations and in particular the safety standards which it maintains. The Sellafield visitors' centre, developed at a cost of £5.4 million is advertised on TV and receives 150,000 visitors each year, making it the single most popular tourist attraction in the Lake District! BNFL have had to change the natural secrecy of a large industrial organisation into one of total openness and honesty and it is correct to say that most visitors to Sellafield do emerge totally reassured about safety at the plant. However, BNFL believes that it will have solved its image problem only when it no longer feels the necessity to spend such huge sums of money on advertising and PR each year and, at the time of writing, it appears that they are still some way from achieving that objective.

16.5 Social Marketing

In his book *'Marketing Management'*, Philip Kotler seeks to marry marketing and consumerist principles through his concept of 'social marketing'. This is an approach to marketing which takes account of consumers' need for wider satisfaction beyond mere product satisfaction. In other words people do place a value on their quality of life as well as their material possessions. For example, although there may be a demand for non-tar cigarettes, its is questionable whether society wants that product to be developed if the research involves the death or suffering of thousands of

Beagles. Equally, although there is a demand for cosmetics, many cosmetics buyers would be opposed to the use of animals in their development. The Body Shop has been extremely successful with its natural cosmetics largely because of the importance people place on these social and humanitarian values.

Although marketing is all about meeting the needs of customers it is possible that the social marketing concept could actually involve depriving them of something they want, at least in the short term, because it is incompatible with something they want, or should want, even more. Earlier in this chapter we looked at the problem of excessive drinking amongst young people. Although there is a demand for drink from young people, society does not want the problems caused by excessive drinking and it is easy to make the case that it is against the interests of the young drinkers, at least in the long term to consume to excess. The principles of 'social marketing' could therefore be used to reduce consumption of alcohol in the under twenty five age group. The unusual step of employing marketing techniques to reduce demand is known as 'demarketing'.

In outline the process would work in exactly the same way as the marketing techniques described throughout this book. It would involve defining one's objectives, in this case perhaps a reduction of 30% in alcohol consumption amongst under 25's. One would then have to do market research, with the objective of developing a deeper understanding of that segment of the under 25 age group which was most likely to consume excessive quantities of alcohol. One needs to understand their buying motives and buying behaviour together with a wider appreciation of their social values. Armed with this knowledge it should be possible to develop one or more campaigns designed to dissuade under 25's from drinking by stressing values which they place more highly than drinking such as health or sporting prowess. These campaigns would then be tested on a small sample group and the most effective one implemented. Its results would be monitored and evaluated, and maybe the campaign would be modified if necessary.

Conclusion

We have now reached the conclusion of this book as well as the end of Chapter 16. It is an appropriate chapter with which to end, partly because it raises the important question of marketing's role in a wider social context but also because it leads us right back to where we started the book.

In Chapter 1 we said that marketing is about meeting the needs of customers through exchange relationships. The firm of course wants to make money out of this exchange process and we suggested in Chapter 2 that those firms which most successfully respond to changing environments are likely to meet customers' needs more closely and therefore make more money. These firms will do marketing research, they will segment the market and they will become 'closer to their customers', thus making it easier for them to respond to changing customer needs.

However, there are two aspects of making profits out of meeting customers' needs. There is short term profitability and long term profitability, and the requirements of these two objectives do not always coincide. As a result we pointed out in Chapters 5 and 7 that companies must aim for long term returns even if that means supporting projects which are not profitable in the short term. The profits from today's breadwinners must be used to finance tomorrow's breadwinners, and as the BCG matrix demonstrated, new ventures, classified as 'problem children' and later as 'stars' may not become profitable for some time.

Of course, it is often tempting and sometimes essential to seek short term profits at the expense of long term profits, but it is often such short term expediencies which are responsible for causing objections from consumerist groups. The examples given in this chapter illustrate this point. Although in the short term, sales of drinks to young people will boost the profits of drinks companies, promotion of consumption in this segment may be against those companies' long term interests if it is felt by the public to be against the interests of society at large. The cigarette manufacturers realised many years ago that consumption of their product was in inevitable long term decline and as a result most have embarked upon successful diversification strategies.

Firms must therefore take the long term view. Expedient decisions taken to boost short term profits can sometimes be at the expense of goodwill and may consequently harm long term profitability. However, it will normally be the case that the firm's concern for long term profitability will be totally compatible with the maintenance of wider consumer satisfaction. Therefore, the social marketing concept with its allowance for consumers' views should coincide with the marketer's desire to provide total customer satisfaction.

Assignment

Southwich Against Smoking S.A.S.

Although smoking has declined significantly amongst adults in the last twenty-five years this trend has not extended to young people. Joan and Eileen were commenting upon this very fact as they drank their coffee in the cafeteria at the Southwich Technical College, enveloped by smoke.

Joan Child and Eileen Entwistle were both in the early years of their retirement. Both were pillars of the community, supporting organisations like the local church, the Ramblers Association, Probus (a club for retired professional and business people) and various other good causes. Both were extremely active. Part of these activities included attending a local history course at Southwich Technical College. Although both ladies liked to consider themselves fairly broad minded, one of the things that horrified them was the number of young people in the college corridors and refectory who seemed to be smokers. Joan and Eileen had both been smokers when they were young but had both given up the habit many years previously as the damage to health caused by cigarettes had become common knowledge. Few people have as much reforming zeal as people who have overcome a bad habit. Joan and Eileen fell into this category. In their coffee breaks from the history class they would discuss this problem of young smokers and wondered if there wasn't anything they could do to reduce this habit at least among the young people who attended the college.

One day they struck up a conversation with Patricia Fraser, a student on the college's pre nursing course. In common with many of the other students on that medical course, Patricia was a dedicated smoker, getting through around twenty cigarettes a day. Joan and Eileen began talking with Patricia and asking all kinds of questions about students' smoking habits. Did many of Patricia's fellow students smoke? How much did they smoke? How much did they spend each week on cigarettes? Did they all want to smoke or would many prefer to give it up?

Patricia's answers were very interesting. Yes, a large majority of the students on her course did smoke. There were sixty students on this course, mainly girls in the 17 - 20 age range, and Patricia estimated that 80%, if not 90% were smokers. She thought that there were all kinds of reasons why they had developed the habit. Some had started when they were younger because they thought it made them seem more grown up. Others had developed the habit in a social setting such as discos or pubs. Others felt that it helped them to work and calmed their nerves, whilst other girls believed that it helped them to keep slim. However, according to Patricia there was one overriding reason why all the girls continued to smoke. They wanted to be like everyone else. Most people wanted to be part of the group and were afraid that giving up smoking might set them apart.

Patricia believed that most of the girls would prefer to give up smoking if only everyone else in the group also gave up. Patricia said that she was more worried about the harmful long term effects of smoking on her health than she had been when she began the habit four years earlier and she was sure that most of her fellow students would feel the same, even if they might be reluctant to admit it in a group setting. They also couldn't really afford to smoke. Spending around £10 each week on cigarettes was a large part of the discretionary income of many of these girls.

Joan and Eileen were very interested in the conversation and discussed it later amongst themselves. They couldn't really understand why these girls continued to smoke. They decided that they should test out Patricia's theories that most of the girls would actually like to give up, but needed someone to take the initiative. They thought that if they could launch a successful anti-smoking campaign amongst the girls on the pre-nursing course, it could perhaps be subsequently extended across the whole college.

The following week they sought out Patricia in the students' refectory. They outlined their plan to her. Patricia agreed to help them to tackle the pre-nursing group with their anti-smoking message. However, she was sure that the critical factor in the success of such a campaign would be the way in which the initial approach was made. Unless it was sufficiently powerful, and at the same time sympathetic and not over moralistic she didn't think that it would succeed.

From this point of view, having Patricia on their side would be particularly useful but all three realised that they would have to bring in some much more authoritative figures to lend weight to their message. They discussed various ideas. Perhaps they could call themselves SAS (Southwich Against Smoking). Eileen pointed out that ASH could provide speakers or horrifying videos of young people crippled by smoking related diseases. Such shock tactics would be needed to win the students' attention for the anti-smoking message at the outset of the campaign. But how could it be prolonged? Even if everyone did agree to give up smoking, how could they prevent them from drifting back to the habit?

Before they made any announcement to the pre-nursing group, these matters would have to be discussed in great detail by Joan, Eileen and Patricia. They would have to plan a demarketing campaign. It was now December. They decided that they should begin their campaign after the Christmas holiday.

Task

Plan a demarketing campaign for Joan, Eileen and Patricia. The objective is to convince all smokers in the pre-nursing group to give up the habit, and to ensure that nobody starts smoking again at least for the remainder of the academic year. Your plan should attempt to ensure that the group get their message across strongly enough at the outset of the campaign and generate enough commitment to the concept over a period of six months.

Index

The following books are also published by Business Education Publishers Limited and can be obtained either from your local bookshop or direct from the Publisher by photocopying the order on the next page or by telephoning 091 567 4963.

THE BTEC SERIES FOR STUDENTS

Core Studies for BTEC (2nd Edition)
Aug 1989 £16.50
Paperback 680pp A4 format

The first edition of this text was published in 1986 to cover the first and second year core areas of BTEC National Courses in Business, Finance and Public Administration. With its substantial coverage of the core areas, Organisation in its Environment, Finance and People in Organisations and its case study based assignments, it has proved to be the most popular book used on BTEC courses nationally. The new edition is an updated version of the first book retaining a large number of its most popular features.

Business Law for BTEC
Nov 1987 £14.95
Paperback 368pp A4 format

This book provides a comprehensive coverage of Business Law taught on BTEC courses at National and Higher levels. It incorporates a range of assignments for which a lecturer's manual is available to Educational Institutions free of charge from the publishers.

Marketing for BTEC
July 1989 £16.50
Paperback 340pp A4 format

This is a new text suitable for students studying marketing as an option module on BTEC National level courses or marketing as a full or part unit on BTEC Higher National level courses.

Information Processing for BTEC (2nd Edition)
March 1990 £13.50
Paperback 300pp A4 format

A new edition of a popular text which covers the BTEC Information Processing Option Modules One and Two. It incorporates a range of assignments for which a lecturer's manual is available free of charge from the publishers.

Transferable Personal Skills for BTEC
Feb 1989 £12.50
Paperback 311pp A4 format

A new text which covers the range of personal skills identified by BTEC in its statement of common skills. It is written in an easy to read style which students will find stimulating and informative. The text facilitates the development of a transferable personal skills training programme.

Computer Studies for BTEC (2nd Edition)
Aug 1990 £17.95
Paperback 608pp A4 format

The book was written specially for the first year core areas of the BTEC National Computing course. This new edition contains extra material designed to cover extra depth in computer courses.

Small Business Computer Systems for BTEC
Aug 1989 £12.50
Paperback 256pp A4 format

A new book designed to cover the SBCS module on the second year of BTEC National Computing courses. The book contains a range of practical skills based assignments which can be used to form the basis of an assignment programme.

Travel and Tourism
Sept 1989 £16.50
Paperback 320pp A4 format

A major new textbook designed to cover the course content of Travel and Tourism modules at BTEC National and Higher National levels and to be used as an introductory text for undergraduates.

Getting Started with Information Technology
Oct 1988 £11.50
Paperback 302pp A4 format

Aimed at students who are new to information technology, this practical book takes a step by step approach to introducing word processing, data bases, spreadsheets, accounting and integrated packages.

THE BTEC SERIES FOR LECTURERS/TUTORS

Marketing : A Tutor's Guide
Sept 1990 £17.95
352pp A4 format

Small Business Computer Systems : A Tutor's Guide
Sept 1990 £15.95
320pp A4 format

Trasnsferable Personal Skills: A Tutor's Guide
Feb 1989 £16.95
500pp A4 format

OTHER PUBLICATIONS

Transferable Personal Skills: A Student Guide
Jan 1989 £12.50
311pp A4 format

Community Health Services
March 1990 £16.95
560pp A5 format

Law for Housing Managers £14.95
468pp A5 format

Government and Leisure
Sep 1990
Royal 8vo

Business Education Publishers Limited
10 Grange Crescent   Stockton Road
Sunderland SR2 7BN
Tel 091 567 4963

ORDER FORM

THE BTEC SERIES FOR STUDENTS	Retail Price	Quantity Required
Core Studies for BTEC (2nd Edition) 1989	£16.50	
Business Law for BTEC 1987	£14.95	
Marketing for BTEC 1989	£16.50	
Information Processing for BTEC 1990	£13.50	
Transferable Personal Skills for BTEC 1989	£12.50	
Computer Studies for BTEC 1990	£17.95	
Small Business Computing Systems for BTEC 1989	£12.50	
Travel and Tourism 1989	£16.50	
Getting Started with Information Technology 1988	£11.50	

THE BTEC SERIES FOR LECTURERS/TEACHERS/TUTORS		
Transferable Personal Skills - A Tutor's Guide 1989	£16.95	
Marketing for BTEC - A Tutor's Guide 1989	£17.95	
The Abbotsfield File - A Business in Action 1984	£39.95	
Small Business Computing Systems - A Tutor's Guide 1989	£15.95	

OTHER PUBLICATIONS		
Community Health Services 1989	£16.95	
Law for Housing Managers (2nd Edition) 1986	£14.95	
An Introduction to Marketing 1990	£16.50	
Transferable Personal Skills - A Student's Guide 1989	£12.50	

Surname

Initials   Mr /Mrs / Miss / Ms

Organisation

Tick Box as appropriate

Please Invoice :

☐ Individual

☐ Organisation (Please quote order number or reference)

Post Code
Tel:

* *All books are available by placing an order directly with the publisher (B.E.P.) or through any bookshop.*
* *For orders received from any Educational Establishment for books in the BTEC series an additional book will be supplied free of charge for every ten books ordered.*
* *For all books supplied postage is paid by the publisher (B.E.P.) .*